DOWN TO THE SEA.
A CADET'S TALE

Brian George

authorHOUSE

AuthorHouse™ UK
1663 Liberty Drive
Bloomington, IN 47403 USA
www.authorhouse.co.uk
Phone: UK TFN: 0800 0148641 (Toll Free inside the UK)
UK Local: (02) 0369 56322 (+44 20 3695 6322 from outside the UK)

© 2023 Brian George. All rights reserved.

No part of this book may be reproduced, stored in a retrieval system, or transmitted by any means without the written permission of the author.

This is a work of fiction. All of the characters, names, incidents, organizations, and dialogue in this novel are either the products of the author's imagination or are used fictitiously.

Published by AuthorHouse 01/25/2023

ISBN: 978-1-6655-9014-3 (sc)
ISBN: 978-1-6655-9013-6 (hc)
ISBN: 978-1-6655-9015-0 (e)

Print information available on the last page.

Any people depicted in stock imagery provided by Getty Images are models, and such images are being used for illustrative purposes only. Certain stock imagery © Getty Images.

This book is printed on acid-free paper.

Because of the dynamic nature of the Internet, any web addresses or links contained in this book may have changed since publication and may no longer be valid. The views expressed in this work are solely those of the author and do not necessarily reflect the views of the publisher, and the publisher hereby disclaims any responsibility for them.

For us.

From a Presentation by E. J. Smith in 1907.

"When anyone asks me how I can best describe my experience of forty years at sea, I merely say.... Uneventful. Of course, there have been winter gales, storms, and fog and the like, but in all my experience, I have never been in an accident of any sort worth speaking about. I have seen but one vessel in distress in all my years at sea......... I never saw a wreck and have never been wrecked, nor was I in any predicament that threatened to end in disaster of any sort."

On April 14th, 1912, the RMS Titanic sank with the loss 1500 lives.... One of which was its Master, Captain E.J. Smith.

EXPECT THE UNEXPECTED

The New Zealand Star

Authors Note

Having been asked on many an occasion by Uncle Ged, Aunt Michelle and the rest of these gentlemen, all coastguard officers of note, to record my nautical adventures, I have decided that now is the time to give in to such demands and make use of my retirement and set pen to paper… or finger to keyboard, as some literary folk would have it.

However, I must first thank Ged, Mike, and many others in Her Majesty's Coastguard for setting me on this path. Their support and guidance has been invaluable, not only in my literary endeavours, but also in my work as a Watch Officer at Liverpool Marine Rescue Co-ordination Centre.

This tome is based on the experiences of a first trip cadet at sea, in the British Merchant Navy during the early nineteen seventies. That cadet is, of course, me.

I say based on, because although all the incidents described did actually happen, I have used some, shall we say, poetic licence and storified it to make the narrative flow a little easier. You can, however, be assured that the voyage described is a typical voyage on a typical ship of that time and I was a typical cadet. Well, no, that is not true. I was a little thicker between the ears and made a tad more mistakes than most. But then, that's all to the good, just gives me more to write about! The characters herein are loosely based on people I worked with and met over several years, their descriptions and names being entirely fictitious and any likeness to anyone on the planet is entirely coincidental. Those descriptions belong to other people entirely.

I was lucky really to have worked for Blue Star Line. It was a well-known shipping company with a proud history, sleek vessels, and professional, competent people to run them. But the thing that stood out most of all was "The Way". This was not unique to Blue Star Line. It was evident throughout the British Merchant Navy and incorporated a professionalism, a sense of humour, a toughness, an acceptance of hardship and an expectation of adventure. That is the only way I can describe it. To understand it, you had to be part of it, and I thank *all* the people I sailed with for showing me "The Way."

I can say, with hand on heart, that I never sailed with anybody I disliked or had any issue with. I can't, of course, say that I never sailed with anybody who didn't like *me*, but that comes under the heading of T. P. (Their Problem)!

Brian George

Contents

Foreword..xiv
Prologue..xvii

Chapter 1:   On My Way 1
Chapter 2:   Arrival... 9
Chapter 3:   Cathy 17
Chapter 4:   Steven.. 26
Chapter 5:   Captain Jonathan McHale 36
Chapter 6:   The Film... 46
Chapter 7:   An Invitation... 59
Chapter 8:   Norwegian Barry.. 68
Chapter 9:   A Bloody Nose 79
Chapter 10: An Assignation 88
Chapter 11: Promotion to Barman!... 98
Chapter 12: Sailing…Maybe?..110
Chapter 13: Last night 123
Chapter 14: Sailing...135
Chapter 15: A Bit Rough 145
Chapter 16: A New Ambition 155
Chapter 17: Seeing To 160
Chapter 18: Caribbean 167
Chapter 19: Crocs..178
Chapter 20: The New York Bar 187
Chapter 21: Homeward Bound..198
Chapter 22: Crocodile 207
Chapter 23: Over Easy...214
Chapter 24: Into the Big Ditch 222

Chapter 25: Pacific..231
Chapter 26: Paint... 241
Chapter 27: Land of the Long White Cloud 249
Chapter 28: Party 258
Chapter 29: Scousula.. 266
Chapter 30: Kiwi Star Cavalry... 273
Chapter 31: The Letter... 282
Chapter 32: Gisborne... 294
Chapter 33: Another Party.. 303
Chapter 34: Driving Lesson 309
Chapter 35: A Normal Night of Passion 319
Chapter 36: Briefly Bluff... 325
Chapter 37: Oops!.. 332
Chapter 38: Ropes 341
Chapter 39: Last leg...352
Chapter 40: Channels.. 362
Chapter 41: So… Home again.. 372
Chapter 42: My Cathy?... 381

Acknowledgements... 389

FOREWORD

Philosophers! They think deeply and seriously about what they observe in life and nature. They ask questions and draw attention to the human condition in its environment. They tantalise our curiosity and cause that spark that initiates a collective appraisal of their musings. Of necessity, they are master raconteurs.

Brian George is a master raconteur. He is an observer of life and has that rare ability to articulate what he sees in ways that has his audience spellbound and roaring with laughter. Regrettably however, because of his uncanny ability to put one and one together and come up with any answer but two, I have to say that he's not quite up there with Plato and his mates - yet!

This book gives an insight into life in the British merchant navy during a unique period of time. It was a period of time that many-a-seafarer has sentimentally acknowledged as being the best time ever to have been at sea. It is the period of time that existed during the transition from the traditional merchant navy to the modern merchant navy. It lasted for roughly two decades - the 1960's and the 1970's – and coincided with the youth revolutions and pop cultures that emerged during that time. It was the time of The Beatles and Dylan, mini-skirts and the pill, a sexual revolution built on the "make love not war" credo, hippies and drugs, demonstrations and anti-establishment. War was over, the future looked bright and optimism ruled the day.

How this coalesced on British merchant ships where the older seafarers had been through the ravages of World War and the younger ones - inherently rebellious - saw life through a lens of sex, drugs and rock n' roll, was strange – to say the least. But strange in a way that reflected the characters that manned these ships. Irrespective of age, they were, in the main, adventure seekers. They were care-free, affable, happy-go-lucky and fiercely individual. They were non-judgemental, tolerant and extremely loyal to each other. Their guiding principle in life was "have fun" - and "fun" they had!

There is a view among younger people that the more rules there are, the more rules there are to break, and the more rules you break, the greater the fun. During that time to which this book relates, British ships were regulated by the British Merchant Shipping Acts and, it was generally the case that the older, hardened seafarers, abided by the rules and the younger ones gave scant regard to their disciplinary constraints.

Officers wore uniform and called those senior to them "Sir". Crew wore flared jeans, floral shirts, had shoulder length hair and invariably puffed on a joint. Cadets and junior officers yearned for what appeared to be the non-conforming freedom of the crew but this, of course, would be harmful to one's career. As the years passed and the older ones retired to be replaced by those once-junior officers, the merchant navy had transformed.

Brian George captures this time perfectly with his inimitable style of storytelling. It is a style intrinsic to his personality. I clearly recall being in pubs with him during our youth when he would hold court and regale us with stories of his adventures and misadventures and have us rolling around the floor laughing. Fifty years later at a class reunion he was still doing the same.

Warsash is a village that lies on the confluence of Southampton Water and the Hamble River. It is nine miles outside Southampton and home to the Southampton School of Navigation. Better known to seafarers all over the world, simply as, "Warsash". It is a quasi-military establishment that takes boys and turns them into men, ready to undertake the rigours of life at sea. It was here I first met Brian. We were employed by the same shipping company and that made us kind-of brothers. We were family. We used to boast to other families of cadets – P&O, Clan Line, Cunard etc – that our company was not choosy when it came to picking cadets. No need for any lengthy selection process or strict entry exams for us; all we needed was a pulse and the ability to stand upright.

Brian has a kind of Surrey accent with heavy cockney undertones. Early on in the piece, fed up with fellow cadets who could not remember whether his name was "Brian" or "George", he gathered the class around the blackboard and wrote in huge capital letters "GAWGE". "That's what you call me", he said. And the name stuck.

Gawge has been a friend since those college days and, I had the good fortune to sail with him some 9 years after I first met him. He is the eternal sailor, a great shipmate and an officer of the highest calibre embodying all those traits that made sailing so much fun. He's never lost his wit and has amassed a body of experience that has provided him with the material to tell his story as only Gawge can.

So, buckle yourself in and prepare to join Gawge as he sets sail on his first trip to sea from London to New Zealand and back to the UK. With his philosopher-like skills of observation and analysis of the human condition, and his not-so-skilled interpretation of the situations in which he finds himself, you will be absorbed into his adventures which he describes with just the right amount of detail to have you are there with him, experiencing the helter-skelter ride of emotions. From the drab streets of London's docks, to the Atlantic rollers, the girlie bars of Panama, the calm blue waters of the Pacific and the dusky maidens, native to the land of the long white cloud, you will be exhilarated.

And there is, of course, Kathy.

You will thoroughly enjoy the story printed on the pages you are about to turn.

Captain Steve Pelecanos
Brisbane, Australia
23rd January 2023.

PROLOGUE

"V ests...."

"I can't find your vests…"

My Mother stood in the doorway, hands on hips, green eyes staring intently at my expandable suitcase as though she could see through the lid.

This was, of course, highly likely as all mothers possess superwoman like x-ray vision. It goes with their extra set of rear facing eyes, steel fingers, Sherlock Holmes like detecting skills and their unerring whip like leg smacking abilities.

I had, but a few minutes previously, managed to jam the thing shut and had no intention of undoing the catches and watching it fly open like a demented Jack-In-The-Box. Anyway, I had no need of vests. Was I not a rufty tufty seadog of vast seagoing experience? Wild storms in the Bay. The rounding of fog enveloped headlands in the far-flung corners of the globe….

Well… no… actually. I had only done twelve months at the nautical college… but I had read a lot of 'Hornblower' books.

"I'll get the vests," said Mother.

"No, it's ok I won't need them," I said.

"Of course, you will." She snorted, turned on her heel and marched out of the room.

I sighed, looking swiftly around our large lilac coloured living room wondering where I could hide vests……

It was eight fifteen on a cold January morning in nineteen seventy-one. I had finished my year's pre-sea college course at the School of Navigation at Warsash near Southampton and having had Christmas at home for what turned out to be the last time for twelve years, I was off to London to join my first ship.

CHAPTER 1

ON MY WAY

Stepping on the train meant something. It meant I was leaving. Going away.

It meant the start of something. Everything from that moment on would be different.

The start.

A new beginning.

A thousand fears tried to crowd out the thousand wishes and wants that filled my thoughts. There just wasn't room for them all.

They were all crammed in the back of my brain somewhere, out of the way. Said brain was, in reality, too busy coping with getting my two oversized expandable suitcases on the train.

At that point it had already had to cope with opening the heavy carriage door. Already had to cope with organising my right upper limb to pull and turn the door handle that always goes in the opposite direction to the way you turn it first. Already had to cope with that sudden rush of panic that floods over you when you think the door won't open in time. Already had to cope with the ridiculous notion that the train was going to suddenly race off and leave me behind.

I could feel the sweat on my brow and great puddles of the same drenching my shirt which started to cling instantly to my torso.

The door, having become tired of playing with me, flew open taking me and my brain by surprise. I staggered backward nearly toppling over my expandables. This gave my father, who had been standing sensibly further back from the edge of the platform, room to move forward and throw two further items of luggage onto the train. There was then, what can only be described as a bit of a pantomime routine, while we both tried to load luggage of various sorts, and of course me, through the door. Me rushing, sweating, and panicking. My father all cool efficiency. In fact that's how it always was with any task we did together. I had never quiet mastered his ability to analyse situations and form an efficient plan in naught point naught, naught two microseconds. Or carry it out, for that matter.

The farce continued while bags and suitcases were heaved, shoved and pushed into every available space around the double seat which was to become my home for the next twenty minutes. All the way from Chertsey to the mainline station at Weybridge.

We said our goodbyes. Both of us awkward as usual. Father was not the huggy, huggy type and really, neither was I, so we shook hands in a formal sort of way.

"So… anyway," he said "look after yourself. Be careful." He looked sombre for a moment. Staring at the floor. Perhaps wrestling with his emotions? He gripped my hand tighter. "Don't forget to write, will you?" I briefly, fleetingly, thought I noticed a hint of sadness in his eyes. A tiny bit of concern. Both of which he had of course, after all, his son *was* going off to sea. Away somewhere. Somewhere where he could not look after me.

Somewhere I would be at the mercy of God knows what. Out with his protection.

He lifted his head suddenly. "Your mother would like that… she worries a bit you know." Dad was always particularly good at keeping his emotions in check.

So… that was the end of that touching father son moment! Actually, all this only came back to me later. Much later. Years later in fact. When seeing my own son off on some adventure or other and me acting in exactly the same way. However, at the time, on that day my mind was full of the moment, of trains, uncooperative doors, and luggage.

I sat down heavily in my seat; the train lurched and began to move. I waved goodbye. Father stood and waved. He was still waving as the platform disappeared from view.

I looked round the carriage. I hadn't even noticed when I opened the door whether there was anybody else in the compartment.

One business gent had flicked his newspaper down and was watching me over the top of his half-moon glasses. A woman with a blue rinse and sour expression was looking straight ahead and making every effort not to look at me and two small children had stopped in the centre isle and stared with fascination at the loading procedures.

As soon as I sat down one of them, a girl of about seven with curly red hair stuck one finger up her nose, frowned and said.

"You goin' on your 'olidays?"

"No." I said, smiling that 'speaking to a small child when you are worried what they are going to say next' smile.

"Oh," She transferred her gaze to the finger that she had extracted from her nose, examined it and said, "that's the biggest bogie I've ever got!" There was a note of genuine triumph in her voice as she waved it in my direction. She ran off, followed by the other child of about half her age who fell over as the train lurched, picked himself up, peered closely at his hands, decided there was no damage and galloped after the red head.

I stared out of the window at the mist shrouded countryside rolling past, but try as I might, I couldn't quite get rid of the image of the little girl and her finger out of my mind.

In nineteen hundred and fifty three a New Zealander by the name of Edmund Hilary, along with a Nepalese mate of his had taken a hike up Mount Everest. Also that year Elizabeth had been crowned Queen Elizabeth the twoth. But the main event was happening at Woking Maternity Hospital in Surrey, at one thirty in the morning on the fourteenth of May.

I was born.

Apart from Mr and Mrs George not many people noticed. Mind you, Pierce Brosnan was also born that month. Not many people noticed that event either. But fate was to lead him to become James Bond. Fate was to lead me to be presented with 'The biggest bogie I ever got.' The glamour attached to my life, to that date, knew no bounds!

The rest of the train journey from the genteel niceness of the flower gardened, two platformed little station at Chertsey to the harsh austerity of London's docklands was the nightmare you may imagine. The twenty-minute ride to Weybridge station was simple enough. Then it got messy. Then it got sweaty.

Getting from one train to another was the first hurdle. The one I was on came to a stop by the platform that serviced the branch line to Chertsey exactly twenty minutes after we had heaved all my bags into the carriage. Now came the difficult bit. How to transport seven pieces of luggage and a carrier bag containing two ham sandwiches, a bar of chocolate and a can of lemonade, across the platform and on to the next London bound train. There were, of course, no trolleys. So, sweating profusely again, I heaved all the luggage off the train. Then I galloped back and forth transferring suitcases (expandable), bags and various essentials between platforms. Luckily there were no stairs involved.

I managed to get all my bags and baggage assembled in one place when the London bound train pulled in. As soon as it juddered to a squealing halt, I attacked the nearest door handle. I was quite surprised that a door was on offer exactly where I stood. Normally whenever I used trains the doors managed to avoid the bit of platform I was standing on by the maximum distance, which meant I was always the last one on the train and the passenger most likely not to get a seat.

I started tossing bags into the carriage as soon as I had got the door open, and was, again, pleasantly surprised to find it was an empty compartment. You never see them nowadays, but it was one of those carriages with about six compartments and a corridor running down one side. MI6 and Nazi Spies used to chase each other up and down them in old forties films!

All the baggage on board, I leapt on and managed to heave some of the stuff onto the luggage racks above the seats before the train lurched away from the station amid a cacophony of whistles, banging doors and shouts. The sudden movement causing me to sit down with a thump on the bag containing my sandwiches.

I cursed, sulked for a few seconds, then extracted the squashed sandwiches from underneath me and stared moodily out of the window.

I continued to gaze as the countryside flashed by. The train speeding towards London, whisking me towards my great adventure.

Well, actually, there would have been countryside flashing by and lots of speeding towards great adventures, if I had got on the right train. As it was, it soon became obvious, as the carriage came to a shuddering stop next to a field full of curious cows, then rumbled slowly forward into the next station after Weybridge, that, in my panic, I had shovelled my luggage and myself onto the slow train to Waterloo. The one that stops at, at least, five hundred stations before reaching the capitol. Had I waited a while; I could have caught the fast train which would have had me there in about half an hour.

I was just beginning to entertain thoughts of abandoning a career of adventure at sea when the door was flung open and someone leapt in and sat down heavily opposite me. Two more people followed in quick succession, the door slammed shut and the train lurched away causing the last person to stand heavily on my foot.

"Ow!" I shouted and glared at the offender.

"Sor...!" he started to apologise then stopped and stared at me for a second.

"George!" He exclaimed.

The other two newcomers turned suddenly and stared at me. "George!" They both said loudly in unison.

I stared at each one in turn. Jimmy, Freddy and Gilmot. All of them acquaintances from school. I couldn't really call them friends. They were from a different form and year, but I knew them well. They were always together, always moving at speed and always, but always, in trouble. In fact, the way they had jumped on the train at the last minute, I could more or less guarantee they were here with no tickets. I prayed silently that they weren't going all the way to London.

"What are you lot doing here?" I said. "What's more, why are you getting on a train in Hersham? "It's in the middle of nowhere."

"On our way to London." Said Gilmot causing my heart to sink to point near my shoelaces.

"Goin' to the pictures." Said Jimmy.

"Yeah, pictures." Said Freddy, his eyes going immediately to my sandwiches. "You eating those." He said, smiling hopefully.

"No, you can have them." I didn't mention I had sat on them. "But why are you here? Hersham? There's nothing here?"

"Got thrown off the last train." Said Gilmot.

"Train." Said Freddy, ripping the cover off the flattened sandwiches.

"No tickets." Said Jimmy, shrugging his shoulders.

"Tickets." Said Freddy.

I had been away from the County Secondary School for a year and three months while at the Nautical School in Southampton and I had forgot all about these three. They were actually quite famous to a particular era of pupils. As I said, always together and always in trouble. Jimmy was the leader, purely because he had the most swagger. Gilmot was a nickname and for some reason no one seemed to remember his real name. Freddy was known as 'Freddy Reps' due to his habit of repeating the last word that the other two said.

"Got thrown off," said Jimmy. "So, we waited for the next one in the bushes and climbed over the fence."

"Fence." Said Freddy, still wrestling with the sandwich packet.

Gilmot looked around the compartment and frowned at each of my bags in turn. "You goin' on 'oliday?"

I was about to answer when there was the sound of a door slamming somewhere along the corridor.

"Tickets please." Said a voice from the same direction.

"Shit!" Exclaimed Jimmy.

"Shit!" Repeated Freddy.

"Fuckin' conductor!" said Gilmot leaping to his feet. And heading for the door.

"… 'Ductor!" Shouted Freddy also jumping up, hurling my sandwiches to the floor and knocking Gilmot back onto the seat. Jimmy was already up but sat back down with a bump as the domino effect took hold and he was shoved by Gilmot.

All three of them managed to get back to their feet at the same time. All three of them tried to open the door at the same time and all three of them tried to leave the carriage at the same time. The result was a series of crashes, bangs and flailing arms laced with colourful language, followed by a stampede along the corridor.

Almost immediately they had disappeared from view the conductor arrived at the door looking along the train towards the departing youths.

He slid the door open, looked at me with a scowl which quickly turned into a glare. "Well, young man." He said. "What sort of behaviour is this?"

I stared at him open mouthed. *'Why is he shouting at me?'* I thought.

"You can't just throw your litter anywhere, you know!" He was shouting now. "You get that sandwich packet picked up!"

Unable to comprehend what was going on for a second, I continued to stare, blushing furiously, which, of course, only served to highlight my guilt.

"Good God!" He exclaimed. "You haven't even eaten them!"

Finally understanding, I leapt up and picked up the sandwich bag from where it had fallen when Freddy had abandoned it. "Sorry." I said. "… But they…"

"No use giving me any excuses!" railed the Conductor. "Bloody youth of today!" He took a step forward. "Anyway, where's your ticket?"

I hunted through all my pockets, finally locating the ticket in the very last one., The man watched with every movement muttering to himself, then snatched it out of hand clipped it and left the compartment shaking his head as he went.

Flopping back into my seat and suddenly feeling very weary, I started to wonder if I was mentally fit enough to travel to London. Never mind across the globe in Merchant Ships!

Perhaps Jimmy, Freddy and Gilmot would be better taking my place. They seemed better equipped to take on life's challenges.

This line of thought had just started to take root in my mind when the trains' arrival at the next station, amid all the usual noises, was, this time, accompanied by sounds of angry shouting and pounding feet. I looked out of the window and along the platform. My face pressed against the glass to get a better view. The carriage was still squealing and shuddering to a stop but I could hear doors being flung open up ahead as well as the shouts and sounds of running.

The source of the commotion was soon explained when Gilmot hurtled past the window closely followed by Jimmy. Both of them with bell bottomed trousers flapping furiously around heavy platform shoes. Seventies style hairdo's flying out behind them!

An uncharitable smile began to play across my face. This increased markedly when I saw a forlorn looking Freddy being led along the platform by the conductor who had him gripped firmly by the ear.

So, no pictures in London for them! The thought cheered me up.

In fact, that was the last I ever saw of them. I did hear a rumour, years later, that they had all become bricklayers and had disappeared in Germany during the building boom in the nineteen eighties, but that was just a rumour. As I was to discover, though, you never know who you will meet, under what circumstances, or when. Life will always, always beat you to the punch.

The eleven o'clock slow train to Waterloo rattled, clanged, and squealed its way towards London, stopping at every station on its route. All of them becoming larger the closer it got to the mammoth terminal it was bound for. I sat staring out of the window becoming increasingly nervous the closer I got to the ship that was going to transport me to distant lands.

I couldn't really complain. I don't mean about the train; I mean about my life up to that point.

Raised in the leafy lanes of a small Surrey village, in a large bungalow with over an acre of garden to play in. I had been educated well. Firstly, in the village Primary School which only had three classrooms for three classes. Namely Bottom Class, Middle Class and Top Class. A simple system. Two years in each class from the age of 5 upwards. Resulting in transfer to 'Big School' in nearby Chertsey sometime between the ages of eleven and twelve. Unless of course one was bright enough to pass the 'Eleven Plus' exam. In which case (horror) one was shipped off to some obscure 'Grammar School'. Away from friends and children you had known for ever. Well, from the age of five anyway.

Luckily, I was nowhere near clever enough for such a lofty education and had to settle for 'Secondary Education' and normal 'Big School'.

So, now, rattling towards London to be transported to the roughest part of the city, to the docks, no less, to enter an alien working environment that, I was continually being told, no amount of Nautical School training would prepare me for, this inexperienced country boy felt extremely nervous, lonely and a long way outside his comfort zone.

CHAPTER 2

ARRIVAL

So 'twas with mounting fear and trepidation that I stepped on to the quayside of the King George 5th Dock in London on that cold, foggy afternoon in the January of Nineteen Seventy-One.

Standing near a warehouse the size of a small African country, surrounded by my worldly goods, I stared forlornly across the bustling dock towards the grey, glistening hull of the New Zealand Star. Blue Star Line's refrigerated cargo vessel of some twelve thousand tons that lay snugly in the southwest corner of King George V Dock in the London dock complex.

I looked at my watch… three o'clock.

The rest of the journey to Waterloo had been uneventful. The train arrived on time, squealing, and screeching to a halt beside platform eleven. I had managed to heave all the luggage off the train and onto a British Rail trolley that a kindly, extremely well spoken old gentleman in a tweed jacket and a trilby had just finished with. He helped me get the smaller of my bags off the train and I helped him get his three enormous suitcases on the train.

Before he climbed on board he stared at my baggage for a moment and asked me if I was going far. While I loaded up the trolley, I told him I was off to sea and that I was going to New Zealand. I even told him a bit about the company I was working for and where I was from. He nodded throughout my tale, appearing interested and eager to hear more. However,

I began to suspect something was not quite right when a glazed expression came over his face. He then peered at me and while I was still in mid-sentence put his hand to his ear and pulled out a hearing aid which made a horrible squelchy popping noise as it came out. He unhooked the wire to the battery from behind his ear, twirled it round his finger and said, in the poshest 'Lord Fauntleroy' accent I had ever heard.

"Fuhhking battery has gawn! Can't hear a fuhhking thing!" With that he clambered aboard the train, slammed the door shut. Pulled down the window and stuck his head out. "Do have a wonderful holiday old chap. Chin, chin!"

I had wheeled my trolley away after that wondering what else could happen. Surely not much. After all it was nearly two o'clock in the afternoon. There was only ten hours of the day left!

Little did I realise!

Anyway, I managed to get a taxi easily outside the station and me and my belongings were whisked, at breakneck speed, across London. All the time heading east towards the Royal London Docks and so at precisely three o'clock in the afternoon there I was. On the docks, staring at my first ship.

My thoughts briefly drifted towards wondering how on earth they managed to get this huge …thing… in to such a small corner, but my ruminations were quickly curtailed by loud squealing of brakes and an even louder angry sounding horn.

"Get art the faaarkin way" said a rotund, be-whiskered, docker perched somewhat precariously on top of an empty forklift truck.

"Sorry…" I started to apologise for my thoughtlessness, but my words were instantly drowned out as he gunned the engine and flung the forklift, at speed, in an exaggerated arc around my baggage.

Ah yes…my baggage. This had already caused me some embarrassment. I had unloaded it piece by piece from the taxi starting with my small holdall, followed by my bigger holdall, then my even bigger holdall, my rucksack, two suitcases (expandable) and a duffle bag emblazoned with the legend.

MEADS COUNTY SECONDARY SCHOOL. PE KIT.

I had made the usual mistake of dragging the stuff from the baggage bay in the front of the cab and placing it on the ground between me and the vehicle. So, I then had to lean in an ungainly bottom protruding manner across the luggage in order to pay the driver who, once he had grabbed his cash rocketed away leaving me to topple forward so I was arched across my belongings, feet on one side, hands on the ground the other side.

The physical makeup of the human body is a marvel of natural engineering making it capable of running at speed, jumping to incredible height, doing all manner of awe-inspiring acrobatics. However, when faced with the task of recovering from a bum in the air arched across some suitcases type position in a manly fashion, it is completely useless!

The problem was exacerbated by the fact that that morning, whilst nervously putting on my tie, I had left the thick end far too long, so as I toppled forward, this thick bit had become detached from the waistband of my trousers, where I had hastily stuffed it earlier and it had landed on the floor seconds before my right hand... which landed on top of it... so... when I tried to raise the upper part of my body the tie, trapped by my right hand, prevented any upward movement and caused me to topple sideways into my luggage whilst emitting a strangled squeaking noise.

I finally managed an upright standing position by rolling across the cases and bags and leaping to my feet in what I hoped looked like an athletic lunge to the sniggering bunch of cockney loiterers that had observed my arrival. As their sniggering had become, by now, loud guffaws, I could only assume the hoped-for athletic lunge had looked more like Bambi on ice.

The next task was to get all this stuff from my position by the warehouse to the bottom the ships gangway across a dockside strewn with ropes, boxes, wires, puddles and cranes. All of which were already being skilfully avoided by speeding forklifts and trucks.

This, I achieved, over the next ten minutes or so by a series of ungainly gallop like lurches amid the traffic, hampered by my having to explain several times to amused dockers that ... a. No, I did not have a kitchen sink amongst my belongings and ... b. No, the rucksack did not indicate my intention to go camping any time soon.

Finally bivouacked at the bottom of the gangway, the New Zealand Star was looming over me like a... a... well a huge looming thing, really.

Twelve thousand tonnes of iron, steel, plastic, wood and Formica. All put together in 1967 at Yard Number 109 of the Bremer Vulcan Shipyard, Vergesack, in Germany.

I looked slowly along the entire 168 metres of ship. Then I stared skywards wondering how to get my bags and baggage to the top of the gangway which now towered parallel to the ships side in a, what appeared to me to be, an almost vertical three-mile incline.

As I stared upwards a head appeared next to the top of the gangway supported by an epaulette clad pair of shoulders.

'At last,' I thought… a figure of authority to help me.

"Who are you?" growled the head.

"Brian George, cadet" I bellowed at the same time as a forklift truck raced past at full throttle.

"Who?" said the head.

"Brian George, cadet" I shouted as a crane rattled and squeaked loudly into a new position.

"What?"

"Brian George, cadet" A ship announced its arrival with a blast on the whistle.

"Can't hear," said head.

'You don't say' I thought.

"BRIAN GEORGE" I roared at exactly the same time as an uncanny period of complete silence descended upon London's dockland. Five thousand London dockers for a radius of two miles stared in my direction.

"Come up," said head.

So off I went again up and down, transferring my never-ending display of luggage, depositing it in an untidy heap at the top of the gangway.

Head watched each trip with interest. Any hope I had of him helping evaporated after the third stumbling, sweaty, muscle jarring journey.

"You're just joining I take it" he said.

I stood transfixed at his powers of deduction as he grabbed the smallest holdall and disappeared through a door marked 'OFFICERS' throwing a muffled "Follow me" over his shoulder.

The door slammed shut.

Picking up the nearest suitcase (expandable) I grabbed at the door handle wrenching the heavy wooden door open in a superhuman feat of

Down To The Sea. A Cadet's Tale

strength, simultaneously leaping over the large door sill, suitcase in hand landing, sweating, panting and panic stricken inside the looming thing.

The door slammed shut.

Now separated from the rest of my belongings I cast around despairingly, searching for any sign that would indicate where Head had gone. A fleeting glimpse of the heel of a black shoe disappearing at the top of a short flight of stairs facing me gave a glimmer of hope. Letting go of the suitcase (expandable) I bounded forward leaping up the stairs four at a time, arriving at the top sweating and panting again, but all to no avail… there he was… gone.

I went back down the stairs to what I now considered to be base camp. The alleyway at the bottom of the stairs was, as far as I could tell identical to the alleyway at the top of the stairs. Standing by the door through which I had hurtled a few seconds before I could see I was in a broad alleyway about fifteen feet wide running across the beam of the ship. To my right a metal and plastic wall containing two large double doorways with frosted glass stretched across the ship. To my left another, narrower, darker alleyway disappeared into the gloom towards the stern of the monster, again with rows of doorways on either side. My brief visit upstairs had revealed a similar sort of layout.

My already panicked brain took another lurch towards total insanity. How would I ever find my way around? Everywhere looked the same!

There was a continuous noise of machinery buzzing and humming coming from somewhere deep within the looming thing.

I turned slowly and opened the door behind me and stepped back out into the misty London air, relieved to find the rest of my baggage had not been purloined by gangs of Pearly Kings and Queens. My befuddled senses had led me to imagine I would see my belongings being toted down the quayside by cockney near-do-wells shouting a hearty "Gawd blimey guv'nor and no mistake" in best Mary Poppins style.

Resigned to my fate I heaved the bags into the alleyway one by one trying to decide my next course of action. Thinking it best to trail in the wake of Head I started the climb to the upper alleyway where I had spotted Head's shoe. Several trips later, heaving the last but one of my bags halfway up the stairs my day suddenly brightened when I saw Head standing at the top.

"Where have you been? Follow me" he said grabbing another of my holdalls spinning round and disappearing again.

Taking the remaining stairs in two panic stricken despairing bounds, determined not lose him and vaguely wondering where he had put the small holdall of mine he had been carrying the last time he disappeared, I arrived at the top of the stairs wild-eyed and panting… all to no avail, there he was… gone… again.

A career in the British Merchant Navy was now beginning to take on a less attractive appearance than my original youthful enthusiasm had given me.

"Hello" said a voice behind me. I whirled around to come face to face with entirely different sort of being. This one was covered in oily streaks, had black hands and was wearing what was once probably a white boiler suit. The being had come up the stairs behind me carrying the duffle bag. The last of my baggage.

"You must be the new Engineer Cadet, follow me".

I tried to explain I was actually a Deck Cadet, but Boiler Suit had raced away down one of the darker alleyways with my duffle bag.

Determined this time not to left behind or be separated from my baggage I grabbed my entire remaining luggage and galloped off in pursuit, bouncing suitcases (expandable) into various doors in the process.

"Come in" shouted a voice from behind one door.

"What?" Bellowed another.

I was, once again, panting hard by the time we arrived at the end of the alleyway outside a door marked 'Engineer Cadets'.

"OI!" Shrilled an agitated voice from the other end of the alleyway from whence I had just galloped.

"What are you doing down there?" It was Head, minus my middle-sized holdall.

"This is the new Engineer Cadet" shouted Boiler Suit.

"No, he's not," roared Head… "He's the Fourth Mate. Head was now stomping down the alleyway towards us.

"No, I'm not." I protested.

"See, I told you." Said Boiler Suit, looking smug.

"No, I mean I'm not an engineer……."

"Aha" shrilled Head in triumph as he arrived at our position at the far end of the alleyway.

"…Or a 4th Mate" I continued. Both Boiler Suit and Head stared at me blankly. Completely at a loss in the face of this confused alien being that had somehow invaded their warren.

"Who are you then?" Hissed Head, frowning.

"I'm a Deck Cadet" I whispered.

"Well why didn't you say so" wailed Head and Boiler Suit in unison. They both turned and raced off back the way we had come.

"You're in the wrong place." said Head over his shoulder.

"You should be in the starboard alleyway" said Boiler Suit, also over his shoulder.

I cantered off after them again, goods and chattels, once again, crashing and bouncing off walls and doors alike.

"Come in," shouted a voice.

Halfway along the alleyway, with which I and my luggage were, by now, totally familiar, Boiler Suit came to abrupt halt and opened a door on the right-hand side. The constant buzzing, humming noise I had noticed earlier suddenly became a deafening roar as he stepped through the opening and was swallowed whole. The door slammed shut. The noise returned to buzzing and humming again.

Head, in the meantime, arrived at the end of the alleyway, turned right into the wider alleyway where the stairs were and disappeared again. I increased my pace to a full sprint and turned the corner just in time to see him, again, disappearing down another alleyway on the other side of the ship. Strength fading fast I managed a final burst of speed and hurtled round the final bend into this new even darker alleyway.

"Hello… come in" shouted someone from behind a door as my stuff crashed along this new alleyway.

After what seemed about a mile, we came to a halt outside a door at the end of the corridor marked 'Deck Cadets'. The relief was indescribable. Particularly as there, outside the door was my smaller, and middle-sized holdalls.

I was finally reunited with all my belongings!

"This is where you live" he said.

"Thank you" I puffed, genuinely grateful.

"Now then" he continued. "What you'll have to do is…" At this point I lost him completely as he reeled off a series of instructions.

It sounded like…

"Gethekeesfromthemateandsumlinenfromthecheefstewoodthenget unpackedandcumandfindmeilebeinumbertwohatch"

"Pardon" I said to nobody in particular as Head had yet again scuttled away into the distance.

I had heard the word 'keys' mentioned so I assumed the door would be locked but as all male humans do when faced with a locked door, I tried the handle first.

Now then… as with the taxi scenario that now seemed three lifetimes ago… my luggage was between me and the door. So, I had, once again, to lean over it to reach the door handle. Not much of a lean, but a lean none the less. This would not normally cause any problems, that is, it would not cause any problems if, as Head had led me to believe, the door had been locked.

It was not. It was unlocked.

So, as I tried the handle, pushing at the door in the process, to my complete surprise, it flew open. The top half of my body was now able to enter the room beyond.

However, as before, at the taxi, the bottom half was restricted by the heap of luggage between me and the doorway. The result was, as gravity took hold, my top half rocketed into the cabin arms flailing. My feet becoming entangled in the various straps and handles attached to my bags. I landed bum in the air, face on the floor in the cabin, feet across the luggage outside the cabin… *'Again?'* I thought… *'Good job there is no one around this time.'*

"Hello" said a new voice. A new female voice.

CHAPTER 3

CATHY

Twisting my neck into an impossible position I was able to look up into the wide, deep blue eyes of a girl.

"You must be the new cadet. You've arrived then. I've been waiting for you."

"Urguff!" was about all I could manage by way of a reply. At the same time lashing out with my feet in several directions at once like a demented break dancer in an attempt to free them from the luggage.

"Here, let me help you" said the vision of beauty, grabbing me by the arm. "What's your name?"

"Brian George" I squeaked staggering to my feet and falling instantly in love.

"My names' Cathy" she said.

"Oh." I breathed. Whenever I was faced with a beautiful women I would always fire off a smooth, witty one liner like that.

'Cathy' was beautiful. She had long blonde, straight hair that came down to her waist. Her face was alight with a captivating smile underneath a cute button nose, all topped off with wide pale blue eyes. Actually, I didn't notice that her eyes were blue at that particular moment. That came later.

"My names' Brian George" I repeated, desperately trying to think up something better to say and offering up prayers to the almighty not to let me start blushing.

"I know, you just told me, "She giggled "You're blushing."

"No, I am not" I said going redder still. Then, amidst very unholy thoughts about the Almighty and his abilities, I began a round of loud coughing as though a sudden bout of apoplexy had caused my change in hue.

My life's ambitions changed in a matter of seconds at that point. Whereas before I had intended to go to sea, work my way up through the ranks and eventually become Captain of one of these mighty vessels. Now, in an instant, my sole ambition was to go out with this vision that stood before me.

My confusion was complete. The very last thing, the one thing that is completely outside the realms of possibility… The situation that a boy of seventeen, arriving on a ship in London's dockland, with virtually no life experience would least expect himself to be in, is to be clambering from a pile of luggage and staring into the eyes of a beautiful woman.

"Yes, you are. Anyway, here, let me help you with these." She grabbed the small duffle bag and went to move into the cabin. Again, I was let down by whichever Gods look after the 'looking cool' section of life. They failed to notice one part of the duffle bag cord was still caught in my foot. The result was Cathy took two steps into the cabin dragging my left foot with her before she had to stop. So, I did a sort of half split. One foot still outside the cabin in the luggage, the other foot inside the cabin. My head now level with Cathy's shoulder.

"Oops! Sorry!" She laughed. Really, a captivating giggle that felt as though she was laughing at us both, me and her, in a silly situation. Rather than just laughing at me looking an idiot.

I could only manage a sort of snort which made me sound like that very idiot.

The situation was rapidly getting out of hand. So, I did an ungainly skipping manouvre to untangle my foot, grabbed a suitcase and attempted a manly couple of strides past Cathy into the cabin.

Then… I employed the services of Clint Eastwood!

That may sound like a strange statement but I shall explain.

When I was a mere boy of fifteen, I was told by a vastly more experienced seventeen-year-old that women of all ages could not resist strong silent Clint Eastwood types. I had therefore spent several months in front of the mirror perfecting my 'Clint' look. I could screw up my eyes, leer, curl one corner of my mouth, wrinkle my forehead and become the very image of Mr. Eastwood.

Actually, it made look more like a short-sighted wildebeest with piles but I didn't realise this until much later in life. I actually spent a long time at parties standing on my own being 'Clint'. Girls would wander past me asking each other who the weirdo with the bad eyes was in the corner.

Cathy had reached out and grabbed another bag and was putting it down in front of me. She looked up and stared at me for a second.

"Is there something wrong with your eyes" she said frowning.

"No" I said.

At that moment I was saved from further questioning about my facial expressions by the arrival of a man, approximately the size of a medium Alp, who lumbered into the cabin carrying one of my suitcases and a holdall.

He stood still, staring at the scene, not speaking.

I stared back, not knowing what to say.

Cathy glanced at him and then resumed looking at me and said, "This is Jim, he is the cadet you are replacing."

My gaze shifted in her direction. She seemed unhappy to see him, as though he had intruded, but she smiled sweetly at him.

"He's my sort of boyfriend."

'Sort of...' I thought.

"He's the cadet you're replacing."

Devastation set in and Clint left in a hurry.

"Ullo" rumbled the Alp.

"This is George." said Cathy.

"Oh right" He looked at me quizzically trying to decide if my eyes were deformed in some way. "My names Jim." He said unnecessarily and stuck out a giant paw.

"I'm Brian" I said, taking his hand and having mine crushed to a pulp while he shook it vigorously.

"You said it was George" Cathy said, looking puzzled.

Jim glared at her "Shut up" he said, rolling his eyes "I think he knows what his name is".

"Don't talk to me like that" shouted my vision of beauty. There was obviously a bit of a domestic situation going on here.

"Well don't be so stupid then" stormed the Alp, while grinning at me and rolling his eyes again.

All this was not what I had been led to expect as a professional handover of duties.

"Get Stuffed" continued Cathy. Jim went purple puffed out his chest and became positively Himalayan in appearance.

"You get stuffed" He muttered sulkily which didn't go with his mountainous appearance.

"I'm off" muttered Cathy and headed for the door. "I'll see you later Brian." She said over her shoulder, then paused, smiled at me, glared at her 'sort of boyfriend' and then flounced out.

"Good… make your own way home" shouted Jim as the door slammed. Then he frowned and turned towards me. "What did she mean 'See you later'?"

I, of course was mortified that anyone would dare to speak to my Vision in such a manner, so I grabbed him by the lapels, slammed him against the wall and told him to mind his manners.

Well, that's not quite what happened…that's what went through my mind.

Instead, I did the next best thing which was to shuffle sideways and develop a deep interest in my shoes.

"Dunno." I said.

"Bloody women" stormed Jim. "Anyway, I'm off, have a good trip" and with that he flung open the door and stomped off down the alleyway.

Alone again I thought.

"By the way" he shouted over his shoulder "The third mate wants someone to help him down number …" A door slammed shut somewhere along the alleyway "… hatch".

I hurdled my luggage again in, yet another despairing bound.

"Which hatch?" I shouted but Jim had disappeared around the corner. I heard a muffled "Yes… that's the one" float back as he reached the lower deck.

Back in the cabin after retrieving the rest of my baggage, I slumped dejectedly into the only chair amidst my battered gear and contemplated my next move. Going back to nice calm quiet Surrey seemed a promising idea. I gazed around my new home. So much had happened over the last few minutes I had had no chance to take in my surroundings.

The cadet's cabin was a square space with a double bunk along the wall adjacent to small bathroom which, in turn, was adjacent to the alleyway with the cabin door at right angles to the bathroom door. The panel at the end of the bunk and the bathroom door formed a short vestibule type space with a double wardrobe on the far side. The main part of the cabin was taken up by a desk, a chair, two small chests of drawers and a settee (daybed in nautical speak) which butted up to the pillow end of the bunks. The floor space in the middle was about the size of a bathmat.

I spent the next half an hour 'stowing' my vast array of uniforms, work clothes and trendy going out gear into various drawers and wardrobes. 'Stowing' is a nautical term that means 'stuffing in small spaces.'

As for the cases, (expandable) holdalls, rucksack, and duffle bag, I managed to get them all into the wardrobe by the cabin door by holding them in with one hand, then quickly removing that hand, at the same time slamming the door shut with the other one before they all fell out.

Anyway, the time had come to venture out and hunt down the Chief of all the Officers. He was actually simply known as 'The Mate' and was in charge of all 'deck' type things. The Chief Engineer being in charge of all machinery type things.

Now then… what to wear? I hunted down one of my sparkly new crispy white boiler suits and struggled into it.

It positively shone.

If I go out in this thing… glowing like a supernova, a multi coloured neon sign would appear above my head saying, 'LOOK AT THIS PRAT… HE'S NEVER BEEN ON A SHIP BEFORE'. So, I had to make it look older. I didn't want to take it off after struggling into it so I dived on to the floor and rolled around trying to get as much dust and muck on it as possible.

The door opened. I just had time to leap into a kneeling position.

"What on earth are you doing?" It was Cathy again. Even my feet blushed this time.

"Lost something" I muttered, clambering on to my red feet and looking pointedly at the floor.

"Oh" she said giving me a look that said, 'I don't believe you'.

"Left my scarf" she said opening the wardrobe door. She was, of course, then immediately attacked by my luggage. Holdalls, suitcases (expandable) rucksacks etc. cascaded around her.

I was at a loss to understand why, whenever this woman appeared, I was visited by all manner of face reddening, limb twisting, tongue cleaving, plagues. I concluded that the Gods were conducting a personal vendetta against me. I must have done something hideous in a former life. Ate people's babies or shot Bambi.

Cathy found the errant scarf and was heading back out the cabin when she stopped, paused then turned to face me. I started to go red again.

"He's not really my boyfriend." She said tipping her head slightly to one side and smiling a sad smile. "He lives next door. His parents and my aunt know each other." She paused again, looking directly into my eyes.

"Ah." I said.

"Well, actually my Dad and his Mum and Dad know each other as well." She elaborated.

"Ah." I said again nodding, hoping my face didn't give away my feeling of complete elation that she had come back into the cabin and the sudden return of an uncontrollable longing.

She nodded in return and we looked at each other awkwardly for a few seconds.

"My father goes to sea."

"Ah."

"I don't live far away."

"Ah." My mind was racing, conversational data banks working at full capacity, seduction techniques being worked up to full operating mode, quick-fire repartee abilities ready for instant use. Unfortunately, all to no avail. All I seemed to able to come up with was…

"Ah."

Suddenly, conversational ability returned.

"I'm from Surrey." I said.

"Ah." Said Cathy.

"Chertsey"

"Ah." She frowned, looking away. Then she raised her eyebrows and looked at me again. "Is this your first trip?"

"Yes."

"Have you met the captain yet?"

Now it was my turn to frown. *'Strange question'* I thought.

"Erm… No. Just got here."

"Oh yes, of course." She said with a small chuckle. "Anyway, I'm off."

"Are you coming back?" said a voice. I looked round, then realised it was me! I blushed again.

Cathy grinned, her face taking on an impish look. She stuck one hip out, tilted her head again and said quietly "Do you want me to?"

"Ah…Yer… Whoa… No…Ah…Yes, YES!" I nearly shouted the last word as my mind battled with my mouth causing it to do verbal somersaults.

I tried to recover my composure. This was, of course a complete waste of time as I had no composure in the first place.

Her grin widened. The result of realising she had me under her complete control again. "Well, I might then." She turned and disappeared out the door.

It took me several minutes to recover from all this. The medical term for this, is, I think, shock. Everything that had happened to me since I stepped out of the taxi, only… I looked at my watch… twenty minutes ago! Twenty minutes! Everything, everything was chasing around in my head.

'My God' I thought. *'Twenty minutes! What's three months going to be like?'*

I managed to pull myself back to something approaching together and paced up and down for a few minutes until I remembered the problem of the sparkly white boilersuit had not gone away. I looked down at it. After my frantic gyrations on the cabin floor, it was now faintly streaked with dust. So, back to the floor again, more gyrations then back to my feet. A mirror was the next problem. I needed to inspect my handiwork. Unfortunately, the only mirror in the place was at head height and only about four inches square, so the only way I could view my ensemble was to stand on the chair. Even then I could only see one sleeve and the left breast pocket, due to only being able to move the chair so far to the left before it was hard up to the desk. However, I thought, if I leapt forward and to the left at the same time, I would be granted a fleeting glimpse of the entire ensemble. So, I leapt forward and to the leftward trying to keep my arms by my side so as to see as much of the outfit as possible and succeeding only in taking on the appearance of a kangaroo in mid hop.

The door opened! (Doesn't anyone ever knock?) In strode another large man. This one had a huge beard and three gold stripes on each shoulder of his navy-blue jumper. The Chief of all the officers.

"Ah, you must be the cadet" he said. Another nautical person with amazing powers of deduction.

He looked me up and down. "You're in a boiler suit then."

'Yes, definitely a descendant of Sherlock Holmes'. I thought.

"Wondered where you'd got to." He fished around in his jacket pocket and produced a 'Yale' type key attached to a small yellow tag and tossed it my direction. "Cabin key." He said. "Did Jim show you anything?

"No." I said. *'Apart from his ex-girlfriend'* I thought.

"Prat!" He said. "He was supposed to show you round. "Gone now, has he?"

"Yes, just left… Err." I hesitated. … "Sir."

He grinned "It's ok, you don't have to call me sir. Chief or Boss will do." He paused, looking thoughtful for second. "Mind you some Mates prefer to be called Sir. Anyway, Follow me." He turned and raced out of the door. "I'll have to show you round."

I galloped out in pursuit thinking it was a good job he didn't see me leaping off the chair.

"By the way, why were you leaping off the chair?" he shouted as we passed a group of leering engineers standing at the end of the alleyway. "I bet you were trying to see what your boiler suit looks like in the mirror, weren't you?"

"No!" I lied. Chortling noises came from the engineers.

"Yeah, bet you were!" he said laughing.

My brain in overdrive again, I was about to indignantly insist that I was really changing a light bulb or something when we came to the stairs where I had first lost "Head" (my initial guide). The Chief of all the officers went down them six at a time. As there were only twelve steps it didn't take him long. I was about to attempt the same death-defying feat when a white coated steward swung into view carrying a large tray of cups. I stopped, my leader continued, through a door and away. I was now sure that these people had all trained under Paul Daniels and were experts in illusions involving their disappearance. The steward and I did a soft shoe shuffle around each other at the halfway point on the stairs, the cups wobbling precariously. I reached the door and flung it open and there to my utter delight was my guide, staring in my direction, exaggeratedly tapping his fingers, and leaning against the bulwark.

"Oh, you have decided to join me then" he muttered. "Now then, listen carefully and I will explain these things as we go around". He then launched into a monologue that must have come from the Greek classics. It was nothing that I understood. In fact, he could have used one of the more obscure Urdu dialects for all the good it would have done! On the upside there were one or two words I recognised like "the" and "it". Just to help matters the tour was conducted at the same breakneck speed throughout.

We finally arrived back at my cabin where he said "Right, get changed into your uniform it's time to eat." And off he went.

I looked at my watch. Five o'clock. At three thirty on this January day, I had been on the dockside staring up at the ship. I had thought of it as *'This great looming thing.'*

When, several weeks ago, I had received my letter of appointment, it had said that I was to join the **M.V. New Zealand Star** for her forthcoming three-month voyage to New Zealand. Well, I had now been on the **M.V. New Zealand Star,** the 'Looming Thing' for one and a half hours. That left only two months, three weeks, six days and seven hours to go.

I sighed and looked around my new home.

CHAPTER 4

STEVEN

About twenty minutes later I peered out of my cabin, ensured the alleyway was clear of leering, micky taking engineers and took a few tentative steps, resplendent in best uniform, along the alleyway. It had taken me some time to gather together the complete ensemble that was my uniform. There was no time for a shower, so I had had a quick wash and thrown on the white shirt, black tie, black trousers, and uniform jacket with my single cadet stripe on each sleeve. A brief moment of panic had ensued when I couldn't find my black uniform shoes. An all-enveloping horror being replaced by waves of relief when I found them underneath the mountain of luggage in the wardrobe.

The next step was, of course, to find the eating place. The saloon.

I remembered, during my frantic gallops around the alleys earlier seeing a sign over some glass doors opposite the stairs that said **SALOON**. So, I trotted along the alleyway to the stairs, went down them and was rewarded by the sight of white coated stewards bustling around carrying dishes of food and the sounds of cutlery clinking on plates and scraping around bowls.

I walked self-consciously through the door and into a large room that contained two large round tables that seated about eight people each and four smaller square tables with four seats each. There was nobody at the smaller tables, but the two round ones had about four people at each. All engaged in earnest conversation.

All engaged in earnest conversation that is until I entered the room. At that point, all earnest conversation stopped and all earnest staring in

Down To The Sea. A Cadet's Tale

my direction began. I made my way to what I thought would be a suitable place to sit on one of the round tables. I didn't want to appear unsociable and sit at a corner table on my own.

The staring continued.
The silence continued.

My chair made a loud scraping noise as I pulled it towards me and sat down at the same time nodding a 'hello' at my table companions in what I hoped was a nonchalant confident manner. Thinking about it later it probably looked more like an involuntary twitch.

The staring continued.
The silence continued.

I was just thinking that perhaps I had, whilst dressing, mistakenly slipped a wellington boot on my head, when the steward that I had briefly danced with on stairs earlier appeared at my left elbow.

"Ooohhh" he breathed "you can't sit there dearie. That's the third engineers place."

The staring continued.
The silence continued.

My chair scraped noisily across the floor as I stood up. The occupants of both tables watched as the steward led me by the sleeve to one of the corner tables for four.

"This is the cadets table" he twittered as I sat down "What would you like to eat?"

Conversation at the other tables resumed. I was no longer of interest.

In front of me I found a piece of dog eared card with the word 'menu' typed at the top. At least that is what I assumed it was supposed to read. What was actually printed was:

M eNU

I picked the card up. The next word read SOUP.

"Soup please" I said. The steward departed, hips swinging, only to return almost immediately with a bowl of a thick brown mud like substance. I was about to enquire as to the nature of this gastronomic delicacy, but the steward beat me to it.

"Don't ask me what it is" he whispered. "The cooks been on the bottle all morning… he's drunk as skunk. We're trying to make do"

I closed my eyes and thought 'If I leave now, I could be home in time for the 9 o'clock news'.

Instead, I consumed my mud, thinking I had obviously been in a train crash or a car accident recently, died and this was the hell to where I had been sent.

My thoughts were interrupted by the sound of a telephone ringing in the alleyway outside the saloon. The steward answered it.

"Ullo… who… Brian what? … Jones? … George?... The cadet? … Just a minute." I could feel my face turning pink. He took a couple of paces towards the door and leaned into the saloon. The telephone cord stretching tautly across the alleyway.

"Are you Brian George?" he bellowed, looking at me with expression like Genghis Khan might have on finding a member of his mighty conquering horde receiving a parcel of clean underwear from his mum.

The staring resumed.

The silence resumed.

I had, once again become the centre of attention.

"Well, there's some woman on the phone for you." He sniffed, looked me up and down and stuck his left hip out in a disapproving manner while pushing the handset as far as he could in my direction. "Called Cathy".

I went red and stood up, my chair doing the loud scraping thing again only this time in what sounded like surround sound.

All eyes followed me as I took the handset from the steward and walked the five miles to the telephone which was situated right opposite the saloon door in full view and earshot of all the starers. I hadn't noticed it before, but it was, actually a public telephone. Obviously minus its red telephone box. It looked strange and out of place somehow and was another thing to get my poor befuddled brain around!

"Hello" I said, once again traffic light red.

"Ah, there you are." Shouted Cathy." The steward hovered, cleaning a clean plate with a tea towel. The occupants of the round table in the saloon leaned towards the doorway. Staring eyes dropping to gaze at their food to try and look disinterested.

"Yes" I whispered.

"What!" She shrieked. "I'm in a phone box... can't hear you".

"I said... yes" I was desperately trying not to let anyone hear what I was saying. Particularly not the starers and, for that matter, the steward, who was by this time, virtually perched on my shoulder trying even harder to look as though he wasn't listening but still cleaning and drying his, by now spotless, bone dry, plate.

"Yes what?" she bellowed.

"Yes, I'm here" I rasped.

"Still can't hear you... Why are you whispering?"

"I'm not whispering." I whispered.

"You are". She shouted in an exasperated tone.

"I'm not." I breathed.

"You are." Her annoyance causing her voice to rise a further ten decibels.

"You are" said the steward flouncing off down the alleyway.

"Anyway" she shouted "I have to come back to the ship sooner than I thought. I've left something in the cabin. I just wanted to make sure I could come and get it. Just making sure you weren't going ashore or anything.

"No" I shouted back. All attempts at secrecy abandoned.

"Why not?" She wailed. "I only want to get something".

"I mean I'm not going ashore" I could hear muffled sniggers coming from the saloon.

"Oh, that's alright then, see you later" The phone went dead.

"Ok" I said into the phone trying to sound as though I had ended the conversation. I needn't have bothered, of course, because the wretched machine had already started making that wailing noise that happens when someone on the other end puts the handset down. This was audible as far away as Peckham, so all the saloon occupants chortled gleefully to each other at my discomfort.

The silence and staring stopped.

The eating resumed.

I walked back to my dining place to resume my mud; however, the steward had already removed the dish and had returned, grinning.

"What would you like now?" he said throwing his head to one side and sticking out a hip. "You can have fish and chips or cold meat".

"Fish and chips please" I was already pre-occupied with piecing together recent events and worrying about what to do next.

Problems of earth-shattering proportions began to build up in my mind. Things like what will I say when she arrives? What will I wear? Should I be standing, nonchalantly leaning, or perhaps sitting? ... Perhaps with one leg thrown over the arm of the chair. A sudden panic gripped me. Did the chair have arms?

A plate of green sludge arrived.

"You did want mushy peas as well, didn't you?" The steward waltzed off without waiting for an answer.

My first meal in The Merchant Navy passed without further drama. I found fish and chips cleverly hidden under the green sludge and I managed to eat it all. It was, actually, surprisingly good so I risked a lump of jam roly-poly and custard afterwards.

Returning to my cabin, I set about the task of preparing for Cathy's arrival. I rummaged deep into my locker and produced a tight fitting bright yellow shirt with a large round cornered collar.…. Also, a pair of blue Loons... Great big low waisted, bell bottom type trousers, the bottoms of which were constantly attracted to large puddles and mud.

I laid the ensemble out on the bunk.

'Next, a shower', I thought. I was actually lucky with my first ship. **The New Zealand** Star was a fairly new ship. So even the cadet cabins were fitted with their own bathrooms.

It consisted of a tiny space with beige floor tiles. There was a shower cubicle in the far corner next to a sink on the wall adjacent to the alleyway. A toilet adorned the rear wall in the space next to the shower cubicle. The only thing that was a bit difficult to cope with was the temperature in there. It was, I felt, fairly close to that at the centre of the sun and I soon discovered that it remained that way regardless of the temperature in the outside world.

I spent the next five minutes leaping in and out of the cubicle in a vain attempt to get a shower with water at a temperature suitable for humans. It wasn't until sometime later in the voyage I discovered that someone had put the shower controls on back to front. So hot meant welding heat and cold meant slightly hotter.

Becoming fed up with all this leaping about *('It's all I seemed to have done since I arrived.'* I thought. *'Leaping… up and down stairs, over luggage, off chairs etc.')* I started to dry myself but gave up after a few minutes. It was far too hot.

I was about to leave for the comparative cool of the cabin, when the cabin door from the alleyway was flung open and someone walked in. When I say walked in, I mean crash in really! The cabin door banged heavily against the wardrobes opposite the bathroom door, and something cannoned into the door itself. There was a loud "Ooofff!" from the cabin crasher then silence, except for the sound of an exhausted human panting.

Flinging a towel round myself, I opened the door and looked out, but, of course, could only see as far as the wardrobe opposite, so was about to step out of the bathroom when a familiar female voice wafted into the cabin. I tensed suddenly causing the towel to drop to the floor. The voice, as far as I could tell, came from the cross alleyway (the one with the stairs).

… "I'll come down to the bar in a bit…just got to get some stuff from the cabin…got halfway home… forgot it… …see you later."

Horror! Cathy had arrived!

'Oh God!' I thought, turning a full circle as I picked up my towel, wrapped it round me and leapt out of the bathroom, … *'That's all I need… she's early'.*

I charged into the cabin flinging the towel ahead of me and lunged in the direction of my trendy 70's clothes which I had laid out carefully on the lower bunk.

In that brief millisecond between opening the bathroom door and hearing the voice of the vision, in my panic, I had completely forgotten the sounds I just heard of someone entering the cabin.

I skidded to a stop. An all-enveloping sense of horror and bewilderment overwhelmed me. They weren't there! The trendy clothes! They weren't there!

Instead, I could see a large, well, huge actually, battered brown suitcase.

I stared, transfixed. My mind unable to take in what my eyes were telling it… battered brown suitcase… trendy gear…not there!

"Oh, hello…Are you the other cadet?" I whirled round, eyes popping. My mouth making a sort of strangled squeaking noise.

A youth with a pimply face, a protruding Adams Apple and the biggest ears I had ever seen atop a tall gangly body stood staring at me. I stared back, mouth opening and closing, unable to make any sound.

There was a loud knocking at the door. Our heads turned in unison.

"Can I come in?" Cathy!

"No!" I shrieked.

"Yes!" shouted Big Ears.

Off I went again, leaping across the cabin in the nude, eyes bulging, muscles straining, doing a passable impersonation of the Wild Man of Borneo and grabbing at the towel which had landed on the desk when I had flung it off during my entrance.

The vision, Cathy, the girl I had planned to impress with my nonchalant behaviour and trendy dress sense, walked in just as I managed to drape the towel round me. I stood looking at her, mouth open, panting, dripping wet, wild eyed and, of course, blushing like a California sunset.

"Have you been running?" said Cathy.

"No" I puffed.

"Why are you panting then?" she asked, looking cute and doing the head tilting on one side thing.

By this time, I was beyond caring… My plans of nonchalant leaning in trendy 70's clothes were in ruins. I became irrationally angry. "Because it's Thursday" I raged. "I always pant on a Thursday. I come from an extensive line of Thursday panters!"

For some reason Big Ears thought this was hilarious and laughed, making a noise like a water buffalo with tooth ache.

Cathy and I stared at him, waiting for the noise to stop. There was then a long silence while he gathered himself.

"By the way I'm the other cadet." He said sticking out a hand in my direction, which, in a natural reaction, I took.

Cathy grinned and looked at me… "I'll get my thing" she said, "It's only a scarf." With that she turned on her heel and marched over to the cupboard.

'She's forgotten what happens when you open that door' I thought.

She opened the door.

Suitcases (expandable) and holdalls cascaded around her. She looked annoyed and the water buffalo noise started again from Big Ears. We both stared at him until he stopped. Cathy muttered something unladylike, glanced in my direction raising her eyes heavenwards as she did so and deftly piled the luggage back into the cupboard where, of course, it stayed, showing no signs of toppling back out again. *'How did she do that?'* Was the thought that briefly crossed my mind but got no further because she was speaking again.

"You can let go now if you want." She said, laughing and looking at my right hand that was still grasping Big Ears' giant paw.

"Right," she continued, "I'm going down to the bar, see you in a minute Brian."

I threw the hand I was holding away and tried to look nonchalant in the second I had left before she reached the door.

"OK beautiful, see you there." said my mind. "Okrermuphligabiddle" muttered my mouth.

"Pardon?" said Cathy, her hand on the door handle.

"Nothing" I said.

She stared at me for about three years whilst I, once again, went red, then she left.

"You're blushing" said Big Ears.

"No, I'm not."

"Yes, you are."

"Where's my clothes?" I stormed. "They were on the bed".

"Bunk" said Big Ears.

"Pardon?"

"Bunk" he said again. "It's called a bunk" A superior tone had crept into his voice.

"I don't care!" I ranted. "My clothes were on it…now your tatty suitcase is on it…so… where are my clothes?"

"Oh…sorry" he looked sheepish. "I think they are underneath the suitcase."

I grabbed hold of the case and dragged it to the floor. We both stared at my wrinkled, grubby, trendy 70's clothes.

"Sorry" he said again "Didn't see them".

"Didn't see them! … Didn't see them! …" I was now in full rant. "How… How… How can you miss bright yellow shirts and light blue trousers?" "How?"

"Is she your girlfriend?" He said.

"What!?" I was completely thrown by his complete change of direction.

"That girl ... Katy ... is she your girlfriend?"

"What... No ... No, she isn't" I said grabbing at my wrinkled trendy Loons. "Be careful where you put your suitcase in future ... and her name is Cathy ... not Katy."

"Alright ... alright" he said. His head bobbing from side to side. "Keep your shirt on."

"I would do if your suitcase wasn't on it!"

Big Ears thought this highly amusing, and I was once again visited by the dentally challenged Water Buffalo.

When he had regained his composure, he dragged his suitcase over to the cupboard to start the ritual stowing ceremony. He also became somewhat annoyed at being showered with luggage as he opened the door.

I hastily put on my trendy clothes and attempted to smooth out the wrinkles and brush off the dust.

"What's your name" I asked.

"Steven" he said, "Steven Waddington...Ow! ... Ouch!" A suitcase (expandable) fell on him.

"Is this your first trip" I asked.

He drew himself up to his full height, which must have been at least six foot and an inch or two, puffed out his chest and said.

"Good heavens ... no! I was on the Townsville Star last trip."

More chest puffing. "Really wild it was ... we did the Kiwi coast!"

"Oh" I said. "How many trips have you done then?"

"Only one ... on that ship" He added the 'on that ship' quickly, as if it was an afterthought.

"You?"

I thought about bluffing and saying this was my third trip. But then decided against it. "No" I said, "First trip."

"Oh" he said in a fatherly tone, looking superior "Don't worry ... you will soon get the hang of it" He headed for the door. "Let's go and find the bar."

"Ok." I said. I had finished dressing by then, even down to donning my brown platform shoes and I had calmed down a bit. So, I followed after him as he left the cabin and we both trotted off down the alleyway with me grateful that I didn't have to find 'The Bar' on my own. *'He's been to sea before'* I thought. *He'll know where it is.'*

"Where is it … do you know?" he said.

"Dunno." I said, starting to worry again.

We got to the stairs and went down a deck. The saloon was all closed up but next to it was another set of glass doors with a sign above saying:

Officers Smoke Room

"Here it is," said Steven.

"Of course," I said. Trying to sound as though I had known all along.

One of the doors was propped open by a chair. Steven paused, peered in, and then strode forward. I followed.

The room was large … about the same size as the eating place, but furnished with green low, curved backed chairs placed around Formica topped round tables. Chintzy looking light brown curtains tied back with tasselled cords adorned the port holes. Two long green sofas were pushed up against the far wall.

At first sight the place looked empty. But off to the right in the corner was 'The Bar'. A small Formica topped curved surface with a gap at one end. It was held up by a solid angled base covered in that studded black leatherette look plastic which was popular once in the dim and distant past. Squashed around 'The Bar' were about ten people. Nine of them in trendy seventy's clothes surrounding the tenth person … Cathy. *'She hadn't gone home after all'* I thought, immediately swivelling my head this way and that in case the alpine Jim was lurking in a corner.

She was holding forth about something. With the nine men, drooling and hanging on every word, craning forward to get as close as possible.

She turned in our direction as we came in.

"Here they are now" she said.

The droolers also turned and looked in our direction. The silence started. The staring started.

CHAPTER 5

CAPTAIN JONATHAN MCHALE

"Hello" said the man behind the bar. "Cathy says you're both cadets"

"Yes." We said in unison.

"Deck or Engine?"

"Deck" we harmonised.

"Are you two a double act … or do you come in individual packets?"

Steven thought this hilarious, and it set him off with the water buffalo thing again. All the sea dogs at the bar stared at him until the noise stopped.

. "Yes … well … what would you like to drink?" said the barman.

"Can of Fosters please" said Steven in his best 'I've been to sea for ages' voice. He leaned manfully on the bar.

"What about you?" said the barman, looking at me and frowning.

"Erm … the same please." I didn't really know what 'A can of Fosters' was, but everybody else seemed to be drinking one, so I didn't want to be different.

Two cans were shoved along the bar at us and a rusty can opener followed which Steven grabbed and proceeded to open both, which I was quite happy about as one of them must have been shaken a bit and showered him white froth.

Anyway, I was still trying to look the rufty tufty sea dog so once I had been given my beer Clint Eastwood started to creep into my face. Until, that is, I saw Cathy looking at me with concern.

"Have you got something in your eye again?" she asked.

"No" I said. Eastwood fled and I aimed an elbow at the bar intending to commence the manfully leaning thing. Unfortunately, being preoccupied with expression changing, I badly misjudged he distance between myself and the bar. The result was my elbow missed the bar altogether and my upper arm thumped painfully into the edge, leaving me leaning at ridiculous angle. My head level with everybody else's shoulders.

All the seadogs now stared in my direction, so I gave it my best effort in trying to look as though this was the way I always leant on the bar. Unfortunately, my efforts were doomed to failure as it meant a lot of contorting and twisting of my body without moving my shoulder to reach my can of beer. After a lot of wriggling my fingers just managed to touch the edge of the tin and I finally got a proper manly grip of it after a few finger scrabbling seconds of inching the thing towards me. The seadogs … and Cathy … watched, transfixed by my contortions.

Cathy opened her mouth to speak but shut again quickly as her attention was suddenly drawn to a loud clattering noise outside the smoke room, at the bottom of the stairs.

"SOMEBODY!" roared a voice.

All the men turned to look towards the door to the smoke room. Cathy looked horrified suddenly and ducked down behind the bar. I was still manfully leaning, facing the other way. So, all the occupants of the bar were now staring over my head.

"SOMEBODY!" screamed the voice again, obviously becoming agitated that 'somebody' hadn't immediately materialised in front of him.

All eyes shifted from looking over my head at the door, downwards to look at me.

"He means you" said the man behind the bar.

"Why me?" I said frantically wondering how I was going to get upright.

"Because" he said with exaggerated patience, "You are the most junior of beings on the vessel and that is the captain who, whenever he wants someone to do something for him shouts 'somebody' and continues to shout 'somebody' until a 'somebody' arrives to do his bidding. Therefore, in this case 'somebody' is you.

"Oh" I said. Actually, it came out more like "Ohoofpshsh… Ah!" because at the same time I attempted a herculean shove with my shoulder and achieved an upright position.

"SOMEBODY … SOMEBODY … SOMBODY!"

"He's waiting," said Barman. "By the way, his name is McHale … Captain McHale … 'Black Mac'!"

'Oh God' I thought as I hopped off the stool and raced into the alleyway skidding to halt by the door where I had first entered the Looming Thing and came face to face with Captain Black Mac McHale. The Head of Everything.

Now then … I had imagined that the captain … the Master … of one of Great Britain's Mighty Merchant Ships and having a name like 'Black Mac' would be, at the very least a huge piratical looking man with great bushy black beard, eye patch, parrot and wooden leg. Well, maybe not the parrot but the rest of the image was surely a possibility. However, I was somewhat taken aback to be confronted with a small rotund being sporting a tiny goatee, a large anorak that nearly reached the floor and the biggest bobble hat you ever did see! The whole thing gave him the imposing air of a… a… well… tea cosy, really!

"Ah … at last!" he muttered, beard bristling "Who are you?"

"I am the cadet" I squeaked. He looked me up and down with distain, then, obviously deciding that in the absence of a real human being, I would have to do, turned and stormed up the stairs.

"Bring my cases to my cabin" he shouted over his shoulder.

I gathered up his two large suitcases and mounted the stairs. The Tea Cosy had galloped off apace taking one small travel bag with him. Of course, the usual thing happened … by the time I had reached the top he had disappeared. However, several of the seadogs from the bar had come out and were standing at the bottom of the stairs looking up at me, grinning, beer cans in hand. All finding great amusement in my struggles to carry the Head of Everything's suitcases up the stairs.

Remembering my previous excursions around the interior of the Looming Thing, I deduced that there must be another place higher up that accommodated Captains and such. This piece of detective work was confirmed by the sound of a door opening and then slamming shut somewhere above my head.

"Where's the stairs?" I said looking back and forth.

"Behind you" said one.

"You've just gone up them," said another.

I heard Cathy's voice "Don't be cruel" she said to my tormentors. "They are through the door … to your left … the one with the sign over the top that says **STAIRS**."

Could life get any worse?

"CADET!" Tea cosy had come out of his cabin and was standing at the top of the stairs. "WHERE ARE YOU WITH MY CASES?" he roared.

"Coming now … sir" I said.

"Well, hurry up!"

I heaved, tugged and dragged his bags up the stairs crashing one of them into the wall.

"Be carefull!" He stormed. "There are fragile items in that case".

What he meant by fragile items escaped me. Ming vases perhaps, or balsa wood trousers.

I continued upwards, gaining another two steps when the inevitable happened … a handle broke. The front end of one of the cases crashed down onto the stair below the one I was standing on. This meant I could no longer proceed upwards.

I looked up. The Tea cosy stared down.

"The handles broken" I could hear chortling coming from the loungers.

"Broken … broken … what do mean … broken?!" He had gone a worrying shade of deep red and danced up and down in agitation. (If you imagine a tea cosy with polished brown shoes protruding from underneath, hopping from one foot to the other and remember the children's rhyme *'I'm a little teapot short and stout'* then you will get the general picture.)

I took a step back causing the case to crash down another step. This really sent him into a rage.

"What are you doing … stupid boy? He shouted. "Put one down and bring them up one at a time".

I let go of one and it thudded down three steps to the alleyway.

"No … no … no … the other one you fool!" He was in full disco dancing mode now.

I let go of the other one and it thudded down four steps to the alleyway. There was a sort of strangled squeaky gasp from the top of the stairs and when I looked up, he had disappeared into his cabin. It was all obviously too much for him.

Watched closely by chortling seadogs peering up the stairs from the deck below, I spent the next few minutes transporting the cases up and depositing them outside the door marked '**Captain**' which was firmly shut. I did think about knocking and announcing the arrival of the luggage but reflecting on the preceding events I decided against it. A quiet tactical withdrawal seemed a better plan. This I did, tip toeing down the stairs and back to the bar. The seadogs, who had all returned to their respective positions at or behind the bar, couldn't help grinning at me. I took a swig at my beer.

Cathy laughed. "Never mind" she said. "He spent most of last trip screaming and shouting at the cadets apparently." She took a delicate sip of her drink "According to Jim".

The same thought occurred to the man behind the bar and me at the same time.

"Ah yes" he said. "That reminds me … where is Jim, has he paid off and gone home?"

"Dunno" said Cathy. "Don't care either. … He's a prat" There was silence. All the seadogs stared at her.

"Am I to take it then" said the man behind the bar "That young Jim is no longer your boyfriend?"

"Correct" said Cathy. "Actually, it was nothing serious in the first place" She waved a dismissive hand. "We live in the same street, next door actually."

I felt a faint smugness because I already knew this. However, her statement did not actually explain anything to anybody, but I and all the seadogs nodded sagely as though we all understood.

The man behind the bar was not to be put off.

"I think then" he said leaning towards her and putting his hand over hers. "I should take you out later and console you over a meal".

"No thanks" she said, snatching her hand away. "I don't need consoling. Anyway, I'm going home now" She hopped off the bar stool and headed for the door where she stopped, turned, grinned sexily at me and said, "Can you open the cabin door for me Brian?"

I stood transfixed. Cathy waltzed out the door.

"Well … go on then …" said one of the sea dogs loudly. "Looks as though you're in there".

All agreed and made their thoughts plain in a series of loud noises and suggestive remarks.

I went red ... again.

Cathy was waiting for me just outside the door, so she must have heard all the remarks from within. Luckily, my face was as red as it could get so it couldn't get any worse.

She laughed "Take no notice ... I think your sweet."

Now ... if there is one thing I didn't want to hear it was a woman telling me, a rufty tufty seadog, that I was ... sweet! What I wanted to hear were the words ... handsome, rough, tough, hard, manly or even interesting would have done. But not sweet!

By now Cathy had marched off towards the cabin. I trotted (manfully) behind with the commanding presence of a Labrador puppy.

"Once I've got my scarf I'll have to go" she said over her shoulder.

"Oh, you don't have to go straight away, we could stay in my cabin for while... have another drink... get to know each other... see what develops...," said my brain.

"Oh" said my mouth.

We reached the door, which I opened. Cathy walked in ahead of me swinging her scarf around her neck.

A tiny light went on in the back of my brain... scarf... scarf. Cathy had said she wanted to get her scarf. ...She already had it round her neck! Why was she saying she wanted to get into the cabin to get it? 'Stupid woman' I thought.

Perhaps at this stage I should remind everyone that up until that point I had led a sheltered life, with my experience of the behavioural characteristics of females of the opposite sex being limited to a few giggly schoolgirls and an extremely large mature woman with varicose veins and a schoolboy fetish. I had no knowledge of confident young women of this ilk whatsoever. Therefore, it did not enter my muddled brain that there might be the remote possibility that she could; a. be generally flirting with me, b. be trying to seduce me, c. just wants to use me for perverted sexual practices or d. wish to engage with me in intelligent conversation for a few hours. I just thought she was stupid for forgetting she had the thing round her neck!

"You've got it round your neck" I said, tripping over the outsized sill between the cabin and the alleyway.

"Pardon" she stopped and whirled round to look at me whilst I was in mid trip, causing me to stumble into her.

"Round your neck… scarf" I mumbled, doing a sort of foxtrot with her as we twirled into the cabin.

She grinned at me, holding onto my shoulders "Oh", she breathed, "so it is, silly me".

On went the traffic light.

"You're blushing again" she squealed, obviously delighted.

"No, I'm not" I said getting angry with myself again.

"It's a shame I have to go".

I stared at her, saying nothing.

She raised an eyebrow and tipped her head on one side. "I said, it's a shame I have to go".

I still said nothing.

An exasperated sigh escaped her lips… "I said …"

"I know …I know what you said" …I said.

"Well…?" her head tilted further, the eyebrow managed another millimetre and her hands went to her hips.

I imagined my arms round her back, one around her waist the other round her shoulders as I tipped her backwards and kissed her long and hard on the lips, feeling her tongue probing.

"Well, what?" I said with sulky expression and my hands in my pockets.

"Aren't you going to kiss me goodbye?"

I stepped forward quickly and aimed a peck at her cheek, hoping not to set fire to her hair with the heat from my bright beetroot face and glowing ears. She turned her head, so her lips were in line with mine. Our noses butted each other with some force.

"Oww!" She wailed.

"Sorry!" I said.

"Come here." She said, cupping my face in her hands.

My brain went numb. My eyes started to water as a result of the nose butt. Her face came close to mine. There was silence… apart from the humming of machinery and a distant thud accompanied by inaudible cursing. The outside world began to fade away. The machinery noises drifted away. The thuds and bangs diminished. Her face came closer. Her soft hands cupped my face a little more passionately. I tipped my head to one side. She tipped her head and began to close her eyes...

"SOMEBODY!" Screamed a familiar voice. "SOMEBODY! ... SOMEBODY!"

My universe imploded. I felt Cathy's shoulders sag and she let go of my face. In a panic I turned and ran to the door

"Wait!" I said over my shoulder... *'Wrong thing to do'* I thought and ran back to Cathy who was frowning. Giving her a quick peck on the cheek again, I said.

"Don't go away!" Which sounded more like "Done goofoof mwawhay" due to my lips trying to peck at the same time. I galloped for the door again.

"What?" shouted Cathy.

I galloped back towards her. "Don't go away." I skidded to a stop, turned again and headed back to the door.

"I've got to go in a minute... don't be long" she shouted after me. I turned again, my panic getting the better of me, ran back a few paces... thought better of it... turned again and headed off down the alleyway my trendy loons flapping around my stacked heels.

I reached the bottom of the stairs at the same time as the 'Head of Everything' in angry teapot mode appeared at the top.

"Who left my suitcases outside the door?" he roared hopping from one foot to the other again.

"Me..." I said looking up forlornly "I thought that was..." I started to explain but he had now worked himself up into a full dancing frenzy.

"Stupid boy... I have just nearly been killed tripping over them!" He discoed back into his cabin. "Bring them in at once".

I raced up the stairs and gathered up one suitcase, the appealing vision of Tea Cosy lying in a crumpled heap at the bottom of the stairs forming in my mind.

"Carefully... One at a time!" He said, suddenly appearing at the cabin door.

I dropped the suitcase, startled "Pardon" I said.

He made a sort of squeaking noise; the bobble on his bobble hat flew back and forth alarmingly. "One at a time! ... One at a time! ... He squealed. "Carefully! Then perhaps you won't destroy my belongings!" He turned on his heal and marched back into the inner sanctum.

I made a face and gingerly picked up the first suitcase again.

Having managed, finally, to deposit the suitcases in the cabin without destroying Tea Cosy's 'belongings.' I hurtled out of his cabin and headed back down the stairs.

"Come back here boy!" I shuddered to a halt, turned and raced back up a couple of steps. "Only leave when you are told to" he said. "I remember when I was cadet…" *'Yes',* I thought *'When Noah was a Second Mate!'* He paused and looked at me as though he could read my thoughts then continued slowly "On my first trip…" At that point, my attention was taken by the sounds of the outside world coming from below. I could hear footsteps in the alleyway below and the smoke room door scraping along the floor as it was opened, then the unmistakeable voice of Cathy.

"Where's Brian?" she said. "Is he still upstairs?"

"Yes" said the man behind the bar "He'll be up there all night" I could imagine him leering.

Tea Cosy waffled on.

"Oh well, tell him I waited as long as I could" said Cathy in resigned tone.

I could feel a deep loathing of bobble hats growing within.

"Never mind" said the man behind the bar. "I will walk you to the gate… unless you would like to come to my cabin for a night cap" I could imagine more leering.

"No thank you," said Cathy.

Relief.

"You can walk me to the gate though".

Depression.

"So… what do you think of that, young man?" Tea Cosy had finished his tale and was waiting for a response.

"Oh …erm… yes… of course… I'll remember that" I said.

"Mmmm." He said peering at me suspiciously. "Off you go then" He had obviously had enough and had decided that I was not worthy of any more effort.

I leapt down the stairs, raced to the smoke room door and wrenched it open. Steven and the engineer I had encountered when I arrived turned and stared at me.

"Where's Cathy?" I panted.

"Gone ashore with the Chief Engineer" grinned Steven smugly.

'So that's who the man behind the bar was' I leapt back into the alleyway.

I managed to find the way to the real world, wrestled the heavy oaken door open and jumped over the storm sill onto the deck outside. I ran to the gangway and stopped. Horror and depression set in. The darkness was broken by the harsh white dock lighting that flooded the quayside. I didn't notice the light winter drizzle that had started to fall.

Cathy, arm in arm with the Head of all Machinery, was walking away into the gloom towards the dock gate. They disappeared around the corner of a shed. My shoulders slumped and I stood staring towards the spot where my Cathy had disappeared, water dripping off the end of my nose. I looked at my watch… eight o'clock… I had been on the looming thing for a mere five hours.

CHAPTER 6

THE FILM

My life on board the New Zealand Star to that point, had, been full of incident. Never a dull moment as they say.

Watching Cathy disappear around the end of the building, arm in arm with the Head of All Machinery had been a particularly low point. I had stood, utterly wretched, on top of the gangway, rain dripping off the end of my nose. Thinking what might have been.

"Don't think you'll have much luck there" Steven had come up behind me. I turned slowly and glared at him.

"Not bothered really" I said loftily. "Not my type".

"Yeah, right" said Steven sounding superior. Then seeing my face darken he broke nervously into the Water buffalo laugh thing.

"Anyway … the Mate wants to see you." He said turning quickly on his heal and diving into the accommodation.

'Now what' I thought. *'Perhaps I should just throw myself in the dock.'* That would, of course, have looked pretty stupid.

Imagine the headlines.

UNREQUITED LOVE DISASTER!!! "SOMEBODY" LEAPS TO DEATH OVER GIRL AFTER VOYAGE OF FIVE HOURS!!!

I trudged dejectedly back through the accommodation door, past the Smoke Room, which sounded full of fun and laughter that was denied to me, a poor lowly cadet, his love life in tatters, then on up the stairs to the Mate's cabin.

Not for the first time that day I thought *'If I sneak off now, I could be back in Surrey, in our living room, in time for the late news'*.

The Mate, John Toobody, he who had given me the whistle stop tour of the ship a few hours earlier, was sitting in his palatial cabin, feet on desk, reading a newspaper.

"Ah, there you are" he looked at me for a few seconds, decided I was worth the effort and continued

"See you had some fun with The Old Man's suitcases!" He chortled, obviously delighted at my discomfort. "Still, don't worry about it. He will have forgotten all about it by the morning".

This, I doubted. Particularly as one of his precious cases now had a broken handle. Not to mention his 'Fragile Items' which may be damaged beyond repair, after all, it was a long way down those stairs.

"So, it should be alright then" I said hopefully.

"Yeah …" he said. Turning his attention to his desk and muttering "Maybe".

"Anyway… young George … the routine now is… in the morning you and the senior cadet will be up at seven and work the cargo with the Third Mate and the Second Mate. They'll have you doing the cargo times and that sort of thing" He stood up and grabbed a heavy leather jacket from the back of the chair and headed for the door, ushering me out. He locked his door, turned on his heel and headed for the stairs "I've left them a list of other jobs for you both as well" he said as his head disappeared below deck level.

I had about five hundred questions for him, but, as seemed to be usual, there was no time to ask anything before the Knowledgeable Ones disappeared.

I wandered along to our cabin still thoroughly dejected. Steven was already in there sitting on the chair reading.

"Chief Engineer just came; he says there is a film in the bar after."

I stared at him. "Film?" My brain was, once again, playing catch up.

"Ah yes" His nose went an inch further in the air. "Sorry, I forgot, it's your first trip isn't it".

Having just lost the love of my life, I was in no mood. *'One trip to sea and he's Cap'n Ahab.'* I thought. My face must have betrayed this mood and the Water Buffalo made a brief appearance, then disappeared.

"We have a projector and a box of films" he said, still looking faintly superior. "In fact, it'll be our job to show all of the films to the officers one night then the crew another night while we're at sea."

"All of the films?" my mind started to boggle.

"Yes" He continued. "Usually there are three films in each box, we get one box between each port." He moved back into the cabin as I advanced through the door. "Last trip, on the Townsville Star, we had 'Ned Kelly'. Mick Jagger was in that! Would you believe?" The Water buffalo surfaced briefly again. "It was awfull!" His smile faded as bad Mick Jagger memories came flooding back. "I saw it four times" his face dropped further. "We broke down." Shoulders sagged. "We were at sea for ages." A glassy look passed over his eyes as though the full horror of being force-fed a bad Mick Jagger film four times over had just begun to dawn.

There was a silence while Stevens' horrors revisited him and I stared, waiting for more cinematic revelations.

After what seemed like an age Steven sighed.

I sighed.

"When does this film showing thing start?" I asked, waving my hand in front his face to get his attention.

He lifted his head slowly "Eh?" The glassy look was still there.
"Film!" I said. "Start! When?"
"Oh… erm… Half eight I think he said."
"Who said?"
"Him… Chief Engineer." He frowned. "Ian."
I looked at my watch. "Well, its past eight now. Shall we go down?"
"OK… but I want to change first".

I noticed then that he was still wearing the same clothes he had arrived in. Which were very, for the era, how shall I say? Conservative… A white shirt with a normal sized collar. Blue normal sized tie. Brown straight trousers, with normal bottoms and a dark brown small check jacket with elbow patches.

Elbow patches! To finish off the look he had sensible brown shoes.

I started to smile to myself, amused by his choice of wardrobe, given the era in which we were living. My smirk quickly disappeared, however, when I remembered what I had been forced to bring with me! My mother's voice echoed in my head.

"You haven't packed any vests".

"Ok" I said. "You change and I'll wait for you" I suddenly felt exceedingly small and vulnerable. Frightened even. The thought of having to go back into the bar and facing all those ancient mariners. The same ancient mariners that had witnessed my 'Cathy' catastrophe. I could feel the sweat starting to form on my brow and the panic rising.

"It's ok" He said, "I'll follow you down."

"No" I said emphatically. "I'll wait". Vivid caricatures of leering, loud, beer swilling, lecherous, staring engineers filled my mind. My face must have portrayed some of the horror.

"Ok" Steven was looking at me frowning as he spoke. "You alright? Your eyes have gone big and your face is funny"

His comment jolted me from my nightmare thoughts. "Never mind my funny face!" I said. Full of bluster to hide my horrors. "Get your trousers on!"

Steven again found my choice of phrase hilarious.

First, he snorted. Then he made a sort of raspberry noise with his lips. Then I was treated to the full water buffalo!

"What?" I said. Steven could not speak. He just emitted the strange noises that made up his laugh. His face became red and his mouth opened wider and wider until I thought his jaw would break.

"What? ... What?" I said starting to grin myself. This only served to send him into even more paroxysms of uncontrolled laughter. He staggered about howling, finally holding onto the cupboard door handle for support.

By this time, I had started to laugh as well. Why, I don't know. It still had not occurred to me that I had said anything remotely amusing.

Seeing me laugh sent him into another staggering journey around the cabin. Howling at the top of his voice. This then started me off properly! Tears started to roll down my cheeks as the pair of us continued an uncontrolled sort of dance around the tiny space. Staggering from one piece of furniture to the other howling with laughter for no real reason at all.

There was knocking at the cabin door, which was still wide open. In walked the head of all machinery. The Chief Engineer. The man behind the bar. The Cathy stealer!

"What's the matter with you two?" he said. Looking from one to the other and back again.

We both stopped and stared at him for a second or two. He was wearing a sort of quizzical frown.

Again, for no clear reason, this set the pair of us off. Steven water buffaloing and me howling.

He looked from one to the other several times until we came to a stop with me holding on to the chair and Steven gripping the cupboard handle again.

"What?" He said.

That did it! Off we went again. Round the cabin, howling and buffaloing. Unfortunately, this time, as Steven left his starting point, holding on to the cupboard handle, he pulled on it slightly, not hard, but enough to open it.

Out came the luggage.

Two large suitcases (expandable), two holdalls, one rucksack, one kitbag, one battered brown suitcase and two duffel bags. All of which landed at the feet of the Head of all Machinery who had deftly leapt backwards as soon as the avalanche had started.

We stopped laughing suddenly.

I could see the Chief Engineer shaking his head. "Film starts in fifteen minutes." He said, "That's if you two hyenas want to watch it" With that he was gone.

There was a short silence while we stared at the empty doorway, then the laughing started again, a bit more subdued this time as it was beginning to hurt.

We finally came to our senses and calmed down. I put away, yet again, the luggage and Steven changed his clothes to… well actually his casual wear looked much the same as the stuff he had arrived in. Even a tie! Not for him frivolous loons and trendy yellow, big-collared shirts!

It took about ten minutes to get sorted and ready. "Better lock it." Said Steven, as he stepped over the storm sill and into the alleyway. "Have you got the key?"

"Erm..." I rummaged in my pockets. "Yes. Here it is." A thought occurred to me. "Haven't you got one?"

Eh? ... Oh... erm ... No," he said. "I went to the Chief Steward when I got here but he said there was only one other key, apart from the one you had." He looked forlorn again "He thinks the last cadet has gone off with it".

"Oh great!" Cathy's alpine sized boyfriend filled my mind. "We'll have to lock the door and hide it somewhere".

"Where?" said Steven.

"I don't know" I said. Sarcasm peeped its head above the parapet. "It's my first trip remember" I grinned a cheesy grin to add effect. "You're the one with all the sea time!"

He looked annoyed. "...Mmmm..." He said frowning in either annoyance or thought. "I know." His face brightened. "We'll keep it above the door." We both looked up. "On top of the trunking."

"Trunking?" I said.

"Yes." Said Steven. "Here, I'll show you." With that he reached up and placed the key on top of the aluminium... erm... thing... that ran the entire length of the alleyway. 'Trunking', apparently. It was about eighteen inches wide and a foot deep and was conveniently situated about three inches below the ceil... sorry 'deck head'. There was just enough room to get your hand in and stow a key. I found out later that this 'Trunking' actually carried pipes for the air conditioning... probably other stuff too, but I was never interested enough to delve into the mysteries of it.

So, that done, we went off to the bar. Stephen in front confidently striding down the alleyway in a salty seadog sort of way. Me trotting along behind in a first trip cadet sort of way.

The bar door was closed when we arrived. Stephen grabbed the long upright metal door handle and pulled. Nothing happened. He pulled again. Nothing happened. I could see his whole-body tense for a second while he gathered his strength. Then with a sharp intake of breath he put all his effort into one mighty tug. Nothing happened.

"Can I be of some assistance?"

We both whirled around.

A large heavily built man with unkempt blond hair, a round cheerful face and a flowery shirt was standing just behind us. His head tipped to one side and there was an enquiring look on his face.

"It won't open" said Steven.

"Ah, let me guess, you're deck cadets, aren't you?"

"Erm… yes" said Steven.

"Thought so" said the newcomer. It was at that point I realized the hubbub previously coming from the bar had stopped. All was quiet save for the sound of the occasional snigger.

Newcomer was still talking. "Well." He said. "In that case I will explain how to open a door" He pronounced each syllable slowly as though talking to children. His head bobbing up and down in time to each word.

Stepping in front of us and with exaggerated movements he reached forward and slowly grasped the door handle. "First." He looked back at each of us in turn. "Firmly grasp the door opening device in a hand of your preference. Then…" He continued to look at us. A pained, pitying expression on his face. "…Gently but firmly push… please note… push, push… the door open and enter the space beyond." He carried out each movement slowly as he spoke and moved with exaggerated grace into the room and stood to one side holding the door open. Steven stared into the bar. I stared into the bar. "Well?" said Newcomer. We both looked at him. "Well?" he said again, raising his eyebrows. "Are you coming in…?" He stuck his chin forward. A frown beginning to appear. "…Or do you want to practice your new door opening skills for a while?"

I hurried forward quickly and trod heavily on Steven's heal. He leapt forward with a yelp, leaving his shoe underneath the toe of my trendy platform boot.

Amid howls and hoots of laughter from the multitude gathered in the bar we both hopped and stumbled in. Steven minus a shoe.

"So…" The Head of All Machinery was back behind the bar watching us. "…this is who they have found to help navigate us across the globe!" He said, with a pained expression and a shake of his head. More howls of laughter. "By the way," he said, turning to me, "your can is still here where you left it."

At first, I didn't know what he was talking about. Then it dawned on me. My can of Fosters. The one I had been drinking when Captain McHale had summoned 'Somebody' to his presence. I looked at my watch again. Not yet eight thirty. Less than an hour since I had seen Cathy disappear around the corner of the building. Less than an hour...... It seemed a lifetime away.

In fact, I was to discover, over the next forty something years, incidents, some funny, some tragic, would happen within minutes of each other and yet seem completely unconnected. As though taking place in different universes. Fate, happenstance, call it what you will, had zero respect for the passage of time.

The general hubbub returned, and most people returned to their conversations. Steven hopped around looking annoyed, hunting for his shoe. I started to apologise but he suddenly did a sort of twirl on one foot as he spotted his errant footwear by the door.

I went to the bar, reached between two people, one tall angular looking bloke with jet black medium length hair who watched my every move with a wide friendly grin, which revealed remarkably perfect dazzling white teeth, and retrieved my beer. "You just joined?" He said.

"Erm... yes... this afternoon."

"Ah right... Yes." He chortled lifting his glass and looking at his companion knowingly. "Huff the Puff told me about your arrival." He took a sip. "Ended up in the wrong alleyway". He said starting to laugh.

This was another valuable lesson I learned in the first few hours on the ship. Everything... and I do mean everything... you say or do from the moment you step on the thing is noticed and filed in everybody's memories for future amusement purposes! Nothing escapes attention.

"Ha! Yeah," said his friend, "Da moosta bin yoo, kerashingg abohw di savvy."

I stared at him, my brain going into overdrive. Must be foreign I thought. I had no clue what language he was speaking. Arranging my features into their friendliest look, I smiled. "Ah... haha... oh ha" I said, nodding furiously and trying to make him think it was part of the conversation. They both looked at me with puzzled expressions.

I felt a tap on my shoulder. "I found it!" exclaimed a flustered looking Steven.

"What?" said the bloke with the black hair.

"My shoe." Said Steven.

The two men transferred their puzzled expressions to him.

The younger of the two… him with dark hair and perfect teeth continued to stare. The other man, the foreigner, a dumpier, shorter being with unkempt fair hair who was also grinning but showing an entirely different set of gnashers, some of them broken and missing which gave him the air of a tougher more experienced individual, started to say something but was interrupted by the Head of all Machinery who was still behind the bar. "Well?" he said impatiently. "Are we showing this film or what?"

The "Smoke room" had, over the few minutes since Steven and I had made our grand entrance, started to fill up. There was now about fifteen or sixteen people in the room most of them talking to each other, some just sitting, but nearly all of them smoking so the atmosphere in there was fairly dense. Helped along, of course, by a permanent 'bar' smell. Something I came to regard over the years with a warm homely feeling! Not a good thing to have a warm homely feeing about I know. But nevertheless, it was there. A heady mixture of spilled beer, after shave, sweaty humans, whiskey and companionship. A particular… *'Something'*… that I suspect only merchant seamen would recognise. Well, only in the same way that Welsh miners or steel workers or maybe fishermen would recognise the atmosphere in their bars and pubs.

"Who's going to show it then?" someone asked. Everyone started looking at everybody else.

It was then I noticed the projector. Quite how I had missed seeing it when we came in, I don't know. Anyway, there it was, a sixteen-millimetre standard film projector. With spools already attached, the front, higher one, full of film. The rear, lower one, empty save for the few loops where the film was attached to it. The machine had been set up on a coffee table in the middle of the Smoke Room floor pointing away from the bar towards the three curtained portholes above a fixed settee that ran across the short wall (sorry… bulkhead) on the left hand (sorry again…port) side of the ship. Not that you could see the port holes because they were covered by a cinema screen supported on a tripod.

To say I was impressed would be an understatement. I was then, am now and always have been a film fan. Throughout my teenage school years my sole purpose for existing was to go the pictures, very often twice, on a Saturday afternoon. In fact, I had, to many, become an annoying 'proper little know all' when it came to films and filming. Luckily, I discovered very early on in my time at the nautical college, that to be an annoying know all about anything was not a good idea and had given up pontificating about the wonders of the cinema soon after arriving at said college.

"Well, I set the thing up so I'm not fucking doing it!" said the big bloke with blonde mop of hair and the flowery shirt that had given us a lesson in door opening.

The Head of all Machinery looked in my direction. A grin began to appear. "There are two bloody deck cadets here" he said. "They can do it."

Panic entered my being. "I've never done it before." I squeaked quickly.

Steven was halfway through a hefty pull on his pint. He spluttered, unable to speak.

"Steven can do it then." Said Head of all Machinery.

"Ah… Yes… No… but…" Steven had found his voice "I…".

"Never mind …Yes-no-but" said Flowery Shirt. "You're it pal!"

Everybody looked at Steven whose gaze darted from person to person. His face, at first, a mask of panic and misery, slowly became one of defeat and resignation.

"By the way" Head of all Machinery had lost interest in Steven's agonies and was talking to me. "What's your name?"

"…Oh, erm.. Brian George" I stuttered.

He looked puzzled. "So…" he paused, frowning. "What's your surname?"

"George"

"What… Brian George, George?"

"No." I said. This wasn't the first time this had happened. Having a surname that was also widely used as a Christian name meant that frequent explanations were necessary. Cathy had had the same problem with it. "Brian first name, George surname."

"Ah… I see." His reply took me aback slightly. I had expected some comment or other.

Instead, he grinned. "My name's Ian, Chief Engineer."

We shook hands. I was still upset about his waltzing off into the night earlier with my future bride. But as my future bride was now gone and not my future bride anymore, then, I reasoned, I should forgive him. So, I did.

"Nice to meet you." I said.

"Yes." He said. "Anyway, I have your next mission for you." He was still grinning.

If there was a smile on my face it began to fade. "You can go up and tell the Old Man that the film is about to start." The grin got wider.

I stared at him, smile beginning to turn into a look of horror. "Umm… now?" I said. He nodded slowly. "Upstairs?" He nodded slowly again. "In his cabin?" Another slow nod.

I sighed.

The heavy-set bloke, the younger, more youthful man with the black hair and Steven were all looking at me. Steven had a pitying, worried look on his face. The other two were making sucking noises through their teeth and shaking their heads slowly. Both with a solemn expression spreading over their features.

"Ok." I said, turning from the bar. Ian reached over and pushed my beer towards me. "Here," he said, "I should have a quick sip of that first if I was you." He pursed his lips and frowned in a knowing brotherly fashion, nodding at the same time. I looked at him and picked up the can. Both Black Hair and Heavily Set wore the same expression and were both nodding. "…Quick sip" said one. "… Beer." Said the other. Steven continued to watch with his worried look.

I took a sip, placed the glass down and walked away from the bar like a condemned man and stepped out into the alleyway.

"Oi!" It was Ian. "…Word of advice." I turned. "Try not to throw anything of his down the stairs!" He said loudly.

This, of course, amused the assembled masses greatly. Cue loud guffaws.

I went slowly up the stairs wondering what sort of reception I was going to get. I started, ridiculously, thinking how to say, 'The film is starting'. "The film's starting sir." No. Perhaps. "Sir. The film is starting." No. "Evening sir. The film is about to start." No. That sounded stupid as well. I started to panic. Even when I arrived at 'His' door I was still wondering how to tell him. I knocked timidly; words quite unconnected with films flooding my mind.

The door crashed open almost immediately. There it was again. The bobble hat. It was level with my nose. I looked down, Captain McHale stared up at me, mouth turned down and a deep frown forming. "Yes?" He bellowed.

"Erm…" My mind now devoid of everything except the hat that filled my vision "Hat" I said.

The frown deepened. He pointed his beard at me "What!"

"They've started filming!" I said.

His head shot further forward as the frown deepened further and a look of questioning incredulity spread rapidly across his face. The sudden movement caused the bobble to whiplash forward coming close to striking me in the chin.

"I mean the film's starting" I squeaked.

"…Mmmmm." He looked at me for a second or two. I held my breath. His features began to relax. "OK, I will be there shortly." I opened my mouth to speak but the door was suddenly slammed shut and I was on my own again.

I went back down the stairs.

"Is he in?" I looked up. Someone was coming up the stairs.

"Yes… yes he's in" I said.

"Oh good" he said. "Need to see him before I go." He stuck his hand out. "Anyway, I will see you again probably. Have a good trip." I shook his hand briefly as he went past… desperately trying to think who he was. He looked familiar. "Erm yes" I said. "See you again."

It wasn't until I reached the bar door that I realised it was Head. The Third of all the Officers. He that had appeared at the top of the gangway when I first arrived and had watched me drag my belongings up the gangway. *"You just joining then?"* He had said.

"Well?" Everybody was looking at me as I walked in. It was Ian who had spoken.

"Says he will be here shortly." I said retrieving my beer.

A few minutes passed while everybody found themselves a seat then Captain McHale arrived in the doorway. He surveyed the scene and then sat in one of the two high wing backed swivel chairs that had been placed in prime viewing positions. "You can start." He announced. "What are we watching?" He looked enquiringly at Steven who was busy checking the projector.

"Erm… err… don't know Sir," said Stephen. "It was already laced up." He looked at Ian for help.

"Yeah." A voice piped up from one side of the room. "What are we watching!?" Everybody looked at Ian.

"Oh, well, it is…" He rummaged behind the bar disappearing briefly as he ducked down then reappearing suddenly holding a thin empty film box. "The Townsville Star is over in the Victoria Dock. So, I swapped films with them." I saw Steven suddenly sit up at the mention of his previous ship. A look of unease on his face.

Ian continued. "It is…" He said again looking at the end of the box "Ned Kelly… starring Mick Jagger."

There was a sort of strangled squeak from Steven.

CHAPTER 7

An Invitation

The public telephone in the alleyway outside the saloon, which was next to the smoke room was ringing.

Ned Kelly, in the unlikely shape of Mick Jagger, was just riding away from his farm at sunset to carry out some nefarious deed to the sound of some mournful crooner singing "Daddy does his huntin' in the evenin.'"

"Somebody going to answer that?"

Everybody had settled down about half an hour before and a still shell-shocked Steven had set the projector in motion. When the film started, I was taken completely by surprise to see a modern cargo ship appear on the screen accompanied by a crash of tinny dramatic music. Then, over the cargo ship the words….

WALPORT PRESENTS.

…. Appeared on the screen. The scene changed suddenly to the ships galley where several catering staff were going about their everyday business.

'Doesn't look like Ned Kelly to me.' I thought.

The music became louder, more dramatic and tinnier as the scene progressed and reached a deafening crescendo when one of the stars of the show threw a very sharp meat cleaver into a bowl of soapy water. Everybody watching knew it was very sharp because every few minutes the camera had shifted from ordinary scenes of ordinary catering persons doing ordinary galley stuff to one character sharpening the meat cleaver. Despite the fact that he never appeared to actually cleave anything he then decided to toss it in the water. That was the signal for the youngest looking person in the galley to approach the soapy water and thrust his hands in it, accompanied by a full orchestra.

A final, ear splitting crash of cymbals with some wailing violins and the poor boy fell back clutching his hand with blood cascading all over the floor (sorry…deck).

The moral of the story? The safety aspect being put across to us professional seamen?

Don't wash up when there is an orchestra in the room. I suppose.

Anyway, this turned out to be what was known as a 'Walport Horror'. It was a short safety film attached to the front of all the films distributed by Walport. The humble beginnings of '…Elf and Safety'.

Ned and his gang had commenced hostilities as soon as this little epic had been played out…

"Well?" It was Ian, behind the bar who had asked. "The phone." He said loudly over the sound of gunfire from 'Ned'.

I looked up and immediately realised that everyone was looking at me "Oh… me?" I said.

"Yes!" said everybody at once.

I stood up and made my way to the door. The phone stopped ringing. I went back to my chair and sat down. Almost immediately the smoke room door opened, and a head appeared.

"Phone call." Shouted the head. All eyes turned towards the door. Mick Jagger attempted a heroic pose on a horse. "It's a Cathy… for a Brian." All eyes turned towards me. Mick got off his horse.

I leapt up and headed towards the door tripping over something as I raced out.

"Ow!" Captain McHale glared at me with his 'Stupid boy' look. "Be careful." He shouted over more gunfire. "Nearly broke my ankle!"

I could hear his thought processes.

'Boys' an idiot.'

Reaching the phone in two strides I snatched the handset from the top of the arched wooden box that sat on the floor of the alleyway.

"Hello."

Down To The Sea. A Cadet's Tale

"Well?" said Cathy.

"Well, what?" I said frantically thinking, already convinced I had forgotten to do something she had asked of me. *'Rescue her from a fire breathing dragon? Meet her in a pavement café on the Champs Elyse?'* No. Nothing came to mind.

There was an exasperated sigh from the phone.

"Are you coming or what?"

"Coming?" *'Ah… the Champs Elyse perhaps?'*

"Yes!" she was almost shouting now. "I am at the phone box by the gate."

'Well, that explains everything then.' Paris drifted away rapidly replaced by total confusion.

"I'm on the ship." I said. My ability to state the obvious not letting me down.

"I know that you idiot." She hissed. I could imagine her clenched teeth. "Aren't you coming ashore?"

"Ashore? Now? Off the ship?" I was totally confused.

There was a long silence. Then she said. "He didn't tell you. Did he?"

My turn for a long silence. Being posed questions by the intended mother of my children and coping with total infatuation for this cute blonde vision, albeit an angry cute blonde vision, not to mention a cute blonde vision that was expecting to meet me, rendered me speechless.

I took a deep breath. Time to gather my thoughts, rapidly process the information and formulate a quick-fire positive response.

"Errr…" I said.

"No, he didn't, did he?" She continued. "I told him to tell you I would be by the gate at nine." Anger and exasperation sounded in her voice. "Slimy git!"

"Who… who!?" Now I was raising my voice.

"That… that… that …" Anger was getting the better of her now. "… that Chief Engineer… You know… thingy…?"

"Ian?" I said.

"Yes!" she replied immediately. "Him… him… I told him, to tell you, to meet me by the gate!" She was really shouting now and obviously very, very angry that her instructions to senior British Merchant Navy Officers were being ignored.

"…Oh sorry. He didn't say anything." *'Why am I apologising?'* I thought.

"What're you apologising for?" she said. "Where's Captain McHale.?"

61

"…What? …Captain… Erm…" The sudden change in subject threw me. "…Errr, he's watching a film."

I stammered back. Wondering what on earth Captain McHale had to do with anything. "Why?"

"Oh nothing." She said quickly. "…Just a minute." I could hear voices in the background. The phone box squealed and squeaked its unmistakable door opening fanfare that every British phone box in the world had built into it. The mouthpiece of the handset was covered and I could hear only muffled voices.

"Hullo." I said unnecessarily.

The mouthpiece was uncovered. "Just a minute." She said. It was covered up again. I waited. Life carried on round me. The door to the smoke room opened. "…Get back inside…it's the Peelers!" shouted Mick. The door closed.

"Come down to the gate." Said Cathy.

"Hullo." I said. My brain was still trying desperately to keep up with the furious pace that life had thrust upon it. Some of its grey cells were lagging behind a bit.

"Come… down… to… the… gate." I could actually feel the exasperation racing along the telephone line.

"Now?"

There was a silence.

"Ok… Ok." I said quickly. "See you in a minute." The line went dead. "Hullo." I said again.

I stood for a second, my mind full of questions again.

'Should I just go? Should I tell them in the bar I was going to the gate to meet a woman? No… no… in the middle of the film? Stupid idea!

Mind buzzing, I walked up the stairs and down the starboard alleyway to the cabin, retrieved the key, and went in. Still not sure of anything I was doing, or about to do, I grabbed a jacket, checked pockets to make sure I had money, took a deep breath and set off.

"There you are!" exclaimed Cathy as I walked round the corner of the warehouse and towards the gate. She trotted up to me and grabbed my arm. "Thought you weren't coming." She grinned at me, obviously pleased that this time her instructions had been obeyed.

I looked at her as we walked. She was bundled up in a heavy suede coat with a fur hood hanging at the back and hairy stuff, which could also have been fur, sticking out from under the cuffs. On her head she had a dark bobble hat that only served to highlight the cuteness of her face.

I fell in love again! I should really have been freezing, only having a thin jacket on, but I was infused with a warm glow all over that started with my usual blushing face. That didn't matter this time. It was cold. I was allowed red cheeks.

"Where... where are we going?" I stammered as we walked out of the gate passed a grinning policeman.

"... And why is he grinning at me?" I added in a whisper.

She waved at him "'Night Cath'." He said.

"Oh, that's Tony he's my friend's boyfriend. We know all the coppers round here."

I suddenly had that 'Country boy out of his depth' feeling again.

"... And the Port Bobbies." She added.

The feeling deepened.

"I've got my car down the street, over there." She waved hand in front of her.

We were walking along a road with small, terraced houses down each side. The street ran directly from the opposite side of the road that ran straight past the dock gates, so when I looked over my shoulder I could see past the gates and into the port. In fact, I could see the stern (back end) of the ship and the mooring ropes coming from the ship before they disappeared behind the warehouse. All this lit by harsh white floodlights that towered above on tall, rusted metal gantries. I turned back and looked at the dimly lit street we were now halfway along. It looked Victorian by contrast. If it weren't for the cars parked at random by the pavement it would have looked positively Dickensian. I half expected Bill Sykes and Fagin to leap out of the shadows with gang of footpads in tow! I put my hand in my pocket and curled my fingers around the few crumpled pound notes I had bought with me.

"Here it is." Said Cathy suddenly. She stopped by a Mini of indeterminate age, fiddled with a key then opened the door which made a horrible crunching, grating noise as it moved. "Get in." She ordered as she reached through and flipped the locking button up on the passenger door.

I got in.

"Where are we going?"

She looked at me and smiled. "Well, There's a party, it's not far from here' only a few streets away, actually." She said all this in a rush while starting the car and pulling away from the kerb far too quickly.

"Party?" Something was not quite right. There was something going on that I did not know about. Country boy I may be, but I was not completely stupid. Close perhaps… but not completely!

"Yes." She glanced at me, her eyes flicking back and forth as she tried to watch the road at the same time. I was doing the same thing. Our heads bobbing back and forth. I could see her face taking on a worried expression as she tried to gauge my reaction to this new, and completely unexpected piece of information.

"Party?" I said again while I tried to make sense of it all.

Beautiful women with cars, picking me up, wanting to kiss me, calling me sweet and whisking me off merchant ships in London's docklands, was an awfully long way outside my experience. In fact, it was also a long way outside my imagination!

…And now parties?

"Err… Yes." Her worried expression deepened, and her voice became plaintiff. "Don't you want to go?"

I managed to tear my eyes away from the road and looked at her. Her eyes were wide with worry.

'Definitely something wrong here.'

"Well," I said still looking at her, I have only just got on the ship. Only just met you. And… and I have been on the go since about eight o'clock this morning!" saying that last part brought visions of expandable suitcases and trains into my mind.

The car slowed. Cathy's face took on a strange, worried, yet annoyed expression. She pulled the car over to the kerb and stopped suddenly.

She stared at me and I stared back for what seemed like an age.

What happened next was even further outside my experience. A million miles outside.

She started to cry. Her eyes squeezed shut, her head went down, and her shoulders shook.

"You're going to hate me now!" she sobbed.

I did not have the faintest idea what she meant. Nor did I have the faintest idea why she was crying. Nor did I have the faintest idea where I was. Or how to get back to the ship, for that matter.

I put my hand attentively on her shoulder. She immediately shied away, and I withdrew my hand quickly.

"I am no good at this." She said after a while.

"No good at what." I said gently. Truth be known, I was getting upset at all this sobbing. My only experience of sobbing females to that point was my sister when I occasionally snitched on her and got her into hot water with mother.

She took a deep breath. "This party we are going to."

She paused.

"Yes." I said.

"Well, it's a nurse's party." She stopped again and stared at me.

"Yes."

"Well, we all had to bring a bloke."

"Yes."

"Bring a strange bloke."

I frowned. "A strange bloke?"

"Yes… Well… You know… Not strange, odd bloke… just a strange… you know… someone."

I looked at her with a completely blank expression.

"Like… not a boyfriend." She flapped her hands up and down as though that described what she meant.

"Oh." I could feel devastating unwantedness creeping up and an empty space in my 'what to say next' locker.

'Come on George, think! Merchant Navy Officer… remember! Rufty tufty seadog! Girl in every port… all that stuff!'

"Oh." I said again.

Cathy's shoulders sagged and she wiped her cheeks.

"So, what happens if you don't get a strange bloke?" There were probably better questions to ask like "Where's my ship?" or "Shall we have wild sex in the back seat?" or something, but none of these came to mind just then.

She looked up and frowned. "Erm… Well… nothing really, I suppose."

Her face looked pale and drawn in the light of the streetlamp across the road as she turned and looked at me.

I should have been annoyed, angry, even, but I couldn't. She looked too miserable. So completely different from the confident Cathy that had grinned down at me after I had fallen over my luggage in, what seemed like, another lifetime. Actually, I started to feel quite the boyo! I now had the upper hand. I was the goody. I held the moral high ground. Aha! I could physically feel confidence flooding through me.

"Should have told me." I said trying and failing to put a harsh tone in my voice. Instead, I sounded like a sulky schoolboy.

"I do like you though." She said giving me a sheepish grin.

"I like you too." I was blushing again. Mostly because I sounded like one of those drippy posh blokes in a nineteen fifties love film. I frowned at myself. *'Like bloody Charles and Fiona.'* I thought. *'Kiss meh Charles, kiss meh like you've never kissed a gel before.'... Oh Fiona, Fiona, I lurv yoh."*

"Oh, fuck the party!" said Cathy. Charles and Fiona disappeared.

"Pardon."

"I said fuck the party. I'll drop you off."

She started the engine, rammed the gear stick into first and flung the car round in a squealing 'U' turn.

"Can you come on the ship?" I was rubbing my head where the sudden 'G' forces had slammed it against the passenger door window.

"No." she said, looking at her watch. "I am going home."

"Oh." It dawned on me then that she had said 'Fuck.' I was not used to girls swearing. I found it strangely arousing somehow.

"Fuck the party?" I said grinning at her.

She looked at me and started to giggle. Her face alight again. My confident Cathy had returned. I fell in love again. It was becoming a habit.

The drive back to the ship was wonderful. Cathy told me about herself with extraordinarily little prompting from me.

She had been brought up in a village in Lincolnshire and was now training to be a nurse at the London Hospital. She was staying with an aunt who lived close to the hospital, so she didn't have to stay at the nurse's home. Her father was in the Merchant Navy and was away a lot.

"What does he…?" I started to ask what her father's job at sea was, but she interrupted me suddenly and said. "Jim, the bloke you met lives next door to my aunt. I've known him for years. Since we were little actually." She paused and frowned. "Thinks we're together, but we never have been really."

"Big bloke." I said.

"Yeah, he's all into boxing and stuff."

'Wonderful, just fucking perfect!' I thought. *'Why couldn't he have been a five-foot six-inch wimp?'*

"Oh." I said.

She grinned again. "Don't worry, he's a pussy cat really."

'Yeah, I'll bet!' I thought but said nothing.

Cathy brought the car to a skidding stop outside the dock gates.

"Right." She said. "Here we are then, sorry about before, the party and that." She leaned towards me as I clumsily did the same thing.

"Ow!" She grimaced as our noses butted for the second time that day.

We kissed each other and everything melted away. The docks, the ship, the party, films, Ned Kelly, everything. I didn't want it to end.

"Oi!" But, of course, it did. "You can't park that there!"

It was the grinning policeman.

"Better go." Said Cathy. "Quick get out before he gives me a ticket.

I opened the door and almost fell out. Turning, I started to say, "Can I see you tomorrow?" But only got as far as "Can I…?" when the Mini rocketed away from the kerb, the door slamming shut as it went.

"Oh, it's you." The policeman peered at me briefly, still grinning, then turned on his heel and walked away.

I stared at the space where the car had been then looked up the road. Cathy and her car had gone. Disappeared round the bend at the end of the road.

If it weren't for the sound of the engine receding into the night, I would have sworn I had dreamt the whole episode.

I turned and walked back towards the ship. It started to rain again. For the second time in a few short hours, I had seen my vision of beauty disappear into the night.

In the rain.

CHAPTER 8

NORWEGIAN BARRY

I had a fitful night's sleep that first night. I had put the small, battery driven, digital alarm clock that had been a gift from my father, by my ear, terrified at the thought of not waking up on time on my first day.

It was not necessary.

I woke at one thirty-eight am.

I woke at three forty-two am.

I woke at four twenty-one am.

Finally waking for good at five fifty-eight am, with a deep hatred of digital clocks, two minutes before the bloody alarm went off causing my heart to leap out of my chest and my elbow to crash painfully into the wall while the rest of my body convulsed into a terrified sitting position.

Several noisy seconds then passed while I tried to turn the thing off. Whatever button I pressed seemed to be for something other than to shut it up. Hands spun round. Lights went on and off. Different lights even started flashing at one point. I finally managed to silence the irritating little demon by pressing the big red button skillfully placed on the top for easy access. The one marked OFF that all ten of my fingers had somehow managed to miss.

I sat still, holding my breath and listening for sounds of life. There was nothing save the buzzing hum of the generators. I let out a long slow relieved breath. '*So*' I thought. '*The entire planet has not been awoken by George's alarm clock after all.*'

Steven was still asleep, oblivious to alarm clocks, buzzing machinery and my poor tormented mind. I lay there frowning listening to his even, calm, annoying breathing.

I had trooped back to the ship in the rain, thoroughly dejected yet again, up the gangway and into the accommodation.

"That was a long phone call." Steven had said coming out of the Smoke Room as I was heading towards the stairs. I looked at my watch. Eleven thirty. Eleven thirty! I had only been gone an hour and a half. It felt as though it should be at least three o'clock in the morning. My mind, obviously thought it had actually been to a party, rather than just heard about one!

I had muttered something about lunatic women, declined an offer of a beer and clambered up the stairs towards the cadet cabin with Steven following behind trying to tell me about the horrors of having to watch Ned Kelly for the fifth time in three months.

So, there I was. My first morning on a ship.

Swinging my legs over the edge of the bunk, I dropped down to the cabin floor with a thump, hoping it would shake Cathy loose from her grip on my brain. It didn't.

She was still there. In fact, she was still there after I had been to the toilet. While I was on the toilet, even! In the shower, while I was drying, finding clothes. (Mind you, the shower thing wasn't so bad. I just wish she hadn't been with me on the toilet!)

Ablutions complete I came out of the bathroom to be confronted by the truly hideous sight of a sleepy looking Steven standing by the bunk, gazing into the middle distance, one hand down his Y fronts, scratching himself. That did it! Cathy released her grip and fled.

"Morning." I said, opening the wardrobe and staring at the contents.

Steven just stared at me, eyes wide, still scratching. His mouth opened briefly as though words were making an escape attempt from his brain but had been apprehended somewhere around his nose.

"Morning." I said again.

"Urrfff." Grunted Steven. A couple of words must have made it as far as his mouth but then tripped over his tongue and got all tangled up.

I started rummaging about in the wardrobe not really knowing what

I was looking for, almost immediately realising that I had not the faintest idea what I was going to be doing. Or when I was going to be doing it.

"What are we doing this morning?" I was looking directly at Steven when I said this and Steven was looking directly back. However, there was nothing in his face that constituted any form of comprehension as to where he was, the question he was being asked, or even who he was.

"The mate said something about cargo times?" I said it like a question, hoping for some sort of response.

Nothing. Steven continued to stare. His mouth did open briefly but nothing came out.

"Boiler suits?" Another enquiring statement. I added a tilt of the head to help indicate that I was asking something.

A tiny piece of the life going on around him must have begun to penetrate because he suddenly shivered, looked around him then stared at me again.

"Eh?" He said.

I rolled my eyes. "Boiler suits? Do we put on boiler suits this morning?"

"Urr." He said nodding his head.

Steven, I discovered, was not a morning person.

It took roughly another thirty minutes of bathroom time, rummaging for clothes and dressing before the pair of us were ready to emerge into the world.

However, about fifteen minutes in, the world came to life with a crash. Well, several crashes actually. All accompanied by bangs, thumps, shudders and shouts.

Obviously, I didn't realise it at the time, but I was being taught another lesson on 'Life at Sea.'

In port, at certain times, which would vary drastically depending on the country, life would attack the ship. This would happen suddenly and mercilessly with no regard whatsoever for a person's personal traumas, their delicate constitution or indeed the on-going state of hangovers etc.

Cargo hatches were being opened; dockside cranes were being moved into position. Men by the dozen were clattering up the gangway. The ship shuddered and shook itself into life. A new thud found its way along the deck, up through the accommodation and into our cabin every time the

Down To The Sea. A Cadet's Tale

hatch covers crashed into their respective stowed positions. Five hatches, five thuds.

"Have you got the cargo times book?" Steven had managed to dress himself whilst still asleep and was only now coming to life.

"Err… No." I frowned at him. "Don't know what that is."

Steven rolled his eyes and took on a superior look.

"Oh yes, sorry. I forgot. First trip." He mumbled. "Hang on, I'll ask the Mate (That being the Chief of all the Officers), he must have it." He opened the door to the outside world and loped off down the alleyway. I listened to the sounds coming from that same outside world with increasing dread. When I had arrived yesterday my mind was in complete turmoil, full of the fears and anticipations of actually getting on to the 'Looming Thing.' I had taken little notice of the actual work. The thing I was actually here for.

The door opened and Steven rushed back in.

"We had better go." He said, immediately turning around and rushing back into the alleyway. "Just got shouted at for not being on deck already."

Panic set in. *'In trouble already.'* I thought. *'And I have only just got my trousers on.'*

"What about this book?"

"What book?" Steven was increasing his speed as he rounded the corner and reached the stairs.

I did a mental eye roll. "The bloody cargo, book, times… thing, whatever it is."

"Oh yes…Err… No…" his steps faltered. "I forgot to ask."

I crashed into the back of Steven as he came to an abrupt halt halfway down the stairs. My momentum pushed him down the last few stairs and both ended up in a heap on the next deck down.

"Ow!" Steven leapt his feet with a yelp. "My shoe!" He exclaimed clutching at his ankle where I had trodden on it. "Again!" He wailed.

As with last night's little pantomime when we couldn't open the bar door, I had managed to remove Steven's shoe from his foot by standing on his heel.

There was the sound of chortling coming from the alleyway behind us.

"Ahhg Ritesss! Yousetoo doonit agen." I looked round. It was the engineer that was at the bar last night. The tubby one. The one accompanying the bloke with the perfect teeth and black hair.

I stared at him while Steven hopped about looking for his errant footwear.

"Hello." I said. Mostly because I couldn't think of anything else to say. I was now convinced he was of Scandinavian decent. Norwegian probably. I had seen a film not long before joining the ship, a war film. There were Norwegians in that. I was sure this bloke was speaking the same language.

The Scandinavian chuckled and stared at me quizzically for a second, then turned on his heel and walked away.

Steven was speaking again...

"You'll have to go and ask the Mate for the book." He had found his shoe and was sitting on the stairs putting it back on.

"Me?" I said. Panic appearing on my face.

"Yes, quick!" said Steven.

I was about to say, "Why me?" but it was obvious really. I was at the very end of the food chain. Therefore, I was, well, sacrificial, really.

It took a little while to get the panic off my face by which time I was back up the stairs and standing outside the Mate's cabin. The door was open and the curtain was pulled across. I knocked. Not on the door, of course because, as I said, it was open, but on the wall next to it. Sorry, I should say bulkhead. A wall on a ship is called a bulkhead… Don't ask.

"Come in!" bellowed the Mate. I pulled open the curtain and peered in.

"You'll want this." He was holding his hand out in my direction clutching a small dark blue notebook. "Your idiot mate forgot to ask when I shouted at him." He said, grinning without looking at me.

I took the book and galloped off after Steven.

The morning raced by. I was assigned, by Steven to keep the cargo times. It soon became apparent that I needn't have worried about it. All I had to do was to write down the times the dockers started and stopped working at each hatch. I soon got the hang of it.

Breakfast came and went. We took it turns to get showered and changed and into uniform. Then eat. Then get changed again and back on deck.

I soon learned that the life of a Deck cadet in the Merchant Navy was one long round of quick changes of clothes. Rompers one minute, Party frock the next!

The rest of the morning was uneventful. The cranes rattled and squeaked into various positions alongside the ship. Cargo was swung over the ship and disappeared down the holds to be picked up by forklift trucks and stacked on top of boxes of assorted sizes and shapes. Occasionally there was a kerfuffle somewhere with a few minutes of exasperated shouting and swearing as something would breakdown. A forklift or a crane. Mechanics and engineers would descend on it and attack it until it worked again. Steven and I wandered about the ship, sometimes just watching, sometimes scurrying about the place looking for things or information that one of the Mates needed as a matter of extreme urgency. They would hint at some imminent, apocalyptic disaster that would be the consequence of failure to find the 'Thing.'

About ten thirty, Steven told me where the Duty Mess was and sent me for a tea break, so I trotted off back into the accommodation, across the alleyway passed the stairs on my left and the telephone on the wall. The Smoke Room and the Saloon on my right. I glanced briefly at the telephone and of course Cathy popped into my head and with her came a feeling of longing in my chest. I hurried on past, turned the corner into the port alleyway.

The Duty Mess was just a small room with a table and bench seats either side where Engineers and other folk not in uniforms could eat and have breaks whilst working. Usually about now, coffee time, it would be full of engineers.

I walked in. It was full of engineers. Nobody actually noticed my arrival they were all talking about engines. Technical jargon filled the air. Talk of 'Ackermakka' switches and 'FooFoo valves went way over my head.

This didn't last long, however. A wailing sound suddenly sounded over the top of the other generator noise that permeated the bulkheads. An engine room alarm of some sort was going off and an orange flashing light filled the alleyway.

They all leapt to their feet and headed out the door.

"Faahck!" said one of them. "The faahcking faahcker's faahcked again!"

The last two out of the door squeezed through it together and sort of popped out into the alleyway. One of them crashing into the bulkhead opposite. I recognised them from the Bar last night. It was the big bloke with black hair and his mate the Norwegian.

I was left alone to pour a mug of tea (I didn't like coffee. At least, I assumed I didn't like coffee. Mainly because I had never drunk it.) We always drank tea in our house.

"Ah, there you are." I spun round. Tom, the Mate, stood in the doorway. "Second Mate needs you down number two hatch." He galloped off shouting after somebody else that he had spotted.

I plonked the teapot down and went back out.

End of break.

Lunch time came and the dockers had their break, therefore, Steven and I could eat at the same time. First, more changing of clothes, then down to the saloon where I headed confidently to the same table, I had been directed to by the steward yesterday. This time with Steven following me.

I sat down. The steward trotted delicately across the room. He was the same one as yesterday. At the same time, the guy with perfect teeth and black hair arrived and sat down heavily opposite me.

"Where were you last night?" He said in greeting, grinning. "I'm JoJo, by the way." He stuck out a hand the size of a baseball mitt.

"Erm… I… Err… Well, I went ashore." I stammered, bravely sticking my hand inside his giant paw. "I'm Brian."

"Woman?"

"Err… No… Err… I mean yes."

JoJo peered at me closely. "Yes, must be a woman!" He exclaimed far too loudly. "You're blushing!"

It felt as though the entire room was looking at me. I looked round quickly. There was only one other person in the place, over in the far corner. He was intent on shovelling down his lunch and showed no interest whatsoever in anything beyond the edge of his plate. I turned back. Even though there was only that one solitary diner, it still felt as though I was in a room the size of a warehouse, with a hundred or so people looking at me.

"I'm not!" I said, also far too loudly.

"You are!" said the steward who had arrived at the table the same time as JoJo had sat down. "You look like a lovely ripe cherry!" He quipped, patting me lightly on the shoulder. The significance of that remark escaped me at the time. The other two had fits of giggles. I went redder.

Before the three of them could finish their giggling, the phone in the alleyway started ringing and the steward galloped off. Only to reappear in the doorway with handset wire at full stretch. "It's for you." He said, staring at me in the same disapproving manner as he had done yesterday. "Cathy." ...He paused while I got to my feet. ... "Again." He said the last word in an elongated fashion. At the same time rolling his eyes exaggeratedly and throwing in a head toss for good measure.

I stood up quickly, ignored the, now, entire room full of people looking at me, raced into the alleyway and grabbed the phone off the steward. Who promptly flounced off.

"Hello." I said.

"Hello." Said Cathy.

"Hello." I said.

"Hello." Said Cathy.

Long silence.

"Sorry about…." I started to apologise about the previous night whilst thinking *'Why am I apologising?'*

Cathy interrupted "Sorry about last night. I got myself in a bit of a mess."

"No… No… No… My fault." I said… Whilst continuing to think *'Why am I apologising?'*

"Why are you apologising?" she said.

"I'm not!" I exclaimed loudly, thinking *'I seem to be shouting "I'm not!" every few minutes.'*

There was another long pause while we digested the opposing arguments and concluded we were both saying the same thing and further discussion on that particular topic was pointless. At least, that is what we would have concluded if we could muster a working brain cell between us.

Finally, in a feat of superhuman manliness, I managed to whisper into the phone. "Can I see you tonight? ... Again? ... Perhaps? ... If you want? ... Maybe?" I ran out of conversation and hoped she was not put off by the pleading tone that had crept into my voice uninvited.

"Pardon?" She shouted. "Why are you whispering?"

"Yeah." Said another voice. "We can still hear you and her anyway!"

I turned around causing the telephone cord to stretch across my cheek giving me the appearance of startled hamster with a mouth full of food.

There was Steven and JoJo, just their heads visible, peering around the corner at me. Grinning, of course.

I frowned and snarled at them, making me look like a cross, startled hamster with a mouth full of food.

The pair of them disappeared laughing just as I said. "Fuck off!"

"Pardon!" shrieked Cathy into the phone.

"No… No… Not you! Them!"

"Who!"

"JoJo!" I shouted in panic.

"Eh? … What?" said JoJo, his head appearing around the corner again.

"No… No… not you!"

"What's JoJo got to do with anything?" said Cathy.

"Nothing… He… He was just here." Panic took over and shouted into the phone.

"I'll see you tonight. By the gate again. Ok? Bye."

"Bye Cathy!" Shouted JoJo.

"Ok… Gate… eight o'clock!" She snarled back. "Bye, Bye JoJo." She shouted sweetly and cut the line.

"Bye, Bye." I said nicely and put the receiver down quickly before anyone could hear that the dial tone had already started.

"Ah, so that *is* where you went last night." Said JoJo as I came back to the table. I went even redder than I was already and scowled at the soup that had appeared at my place while I was away. *'Can't remember asking for soup.'* I thought, but my brain was in too much turmoil to consider that matter further.

"Err… Yes!" Was all I could say. I was feeling annoyed anyway because I had just realised that, of course, Cathy already knew all these blokes. Apart from Steven that is. I was the newcomer. Why I should be annoyed I didn't know, but I was.

Of course what I should have done was boast about my manly conquest of said fair maiden, but as there was no conquest, manly or otherwise to boast about, I couldn't bring myself to act out that part. If anything, Cathy had done all the conquering!

All that had happened to me in a space of less than 24 hours was so mind bogglingly far outside my hitherto life experience that my brain was having extreme difficulty in keeping up.

Down To The Sea. A Cadet's Tale

Learning the mysteries and mathematics of navigation, the science and problems of ship stability, knots, bends, hitches and splices was all very well, but the history steeped classrooms and training halls of the School of Navigation in Southampton was sadly lacking in lessons about important stuff like women, shipboard cinema, women, parties, Fosters' lager and women.

Beautiful females picking me up off the floor and tricking me into going to late night parties, captains dressed as teapots with delicate things in their luggage and ship mates from Norway, was not what I had expected when I stood looking up at the ship from the bottom of the gangway yesterday afternoon.!

"What's your mate's name?" I said, looking at JoJo over the top of my soup spoon.

JoJo frowned, then grinned.

"Oh, you mean Barry. The other Engineer Cadet."

"Yeah. Him. Seems a nice bloke." I smiled, still looking at JoJo. "Must be difficult for him."

JoJo frowned and looked puzzled. I glanced at Steven who was also frowning.

"What's Norwegian for Hello? Anybody know?" I looked from one to the other and slurped some more soup.

Both of them looked really perplexed. JoJo started to say something, but Steven's face suddenly brightened, and he almost shouted in his excitement.

"Oh!" he exclaimed. "I know!" for a moment I thought he was going to put has hand up!

"My sister goes out with a bloke from Norway. Erm, let me think…" He paused while his frown deepened. "Ah yes, it's… it's… In fact, I can do one better!" Now he was really excited. "It's…"

JoJo was looking at us open mouthed, soup spoon midway between plate and mouth.

"Hei. Hvordan har du det? That's 'Hello? How are you?'"

"Ok, thanks." I said and continued with my soup, repeating the phrase in my mind three times to get it planted firmly in the memory banks.

JoJo had just opened his mouth to speak, soup spoon full of soup still halfway between bowl and face, when the very man himself, JoJo's

Norwegian pal, strode into the room and sat down with a thump next to him. Opposite me.

I smiled at him.

"Hei. Hvorden har du det." I said, raising my eyebrows and nodding my head to emphasize something. I didn't know what I was emphasising exactly but to my mind nodding seemed to add gravitas to the phrase.

He frowned.

"Was… That… Right…?" I nodded again as I enunciated each word in turn far too loudly. The way English people always do when talking to someone from a different country. As though talking louder somehow makes English more understandable.

His frown deepened. He looked at JoJo who looked back at him, shrugged, and shook his head. Barry's gaze then transferred to Steven who did exactly the same thing. Then all three of them looked at me.

Barry leant forward so his face was close to mine.

"WHAT… THE… FOO… OOK… ARE… YOO… OO… TALK… ING… A… FOO… OOK… ING… BOUT."

I didn't know what to say next. That sounded English.

"Erm… Oh… Did I say it wrong?" I was still nodding and talking too loudly.

There was a long silence, while Barry, JoJo and Steven stared at me in complete confusion.

"Say what wrong?" said Barry.

"Oh…" I said. "You speak English!" My turn to look confused.

Everybody now looked the same.

Barry was the first to speak. He grimaced, frowned even deeper and shook his head.

"Eeeerrrm… what Fookin language did you think I was speakin'."

"Well, Norwegian of course." I said, joining him in frowning.

"Norwegian!" he exclaimed. "Norwegian! What makes you think I speak Norwegian?"

"You 're not from Norway then?"

Barry rolled his eyes. The other two collapsed in fits of laughter over their soup.

"No!" He chortled.

"I'm from Liverpool you tosser!"

CHAPTER 9

A Bloody Nose

The afternoon passed slowly.

I, of course, was back in my usual state. Asking myself questions of world-shattering significance, like *'What will I say to Cathy? What will she say to me? Should I touch her right boob first? Should it be the left?'* The usual things that go through the minds of would be Lotharios.

At the same time, I was trying to stay alive amidst the tons of cargo that were swinging across the deck at head height. The New Zealand Star was a relatively new vessel and had been fitted with cranes rather than the usual derricks. So, some hatches were working with ships cranes and some hatches were using shore side cranes. That meant that cargo came at you from all angles. Nifty footwork and plenty of concentration was required to remain uninjured. So, after a few near misses and several polite suggestions from the dockers, like, "Get ahrt the fahkin' way!" and "Mind yer fahking 'ead," my brain decided that imaginary conversations with cute blondes had to be put aside.

I continued as before running about at the whim of various people, all of whom seemed to regard me as their personal goffer. "Brian! Go for this! George! Go for that! At the same time there was that bloody Cargo Times book. Writing down the time of each stoppage and startage. Of each breakdown. Of each change of deck. Of each… well… each everything really.

All seemed quite straightforward. Nothing too taxing for my befuddled brain to cope with. The only fly in the ointment was the nagging feeling of stupidity that ate into my few moments of self-confidence.

Why, on earth, did I think Barry was Norwegian? True, I couldn't understand a word he was saying when he was in full Liverpuddlian mode, but Norwegian! I still don't know! It will remain one of the great unsolved mysteries of the world.

Every so often during the course of the afternoon I would see JoJo or Barry scurrying about, obviously sent on some task or other out in the daylight, their boilersuits, and hands a horrible shade of black that went nicely with the dark oily streaks down their faces. They would both grin whenever they saw me and make Scandinavian language noises. "Yurdle furdle? Barry would enquire. "Nooo. Fooder boodle." JoJo would answer. Then they would both fall about laughing. It all got a bit tiring after a while, but I had to admit it was funny, and, I thought, I deserved it really. Norwegian! Hah!

A working ship is quite a remarkable sight in port. Apart from all that cargo swinging about above deck, then being landed below deck with crashing thumps that caused the ship to shudder from end to end, a myriad other things were happening at the same time. Tons of stores were being loaded and stowed for the voyage ahead. Some of it by crane, interrupting the cargo flow (to the annoyance of the dockers, judging by the language that assaulted my delicate teenage ears), and some it being manhandled up the gangway by anybody the Chief Steward could bully into helping as they passed by.

A thousand things were being repaired or replaced. Sparks flew at all angles at various places as things were welded to other things. Large hammers were used on anything that refused to work after the repairers had failed to repair. That usually seemed to do the trick and the piece of machinery singled out for such treatment would splutter back to life with a few extra grinding noises than it had before, but working, none the less!

Steven found me hovering around number one hatch which was on the ships unusually long sleek foc'sle or forecastle to give it its full title. (That's the bit at the front of the ship that is a bit higher than the main deck.) I was watching, open mouthed, as a large cylindrical, heavy looking tank

Down To The Sea. A Cadet's Tale

attached to a bigger than normal shore side crane by two extremely thin looking wire strops was being lowered into the hold.

"Go and get a coffee if you want." He said. "It's three o'clock." This, I discovered was one of the day's milestones on merchant ships. British ones anyway. Time for tea!

"Ok." I was still staring at the tank, convinced the wires were going to part and send the thing crashing below.

"Go on then!" He said, frowning. "It won't fall down the hatch!" A grin appeared. He seemed to be reading my mind.

I scurried away down the ladder, along the main deck, up to the accommodation deck and through, yet again, the same door I had heaved open when first I arrived. I paused for a second as the door slammed shut behind me. 'It's three o'clock.' I thought. 'Only three a bloody clock! Twenty-four hours. Only twenty-four hours since I arrived! Only one day!' It actually felt as though I had been on the 'looming Thing' at least a week. My mind was, again, having trouble coping with all the things that had happened. *At this rate* I thought *'I will have ten years' experiences inside six months!'*

I peered around the corner into the port alleyway. 'Good' I thought. 'No sign of Barry or JoJo. It was only one pace around the corner and then into the Duty Mess. I turned the corner and immediately turned again and stepped over the sill into the mess.

"Yurdle Furdle!" said Barry grinning from ear to ear again. Teapot in hand. This time he made it sound like a greeting "Yurdle Furdle." His grin suddenly disappeared "Shit!" He said as the alleyway filled with an orange flashing light and that same wailing noise as this morning came drifting up from the engine room. "Fookin' things gone again!" He galloped off.

"Yeah!" I shouted after him. "You'd better go and Yurdle Furdle it!"

"…. Off!" he shouted back. There was a word before "off" but I couldn't quite make it out.

I picked up the teapot which was a metal thing about the size of a small house. It took two hands and some muscle work just to lift it. There was the usual array of white mugs on a large tray in the middle of the mess table and I aimed the spout in their general direction, managing to pour one full mug, two part full mugs and one nearly full tray before I got the thing under full control, but by then I had to slam the thing back to its resting place by the large plate of now soggy biscuits due to the intense pain in both wrists.

"You doing anything?" The Mate appeared in the doorway. He didn't wait for a reply. "Something happening down number three hatch… Think they need you there." He abruptly disappeared. I put down the teapot. End of break.

The day continued in the same vein. The 'something' that had happened down number three hatch had finished happening by the time I got there. Apparently, the apocalyptic catastrophe implied by the Mate's tone when he sent me there had not caused much of a flutter and my presence was not required.

Nothing broke down during that last period and just before five o'clock, with the misty, murky, grey daylight already long gone and being replaced by the harsh brightness of the dockside lights and the sweeping arcs of the shore cranes, work ended.

The great steel hatch covers, stowed upright in their bays at the end of each hatch began to trundle along the greased rails either side of the great gaping openings that were the cargo holds. McGregor hatch covers they were called. Five steel slabs for each individual hatch. Each slab joined to its neighbour by chains and each slab having six wheels each side, designed so when the first slab moved and tipped forward onto the hatch top it would pull the next slab with it. The first one would crash down onto the hatch coaming and begin its journey to the solid metal stoppers at the other end pulling the next cover with it which would pull the next until all five of them were in position. This being a modern vessel, all this was achieved by pushing a black button situated just below the overhang of the hatch coaming, the chest high surround, around the hatch on which the track for the cover wheels was located. There was also, of course a 'stop' button next to it. This one was larger and painted red, just in case the operator became confused by so many buttons.

On this day, no disasters occurred. All the hatch covers stayed on their tracks. None of them became derailed or jammed, which, I was to discover over the course of my nautical career was a rare event. With between five and seven hatches being opened and closed daily when in port, most ships

Down To The Sea. A Cadet's Tale

suffered regular jamming's, derailments, and associated disasters fairly regularly.

I had just watched number two hatch covers crash into place and had begun to wander in the general direction of the accommodation deck, when Steven came hurtling down the ladder in front of me and thudded to stop.

"Quick!" he gasped. "Get down aft and take the flag down. I forgot about the flags!"

"Wha…?" I started to ask. "Quick! Quick!" Steven was panicking now; his eyes were wide with horror. His panic was infectious, and I went to push past him and climb the ladder to the accommodation deck.

"No! No! Not that way!" he shouted. "The Mate's coming! Go up the port side."

I whirled round and went to race off across the ship between the towering accommodation on my left and number two hatch coaming on my right. A narrow-ish space made even smaller by Steven who had sort of danced to his right when he should have sashayed to the left to let me pass. We crashed into each other, my head connecting with ample snout.

"Ooofff." He exclaimed, the panic on his face being replaced by pain as blood spurted from his left nostril. We did a short twirl around each other, he holding his nose and me rubbing my forehead.

"What the fuck are you two doing?" We both looked up the ladder, Steven still firmly gripping his nose and me still rubbing my head. The Mate stood at the top with another, older, taller bearded man.

Steven managed to look forlorn, angry, panicked and in pain all at once.

"Blags." He said.

"Blags?" said the Mate, frowning and looking at Steven with a quizzical expression that said, *'I don't know what you're fucking talking about!'*

"Yeb… Blags." Said Steven.

"I don't know what you're fucking talking about." Said the Mate, unnecessarily and without changing expression. "Let go of your nose!"

Steven let go. Blood flowed.

"Flags!" Said Steven exasperation creeping into his voice.

Both men pulled faces and moved their heads back as they saw the blood flow from Steven's nose.

I stood watching and rubbing my head. I still didn't know what all this flag malarkey was about.

"Thought I told you to do that an hour ago?" His frown deepened.

"Borgot." Said a forlorn Steven, gripping his nose again, his shoulders drooping.

The Mate thrust his head forward. "Eh?"

"Borgot. Borgot!" Steven realised he was holding his nose again and let go. More blood gushed.

"Forgot." He said, then took hold of it again.

The Chief of all Officers sighed. "These two, Albert," he said turning to the bearded man, "are your two cadets for the trip." A sort of pitiful expression spread across his face. "Try and keep them alive until you get back, would you?" He turned slightly and stared down at us. "Not an easy task, I grant you," he sighed, "but the company would be upset if you came back without two of their future Ships Masters."

We both stared up at him, still rubbing heads and holding noses.

"…And I suggest," he continued, "that you two buck your ideas up. This gentleman next to me is the deep-sea Chief Officer." The Mate grinned. "…and he is not as patient as I am."

The new Mate joined in the grinning.

We both scuttled off.

It turned out that, apparently, we cadets were responsible for putting up flags in the morning and taking them down at night. Also, we had to turn off the deck lights in the morning and turn them on before it got dark. *'Doesn't sound too difficult. Think I can remember that.'* I thought to myself later in the evening after all our tasks had been completed. Everything seemed so much simpler, more straightforward, and somehow clearer when the day was done, and one was in the shower.

We had raced away from the scene of our collision and I had followed Steven to the rear of the ship, usually referred to as 'down aft.' Or even more usually as 'the arse end.' There Steven had manfully attempted to instruct me in 'flag lowering' and 'flag raising' procedures while holding his nose.

Once the large Red Ensign had been taken off the mast. He took me up the outside of the accommodation, across the boat deck, on to the

Down To The Sea. A Cadet's Tale

bridge wing then up a short vertical ladder so we ended up on top of the wheelhouse gazing up at the mast on which flew another flag. A stubby thing with a 'v' in the unattached end. It was red with large blue star on a circular white background. The company flag.

I took it down and hurriedly took it off its halyard, the other end of it wrapped round my boots, held there by the swirling, misty drizzle.

"Aagh!" exclaimed Steven, letting go of his nose.

I froze. "What? What?" My eyes moved rapidly back and forth. "What?" I said again.

Steven gurgled as his nose started bleeding again and he rapidly squeezed it close with his fingers.

"You budn't leb id tud de bloor, geb id ub kick!" I stared at him. "Kick! He said again.

I was getting used to his new language by now and understood that the flag should not be allowed to touch the floor (deck) and I was to get it away from said floor quickly!

He frowned suddenly. "Or ib dad de endign?"

"It's more likely to apply to the ensign rather than the company flag." I said.

Steven nodded and we made an agreement to make sure, whenever we handled flags of any sort, they would not touch the deck. That way, we would avoid any type of flag strife.

Duties all finished we went back down the way we had come but stopped at our deck and went along the alleyway to our cabin. Then, it was a case of, yet another, quick change into best party frocks and along to the saloon for dinner. The place was fairly full by the time; Steven and I galloped in and sat at our usual table. No sign of JoJo and Barry though. *'Probably still working'* I thought. *'The fookin' thing that had fookin' gone again was obviously still fookin' gone!'*

There were however one or two unfamiliar faces. Tom, the Mate was sitting at the centre table with several others. One of whom was the man with the beard we had encountered during the 'nose' episode earlier – the new, deep-sea, Mate.

"Must be sailing soon," said Steven. "If the new Mate's here." He had managed to stem the flow of his bodily fluid by the time he had scrambled into his uniform back in the cabin, so he could talk properly at last. "And the 'Old Man'," he added. All ship's Masters were referred to as 'The Old Man,' I discovered.

This last sentence filled me with a sudden attack of nerves. Flocks of butterflies the size of booted sparrows flapped their wings around my insides. 'Sailing! Sailing! We would be leaving London! …Cathy? What about Cathy? I will never see her again. She will meet someone else and run off… and have five children, and a house!' The fact that I hardly knew the girl didn't enter my head. All ridiculous thoughts of course. But not to a teenager with little experience of such matters!

"You going to see that Katy girl tonight?" said Steven. "Might be the last chance you get." He sniggered into his soup.

"Err… Yes. I am." I said. "When do you think we will sail?"

Steven sat up straight and went in to 'Salty Sea Dog' mode. "Ah, well, fairly soon." He said wearing an expression like an old 'I've Been Every Where stroke John Wayne' poster. Lop-sided grin and all.

"Yes, but when?" I persisted.

He nodded sagely. "Within a few days."

I gave up and studied my patch of tablecloth.

"Six o'clock tomorrow night." said the steward coming up behind me.

"How do you know?" said Steven looking annoyed at having his 'superior' moment taken from him.

Grinning, he collected Steven's empty soup bowl, winked, tapped his nose in a conspiratorial fashion and hurried away.

We ate mostly in silence. Me, deep in thought. Steven delicately touching his nose, making sure it wasn't spouting blood over the tablecloth. There was still a fair bit of hustle and bustle coming from the wide cross alleyway outside the saloon door and occasionally a new face would wander in. At least they were a new face to me. It was only now, since Steven had mentioned sailing that I could feel that the mood on the ship had changed. It was somehow different from last night. The fresh faces, the stores being loaded, the phone outside the saloon was constantly in use. The main thing though was all the greeting that was going on. Deck and engineering folk were coming and going, but everyone knew everyone from somewhere else! They had all, well, maybe not all, but most of them had sailed with, it seemed, everybody they met or passed in the alleyway.

All this much to the annoyance of the stewards who were deftly

Down To The Sea. A Cadet's Tale

avoiding groups that suddenly formed as old acquaintances met again for the first time in a hundred years. Trays full of food wobbled and tilted alarmingly as they swerved around the hand shaking, storytelling throngs.

That was another thing I had noticed about seaman. The instant, the very instant one sailor, or group of sailors meets another, stories of past voyages are told. It matters not where the meetings take place. It could be in an alleyway, on a deck, in a pub, in the middle of a zebra crossing on a busy street, anywhere. Brief hello. Then… "Hey d'ya remember old what's his face on the whatever?" Some story is then related amid peels of uncontrollable laughter which overcomes both of them regardless of the fact that they were both there at the time so they both know what happened and even sillier, they have both told the same story umpteen times, usually to each other, every time they meet!

Steven and I left the saloon at the same time, leaving Barry and JoJo to finish their large dollops of rice pudding and went back to the cabin where I immediately leapt into the bathroom, stripped off and got in the shower. The thoughts about flags and cargo were soon replaced by the more normal 'Cathy' thoughts. Imaginary conversations with cute blond girls started again. In fact, I stopped these conversations a couple of times during my shower wondering whether I had started talking out loud. Each time I would stand very still listening for some clue as to whether Steven would have heard me if I had been. Each time there was no sound save the usual generator noise and the odd scraping noise as Steven moved our only chair along the floor.

I finally emerged from the bathroom amid a cloud of steam.

"Was that you talking in the shower?" asked Steven.

CHAPTER 10

AN ASSIGNATION

My Platform shoes clattered down the gangway four steps at a time. My momentum increasing rapidly the nearer I got to the bottom so by the time my feet touched the dockside I was travelling at a bit of a rate causing my arms to windmill in order to keep the rest of my body upright. So, I did that, sort of, out of control run thing as my feet tried desperately to catch up with my body.

However, as I had taken exceptional care to look my best, my brain made an extraordinary effort to make the rest of my being behave and not sprawl on the ground. Therefore, I remained in an upright position, albeit an ungainly, arm flapping, upright position. It was a close-run thing and I continued to jog a few paces, in case anyone was watching, as though I meant to come down that way, then slowed the pace gradually.

Once I had stopped the jogging subterfuge, I risked a quick glance over my shoulder to see if anyone was watching. No one. I was in the clear, so I went back to walking normally and trying to make my hair behave. My hair had, in recent months, well, in recent years actually become a complete pain in the arse. The problem was I didn't have the right hair. I had been given someone else's. It curled up at the ends. I didn't want hair that curled up at the ends, I wanted straight hair. Long straight hair. It had to be long because it was nineteen seventy and all hair was long in the nineteen seventies. Unfortunately, the 'Hair Gods' had decreed that young George should be given thick chunky hair that curled up at the ends. This, of course, was the most ridiculous looking hair imaginable. It made my head look much too large for the rest of my body and the curly up bits looked really girly. The fact that I exacerbated the look by wearing equally ridiculous looking seventies trendy clothes escaped my notice. I was, therefore, forced to be forever worrying about these curly up bits (and an overlarge head) and had to walk round trying to smooth them down every few minutes. My anger at the 'Hair' Gods remained with me for many years, until said Gods became tired of my petulance and made it all fall out,

Anyway, I continued on, rounding the end of the shed, walking past the police hut and out through the gate.

I looked up and down the road, then moved along to my left a few paces and peered up the road that met the dock road in a 'T' junction. (Where Cathy had parked her car the night before).

No Cathy.

"Good evening young man."

My feet came completely off the ground as I whirled round, startled, coming face to face with captain McHale.

"Ah... Oh... Erm... Yes sir... Sir yes... Erm... Good morning!"

"Good morning? He queried, frowning.

"No sir... I mean yes... Good night... no... evening I mean!"

I thought he was going to glare at me but he didn't. He just continued to frown while a pitying, sad sort of expression passed over his face. If this had been a cartoon or a graphic novel there would be a speech bubble emanating from his head with "Stupid boy!" printed in it.

A large car came hurtling around the corner and saved me from further embarrassment by coming to a stop next to us. Captain McHale continued to look at me with that same expression while he opened the rear door and got in. He shut the door and the car sped off.

It was only then, while I recovered my composure, such as it was, that I realised he had been in full uniform, with hat. He had a coat on, but it had been undone and I could see his uniform buttons.

I was just starting to wonder where captains went at seven in the evening in full uniformed splendour, when there was a squealing of tyres and another car pulled up alongside me. Cathy. My heart did its leaping thing which caused, as usual, a great big stupid grin to appear on my face. I opened the passenger door and peered in.

"Hello." I said.

"Quick! Get in!" She said. "I can't stay long.

Grin disappearing and disappointment rushing over me, I leapt in. Well, not exactly leapt. You can't 'leap' into a mini. You can do a sort of falling, bum first, jack knifey, ungainly kind of flop motion. So, I did that instead, feeling stupid as well as disappointed. The mini's suspension made a grinding noise, and the door sill came perilously close to touching the ground as I landed in the seat.

"Why can't you stay?"

"I have to go somewhere with my aunt… I forgot all about it… I've got time for a quick drink though… There is a quiet little pub I know not far from here."

The words all came tumbling out one after the other. The last two sentences were more like questions and I realised she was asking for my approval! Me!

My shoulders rose a couple of feet and my chest puffed out.

"Of course," I said. "That's fine… No problem."

Actually, it wasn't fine at all. I was expecting all night out. Well at least until closing time. Even beyond… Maybe? Perhaps?

"I really am sorry." She said. "I would have loved to have a proper night out with you particularly as you're sailing on Friday.

"Oh, that's ok. It's not a prob…" Something occurred to me. "Erm… How do you know we are sailing on Friday?"

"Ah… Erm… Someone told me." She said quickly. Too quickly.

Then something else jolted my mind.

"Well, anyway," I grumped, "we are not sailing on Friday, we're sailing tomorrow night."

"No." she said. "You're sailing on Friday night at six." Then she leant over, grabbed my head, and kissed me, forcing her tongue between my startled teeth. I instantly forgot about wondering how she knew when we were sailing and became lost in her presence.

"Come on." She said, disengaging suddenly, "Let's go to that pub."

'Let's not' I thought. *'Let's go to a posh hotel and engage in a night of wild sex and debauchery!'*

"Ok." I said, still leaning in her direction with my mouth wide open, so my cool "Ok" sounded more like a drunken "Oh ayay."

The car rocketed away from the kerb and my gaping mouth and I were pushed back hard into the seat. As usual the Gods of 'Cool' (who had aligned themselves with the 'Hair' Gods) conspired together to cause my mouth to slam shut before I could get my tongue out of the way. Agony ensued. I made that universal tongue biting face which looks a bit like the face on the bloke in that painting 'The Scream' but with a half-chewed tongue sticking out.

"Ooohahoo... ooo!" I wailed. Cathy looked at me in alarm.

"What's up?" She shouted. Her face a picture of concern.

"Nu...ing." I said. (Very difficult to say 'nothing' without using your tongue.)

"Eh?"

"Nu...ing!" Nu...ing!" I shouted.

"All right, all right!" Shouted Cathy back. "Keep your hair on!"

"It I ung." I said.

"What?"

"IT I UNG!" I bellowed and stuck my butchered mouth furniture in her direction.

"Eeuwgh!" She exclaimed making a face like a deformed pussycat. "You've bitten your tongue,"

The Masonic Arms in East Ham is no longer there. The site now accommodates a housing estate, an office block, and a café. But then, in nineteen seventy-one, the pub sat at the kerbside on the corner of a narrow street just off the dock road about half a mile from the entrance to King George the Fifth Dock.

We sat at a corner table in what passed, I assumed, as the posh bit of the pub. There was carpet and seats and stuff so it must have been the posh bit.

"Any better now?"

"A bit, yes." I answered her question while gingerly moving my damaged muscle around my mouth, trying to find a comfortable place to put it.

"Oh," she said, sympathetically, nodding, "sorry about that, it was my fault, I took off a bit quick."

I thought so too.

"No, no, no!" I said steeling myself against the agony of my tongue scraping across my teeth and clattering into my gums at every word. "It's ok, just a bit sore that's all."

The door on the other side of the room opened and a tall distinguished looking man in an expensive coat wafted in, accompanied by an icy blast of rain lashed wind. He had a pleasant smile and exuded an air of friendliness and good humour. Cathy shivered as the chilly air reached us and put her arm through mine, shifting her weight slightly to lean against me. My shoulders broadened and my chest puffed again. Cathy smiled and waved at the man who had just entered.

"Hi Fred!" she called.

"Well, hello my lovely Cath." The slimy, gaunt, poorly dressed looking git in the cheap coat replied with horrible grin as my shoulders returned to their usual slump and my chest deflated.

Actually, that was the third time she had said hello to different men as they entered the pub, and my ego was being dented. Well, caved in, more like.

"So," I said, trying to sound nonchalant, "you know a lot of people round here. Is this your local?"

"No," she said. "I only come in here if I'm visiting ships."

"Oh." I said. *'This is not sounding good. How many blokes does she 'visit' on ships?'*

"Erm…" I tried to be diplomatic, "you must have been on quite a few ships."

There was a pause, then she stiffened and sat up suddenly.

"What do you mean by that?"

"Nothing, nothing! I just meant that you must have been on many ships." As soon as the words were out of my mouth, I realised that just repeating what I had already said was not going to get me out of appearing to suggest that she frequented dockland pubs and spent the rest of her time on ships with various men. That was obviously what she thought I thought. When, actually, that wasn't what I thought at all. If I had had more experience with females of the opposite sex, I would probably have thought exactly what she thought I thought but lacking that experience I didn't think what she thought I thought at all. …I think!

'This is not going well,' I thought.

Cathy started to look distraught. Her face was a picture of horrified indignation. Actually, I didn't recognise it as horrified indignation. I thought she was going to sneeze.

"Is that what you think of me?" She withdrew her arm from mine and added a sort of pouty frown to her horrified expression of indignation. Again, my total lack of experience with women turned me into a jibbering idiot. What I should have done, of course, was smiled knowingly, slowly letting the smile become a leer, winked, and said "Of course not doll…. Just thinking what a lovely, experienced woman of the world you are, that's all…. Do you know how beautiful you are when you get angry?"

That would have; (a) got me out of trouble, (b) opened up the possibility of safer conversation, and (c) make me sound like a cool, manly person of worldly experience.

Maybe.

Perhaps.

"No, no, no!" The real me stammered, "I didn't think that at all!"

She glared at me "Well what did you mean then?"

I made a sort of half laugh, half whiny whimpering sort of noise and smiled a pathetic smile, immediately aware that I sounded as though I was trying to copy one of Steven's full-blooded water buffalo laughs… and failing miserably.

"No, no, no, no." I said again while I attempted to force my brain into thinking up something suitable to release me from this torment.

"What I meant was… erm… erm…"

"Yes?" She said tilting her head to one side.

"Well… erm… well, what I meant wa…!" The door to the street burst open letting in a waft of hurricane force, rain-infused London dockland wind. We both looked quickly in that direction and cringed away from the noise.

Even though this sudden rush of cold air made me shiver, my shoulders relaxed as I thanked the weather Gods for giving me at least an extra few seconds to think up some form of response to an angry woman's question.

My befuddled mind was just thinking the situation couldn't, just couldn't, get any worse… when it did!

Through the door walked Jim, Cathy's Himalayan sized 'not a boyfriend' boyfriend. He who had had the shouting match with Miss

Pouty face next to me when I had first met her in the Cadets cabin. About three lifetimes ago.

"Oh God!" said a voice which seemed to come from far off. Actually, it may have been me, but my entire body was in a state of confused bowel loosening shock. So, it could have been my mind playing tricks.

I made another squeaking noise as Jim looked in our direction and Cathy slipped her arm through mine again, turned her head towards me, smiled sweetly and kissed me gently on the cheek.

"Oh God!" Said the voice again.

"Hi Jim," shouted Cathy, waving with her other hand.

He stopped and stared, well glared really, in our direction. Then he stomped over to where we were sitting and maintained his glare. Now he was looking down at us. His body filled my entire visual range.

"Oh God!" Although my mouth was open, I was sure no sound came out, so that one must have been in my head.

"What're you doin' 'ere?" His frown deepened with each word, "with 'im?" He gave me a dismissive head nod as he said "With 'im." This was accompanied with a top lip curl that would have made Captain Hook proud.

"We were just leaving, actually." Said Cathy pushing me along the seat.

"Erm… leaving… now… yes…" I waffled quietly while doing that bum hopping shuffle along the bench that you have to do to get out from behind the table.

Jim took no notice of me whatsoever. He continued to stare at Cathy.

"Thought you were going to that 'do' tonight?"

"We are." Said Cathy giving me a hefty shove towards the door."

"Bye." I said to nobody in particular as I was bundled out into the cold.

"Hi Cath, what you are doin' 'ere?" Three large hard looking characters in long furry hooded 'Parkers' were standing outside the door.

"Oh." Cathy came to a halt beside me. "Hi, Jerry… Hi Sid… Hi Mungo." She said, nodding at each one in turn. "We're just going." I was given another shove, this time towards the car.

"Bye." I tried to say politely over my shoulder but being shoved at the same time all I managed was "Boof!"

"Did he just call me a poof?!" Shouted Jerry as all three of them took a step in our direction.

Unfortunately, Cathy's shove had been none too ladylike and had sent me hurtling towards the kerb. My balance deserted me and in order to not end up face down in the gutter I had to employ a 'knee bend whilst walking quickly' technique in order to stay upright. This meant that each knee in turn bounced off the floor leaving large wet puddle marks on the fabric of my trendy light blue 'Loons'.

Cathy shouted back "No! ... Bye!" I could not join in these pleasantries as, by then I had reached the kerb and was trying to fold myself into the mini in a hurry.

Cathy ran around the front of the car, flung open the driver's door and leapt nimbly in. 'G' forces soon gripped me as we rocketed away from the kerb leaving the three scowling Cockney folk standing in the rain and me thinking *'Why is it always me that looks a prat?'*

There was a silence between us for a while. I was wondering about my immediate future and Cathy... well... Cathy was busy scowling at the road ahead, her brow deeply furrowed.

"Erm... so." I said when the silence became too much to bare.

Nothing from Cathy.

Another minute passed by which time we were approaching the dock gates.

I looked at her. "So," I said again, "What's all this about a 'do' that we're going to?" That seemed to shock her back to the same planet as me.

"Oh... erm... I have to go to a... a... thing tonight, In fact I'm late."

"Right, I see." I must admit, despite the evenings' developments, I was a little disappointed. Then another terrible thought entered my already scrambled brain. *'Sailing. We were sailing tomorrow. This would be the last time I would see my future bride. So, therefore,'* continued my overworked grey matter, *'she would not be my future bride.'*

I spoke in a sudden rush of panic "We're sailing tomorrow night."

She brought the car to a halt just before the dock gates.

"No... you're not." She said staring into my eyes and looking lovely. I stared back looking like a startled rabbit.

"We're not?"

"No, you're not."

"But... I thought... well..."

"No. Remember, I told you, you are not sailing until six o'clock on

Friday night." The sentence was delivered with the appropriate amount of eye rolling.'

"How do you know?"

"Oh… erm… well, I just do. I spend a lot of time on ships, remember." She was scowling again.

"Yes, but," I persisted. "But… but…" Then I found I could not produce a suitable 'but'."

She looked slightly confused for a second but then her expression changed when she realised, she had the upper hand.

"Anyway," she said. "What were you accusing me of when said that about me and ships?"

There was a second or two while my brain did some mental gymnastics. The change of subject had taken me by surprise.

"I didn't mean what you think I mean… erm meant." I waffled. It was my turn to start getting annoyed, mainly at myself and my inability to communicate properly.

Her expression softened.

"I know, I know," she said. "Anyway, I've got to dash, I'm late." She leant over and kissed me on the cheek. "I'll give you a ring tomorrow."

I started to clamber out of the car and actually got one leg out. Then, in a sudden rush of romantic bravery I stretched the rest of me back towards Cathy and aimed a kiss in the general direction of her face, hoping to make contact with lips of some sort. Of course, my timing and aiming ability was less than required and I nose butted her in the chin. However, she must have seen the desperation in my face and her expression changed, yet again, to one of delight and, even, a degree of affection. Meanwhile, I gazed up at her like a lost kitten with puckered lips and a red nose. She cupped my chin, tipped my head further back and kissed me full on the lips. While her tongue probed the inside of my mouth. It was a long kiss full of passion, which would have been wonderful, but, because of my position, it put a huge strain on the back of my neck and meant that my chin was jutting forward at a ridiculous angle, straining my jaw to breaking point. This coupled with the brief, but clearly memorable, view up her left nostril as she bent forward, somewhat took away the romance of it all.

My other leg came free from the passenger side well and shot out into the street to join the other one which meant I was now at full stretch with both arms by my side. Cathy disengaged and let go of my chin which left me at full stretch with no support.

My head flopped onto her chest.

So, there I was, on Wednesday the sixth of January nineteen seventy-one at eight o'clock in the evening, outside the gates of King George the Fifth docks in London, stretched across the front seat of an Austin Mini with my feet in the road and my head buried in a blond woman's bosom. Not what I had remotely imagined would happen after my first twenty nine hours as an Officer Cadet in the British Merchant Navy!

CHAPTER 11

PROMOTION TO BARMAN!

I had woken that next morning at the usual time after a fitful nights' sleep, waking every hour or so and trying to make some sort of sense of all the things that had happened to me.

Steven woke at much the same time and we went through all the usual manoeuvres. My knees hurt a bit where I had fallen over during my hasty retreat from the Masonic Arms, otherwise I was suffering no ill effects. Remarkably Steven actually managed to become fully awake before we left the cabin. Well, when I say fully awake, I mean his arms and legs were moving in a co-ordinated fashion. There was still nobody home as far as his brain was concerned. That would come later.

The new Mate, met us in the alleyway. "Right, you two, on deck as quick as you can, number two hatch needs watching. They're loading that big lorry this morning. Bloody thing's turned up early." He was looking at Steven as he spoke and a worried look gradually spread across his face as he obviously concluded that Steven may have been bitten in the night by a Zombie and had become one of the undead. He finished speaking, switched his gaze to me and seemed quite pleased to see an attentive look on my face. "Got that?"

"Erm... Ok." I said.

"Then after breakfast you can both go up to the bridge and give it a good clean and get the flags ready for sailing." He looked at each of us in turn, his frown returning when he looked into the glazed expression on Steven's face. He looked back at me. "Got that?" He said again.

"Yes, got that" I said.

'Ah, so we are sailing today.' I thought.

Horror crept over me as I wondered whether I would see my beloved Cathy before we left London for the far-flung corners of the globe. My heart sank, but there was a tiny light of triumph in my befuddled mind knowing that she had been wrong about our sailing date… and… I… I… had been right!

The Mate's frown remained. "Mmmm." He stared at us for a second then turned on his heal and headed back along the alleyway towards his cabin. "Oh," he said over his shoulder after a few paces, "put the Blue Peter up when you do the flags." He disappeared into his cabin.

Steven continued to stare. I looked at him. "Got that?"

"Eh?" He said after a pause, managing, somehow, not to move one single facial muscle.

"I said, have you… that is you, yourself, got that!"

His head slowly moved in my direction. "Got what?"

My teeth ground together. "Flags, lorry, bridge, cleaning, blue fucking peters!"

He frowned.

'Ah!' I thought, *'something is stirring.'*

"Um, yes, got that." He said. I gave a brief sigh of relief, turned on my heel and headed for the stairs down to the gangway deck.

"Where are we going now?" said Steven.

Another few millimetres of teeth were ground away.

Despite the shaky start, the rest of the day had progressed without too much bother. The lorry, a huge earth mover with wheels about twelve feet tall was lowered into position using the ships own heavy lift Stulken derricks.

Steven and I watched open mouthed as the thing was lowered into position, both of us, I think feeling a sense of awe as the ship moved when the wheels of the monster truck landed gently on the deck of the lower hold. Both of us, after a brief discussion about what we should do next, weaved, and dodged our way through the mayhem of humans, wires, ropes, wooden pallets and swinging hooks to the 'Booby Hatch'. The only access for two legged beings to the lower decks. This 'hatch' was only about three feet square, usually placed at one end of a cargo hold, with a raised edge of about three feet high all the way round it. This meant that to get to the ladder you had to lift a leg over the coaming and aim a foot at the top of the ladder without actually having sight of either your foot or the ladder. Sort of a leap of faith really. In fact, people who were new to ships made themselves obvious by always lifting the wrong leg first, or sometimes the correct leg first, then thinking it to be the wrong leg before finally realising the first leg was the correct one after all and throwing that one over the coaming. So, from behind they would look a bit like a Sumo wrestler at a disco. Designers of ships didn't help by very often putting Booby Hatch ladders on different sides on different ships, sometimes on different sides on the same bloody ship! Anyway, having completed the customary dance moves we clambered down the almost vertical ladders that went to the upper tween deck. Steven went first, but being taller and more ungainly than me, was much slower. However, his ladder descending skills increased rapidly after I twice stood on his fingers. We had to wait on the upper tween deck while several dockers came up the next ladder and then again on the lower tween deck for the same reason, until finally we stood at the bottom, Steven frowning at me and rubbing his bruised knuckles and me gawping at the vast yellow lorry that towered over us. *'Another looming thing'* I thought.

"Eighteen gears." Steven announced, still rubbing his bruised hand.

I looked at him. "What?"

"Eighteen gears, those things have eighteen gears." He had his 'knowledgeable enthusiastic' look all over his face.

"How do you know?"

His facial expression changed to 'smug superior'. "I went on a visit to where they make these things once." He said nodding his head furiously as his enthusiasm for eighteen geared yellow lorries took hold. "We…"

"Get ahrt the fucking way!" A large pot-bellied docker, (to whom I shall be eternally grateful for sparing me horror of a lecture on the manufacturing complexities of the building of large yellow lorries), shoved passed Steven, moving him from his position underneath the ladder.

"Sorry" mumbled Steven. The docker grinned and despite his size, nimbly galloped up the ladder.

"Let's go and look at the front end." I said quickly. We walked towards the front of the truck, taking a roundabout route to stay out of everybody's way and as we did, I could see someone clambering up the side and into the cab. We were both still gawping up at the thing when we arrived by a bunch of dockers standing at a respectable distance from the giant wheel at the left-hand corner of the thing.

One of them turned and looked at me. "Dahn't go no closer mate!" he said sticking out a gloved hand.

There was a deafening roar and the whole ship shook as the lorry's engine burst into life. It took us completely by surprise and one of us emitted a startled squeak that sounded a bit girlie, so I like to think it was Steven. A big cloud of black oily smoke shot from a pipe just behind the roof of the cab and the machine shook violently despite its huge mass. Everybody coughed, spluttered, and moved back away from the monster as, amid terrible grinding noises and mechanical sounding clangs and thumps the truck shuddered forward a few hops, gave a short wheezing sound and clanged to a stop.

An Anglo-Saxon expletive floated gently out the open side window of the cab. There was silence for a while then the beast roared into life again. More gear crunching followed, then, after an ear-splitting whining noise... it stopped.

The same expletive wafted across the lower hold. This time a head appeared at the window. The head had a round, pale, bad tempered face with a deep frown just visible underneath a woolly hat pulled tight over the ears. It peered around then stopped suddenly and stared in our direction "Ah... Steven! The very man!" It exclaimed brightening considerably. The rest of the being followed its head as it clambered down from the cab and jumped of the last rung of the access ladder, landing with a thump on the deck. I was as usual taken by surprise. This new being was wearing a white uniform shirt underneath an open blue anorak. He reached our position, fished in a top pocket, and pulled out a battered packet of Stuyvesant cigarettes flicked one out and lit it with a battered zippo.

He looked at me, a slight frown appearing. He continued looking while he spoke.

"Steven, go and tell the Mate that we'll have to leave this bleedin' great lorry where it is. It won't soddin' well start."

"Ok." Said Steven immediately loping off towards the ladder.

"You must be Brian," he said still staring at me, this time, through a cloud of smoke.

"… Err, yeah."

"I'm Dave… Dave Spiggot… Third Mate…. Arrived last night… I was in the bar… they said you were off ashore tokkin some local bird."

"… Err, yeah." I said without thinking. Then realised with stunning clarity what I had just admitted to! Again, inexperience getting me into trouble. If I had had that experience, I would have said nothing. Or grinned a womaniser's grin and winked. Actually, saying nothing was the right thing to do. Not because of the gentlemanly thing, it's just that nice boys from Surrey aren't good at womanisers' grins.

"Err well…. Err no … err… you see… err… what happened was…" I tried to backtrack, getting redder in the face by the second.

Dave grimaced, rolled his eyes, and said "No… no… it's ok… I don't need all the gory details! He headed towards the ladder. "Come on, breakfast time."

I sat on my own at the cadets table and shovelled down a fried egg breakfast. Steven had already had his. He had been sent to eat by the Mate after delivering the tragic news about the immovable lorry. But it seemed that the news was not that earth shattering and the world had not stopped turning after all.

Dave sat at one of the tables on the far side with a couple of engineers who he had, apparently, judging by the conversation, sailed with on different ships.

Just as I shovelled the last few beans into my face the Mate appeared in the doorway, frowning as usual.

"We not sailing til Friday." He announced to the room. There was a short silence then a sudden hubbub of noise as the information and its numerous personal implications sank into the assembled masses. Well, actually, there was only five people in the saloon, but it was still hubbub making news.

"Ah." He said as his eyes found me in my corner. "You can forget about the flags; the Old Man wants to see you soon as you have finished your breakfast." He disappeared and I could feel the other four occupants looking at me. I swallowed my beans which had lay forgotten in the bottom of my mouth at hearing the latest news and stared straight ahead frowning as the small spark of triumph I had felt, less than an hour ago, at thinking Cathy had been wrong about not sailing, fled from my now even more confused brain. I thought. *'How?... How did she know?... How did she know we were sailing on Friday?'*

"That means now!" the Mate had appeared in the doorway again.

"Eh?" I stared at him. He flapped his arms.

"Now... now...!" He shook his head and disappeared again. I looked at Dave who sighed.

"When the Old Man says... 'When you have finished your breakfast' ...he means... NOW!"

I left quickly and headed for the stairs up to his cabin. A feeling of impending doom descended as I passed the spot where I had dropped his suitcases. The door was opened at my first knock. Captain McHale stood, shoulders back looking up at me.

"Ah, young man, there you are!" The way he said it implied a certain tardiness on my part.

He stared at me, frowning a real frown. "I trust you had a good night ashore last night?"

"Err yes Sir." I said.

"Visiting friends?" His eyes seemed to bore into my skull, and I felt sure he could see everything that had happened since I was born displayed in my teenage brain.

"Err yes Sir." I said.

He peered over his glasses and raised his eyebrows.

"Hope you behaved yourself?" He said, sternly.

"Err yes Sir." I said.

"No shenanigans with the local ladies I trust?"

"Err yes Sir." I said.

His eyes widened. "Yes?" He bellowed.

"Err no, no, erm I meant no!" I shouted. I didn't mean to shout. It just, sort of, escaped my face.

"No need to shout!" He shouted. "Just asking!"

"Erm, err, no... erm... yes... I mean sorry Sir."

He seemed about to say something more but thought better of it. I think actually he had decided that the effort of talking to me was too much.

"Right, I have a task for you." He turned on his heel and marched further into his palatial quarters.

"I want you to…" He turned around and saw me still standing in the alleyway. "Don't just stand there boy, come in!" He bellowed. "I don't bite, and I am not in the habit of shouting the length of the alleyway!"

You are shouting you bobble hatted idiot!' I thought, tripping over the storm sill as I fell into his cabin.

"Now then." He continued. "I want you to put on your uniform jacket, so full uniform, and go around to the other side of the dock where the **Magentic** is berthed." He paused, looking at me. He then obviously decided that being of a lesser species, I would need more information to complete the task. "It is a large white Shaw Saville cargo passenger vessel; you can't miss it." The expression on his face, however, said. *'But you probably will.'*

"When you are there, go aboard and find Captain Williams and tell him Captain McHale on the New Zealand Star invites him on board tonight for a drink or two."

I stared at him, horror gradually enveloping me. *'Full uniform… different ship… other side of the dock… full uniform… in front of all those micky taking dockers… God! Even worse… in front of all those mickey taking engineers!*

"Well…" He was speaking again, "off you go."

"Ye…Yes sir." I stammered, tripping over the storm sill again. I could hear him shaking his head as I went down the stairs. What's more I could feel him thinking *'Stupid boy'.*

Exactly one hour later I was standing on the quayside at the bottom of the **Magentic's** gangway staring upward. Just as I had with my own ship's gangway a couple of days before.

I had gone to my cabin after getting my instructions from our leader, dug out my uniform jacket from the wardrobe and told Steven about my task.

"You're kidding!" He exclaimed. However, he had no time to think about my task as he was instantly given one of his own by the Mate who appeared in the cabin in an obvious temper about something.

"Come with me." He scowled at a frightened looking Steven before he spotted me stuffing an arm into my uniform jacket. "What the fuck do you think you're doing?" His scowl had become an expression of unbelieving incredulousness. This changed to plain annoyance when I told him about my mission, and he stomped off muttering to himself with Steven in tow.

In actual fact I had made it to the ***Magentic*** without too much bother. I managed to get down our gangway and onto the dock without being spotted by anyone. All the engineers appeared to be busy doing engineering things in the engine room. I gathered one or two salutes and "Hello sailor!" comments on the way round the dock, but nothing like the amount of abuse I had expected.

All I had to do now was find Captain Williams and deliver the message. Simple. Back on the ship in time for smoko. Easy.

I climbed the gangway which was even longer and steeper than our own and stood looking lost by the entrance to the accommodation. At least, I assumed it was the entrance to the accommodation. After all the door was opposite the top of the gangway, just like our ship. The trouble was this ship seemed much bigger than ours. A looming thing to the power of four, sort of size.

In fact, this thing seemed huge compared to our ship. There was the same hustle and bustle about the place. The same noises. The same shouts. The same thuds and shaking as very heavy stuff was landed or moved around. Even the same smells.

I took a deep breath, pulled open the door, and went in.

It was dark. Everywhere was wood. Dark wood. Like the inside of pirate ships, you see in films. I would not have been surprised to have been greeted by a bloke with a wooden leg and a parrot.

Instead, I was delighted to see, heading towards me, a uniformed being. He was wearing a full rig, the same as me, except he wasn't carrying a hat, (that's how I had managed to avoid too much mickey taking on the way round. I had carried my hat) and he had two stripes on each arm.

I smiled and opened my mouth to ask whereabouts the captain might be found.

"Where the fuck have you been!?" He glowered at me, obviously annoyed. "You were supposed to have been here yesterday."

My smile fled and was replaced by a look of stunned confusion "Err... Oh... Ah... Well actually I'm..."

He raced passed me and pulled open the door.

"You'd better go see the Mate," he interrupted, "he's in the bar with the Old Man." He leapt over the storm sill and disappeared onto the deck. The door slammed shut.

All this felt unnervingly familiar. This was the second time in a week I had walked onto a ship and been confused with someone else.

"Oo are you?" A door had opened on my left and a tall, stooped, unsmiling, angular faced man with deep set eyes and one huge, full width, black eyebrow glared down at me.

"...Oh... Ah... well... now... I ... ah..." I was stuttering again. It was the eyebrow. It seemed to grow and fill my vision. First it had been Bobble hats, now it was eyebrows... or... well... eyebrow, singular.

"Well?" It said, leaping upwards.

"Captain!" I squawked, backing away. "Looking for the captain."

"In the bar." Said the eyebrow, advancing.

I backed up further. "Where is it?" I did a sort of sideways shimmy and managed to get a bit of space between me and the brow.

"Up the stairs, next deck." He pushed past me and loped along the wide cross-alleyway then suddenly turned left and disappeared from view. "Follow me." His voice had a deep bass tone and sounded like the butler in a haunted house film.

I galloped after him and was just in time to see his feet reaching the top of a short flight of stairs. *'Here we go again'* I thought. *'At least, this time, there are no suitcases.'*

After about five miles of alleyways and stairs I was completely lost and had no clue which way I was actually pointing. My guide, however, loped confidently along in front of me until, halfway down one of the longer wood cladded corridors, he stopped abruptly and pointed.

"In there." He intoned. Then, turning on his heal, he marched off, taking his eyebrow with him.

I looked at the door. There was raucous laughter, a thumping sound and the unmistakeable sound of a glass breaking coming from within. Raucous laughter is always off putting when you going to enter a room. It usually means that all the laughter will stop as soon as you appear and all… all, the merrymakers will stop laughing and stare at you. I started blushing before my hand touched the doorknob.

"Good Luck." Said the Eyebrow without breaking stride as it turned the corner at the end of the alleyway.

All the laughter stopped, and all the merrymakers stared at me as I entered the room. The 'Bar' was just that. A bar. A narrow room with two port holes at the far end and a bar top that started on the left of the door I had just come in and then curved towards the bulkhead (wall) about a third of the way down. There were three merrymakers sitting on bar stools, all oldish looking gents and all in civilian clothes. No sign of any uniforms.

"Fuck me!" said one. "What have you come as?" More laughter.

"Captain?" I said, going redder. "I was looking for Captain Williams."

The man who had spoken continued to stare at me swaying slightly on his bar stool.

"Arthur!" he said loudly, still looking at me. "Someone wants you." All went quiet for several seconds, then from the far side of the bar, where it curved towards the wall, a bearded face slowly rose from behind the bar top,

"Yes." It said.

I stared.

"Yes." It said again.

"Erm… Captain Williams?"

The face stared back without moving, "Yes."

The other three people all moved their heads in unison, looking at each of us as we spoke.

"Well?" The face was frowning.

"Ah… Yes… Erm… I have a message from Captain McHale on the New Zealand Star." I announced. The heads all looked in my direction. I looked at them. There was another silence.

"Yes." The face had not moved.

I looked at it again.

"Erm… He says he invites you over for a drink or two this evening."

The face stared back.

"On the ship." I added for no reason.

The face continued to stare.

"Our ship." I was going redder.

No movement from the face.

"The New Zealand Star." I said.

There was a further pause. We all looked at the face.

"Right!" Captain Williams finally got to his feet and ceased to be just a face. He was huge. My gaze followed his face as it rose and rose and continued to rise, towering over all of us.

"Ok young fellah!" He boomed. Thanks for that, "Get behind that bar and get yourself a beer!" He shouted. "...Don't seem to have barman at the moment." He continued. "...And I'm too old to be clambering under the counter."

Taken completely by surprise, coupled with the fact that it was only ten o'clock in the morning and thought of beer at that hour was something beyond my comprehension. I said nothing.

"Well?" Captain Williams was advancing on me. "Go on, duck under and get one." He ordered.

I did as I was told.

"There are cans in the fridge, just to your left," He said, noticing my wild-eyed hunting after I had clambered clumsily under a gap that served as an entrance to 'Behind the Bar'.

"Err... I have to get back!" I protested.

"Nah." said Captain Williams. "You'll be right!" I noticed a sharp Australian twang in his voice. I knew it was an Australian twang. I had a lot of experience of Australian sounding voices. Well, actually I was a 'Skippy, The Bush Kangaroo' fan when was younger. So, I knew an Australian accent when I heard one.

"The silly old midget won't even notice you're missing!" Everybody laughed. I felt strangely annoyed at having my Captain referred to in such a manner, despite the fact that I had thought of him as a 'Bobble Hatted Idiot' just recently.

I had no time to dwell on it anyway. No sooner had I got myself a can then the rest of the folk all demanded I give them one. So, there I was bobbing up and down distributing beers like an alcoholic jack in the box. An uncomfortable feeling of being trapped swept over me.

"I really will… though." I said to nobody in particular.

"Really will what?" said one of the men.

"Have to go!" I said as I went to duck under the bar top again. My exit was stopped suddenly as the bar door flew open and people flooded in.

"Throw us a beer, pal." Said the first one.

"Yeah, me too!" shouted another one.

"And me!"

I looked pleadingly at Captain Williams.

"It's ok young man, give them all a beer." He said nodding his head and grinning.

"…But." I started to protest.

"Come on! Hurry up! Someone said from the back of the throng.

I went back to bobbing. Now I really was trapped. Four days into a career in the Merchant Navy, it's ten o'clock in the morning and I'm suddenly the barman on a strange ship.

Hornblower books and stories of 'Press Gangs' came to mind.

CHAPTER 12

SAILING…MAYBE?

My tenure as Barman aboard the ***Magentic*** lasted only a brief period, but way, way longer than it should've done.

I could feel the panic rising as I frantically dished out beers to all and sundry, bobbing up and down as the fridge gradually emptied.

Nobody seemed to notice that I was a stranger, nor that I was the only person in the place wearing a full uniform. They were all busy opening cans of beer and all talking at once. The odd word drilled its way through the heavy atmosphere and reached my delicate ears.

"Yeah, the fuckin' disprogonator valve is fuckin' fucked a-fuckin'-gain!"

"Yeah, yah got that right." But it might have something to do with that fuckin' lingmollifiyer switch."

"Yeah?"

"Yeah."

"Yeah… might be right."

"Fuckin'… yeah."

Long pauses punctuated the conversations while beer was consumed in half can gulps.

"Hey Swooper!" The speaker, a small rotund being with a pink face and round spectacles, shouted over his shoulder.

"What." A deep bass voice that sounded as though it came from a giant, (I half expected his next words to be "Fee Fi Fo Fum… I smell the blood etc., etc.), drifted back through the crowd.

"Lingmollifiyer or Disprogonator?" said Pink Face.

"Jakarumber Relay." Intoned the giant. Glasses rattled on the shelves.

I didn't understand a word, nor was I the slightest bit interested. All my attention was focused on working out a way of getting off the ship.

Another short rotund individual pushed his way through the crowd to the bar, stared at me for a second.

"Toss a beer out mate," he said.

I bobbed back down to the fridge.

Empty.

"None left," I said straightening up.

"None left?"

"None left," I said again.

His face bore a look of uncomprehending horror. "None… left…" He said slowly and loudly. This time it was more a statement than a question. As though his mind was having the most difficult of times understanding the empty fridge concept.

I suddenly realised that a deathly hush had fallen upon the assembled horde and all of them were looking in my direction. My face started to get red again.

Captain Williams was the first to gather himself, take command and come up with a dynamic plan to rescue the situation.

"Somebody go and get some more," he said. Everybody looked in his direction. He transferred his gaze to me. Everybody looked back in my direction and stared at me waiting.

"Erm… I don't know where it is." I was aware of the pitiful look on my face and the plaintive wail in my voice.

There was a collective moan, then the small round bloke that had asked for the beer spoke.

"Typical bloody cadets," he said raising his eyebrows. "You must know where the beer's kept!" he said. "How long have been here?"

"Well… actually…" I started to explain I had only been on the bloody thing about fifteen minutes.

"Never mind… never mind." He interrupted. "Follow me, I'll show you." He turned sharply left and headed for the door.

I hesitated. My situation was rapidly becoming worse. I could see myself being kidnapped and sailing on this ship as deck boy or powder monkey or something. It's much like that feeling of horror that sweeps slowly over you when you realise you've got on the wrong train and there are no stops for a hundred and fifty miles.

The door had slammed shut as my new guide to the beer store raced out. I panicked and ducked under the bar top to follow him. Unfortunately, I didn't duck quite far enough and the top of forehead crashed into the edge of the bar. I yelped and stood up rubbing my head. A multitude of faces were still staring at me, only this time all their mouths formed a round shape and their brows furrowed deeply as they all grimaced at the sound of bone meeting wood and a collective "Ooooooooffffff" sound wafted across the bar.

I had no time to wonder whether anybody was actually concerned over my wellbeing as I started to duck down again to recommence the chase.

"Whoa! ... Whoa! ... Stop! ..." Several voices shouted at once.

"Mate..." said the nearest person to me, "try lifting the hinged..." he paused slightly and placed his hand on the bar top, gripping the edge, "...piece of bar top..." another pause, "... conveniently placed for ease of entry to the serving area!" He dramatically lifted his hand raising the top until it was vertical.

Everybody guffawed with laughter as I raced past and plunged out of the door.

The **Megantic**, was even bigger than I had first thought. The alleyway in which the bar was situated was even longer, in both directions, then I remembered from when I had been delivered to the door by the horror film butler not twenty minutes before. My head whipped back and forth as I looked up and down. My wide, bulging, panic-stricken eyes hoping against hope to catch a glimpse of my rotund little helper.

My panic subsided as I saw him disappearing round the distant corner of the alleyway. A brief sprint that an Olympic athlete would have been proud of, brought me to the same corner.

He glanced over his shoulder as I galloped up behind him.

"When are we sailing?" he asked.

"I don't know," I puffed, "I'm not on this..."

"You don't know!" He said incredulously. "Aren't you told anything up there?"

"Erm no... well... I'm not actually..." I started to do the 'not on this

Down To The Sea. A Cadet's Tale

ship' thing again, but he had turned a corner again and disappeared. I sprinted briefly again, cornered dangerously, and caught up just in time to be confronted with stairs, very steep stairs going a long way down into the bowels of the vessel. My mind was immediately taken over by more panic. *'I must keep this bloke in sight at all times'* I thought. *'If I lose him, I'll never find my way back... or out... or off this thing!'* It also occurred to me, not for the first time, that since I had started my career in the Merchant Navy, most of my time had been taken up chasing after people in alleyways.

"In here," rotund man said, coming to a halt suddenly.

What seemed like moments later we were staggering back along the alleyway and up the stairs carrying two cases of beer each. The stairs seemed much longer on the way up than they did on the way down and I was grateful that Rotund Man was, indeed, rotund enough to keep him moving slowly enough for me to keep up.

Once back in the bar and after helpful comments from the masses like "Where the fuck have you been?" and "Did you have to brew it yourselves?" I found myself back behind the bar dishing out the new beer. Once again trying to figure out how to get out of the place without causing any disruption, offence and of course without drawing any attention to myself.

I could, of course, have just said to Captain Williams "You will have to excuse me Sir, but I must return to my ship now." Sounds simple enough, I know, but it just not that easy for a gangly, spotty faced youth in an oversized uniform to say such a thing to a Ship's Captain who is; (a) telling a crowd of fellow seafarers salty sea dog stories, (b) gives every indication that he has forgotten you are there, (c) gives every indication that if he hasn't forgotten about you then he thinks you are a cadet on his ship and (d) is very drunk.

My opportunity came a couple of hours later. I had been nodding and tutting, in what I hoped was sympathetic harmony, every time one of this engineering discussion group looked in my direction with their eyebrows raised in an attempt to solicit my approval. Not an easy thing to do over a prolonged period, I can tell you! You need the concentration of a sniper and the neck muscles of a weightlifter. On the odd occasion I had joined in the conversation, but only when the subject strayed from technical tosh to more mundane everyday subjects like beer or women. However, my diplomatic skills had come under severe strain as time passed as I felt obliged to say yes, every time a beer was offered. Everything was taking on a rosy glow and my teeth started to get in the way of my words.

I seized my chance when a white coated steward appeared at the door, held aloft a triangle, and began to hit it gently with a short metal stick. The resultant tinkling noise was annoying enough for everybody to look in that direction. The steward stood in the doorway, one hip thrust forward, looking solemn and continuing to tinkle his instrument.

"Alright, alright!" shouted an irritated someone. "We get the message... It's lunchtime!"

The steward stopped tinkling and flounced out.

'Lunchtime? ... Lunchtime!' More panic flooded over me. I could imagine the entire ships company on the New Zealand Star searching the ship from end to end, wondering where I was.

The discussion group drifted out of the bar slowly, still talking, after they quaffed down the last dregs of beer.

"You coming?" Rotund Man enquired as he reached the door.

"Err... in a bitimin... mini... minute," I said, frowning. There was something wrong with my mouth, teeth were fighting with words and I had two tongues. Luckily, Rotund Man hadn't waited for an answer and the door clicked shut behind him.

I hopped off the bar stool and tried to lift the bar top to get out, but it slipped from my grasp and crashed down.

"Oh... Oh... what?" It was Captain Williams. He suddenly sat bolt upright from the position he had slipped into a few minutes before, his elbow wedged against the bulkhead with his right cheek resting in the palm of his hand.

"Sorry sir, shipped... erm... I mean slipped."

"Who are you?" He said peering at me and frowning at the same time.

"Cadet from the New Zealand Star sir." I said grateful that my mouth had worked properly that time.

He frowned for a bit longer and then something clicked. "Ah yes, of course." The frown returned. "You still here?"

I took a deep breath to answer but he waved me into silence.

"Anyway, anyway." He continued to stare. "Have a beer."

"No sir, thank me...I mean you ... all the same... sir." I waffled, scrabbling with the bar top, dropping it twice, before finally getting to the bar door. "Have to go." I pulled open the door as it occurred to me that he might not have remembered why I was there. "I'll tell captain McHale you'll be there tonight."

"Yes, yes… jolly good," he said.

I felt a flood of relief. Mission accomplished. Message delivered. I stepped into the alleyway and the door began to shut.

"Who!" shouted the ***Magentic's*** Captain.

I kept going.

It had gone one o'clock by the time I reached my own ship. Finding my way out and off the Shaw Saville ship had proved a little more difficult than getting on and in.

About twenty minutes of alley wandering had ensued after my hasty retreat from the bar and the ship's Captain. This was hampered by the ongoing effect of those cans of beer inside me which caused a strange lack of co-ordination in my walking abilities. Luckily, no body spoke to me as I made my way back around the dock so the impairments to my speaking and walking abilities wasn't apparent.

In fact, when I did reach the gangway to my own ship, I couldn't remember any of the leaping over stuff, dodging forklifts or near misses with swinging cargo that had dogged my journey to the ***Magentic***. So, I may have been nearly killed several times during that return journey and been completely oblivious.

Once back on board I raced back to the cabin and changed back into the boiler suit which lay where I had left it, in a heap, on the floor. Just in time. The door flew open and Albert, the new Mate, stood there frowning.

"Ah," he said, "number four hatch." Then left. That one sentence enough to indicate a whole wealth of information. Something was happening at number four hatch that urgently required my nautical, cargo handling and stowage skills. Actually, I had found, over these past couple of days, that I could solve any problem, sort out any situation, overcome any crisis and generally be a nautical good egg by staring hard at whatever was going on, looking knowledgeable but concerned and smiling. Maybe in instances of extreme difficulty adding a grave looking nod of my head every now and then. The fact that there was always someone else there with authentic experience and ability was, of course, entirely coincidental.

I started for the door and nearly cannoned into the Mate as he turned around and came back in.

"Oh!" he jumped as he found his nose less than an inch from mine. "Your lady friend… what's her name? … Katy or something is it? … Anyway, she called at lunch time… said she would call back later?"

He turned and raced away.

I stood with my mouth open for a few seconds taking in the information. Cathy… Cathy was going to ring! …! I started to float out of the door.

"Oh yes!" shouted the Mate from further down the alleyway. "We are definitely sailing Friday night at six."

'Friday night… tomorrow night!' Thoughts of sailing, oceans, far off countries and of course, Cathy, flooded over me again. She had called. I would see her later. Although now, the excitement of sailing was tempered by the thought of leaving Cathy, which seemed unfair when, by my standards, I was doing so well with her.

All the way to number four hatch the distance between my feet and the deck remained steady at about six inches. This was entirely due to the Cathy effect and nothing to do with the beer. Anyway, the walk in the freezing cold January weather round the dock seemed to have nullified the alcohol by the time I reached the relative calm of my own ship.

I found Steven already at number four hatch and joined him in watching while something was taken out and then put back in again amid some bad-tempered exchanges between some dockers and some suited gentlemen on the quayside. What the problem was I never found out. I suppose I should have asked really and added the experience to my 'learning curve.'

However, I had far more important things to worry about.

"We're sailing tomorrow night." I announced, trying to sound as though I knew about these matters.

"Yeah," said Steven, "I know." He sounded bored. "Anyway, where have you been all morning?"

I recounted my tale of message deliveries and bar duties.

"What was the ship like?" He said. Then, not waiting for an answer. "I think it has Doxfords."

My mouth was open, having taken a breath in to answer his question,

Down To The Sea. A Cadet's Tale

but I let the breath back out again without sound as my mind, again tried to keep up.

I frowned "Wh... what!" I stuttered. "Doxfords? ... What's a Doxfords?" My frown deepened. *'Sounds like something to do with trousers!'*

He tutted and raised his eyebrows "You know..." He said flapping his arms. "Engines!"

There wasn't really anything I could say to that. I was still standing staring as he raced away after hurling the little notebook at me.

"I have to go to the toilet; here you do the Cargo Times Book for a bit."

The rest of the afternoon went much the same as the previous day had gone. Steven and I trotted around the deck, sometimes watching things, sometimes being sent for things and all the while noting down times of things in the Cargo Times Book. The ship shook occasionally as something large and heavy was loaded into a hatch, smaller crates and pallets loaded with cartons of... well... something, swung across the deck just above head height. The noise continued relentlessly. Ships' generators hummed, shore side cranes squealed and clanked as there booms raced back and forth, dockers shouted at riggers, riggers shouted at dockers, harassed, suited gents shouted at each other and amongst this the loud staccato roar of squadrons of forklift trucks being over revved as they transported all those crates, pallets, and boxes from the warehouse to the quayside.

Smoko came and I actually managed to get a whole cup of tea inside me this time before being sent on another errand by the Mate.

"Second Mate wants you!" he shouted as he raced past the Duty Mess door. I hurdled a couple of sets of oily, boilersuited legs as I tried to get out into the alleyway from a sitting position at the back of the Mess.

"Where is he?" I shouted to no one in particular as I reached the door. My head swivelled back and forth as I searched in vain for the elusive Mate.

"Cabin!" I heard his voice, but my head still spun back and forth looking for him. He had somehow reached the cross alleyway in the nought point nought four of a second it had taken me to get out of the Duty Mess. *'Olympic athletes have got nothing on these blokes'* I thought.

It only took a few seconds for me to leap up the stairs and get to the Second Mate's cabin which was two doors along from our cadets' cabin.

"Ah…" said a complete stranger as I arrived in the doorway. "John Able." He announced. "Second Mate… erm… what happened to Jimmy?"

I stared. "Who?"

"Jimmy… Jimmy. You know…Jimmy. The other Second Mate."

Now, I had met Jimmy, the other Second Mate, but I didn't know his name was Jimmy. Nor did I know that anything had happened to him and he wasn't here anymore.

"I don't know." I said.

"Yeah, Mr Hume phoned me yesterday afternoon and asked me to get off the Newcastle Star over in the Victoria Dock and join this one to go deep sea."

"I remember being introduced to him the other night in the bar but… erm… not since." My words tailed off as I realised, I hadn't seen him since the night of the film. In fact, several things hit me then. Not only had I not seen the Second Mate since that night, 'that night' was only the night before last! Also, I hadn't been in the place since then.

"Anyway," said John, "Can you get my other bag from the top of the gangway before someone nicks it? I'm going up to the chartroom… see how far he has got with the courses." He came out of the cabin and locked the door. "Here's the key, dump the bag in the cabin then come up to the chart room." He raced off.

I followed as far as the stairs. He went up and I went down and found his 'bag' on the deck outside the door to the accommodation. 'Bag' was not really an apt description. It was huge! More like a sea chest! Muttering to myself I set about getting this thing inside and was trying to heave it over the storm sill when the phone outside the saloon and smoke room doors started ringing. The steward came trotting out from the saloon, delicately picked up the handset, even more delicately tossed away some imaginary hair from his ear and said, in an equally delicate voice.

"Good afternoon, New Zealand Star here, may I help you." He frowned and glared at me all in one expressive look, putting his hand over his other ear as the monumental, trunk sized, solid, 'bag' thudded down on the deck.

"Oh…" He said into the handset. "It's you!" Still glaring at me, he shouted, less delicately, this time. "Hang on." One hand went to his hip as he tossed his head away from me and held the handset at arm's length.

"It's for you." He said. "Your lady friend!"

"Meet me tonight." Said Cathy.

I had grabbed the phone from the steward who had pouted at me and stomped off.

"OK, where?" I had breathed in a conspiratorial tone.

"What?" She yelled. "Can't hear you. You're whispering again!"

"I'm not whispering." I whispered loudly.

"You are." She bellowed.

"I'm not." I shouted back getting annoyed.

"That's better... can hear you now, what did you say before?"

I had forgotten.

"Erm...

The memory Gods took pity on me and I remembered.

"Erm... where shall we meet?"

"At the gate of course." I could hear her frowning at me. "Where we usually meet." I could also feel her eyes moving heavenwards.

"What ti...?"

"Eight." She interrupted me. "Got to go!"

The phone went dead, but not before I had heard a voice in the background calling her name. A male voice. Not only a male voice but one that sounded vaguely familiar. I couldn't place it, but I was sure I had heard it before. It could have been, perhaps, the voice of her over large previous boyfriend. Or maybe one of the other officers from that first night in the bar. My mind started to work overtime, filling gaps in my knowledge concerning all things, Cathy. 'Who was it? ...was it him? Where was she calling from? ... It was her house, or wherever it was she lived! ... Ah hah! ... That means there was a man in her house! ... Was it that other bloke? Was it the Chief Engineer? ... Yes, maybe it was him. After all, he did walk her to the gate... in the rain... by himself... alone... with my Cathy!' I put the receiver back on its cradle and walked back to the Second Mates luggage and, thinking constantly of my lovely Cathy, heaved it up the stairs to his cabin, shoved it in, locked the door and headed for the bridge.

The Second Mate was bent over the chart table peering at a large chart of what appeared to be New Zealand. He looked up as I entered.

"Now then… Brian, is it? … I need a hand here."

It had, actually taken a while for me to get up there, not because of any physical reason or because of other jobs that urgently required my attention. The sole reason for my slowness was that I had trouble finding it. It dawned on me, as soon as I locked his door, I had not been up to the bridge before. At all. Ever.

The alleyways were full of hustle and bustle. The cross alleyway where the bar and dining saloon was particularly busy. Even while I had been on the phone to Cathy people were queuing up to use it. The queue, getting in the way of the stewards who were hustling back and forth between galley on one side and saloon on the other. It was as though the entire ship and shifted up a gear. As though the ship itself would suddenly depart at any moment and anybody not ready would be left behind. Everybody was rushing. But then, over the years I found this to be normal, whenever a ship was due to depart, even in the remotest, sleepiest little South American ports, there was always this gallop to the finishing line.

Outside, the cargo still swung across the decks and disappeared into the holds, landing with loud thumps that shook the vessel from end to end. All this to the accompaniment of generator noises, rattling cranes, slamming doors and bad-tempered shouting. In fact, thinking about it, every ship I sailed on, visited, or had anything to do with was full of noise. You could tell the ships position on the planet, the time of day, even the way the bloody thing was pointing by the noises that accompanied them around the world.

Actually, it wasn't difficult to find… the bridge that is… I just kept going up stairs until I came to a door that said 'Chart Room' above it.

"What I want you to do is take that folio there…" The Second Mate pointed towards a flat canvas bag with wide flap. It appeared to have been dumped on the floor. "…and put all the charts in the right order." There was a look of hopefulness on his face when he raised his eyes and peered at me.

"Erm yes, right, ok." It seemed easy enough. I bent down and grasped two corners to pick it up but came to a jolting stop. It weighed about the same as small pickup truck!

"It's heavy, mind." He said, smiling and losing the hopeful expression.

Down To The Sea. A Cadet's Tale

I managed to drag the thing into the wheelhouse and began to remove charts and sort out the numbering system.

"Some dick head has mixed them all up." He shouted through the door. "It might take you some time."

A horrible thought began to take hold. *'Did he expect me to stay until I had finished? Come back up after tea!'* The thoughts became more horrifying. *'What about Cathy? Would I be able to finish them in time? It looked as though there was hundreds of them!'*

"Erm... err... err..." I stammered.

"What's wrong?" the Second Mate appeared in the doorway.

"Erm... err... well... erm." I stopped, going red in the face yet again. *'What do you call Second Mates?'* I couldn't remember. *'Second... sec... sir... Mister... whatever his name was?'* I had even forgotten that!

"Erm... well, you see... err, Sir." I plumped for 'Sir.' 'Can't go wrong with 'Sir.' Everybody liked to be called 'Sir.' "You see..."

"Whoa...!" He looked aghast. "You don't have to 'Sir' me. Just John will do!"

With that he turned on his heel and went to the chart table. "You only call the Mate and the Old Man 'Sir.'

"Well..." I started again.

"You can start that job now and then continue in the morning if you haven't finished by five o'clock."

I heaved a sigh of relief.

"So, you can go ashore tonight and meet that woman of yours." He said chuckling.

'Are there no secrets on this ship?' I thought. *'Does everyone already know about Cathy?'*

The answers to those questions were, of course, no... and yes respectively.

I did ask him one question.

"Where are we going? I know we are going to New Zealand, it was on my letter, but where in New Zealand?"

He popped his head round the door.

"Auckland, Gisborne and possibly Bluff."

"Ahh, I see." I said. I didn't actually see at all. Auckland I had heard of but the other two places meant nothing to me and I was still pondering as to their whereabouts an hour later when Steven arrived on the bridge a little before five o'clock, a bit miffed because he didn't know where I was and thought he might have to do the flags on his own. Anyway, his arrival rescued me from the piles of charts I had spread out all over the wheelhouse. His first question was, of course.

"What are you doing?"

I explained the task and he frowned, thought for a bit then said.

"Oh, I see." He clearly didn't see but I couldn't be bothered going over it again. "Well, anyway." He said, "it's knocking off time, so we have to do the flags and lights."

"Where's Buff?" I said as we left the chartroom. He was slightly ahead of me going down the stairs. "Eh? ... ooh, arff!" In trying to turn his head towards me, think of an answer and arrange his size twelve feet to get down the narrow steps he managed to tangle said feet around each other and had to do a sort of gallopy leg waving disco dancing move in order to land the right way up at the bottom of the stairs.

"Where's what?" he panted.

"Buff"

"Buff?"

"Yes, Buff! Buff! The second mate said we might go to Buff."

Steven frowned for a bit then burst into laughter.

"Bluff!" He said, then fell about laughing again.

"Ah yes, of course, you probably have never heard of it."

Frowning at him I realised I had made a mistake. I had given him the perfect opportunity to do his condescending 'I've been everywhere salty seadog' act.

Very annoying!

He carried on across the alleyway and down to the next deck chortling all the way and he never did tell me where it was.

CHAPTER 13

LAST NIGHT

Her mini screeched to a stop at the kerb. Almost, to the inch, in exactly the same place as she had stopped the night before to let me out. She reached over and flung open the door which made the usual terrible grinding noise when it reached the limit of its, now old, tortured hinges.

Some rust fell off the door sill.

Cathy leaned over, peered up at me through the open door.

"Get in, quick!"

I leapt in and the car dipped alarmingly as my weight landed on the seat. Cathy seemed not to notice as she let the clutch out violently, and, violently, the car shot forward, my head bouncing off the headrest as various laws of physics did their stuff.

"In a hurry, are we?" I said sarcastically, rubbing my rear cranium.

"No." she said, but then fell silent while I looked enquiringly at her.

Three corners later I was still enquiringly looking.

Cathy finally returned my gaze. "What?" she said, returning her attention to the road.

"I said, are we in a hurry?"

"No." she said. "Why?"

"You're driving bloody fast for someone who's not."

"Not what." She said frowning, her head turning back and forth several times while she tried her best to concentrate on the road and me at the same time.

"In a hurry!" I said loudly with a large dollop of frustration. Actually,

I had no right whatsoever to criticise as I didn't drive, or even own a car myself. Apart from one single solitary driving lesson and a couple of goes in the family Volkswagen Caravanette, I had never driven anything. But I thought it prudent to keep that piece of information to myself.

"Am I?" she said, nonchalantly. Actually, a bit too nonchalantly. I had the feeling we were running from something.

Perhaps it was because I had been in a state of high anticipation since I stepped out of the shower earlier that evening that my senses were heightened, but I definitely had the feeling I was missing something here.

Steven and I had left the bridge to its silent vigil over the vessel and rushed around taking down the flags and making sure all the deck lights were on, then had a brief war over who was going in the shower first. Steven couldn't come up with a good reason for him going first, so he pulled rank instead and I had to wait while he gurgled and splashed away half an hour before emerging in a cloud of steam and after shave.

"Urgh! ... You smell like a whore's handbag." I said irritably. (You were allowed to say that in Nineteen Seventy-One without being accused of being some sort of 'ist... You know... sex-ist, Chauvin-ist, man-ist, bully-ist, whatever). "You going to that pub?" I asked, trying to sound as though I didn't care.

"Yes." He said. "You?"

"Erm... Nah, don't think so." I had dived into the bathroom and shut the door quickly so I didn't have to answer further questions.

After a quick shower I had scrambled into my uniform and trotted along to the saloon for something to eat. Steven, Barry, and JoJo were already there.

"You're not coming ashore tonight then?" Said Barry between slurps of soup.

I blushed, "No, don't think so."

"He's seeing that girl," said Steven.

I blushed a bit more.

"You're blushing," announced Barry loudly.

"I'm not!"

"Bring her in the 'Masonic'," JoJo was looking at me with one eyebrow raised.

"Yeah," said Barry, "we'll see you in there later."

A sudden silence descended on the room. Actually, it seemed to drift in from the alleyway which was still busy with new crew members of all departments arriving and endless harassed looking individuals rushing about with briefcases.

Captain McHale entered the saloon preceded by his presence. He stopped in the doorway, surveyed the scene and then went directly to his chair at the head of the centre table.

Now, as I described before, the centre table was round. It is difficult, as young Arthur discovered when he got his first 'King job,' to have a 'Head of Table' place at a round table. But, somehow, British Merchant Ships managed it. It was usually the bit of table nearest the sharp end of the boat and had, no matter what sort of ship it was, an aura about it. The cutlery looked shinier and sharper and other cutlery seemed to keep a respectful distance.

"He's going ashore after," Barry was leaning across the table in a conspiratorial manner, whispering.

"Who?" I said.

"Himself," said Barry waving his head towards the centre table. "… Skipper."

I looked over my shoulder and straight into the eyes of our leader. He seemed to have singled me out for some stare treatment. I whisked my head back blushing profusely.

"You're blushing again," said Barry.

"Not."

"Are."

"Not." I said glaring at him.

He opened his mouth to speak but JoJo got in first.

"Will you two ladies pack it in," he said, a deep frown on his forehead, "you give me the headache."

"It's 'im," said Barry.

"It's not me…" I started to say but shut up quickly when JoJo turned his full attention in my direction.

"Shall we go to the Masonic?" Said Cathy.

"No!" I virtually screeched the word. My mind instantly giving me images of, not only Barry, Steven and JoJo, but the Himalayan ex- not a boyfriend and his crew.

"Alright, alright." She said. "We don't have to."

I looked at her. "No … it's ok, I just thought we could go somewhere … you know … together." I frowned at myself. 'What a stupid thing to say. … *"Go somewhere together!"*

Cathy obviously agreed. "What a stupid thing to say!" She rolled her eyes. "Of course, we'll go together."

I frowned. "Yes, I know that, but what I meant was, you know, just us." I wanted to say the word 'alone' but somehow it seemed, well, too much.

She grinned, keeping her eyes on the road.

"You mean, alone." The word, 'alone' she breathed in a mock seductive sort of way. Her grin became wider, and she glanced in my direction with her head tilted towards me. This made her look even cuter than all the other times she had looked cute. I went red again.

"Well… yes… alone." I said, wishing I had said it first.

It was at that point disaster struck.

Cars have wheels.

Around the wheels they have tyres.

Tyres have an aversion to sharp objects.

If you run over a sharp object, you get a puncture.

We got a puncture.

"Fuck." Said Cathy in a ladylike fashion. Actually, as she had obviously been brought up well, she put an "Oh" In front of the Anglo-Saxon bit. This, I have found, always makes "Fuck" sound posher and therefore more ladylike.

"Oh fuck!"

The car came to a slow bumpy stop, the offending front left wheel scraping along the kerb as Cathy steered close into the pavement.

We both stared straight ahead saying nothing. The deserted street was full of derelict houses on one side and old Victorian looking warehouses on the left.

"Where are we?" I asked, not really knowing what else to say.

There was no surprise in my voice because for quite some time I always assumed that any sort of situation like this that I might find myself in would, of course, include at least one disaster. ...and I was right. Here it was. The disaster.

Cathy looked up and down the road.

"Ermine Street." She said quietly. "Why."

"Oh, just wondered." I said matching her quiet tone.

We sat staring out of the window for a bit longer then she sighed.

"Can you change a tyre?"

"Of course." I said. Stupid thing to say really as I had no clue what-so-ever how to change a tyre.

I tried to backtrack a bit. "Well, what I mean is I can help."

"Help?" She looked at me quizzically.

"Yes... Help... You know, help you change it."

"Oh, you can't change it yourself." She was frowning now.

"Yes." I said, elongating the word to give me more thinking time. "But err...." More elongating. "...Erm... It is your car so you will know where everything is and the best way of doing it." *'Hah! Masterfully done George'* I thought. "So, I will help... where's the spare?"

Cathy looked distraught. Her shoulders dropped and she actually blushed. Well, I think she blushed. It was dark so I couldn't be sure, but, as I was the one who usually did all the blushing, I really hoped she was.

"I don't think I have one." She whispered.

"Pardon."

She cleared her throat and puffed out her cheeks before saying, louder this time "I don't think I have one."

I turned and looked straight ahead.

"You don't think you have one?

"No." she said.

"A spare tyre?"

"No." Quieter this time.

I was, I am ashamed to say, enjoying my moment of superiority and was beginning to wallow in the glow that follows a sudden rush of undeniably quick thinking that had enabled me to, finally, feel manly in her presence and, well, sound as though I knew about tyres, cars, and stuff.

"Sorry." She said quietly and pitifully, breathing out at the same and adding a sexy kittenish look to her beautiful face while her eyes began to glisten with tears.

Away went all my superior feelings. (Women, I discovered over the next fifty years, are really, really good at that. Taking away a chap's manly feelings with a well-timed kittenish look, a few tears, and an apology.)

I went back to being a jibbering idiot.

"Oh... no... erm... not to worry... erm perhaps we can get one."

'Perhaps we can get one?' I was definitely back in 'say stupid things' mode.

Cathy looked up the road, turned slowly and looked behind her. Then she looked directly at me.

"Where from?"

I looked up and down the road as well.

"Well, I don't know." I said. "You know this area better than me."

She turned again to look up the road.

"It's half past eight at night and it's raining again."

I twisted towards her and then a little further round to look through the back window. Her perfume wafted over me and I turned back towards her. She was looking at me, her mouth slightly open. I could hear her breath. I could feel her without touching her. Our mouths locked together suddenly. I had no warning, no sudden rush of passion, we just kissed. My whole body relaxed and fell towards her. Her weight pressed against mine, our bodies had their own agenda and seemed to strain towards each other with no conscious help from us. My left arm started to snake over her body and round her back.

There was a loud snapping noise and Cathy's face disappeared into the back of the car. The back of her seat seemed to have collapsed and I briefly, very briefly, fleetingly actually, wondered about the snapping noise. I had no time for further wondering as she kept hold and pulled me down on top of her. Well, sort of on top of her. My seat prevented me from rolling right over, not to mention various inconveniently placed gear levers, handbrakes, dashboards etc. I was twisted in an entirely unnatural position so my head couldn't quite reach hers. The result was I ended up with my nose between her breasts. Not unpleasant, I grant you, but the accompanying pain in the legs from all those handbrakes and stuff added to the wrenched back and side muscles that went with my twisted position, all made my eyes water a bit.

Not to be denied Cathy grabbed my head, her fingers naturally curling around my ears.

"Kiss me." She breathed.

Then she pulled.

"Oh Brian!"

"Ow! Fuck!" My eyes were screwed tightly shut against the pain of neck sinew stretched way beyond its allotted length, but with my head still nostril deep in bosoms my shout was muffled so she only heard the second word.

"Oh, we can't... not here... not like this!" exclaimed Cathy still heaving at my ears.

She stopped suddenly and lifted my head up, another agonising little twist. My eyes gazed up at her and she squashed her head down on to her chest and looked down.

"Have you... you know... got anything?"

I was extremely hurt by that question. I shouldn't have been because in the circumstances it was a very grown up, adult thing to ask.

"Well... no..." I said frowning. "I don't think so."

"You don't think so?" Her breathy passionate voice was replaced by a puzzled tone.

"No... I am sure I haven't." I said. "I had a medical examination after I left college."

"What?"

"Medical... after college... health check and stuff, you know tests and inoculations." I tried to move my head but she held me in a vice like grip, so I was forced to look directly up her nose. "And we had a lecture about V.D. and... and stuff before that." I elaborated.

She suddenly let go of my ears and her head fell back on to the seat.

"No... No... you moron." She said breathing out heavily. "I mean... have you got a condom!"

"Oh, I see." I buried my head back in her bosom to hide my shame. "...Erm, no, actually." I said.

There was a fairly long pause before either of us moved, then Cathy suddenly shifted.

"Never mind, there are plenty of things to do." Her right hand that had so firmly grabbed my ear but a few seconds earlier moved gently down towards my belt and began to pull at the buckle while she heaved herself lower down so our faces were level.

"Kiss me." She said again.

The next minutes, or was it hours, it could have been days or even seconds were filled with legs, trousers, exploring hands, exploring mouths and various body parts. Everywhere and everything became a hot, sweaty, sticky erotic universe of sexual passion.

In a Mini Minor.

The smallest of small cars.

Space played a part in all these passionate gymnastics. As did inconveniently placed gear levers, handbrakes, window winders and steering wheels. All causing many a frustration, not to mention severe bruising. The windows became steamed up completely within seconds and the hooter sounded on several occasions but neither of us cared very much. Neither did we care about the loud squeaking, rattling, and grinding noises that were coming from what little suspension apparatus the poor car had. Nothing mattered but us. Time didn't exist. The rest of the planet didn't exist. Just us.

Inevitably things came to a head and we flopped down exhausted. Well… we would have flopped if there had been any flopping space available. There wasn't, so all the flopping was, sort of, internal. What muscles could be relaxed, were relaxed and we lay there panting. Cathy had, somehow, managed to get her legs past the steering wheel and into the back seat while keeping her head in the same position. However, she had kept her jeans on, albeit on one leg only while I was bent backwards around the edge of my seat which was still upright. My right trouser leg was hooked on the gear lever and my left platform shoed foot was over by the driver's side window. Luckily, said window was still intact. I lifted my head from her left leg and looked along her body til my eyes met hers. She was smiling.

"That was lovely." She breathed and tried to move but gave up at after the second attempt. "Uncomfortable, but lovely."

"Mmmm." Was all I could manage in reply.

It was only a few minutes later that the pain started to kick in. All the afterglow disappeared, and muscles began to complain, joints bent in unnatural angles screamed in agony.

"Shit!" Cathy suddenly struggled upright.

"Ahhh Ahh ooo yah ooff fah hah!" This sudden movement caused my back to bend further round the seat and the knee of my window leg to thump painfully on something metal and pointy.

"What? What?" I said, trying to get my head above the level of the seat.

"Oww! The tyre!" She was rubbing her head, which had come into sudden contact with the rear window, with one hand and trying to wipe something off her chin with the other.

I was trying to look through the tiny rear, misted window.

"What tyre?"

"The spare! She shouted, her face a picture of delight. "I know where it is."

Now, this was another major milestone in my 'Life Education' programme. Women, I, at this point, discovered were able to skip between universes at will. That they had this ability was confirmed to me many, many times in the future, but I made this discovery first on the 8th of January Nineteen Seventy-One in a Mini Cooper on Ermine Street, East Ham, London. Cathy went from the 'Sexual Ecstasy' universe to the 'Car Mechanic' universe in one fifteen second hop.

"Oh." I said.

"Yes, we can change it now and go and have a drink."

"Oh." I said. My feelings were hurt. I felt, dismissed, I suppose you could call it. Cast aside in favour of a tyre.

We attempted to gather items of clothing. Cathy found she was missing a sock and a shoe. How that had happened I could not understand but she gave me no time to ponder on it.

"Come on." She said opening the door and letting in a cold wet blast of air.

"Alright, alright." I muttered as I tumbled out of the door trying desperately to get my clothes to co-operate.

"It's here, look." By the time I had organised myself Cathy was squatting down behind the car.

"There." She said, pointing underneath as I joined her.

"Oh." I said. "How do we get it out?"

She frowned. "…Erm… Dunno."

"Great!" I also frowned.

Brian George

"Well, it's not my fault! She wailed indignantly. "Stupid place to put a spare tyre."

I couldn't help agreeing. Some idiots had decided the best place to put it was on a wire rack underneath the rear of the vehicle. Ridiculous!

The next half hour was pure farce. Neither of us had a clue how to change a tyre. In fact, neither of us had a clue how to get the bloody thing off the rack, never mind change it.

After an endless amount of heaving, tugging, swearing, arguing and frustration I managed to get the spare wheel off the rack. Now all that was needed was for the tyres to be changed.

After another endless amount of heaving… etc… etc. I stood back and looked at the wheel. It appeared to be all right. In fact, it looked perfect. I grinned, feeling very manly and mechanic like.

"Well." Said Cathy. "We did it." She was standing next to me shivering. Her hand slipped into mine.

I didn't think 'we' was an apt description of the work force used to change the wheel, but I decided that now, standing cold and soaking wet in the rain, in my trendy crumpled seventies fashion wear, was not the time to mention it. Particularly after what Cathy had done with various parts of my anatomy less than an hour before.

"Come on… get back in the car."

She pulled gently at my fingers and then kissed me on the cheek.

"Thanks." She said.

I turned to smile at her but she was already walking round to the driver's side.

"Don't forget to put the other wheel back under the car." The door slammed shut a second later as she plonked herself into the seat.

There followed a brief bad-tempered exchange, quite at odds with all the love that had been in the air just before, because I insisted that "The tyre would be put in the back and was fucked if I was going to faff about in the rain with that stupid wire rack thing!"

Cathy drove away from our area of wild passion at her usual rate of knots and as usual I was rubbing my head where it had thumped against the window.

"Well, we can't go to the pub looking like this." I said. "Anyway, I'm soaked and bloody freezing."

"Yeah, me too." She said frowning and obviously thinking hard. "I know." Her face lit up. "We can go to Sid's he's still open."

"Sid's?"

"Yes, Sid's. It's a café near the dock gates."

So, Sid's it was.

Describing it as a café was over egging it a bit. It's actual name was Sidolis Café, (It had a neon sign over the door but the o, the l and one i were in darkness and looked as though they hadn't worked for years) and a scruffier, greasier more run down place you would be hard pressed to find anywhere outside the more run down areas of Casablanca. But it was warm and virtually deserted save one old tramp and a bag lady dressed in a fur coat that, I am sure, had things living in it.

Cathy ordered two cups of tea and a round of toast each. Then we sat, talked, laughed, and warmed up. Then we talked some more. We must have been there for nearly two hours, but it seemed like only a few minutes before she said.

"Well, I suppose I had better go home." She stretched across the table and held my hands in hers and looked at me. "You're sailing tomorrow night."

My shoulders slumped. "I don't want to now." I said in a pitiful voice.

She got up from her chair and turned towards the door but not before I caught sight of a tear on her cheek.

"Come on, I'll drop you off at the gate."

"Can't you come on the ship for a bit?" I managed to reach the door before her and opened it. She stepped outside with her head turned away from me.

"No, no." she said loudly and purposefully. "I must go home… up early in the morning."

I could hear the quiver in her voice, so I didn't argue I just followed her back to the car and got in.

It took less than two minutes to reach the dock gates where we sat and held on to each other for a long time without speaking. Then she let go suddenly and started fishing around in the open glove compartment in front of me.

"Here she said I'll write my address and phone number and you give me yours." She found a pencil and an old envelope which she wrote on then ripped a piece off and handed it to me. I did the same and handed it to her.

"Go on now." She said. "Go back to the ship, I'll come and wave you off tomorrow night."

I leant over and kissed her then got out of the car. I couldn't find any words to say as I closed the door.

Cathy leaned over and wound down the window "Bye now." She tried to smile but I could see the tears. "Write to me… eh? I'll ring you when you get back." She let the clutch out and revved the engine, the car leapt away from the kerb.

She was gone.

I never felt so empty and lost as I stood there in the rain staring after her rapidly diminishing taillights. The lost feeling was replaced by a terrible sadness. I had not even been able to say the word 'Goodbye.'

"Where the fook 'ave you been?"

I looked up. It was Barry.

"Yeah, we've been in the Masonic," said JoJo coming up behind him.

"Oh," I said and stared at them.

Barry rolled his eyes. "Well?"

"Well, what?" I looked from one to the other.

They looked at each other and grinned.

"It's ok, we know where you've been," said Barry stabbing me in the chest.

"You've been with that Cathy. I know you 'ave. I saw her drivin' off."

JoJo stepped closer and peered at me. "Judging by your face you have just been saying your fond farewells." His grin widened.

He put his arm round me. "Aagh, don't worry you'll be fine."

"Yep," said Barry putting his arm round my other shoulder.

I looked at them both. "Where's Steven?"

JoJo laughed. "He had two beers then said he was off back to the ship and disappeared.

"Anyway," said JoJo steering me through the dock gates. "Tomorrow, me boyos… we are off to sea!"

CHAPTER 14

SAILING

There may be, in the history of the British Merchant Navy, some lads and lassies who, at this precise point in their seagoing careers, still had burning ambitions to be really efficient Officers, able seaman or whatever, but I suspect, they will have been few and far between. You have to remember most people go to sea because it's in them to go to sea. They just want to. It's for the pure excitement of it. Well, no, not even the excitement, that also comes later. They just want to and that's it! Once they discover the little extras that go with it... like... going ashore for example, then they become hooked and the pure thrill and excitement of it all takes over. But, at that moment, when they are about to put to sea for the very first time, when everything is firing up, when all around them seem to know what they are doing and are rushing about following, what appear to be routines that are totally alien to first trippers, then all that, 'I've always wanted to go to sea' malarkey, seems a really, really stupid idea. So, no burning ambitions for me. I just wanted to be able to do all this stuff so that I could wander about in a matter of fact sort of manner and feel comfortable, but, most of all, fit in. That's what every youth wants... to fit in. That's all that was passing through my shallow teenage mind. Fitting in is the order of the day. If anybody tells you it was different for them... they are lying through their teeth, speaking untruths and not being exact with facts.

Except, that is, for Steven. Steven was different. Steven actually wanted to learn about nautical stuff all the time. Not only nautical stuff, but, in addition, nautical engineering stuff! The more technical things were, the more interested Steven became. Greenwich Meridians, Sidereal Hour Angles, Declinations, Mercator Charts, and position lines were all joys to him. As were pistons, liners, and crankshafts. He loved to chat about the movement of stars and planets and so on. In fact, earlier that day, he had tried to engage me in a conversation about the apparent retrograde motion of Uranus. Fortunately, an urgent situation down number two hatch had rescued me from the lecture and it was to be a further three years before, sitting in a classroom at the Warsash School of Navigation, I was faced with such motions again.

There was one other thing on my mind of course. Something that could, if I weren't careful, take over completely. That something was Cathy. My Cathy. Or was she, my Cathy? The previous nights' events had been wonderful, but there was still trauma going on in the back of my mind over the voice I had heard on the telephone and one or two things she had said. Now, my head was juggling those doubts, the joy and horror and wonder of being associated with a beautiful blonde woman, doubt over her feelings, the sheer terror of trying not mess anything up while being part of getting this vast machine into open water, the worry over whether or not I would be able to do what I was going to be asked to do and to cap it all, attempting to put to the back of my mind the undeniable fact that I desperately wanted to go to the toilet!

That state of mind, that bedlam of thought, that urgency of bodily function control all contributed to the …erm… somewhat chaotic and terribly slow river passage down the Thames and out into the open sea.

Six o'clock that evening had found Steven and me sitting in our cabin, fully booted and spurred, uniforms, hats and all, waiting for the bell to go to tell us to go to our respective stations. Steven was to go to the foc'sle with the Chief Officer (the Mate) and I was to be on the bridge with the Third Mate and of course, Captain McHale and the Pilot. Neither of us said very much, we were both nervous. Steven was, as usual, reading something technically nautical, but I could see he was nervous. His left foot was bouncing up down at a hundred beats a minute.

All our other duties had been performed. Steven had been on the bridge helping the Third Mate test the bridge equipment and I had toured the ship with a little blue notebook, which, I had been told was the "All

Aboard Book." It was a new one befitting the new voyage and had on the first page a list of all the heads of department, Chief Officer, Chief Engineer, Chief Steward etc. etc. It was my job to go around and get all these people to sign against their name to indicate that all the people they were responsible for were on the ship and all the people visiting the ship they were responsible for were off it. I then had to go and find the Third Mate and give the book to him as he was responsible for making sure that all the heads of department were sure that all the people, they were responsible for were on or off the ship. Mind you, I never, ever, in all my time in the Merchant Navy, actually saw a 'Head of Department' go and check if all these people were on or off anything.

There had been a brief moment of panic when I thought I was going to have to go into the Engine Room to find the Chief Engineer. The horror I felt at the thought of entering that cavernous, machinery infested, smelly, oily, hell pit, was almost too much to take. But my luck held and just as I was going to open the Devil's gate to the fiery pit, said gate was flung open and the man himself appeared, wafted out on a cacophony of deafening generator noise and a blast of really hot, oil infused air. He didn't even pause, he just grabbed the book, searched briefly in a filthy looking top pocket of an even filthier 'used to be white' boiler suit, produced a half-eaten biro, scribbled his signature in my nice new book and galloped off down the alleyway. It wasn't til I had gathered my thoughts and looked down at the now blackened, crumpled page that I saw that he had signed his name against the line reserved for the Chief Steward. Well, actually, it covered the line for the Chief Steward and four other people.

So, there we sat, all ready for the off.

In the end no bell rang. Instead, the Second Mate appeared in our cabin resplendent in uniform and cap, at least, I assumed he had his uniform jacket on. It was underneath the scruffiest looking 'Parka' ever, with the hood, which was up, sporting an inch-long tear that started by the corner of what was left of some fake fur at the edge. It looked as though he had sewn a piece of dead rat to one corner as some sort of fashion statement.

"Stations!" he announced. "Better get a move on, the tugs have arrived."

We leaped to our feet and followed him out of the cabin. Steven turned right heading forward, The Second Mate turned left heading aft. I stood momentarily confused, my head swivelling back and forth before it made a decision and followed the 'Parka'.

'I'll go out the aft alleyway door and up onto the boat deck and then up to the bridge wing.' That was my thinking. *'Then I will be out of everybody's way.'*

So that was what I did. There was a small hurdle to overcome as all the deck lights had been turned off and the boat deck was in pitch darkness, which meant I went across the deck fairly slowly, sideways, with one arm flapping the air in front of me to ensure I didn't bounce off any obstacles. However, all was well, and I arrived unscathed, but before I went into the wheelhouse I looked over the dodger, which is the sort of wall thing that goes from each side of the wheelhouse round the edge of the bridge wing to protect everybody from spray… and to stop them falling off, I suppose… There was a small gaggle of people, on the dock, standing more or less opposite the bridge and as I stepped up to the dodger, a figure stepped out from behind them and started waving.

It took a while before I registered who it was and when I did I started to wave back… couldn't get my arm in the air quick enough… I felt as though the entire world had been put to right! From that moment on I would be the best seaman ever! Captain at twenty-three years old! The sun would shine nonstop from now until eternity. There was nothing I couldn't do!

It was Cathy! Confidence flowed through me!

"SOMEBODY! SOMEBODY!"

Confidence flowed out of me. My arm withered into the sleeve of my jacket as I whirled round in time to see Captain McHale striding out onto the wing.

"Ahh," he said, "there you are. Nip down to my cabin and tell the Mr. Carr, the pilot, we are ready to leave. Tell him the tugs are here."

"Yes Sir." I said and dived towards the ladder to the boat deck.

"Not that way you idiot. Go through the chartroom!"

"Oh… erm… No Sir… I mean yes Sir, chartroom Sir." I couldn't see, it was too dark, but I could imagine the look of disbelieving incredulity on his face at being faced with one that continued to display stupidity to such a degree.

Fred Carr was the choice Blue Star pilot for the Royal Docks in London. He was a tall angular man of indeterminable age dressed in a plain navy-blue beltless raincoat. Actually, it was difficult to tell his height as he was stretched full length on the captain's daybed with a small black peaked cap tipped over his eyes and a cup of tea perched on his chest. I had rushed through the wheelhouse, then the chartroom, to carry out my leaders bidding, tripping over everything that could be tripped over and bumping into everything and everybody that could be bumped into.

"Erm… Mr Carr, the tugs are here, and we are ready to leave." I said in a rush as I stepped gingerly into the already open door of the captains palatial cabin.

"There's no 'urry young'un." He spoke slowly in broad cockney accent as he unfurled himself from his prone position in one deft move. "You're going no-fahkin-where til I get up there." Unfortunately, he had obviously forgotten his cup of tea which was hurled across the cabin as he came upright. We both stood and watched as the cup came to an abrupt stop against leg of the captain's large desk.

He shrugged. "Lead the way boy."

From then on everything happened in a whirl. As soon as we arrived on the bridge things started to happen. Mr Carr was obviously well known to everyone and he was handed a mug of tea by Dave, the Third Mate, as he stepped over the chartroom door sill.

"Tugs fast fore and aft Sir." said Dave, then looking at me said, "Come here you, you can do the book."

I followed him out into the wheelhouse where a small wooden flap held up by two triangular frames, so it formed a sort of table, had been erected.

Dave pointed at a large, hardback notebook that sat, open, on the table. "That," he said, "is the movement book. All you have to do is write down everything that happens, as it happens. You know, engine movements, lines being taken in, pilot orders and stuff." He stared at me briefly. "Got it?"

"Got it." I nodded.

"Sure?"

Err… Yes, sure." I said, not at all sure. It seemed straight forward enough, bit like the cargo times book… but moving. I just wished they didn't all keep saying things 'and stuff' when they were explaining things.

Anyway, there was no time to worry about it as orders started being shouted more or less straight away.

"Let go for'wd spring!" shouted Captain McHale.

"Let go for'wd spring," repeated Dave, and then repeated it again into his Walkie Talkie.

I looked at the book. The page had been divided by a single line drawn down the left-hand side leaving a margin on one side where times had been written corresponding to statements in the other column.

The first one read.

1750. POB.

I didn't know what that meant, but I got the picture, grabbed the biro that sat on the table, looked at my watch and started scribbling furiously.

"Let go the headline!" Again, this was repeated, and I could see people scurrying around on the foc'sle which was illuminated by the harsh, bright dockside lamps that shone from the walls of the warehouses.

After what seemed an age the first helm order came from the pilot. "Port ten!"

"Port 10!" shouted a voice behind me making me jump. I hadn't seen the wheelman, one of the able seamen, leaning on the wheel. "Wheels at port ten!"

"Dead slow ahead!" shouted Mr. Carr.

"Dead slow ahead!" shouted back the Third Mate as he moved the engine room telegraph to the appropriate slot.

He looked at me. I looked back.

"Well?" he said.

"Erm… well what?"

"Well right it down then, hurry up."

"Oh yes… I am, I am!" I said immediately scribbling again.

There was a shudder that ran through the ship at that moment. At the same time a sort of hissing roar rumbled up from below as pistons began to move up and down.

"Let go stern line!"

The ship moved. My first movement. I grinned a stupid grin as I stared out of the bridge window and watched as the ship's bow began to move slowly, majestically away from the quayside towards the darkness of the mist shrouded dock and clear of the ship ahead, which, until then, had seemed oh so awfully close, which, in fact, it was, with its stern right underneath our bow.

"Let go the spring aft."

The last line was let go. There was now no contact with the dock.

I didn't really take much in after that initial movement, it was all too quick. But I did manage to keep up with my movement book and once we had cleared the quay and the other ships, manoeuvred through the narrow dock entrances and out into the River Thames, I was feeling quite the expert in movement book filling in, which may sound silly, but believe me, to a first trip, seventeen year old boy, is a really important milestone in his history! To have had a hand in moving millions of pounds worth of merchant vessel, filled with even more millions of pounds worth of other people's stuff, as a member of a professional crew of stuff movers is a big deal.

I felt part of something.

Anyway, we were off. Mr. Carr and his tugs had gently manoeuvred, nudged, pulled, and teased us out of the Royal Docks.

At some point the pilot had disembarked and another pilot, a river pilot, had arrived. (Now, nearly fifty years later, my memory has let me down and I can't remember when, or how, the pilots changed.) In any event, we were away down the Thames heading for the open sea.

This 'open sea' that we were headed for was, of course, quite a long way off and would take several hours. In fact, the several hours became several more hours as progress was very slow. Fog had arrived. A thick, impenetrable, black-grey wall descended upon us and speed was reduced to a minimum, the vessels very loud whistle blasted out its deep-toned warning every so often while I continued to masterfully write everything down. My sense of worth increasing with each stroke of my betting shop biro. Excitement coursed through me. I was going to sea.

The only regret I had was I hadn't had enough time, enough courage, enough wit to get to know and spend time with my Cathy.

"Cadet!"

Captain McHale was pacing around the starboard bridge wing as we crept down the river. We had only been under way for about half an hour but it seemed like a lifetime to me.

"Cadet!"

"Yes sir." I said, peering out towards the wheelhouse door and trying to locate him in the mist.

"Cadet!" He roared, even louder.

This galvanised me into action and I headed towards the door. However, after taking two or three steps, which, actually took me almost to the entrance, I remembered my instructions from Dave to stay put and write everything down. This caused me to come to an abrupt halt and turn suddenly back to the desk.

"Oooff!" breathed the Third Mate, who, for some reason, had followed me and cannoned into me as I stopped.

"Sorry!" My voice became a squeak of panic induced exclamation, but my focus was still on my movement book and I reached behind him, making a wild grab at it. Unfortunately, this caused me to step fairly heavily on his right foot.

"Ow!" He shouted.

"Sorry." I said again but with less meaning this time as my brain had registered the fact that my scrabbling fingers had found the book.

"Cadet!" A degree of frustrated agitation had now entered Captain McHale's voice and he appeared in the doorway.

"Sorry Sir... Coming Sir!" I shouted, spinning round, book in hand to face him.

That look of amazed incredulousness that always seemed to pass across his face whenever he had any dealings with Brian George Cadet, appeared as he first looked directly at me and then lowered his gaze slowly to the point where my betting shop biro, having been propelled at speed across the bridge as I had spun round, bounced off his jacket.

His attention was then drawn towards his Third Officer who was limping away towards the chartroom.

He looked then back at me.

"What...?" That look remained on his face. "Why...?" He started again. "Why have you got the movement book in your hand?"

"Erm... well... erm... yes Sir... yes." I said, explaining succinctly. "You see... erm... Sir..."

"Never mind!" He said quickly. "Just…" He paused, gathering himself and forcing calm into his words. "Just… please go and make coffee for everyone."

"Yes sir." I spun round and headed towards the chartroom. The Third Mate, standing in the doorway immediately leapt out of the way and hurried towards the sanctuary of the compass binnacle to avoid further injury at my approach.

Now, making coffee may seem a simple task to perform, but it did cause me some concern. I had never made coffee! I had made tea many, many times, but coffee I did not like. So, therefore I didn't make it and under the circumstances I felt that asking Captain McHale "How do you make coffee?" would not be a clever idea.

All the equipment for making beverages was laid out on the chartroom daybed. Cups, saucers, milk, unopened two-pound bag of sugar, (next to a delicate looking sugar bowl with pink flowers round the edge filled to the brim with more sugar) tea bags and of course, an opened tin of coffee powder.

'Now then,' I reasoned, *Normally, if I were making tea, I would put tea or teabags into the pot, pour in the boiling water, stir it and leave it for a bit to brew. So, therefore, it should be the same for coffee.'*

So that is what I started to do. I actually got as far as pouring the water into the teapot, or 'Coffee Pot,' as I now liked to call it, when the Third Mate pushed back the heavy, light excluding curtain that covered the wheelhouse entrance and stepped into my beverage making area.

"Oh," he said, coming to a sudden stop. "Thought you were making coffee."

"Yes, I am, that's what this is."

He looked at the water filling the pot, then looked at me for a second and returned his gaze to the pot while all the time the expression on his face went from 'quizzical', through several muscle contorting phases to 'horror struck'

"Wha… wha…!" He tried to speak. "Tha… that's the teapot!" he finally managed.

I stopped pouring and also gazed at the pot.

"Erm, yes, but there isn't another one."

He continued to stare. "But… but… that's the teapot!"

Just then Captain McHale appeared in the door.

"Where's the coffee, young man?"

I looked at him then at the pot that I was still holding.

"That's the teapot," he said staring at it.

"That's the teapot," repeated Dave, still with his horror-struck expression welded to his face.

"Teapot," I said looking from Captain to Third Mate and back again as, now, my expression changed to one similar to the Third Mate's as I realised, I had made an error akin to triggering a nuclear holocaust or eating the wrong peoples babies.

Making coffee in a teapot!

"You've made coffee in a teapot," said Captain McHale quietly, staring at me.

I'm not absolutely sure whether it was a statement or a question. There was far too much menace in his tone to tell really.

"Fuck me," said Dave.

Our voyage to New Zealand had begun!

CHAPTER 15

A Bit Rough

It was early evening just before heading back to the bridge for my watch with the Dave, the Third Mate, that I noticed a perceptible change in the ships motion.

For all of our passage out of the Thames, around the coast, past Dover on one side and Calais on the other, then on down the English Channel, the ship pitched gently up and down. Not an unpleasant feeling. Rhythmic. Natural. It was as though the sea and weather were gently easing the vessel into a smooth routine of motion designed by the weather Gods to waft us all the way to New Zealand.

Now, however, things had begun to change … rapidly … The pitching motion at once became more violent. More … urgent. Sitting on the daybed in our cabin, I glanced over at Steven, who was at the desk, on our one and only chair, to see if he had noticed the change. Apparently not. He sat there busily turning the pages of his book. First forward and then back. I could see the paper cover he had discarded lying next to the coffee cup that was anchored to the desk by his other hand.

STEAM RECIPROCATING ENGINES
(PRINCIPLES)

Strange reading, I thought, for someone training to be a Navigating Officer. I had, in fact, noticed, in the five days that I had known Steven that he showed, for a deck cadet, an unhealthy interest in all things mechanical. For one thing, he would disappear into the engine room at the slightest excuse. Something that I would go to the ends of the earth to avoid.

I was sitting on the daybed with uniform and coat already on nervously fidgeting and reading a book. Well, not really reading, more staring really. I was just doing that… 'read a page, then read the same page four times again because your nerves are screaming, and you are thinking about something else entirely'… thing! Actually, I cared not a jot for the rough weather, nor did I care whether I would be able to carry out my sea going duties in such weather. Even worries about seasickness passed fleetingly through my thoughts, only to be dismissed and flung on the scrapheap of a thousand other worries that had come to nothing.

No, the thing that was uppermost in my adolescent mind was *'I hope enough time has passed for my coffee making error to have been forgotten about.'* Various sarcastic remarks from some of the engineering staff over the intervening twenty-four hours suggested that it would be sometime before my famed beverage making abilities would be confined to history books.

"Think we've just gone around Cape Finnistere," said Steven without looking up.

I looked at him, impressed by his knowledge "How do you know," I asked holding on to the edge of my seat.

"The Mate told me earlier we should be there about now".

"Oh, right," I said, less impressed. I shifted position slightly to give my feet better purchase on the floor as the ship rolled slightly to starboard, a new motion to add to the increased pitching. The ship rolled slowly back to port just as the bow ploughed into another wave. The sound of crockery hitting the floor in a distant part of the vessel made us both tense a little more.

"Getting a little rougher" said Steven looking up, trying, but failing, to sound nonchalant.

I said nothing, also trying and failing to look nonchalant.

"Anyway," I said, standing up. "Time, I went to the Bridge." I sat down again with a thump as the ship took another roll to starboard, then planted my feet and stood up again. This time with my knees bent and arms out wide'.

"Now?" Said Steven looking up and ducking under my flailing left arm. "Bit early, isn't it?"

I looked at my watch. Quarter past seven. As the title suggests, the eight to twelve watch starts at eight, so he was right, it was a tad early. My rear end was just beginning to lower back down in the direction of the daybed when life changed forever…

The very ground (deck) I was standing on rose up to meet me. I … was on the way down. This had the effect of doubling the stomach-churning effect of the vessel suddenly climbing the very … I repeat …very large wave that had chosen to occupy the same tiny, tiny patch of planet that thirteen odd thousand tons of the New Zealand Star was already using! Hardly fair really … but that's the way it was.

The ship reared up and up … and up. Then instantaneously, tipped violently forward and down plunging headlong at, what felt like, several hundred miles an hour into the trough between that exceptionally large wave and the next, even bigger, exceptionally large wave. At the same time, because the waves were coming from an angle rather than straight ahead, the ship was rolling even more violently to the right - or starboard if you want to be nautical. To make it worse there was that helpless, stomach meeting throat, moment you get when the rollercoaster car begins its headlong brain rattling, out of control rush downwards.

All this felt to me, just that, out of control. The headlong plunge considerably worsened by (what felt like) the vessel seemingly on its side! Actually, of course, it probably was only a ten-degree roll. But seventeen-year-old first trip cadets are not known for their judgment or knowledge of the behavioural characteristics of a ship in a heavy sea.

Down and down went the New Zealand Star until suddenly the world stopped! She ploughed, still pointing downward, still tipped at a crazy angle, into the next wave. This mightily arrested her forward rush and at once began to push the ship upwards and over… ten degrees or so …to the left.

We climbed the next mountain.

All this had taken but a few seconds. The effect on us humans was, to say the least, drastic.

Steven immediately clutched the arms of the chair releasing his hold on the coffee cup, which, along with everything else on any sort of flat surface, slid quickly to the floor with a crash. The chair, which in our naivety, we had failed to secure to the deck, first began to turn in an anti-clockwise direction, then raced to towards the short vestibule (where the cupboards were). There was a strangled squeak of alarm from Steven as the chair spun round. I got a glimpse of the look of horror and bewilderment on his face as, clutching the chair arms in a death grip, he rocketed past me towards the open cabin door. At the same time, I had been thrown towards the double bunk. I tried desperately to regain my balance having been violently interrupted in the mid-posterior lowering manouvre, but only succeeded in fetching up with a thud against the bunk.

Steven was less fortunate. As he and his chair scooted into the vestibule, he flung out an arm, his fingers desperately grasping for something, anything, to arrest his journey. As I hit the bunk with my shoulder my head was poking around the small wall at the end so I could see Steven's face once more as the chair again turned in my direction. It, Stevens face that is, not the chair, had the same bewildered panicked expression on it, except now his eyes stared at me pleadingly. At that instant two things happened to Steven and his transport. Firstly, his fingers found a purchase on the cupboard door handle. This, of course, did nothing to arrest his rapidly increasing speed. Instead, it opened the cupboard door. Out tumbled Steven's battered brown suitcase, followed by my kit bag, duffle bags, rucksack and two large suitcases (expandable). The whole avalanche cascaded around him. He let go of the handle. Secondly, everything, Steven, the chair, and the luggage hit the door sill at the same time. (These door sills or storm sills as they are known can be up to six inches high in some places. This tipped up the chair and hurtled Steven into the alleyway closely followed by the luggage. He was left, briefly, on his back covered in bags with both legs in the air.

Now this was bad enough for the poor boy. But what I should have mentioned earlier was, that, just before we had been sitting in the cabin. Steven had been in the shower. Eager to get back to his Steam Reciprocating Engines, he had not bothered to dress. He had sat down and grabbed his book clad only in a towel... Steven that is... in a towel... not the book. So... Lying in an alleyway covered in luggage, legs akimbo, with the towel, (subject to the same forces as the rest of us, gravity, tipping moments... all that) having departed his midriff and now adorning his head, was… (a) not a pretty sight, and (b) to him, mortifyingly embarrassing.

The sea and the *New Zealand Star* took no notice of our misfortunes whatsoever and continued their wild nautical dance. The ship heaving herself up one side of a towering Atlantic roller, the deck rearing up under our very feet, pushing against gravity. Ankle, knee, and hip joints issuing pain signals in their confusion. Then, at once, cresting the wave and again tipping and plunging down, giving a brief moment of apparent weightlessness followed by that racing, falling, rolling helplessness, and finishing with a slamming, immediately arresting jolt as the huge bulbous bow buried itself in the green blackness of another giant foam topped monster.

All this mayhem was accompanied by the sound of more crashing crockery, slamming doors, unidentifiable banging noises, angry shouts and oaths of extreme linguistic severity! Over the years I came to find that this was entirely normal for the beginning of a passage of rough weather. Every person, on every ship, knows the rough weather is coming. Every person is always prepared for it… but never… ever, ready for it! That may sound strange, but it's true.

Steven tried to regain his feet. Not easy in a narrow ship's alleyway festooned with suitcases and a chair. He managed it by grabbing hold of the wooden rail that ran along the entire length of the inner bulkhead (wall) and hauling himself upright. By that time, we were on our downward trajectory, which meant a severe starboard tilt. This had the effect of catapulting poor Steven over the luggage and back into the cabin. His panicked face turned towards mine as he, once again, raced past me. His eyes… his wide staring eyes… his wide, staring, pleading eyes locked on to mine and one hand flailed in my direction. I managed to grab it and for a brief moment we stood holding hands, eyes locked together as the ship completed the starboard roll. The only thing preventing us ending in a heap in the far corner was my grip on the top bunk rail.

"You two ok?" John, the Second Mate peered in "Oh!" He said his head moving swiftly from side to side as looked at us both.

'Again!' I thought … *'Bloody… again!'* Every time… every time I am in an embarrassing situation, and let's face it holding hands with a naked

man on a ship is pretty embarrassing, there is always some clown there to witness it.

We both started to gabble explanations at the same time. Our heads permanently moving back and forth as we sought reassurance from one another.

"Rolling... ship... chair... towel... in the shower... bunk... alleyway... suitcases... Steam reciprocating Engines!" Our words became one confusing sentence as we desperately tried to explain why the two deck cadets, one naked, were holding hands.

John frowned "Mmm." He shook his head, turned on his heel and expertly used the motion of the ship to negotiate his way down the alleyway over the chair and past one suitcase that had become wedged against the cabin door. He had gone. We were still holding hands. We let go quickly.

Steven went down on all fours and retrieved his errant towel. The violent motion continued unabated.

I decided it was time to leave. To get away. To try and remove the memory of suitcases and hand holding from my fuddled brain.

"Where are you going?" wailed a distressed Steven as I stepped over him, hanging on to the cupboard door as the ship took another wild lurch. This particular lurch seemed worse than the last and the ship stayed at an alarming angle of tilt longer than before. Which meant I had to hang on and remain with one leg over Steven for some time.

"I meant to ...." John had returned and was hanging on to the cabin door post his eyes widening and his question stalling in his throat while his brain took in the sight of me straddling a naked Steven. We both started talking at once again "Bridge... ship...towel...leg over!" words tumbled out.

"Never mind! Never mind!" He held his hand up and looked away "I don't want to know!" He rolled away again, heading back up the alleyway.

I recovered my balance and lifted one leg over Steven's head. Unfortunately, not high enough and I caught him in the right ear with my size ten.

"Ow!" He wailed.

I paid no attention as I tried to hurry into the alleyway.

"The suitcases!"

"Leave them!" I said over my shoulder. I couldn't look round, the ship's motion had, once again got a grip of my balance muscles and I was doing the 'First Trip Heavy Weather Boogie' along the alleyway. This a sort of stepping forward whilst leaning forward movement as though going uphill.

Gravity pulling down, ship pushing you up.

Swiftly followed by a leg waving in thin air canter. As though going downhill.

Gravity still pulling down, but now with the ship disappearing beneath you.

Not a… cool… look at all.

Of course, not forgetting the roll as well. This produced the thumping your shoulder into the port bulkhead (wall). Then thumping the other shoulder into the other bulkhead (other wall).

Put it all together.

Lean… step… pause…thump right… leg wave… three step downhill canter… pause… thump left… pause… lean… step… pause… Thump right… leg wave… three step uphill canter… and so on until reaching the end of the fore and aft facing alleyway.

Then I proceeded to the infinitely more advanced 'Cross Alleyway Quick Step'. Which, actually, is much the same as the previous tango but with a much sharper staccato hip sashay between the leg wave and the downhill two step canter. (Note this is now a two-step. Instead of the normal three).

Add some grimacing, an expletive or two and a full orchestra of bangs, slams, smashing crockery, cascading cutlery, and thumps.

There, you have the whole picture.

I, of course, at that time, was not aware of the humour in any of this. I just wanted to get to the bridge.

The ship took another lurch to port causing me to gallop up the stairs to the bridge deck finally arriving at the door to the chartroom in bewildered state but, nonetheless relieved to have made it without significant injury.

I heaved open the door with one hand and held on tight. My other hand pushing hard on the door post. I waited, in that position, while the ship took another wild plummeting journey down yet another deep trough, then heaved myself through the opening as it crashed and shuddered into the following wall of water. Just in front of me and to my left the chart table offered a place to cling on to. I gratefully accepted it as the roller coaster movement continued. The door banged shut behind me.

My sigh of relief was audible as I looked around the chart room, still with a death grip on the edge of the table. Everything that normally resided on any flat surface had been removed and placed on the long thin green cushion that covered the daybed at the back of the chartroom. Books, trays of coffee stained cups, milk jugs and packets of biscuits all competed for space with sextants, binocular cases, and white peaked caps. At the far end of the room the door to the radio room, 'Sparky's Shack,' was open and hooked back to stop it flying back and forward.

'Sparky' looked up, grinned at me, and raised his eyebrows in greeting. Then instantly lowered his gaze back to his notepad and began scribbling furiously. Morse code beeps emanating from his headphones. I took another staggering step from corner of the chart table to the heavy green, light excluding, curtain that adorned the doorway into the bridge.

Coming from the lights of the chart room into the blackness of the wheelhouse rendered me instantly blind. I couldn't see a thing. The ship took a lurch to starboard. My right hand shot out to find something… anything to hold on to. I found something. It felt strange but I lent on it, squeezed my fingers towards my palm to get grip and pushed against it to stop myself from falling over. My brain now engaged. Too late I realized what it was I was holding on to. It was a shoulder. A shoulder bedecked with an epaulette.

Captain McHale, from his position in the Captain's Chair, the Captain's Chair situated just to the right of the door to the chartroom, turned his head slowly towards me.

"Get ……. Off." I could just make out a face in the gloom.

The human eye is a remarkable piece of engineering and a biological marvel, able to adjust itself to varying light conditions at will. However, the brain it is attached to sometimes has difficulty in fathoming out what it is the eye is actually seeing.

As my eyes accustomed themselves to the darkness, Captain McHale's face came sharply into focus. Hardly surprising really. It was only inches from mine.

"Get!" he said again. "Off!" But it was not his face that drew my

Down To The Sea. A Cadet's Tale

attention. It was the bobble hat. I hadn't seen it since his arrival and my… erm… brouhaha with his luggage.

It had grown! It was the same colour. The same style. But, whereas, the last time I had seen it, it was large and made him look like an angry teapot, now, it was positively enormous! It was that big the bobble was obviously too heavy for the pointy bit causing said pointy bit to bend halfway up.

My eyes moved slowly up the structure and became fixed on the woolly orb which moved hypnotically back and forth in time with the ship's movement.

"What are you staring at boy?" He glared and made his beard bristle a little more. "And let go of my shoulder!" he roared.

I stared at the bobble.

"Boy!" he said again, beard straining at the roots, trying to reach me and stab me in the chest.

I let go and staggered backwards as the ship lurched. "Bobble sir"

"What!"

"Yes sir" I managed.

He frowned "Yes what?"

What did he mean? I had said "Sir." Panic set in again "Yes sir… sir" I said hopefully. I realized then I was still staring at the bobble. He thrust his beard further in my direction "What are ….?" He started to say.

"Cap'n!" … His attention was suddenly drawn by a shout from Albert, the Mate.

"What is it?" He whirled round, now aiming his beard at him…

"I have a target on the radar sir, port side … 'bout twenty degrees… range 'bout eight miles… nothing visual though…" Albert lifted his head from the radar hood and peered out into the gloom.

Captain McHale peered in the same direction. I peered in the same direction. The AB at the wheel peered in the same direction. We all held on to something. Even captain McHale gripped the arms of his chair as the ship reared up suddenly, the bow pointing briefly at the moon as an even bigger wave took control. The ship then began its downward journey almost immediately after we crested the wave. That sudden movement pitched me forward to the edge of the centre consul where I bounced round the corner of it and finally fetched up with my nose perilously close to the bridge window. As I landed there, I saw it.

"There it is." Said someone calmly as they spotted the vessel. What had been just an orange blip on a radar screen now suddenly became a real thing. An actual living thing. Well… not actually living… as in… alive. But you know what I mean. The 'target' the Mate had seen on the radar came into view. No more than a few miles away. A ship. Much smaller than ours. A tanker. Her deck clear of any derricks or cranes. One lump of superstructure at the rear. Even to my untrained eye it was obvious the thing was barely half our size. The front part of the vessels hull, the part underneath its bow was visible as it reared up and tipped downwards, plunging into the trough. That same bow suddenly disappearing altogether under a mountain of black, green, foam encrusted water.

But that wasn't what left me awestruck. I was looking in that direction because everybody else was. But I could have been looking in any direction. The sight before me was just as incredible. The clouds had parted, and a full moon lit up the sky making the fast-moving lumps of black cloud look even blacker but by contrast lighting up their edges with a silver glow. The sea was coming at us in rows of huge rollers topped with white horses and silvery spray. One minute I was watching this army of huge waves, rank upon rank stretching back as far as the blackness that was the horizon. The next, after a stomach, churning, tilted, steep, plunging, downward roller coaster ride, I was looking up at a wall of green, black water as the bow dug a hole in the next monstrous wave. Tons of water cascaded then off the forecastle as that same bow reappeared. Each time this happened the ship would shudder, shake, and begin the climb up the next mountainous lump of Atlantic that stood in its way. All the time there was the howl of the gale force wind that whipped around the wheelhouse, loud enough to make all inside shout to make themselves heard.

To me, staring wide eyed through the wheelhouse window, this was pretty dramatic stuff. All the other people on the Bridge at that time, however, seemed to take it as a normal day at the office, actually to the point of looking bored. Everybody looked in the same direction, moving their heads around to get a glimpse of it as it appeared in the window.

Everybody, that is, except Captain Jonathan Michael Fergus McHale

CHAPTER 16

A New Ambition

Captain Jonathon Michael Fergus McHale hopped deftly down from his tall wooden chair, landed lightly on his feet, balanced himself against the forward tilt of the ship as it thundered into the next wave and put one hand in the top pocket of his anorak. I stared wide eyed as one of the coolest of cool events unfolded. What happened over those next few minutes changed my ambitions forever. It defined my future path in the British Merchant Navy. Not only that, it elevated Captain McHale, despite his being a small round man with an overlarge bobble hat, to hero status. All at once up there with Steve McQueen and John Wayne. Clint Eastwood even. I had turned to look at him expecting some nautical order to be barked. Instead, he stayed silent. Then, continuing to balance himself and look out of the window at the approaching ship, he rolled a cigarette. Not only did he roll a cigarette, he rolled a cigarette with one hand.

Now this may not seem like much, but, believe me, to a seventeen-year-old impressionable youth, this was a much! A ridiculously huge much. He managed, somehow, to firstly extract a small pouch with a thin drawstring at the neck from that top pocket. Then, holding it lightly in his cupped right hand, he used the fingers of the same hand, the same hand mind you, to open the neck and extract a packet of cigarette papers. If that wasn't deft enough, he simultaneously lifted his hand to his mouth and then using his lips pulled out one piece of paper. At this point, he stepped forward, using his other hand on the corner of the consul to steady himself. The packet of cigarette papers remained in his right hand. Admittedly, now, the other, steadying hand was used. But only briefly, and, given the complexity of the operation, he could be forgiven. He let go of the consul and used it to extract the correct amount of tobacco from the pouch still cradled in his right hand. He paused, moved his head slightly forward and peered more intently though the window.

"All ok?" He said slowly out of the corner of his mouth. The rest being occupied with the piece of cigarette paper.

"Aye," said Albert, the Mate, not moving his gaze.

Captain McHale continued his cigarette construction. His right hand moved to his mouth again where the cigarette paper was removed gently from his lips and the drawstring from the pouch placed between his teeth. Then, incredibly, in one, awe inspiring, continuous, movement, the paper appeared, resting along the length of a narrow gap between forefinger and thumb whilst the other hand placed, arranged and patted down the tobacco. Almost immediately the thumb and forefinger moved together and began to roll the paper around the tobacco. Not only that, but his hand also moved back up to his mouth so he could lick the sticky side, complete the roll, and remove the pouch drawstring from between his teeth all at the same time. The result was a perfectly formed cigarette which appeared in the corner of his mouth in four deft movements. The whole performance was topped off by his producing a battered Zippo lighter, flicking it open and lighting the cigarette.

I determined there and then, on that spot, at nineteen forty-five hours Greenwich Mean Time on that January night in Nineteen Hundred and Seventy-One, that I would, one day, attain the impressive ability to roll a cigarette with one hand! My eyes narrowed and Clint began to take over as I thought about my new career goal. Never mind all that navigating stuff. Never mind all those knots and hitches. That was where my future lay. Looking cool with cigarette and Zippo. Women would stare admiringly before ripping of their clothes. Other men would look with envy. That picture was suddenly mixed with one of Cathy with that puzzled expression she had worn in my cabin all those weeks ago. "Is there something wrong with your eyes?" She had said.

"Is there something wrong with your eyes boy?" Captain McHale was looking at me. I must have been screwing up my face while thinking of ciggy rolling and Clint Eastwood type facial expressions.

… "Err, no sir." I straightened my face immediately.

I was saved further embarrassment by a crash from the direction of the bridge door. Everybody looked in that direction to see Dave, the Third Mate almost bury his head in the bridge consul. He had tripped over the storm sill on his way in and been hurtled into the darkness by an accompanying downward plunge as the ship slid into yet another trough.

"Fuck." He enunciated eloquently as he rubbed his hands, which had taken the brunt of the collision, together.

Captain McHale rolled his eyes and clambered back into his chair. Dave staggered over to where Albert, the Chief Officer was draped over the radar, his head occasionally dipping as he looked at the screen.

"Wouldn't like to be on that thing." Said Dave nodding his head in the direction of the tanker.

"Hah!" Exclaimed Albert, "I was."

Dave looked at him. "You were?"

"I was." Albert turned and also looked at the tiny vessel which was now on our port beam and could only be seen occasionally through the window in the door to the port bridge wing. "Third mate I was. 'Bout ten years ago." He turned back to face Dave. "The 'Torino' its' called. Takes fuel oil to Madeira. Runs from Lisbon."

Dave stared at him for a full ten seconds. "Oh… right… I didn't know you worked for the Portuguese." He said. "…thought you were a Blue Star man from the start."

Albert pushed himself upright. "I am…" he started to say, then grimaced and flung out an arm and grabbed the radar again to steady himself as the ship took another crashing dive into the base of the latest water mountain. "…I got a holiday job on it one year, in the summer of course."

"Of course," echoed Dave, still looking bemused.

"Well, I wouldn't go anywhere near it this time of year, would I?" Albert took a last look at his old ship as it disappeared rapidly behind a large green and black water mountain. "Imagine that all the way to Madeira".

"Erm, no thank you. I'd rather not." Said Dave with a shudder still looking puzzled. "What's it doing this far north?"

"Dunno mate," Albert pulled a face while he thought. "Probably some charter or other."

I watched this exchange with fascination. I had only been on the bridge for five minutes and already I had witnessed a life changing event and been made privy to admissions of secret summer jobs.

"Anyway," said Dave, "where's that cadet?" He turned, still holding on to one corner of the radar. And looked in my direction. "Ah, there you are." There was another pause. Another round of crashing noises. Another round of tilting and stomach-churning swooping as more Atlantic Ocean thumped into the ship and lashed itself against the bridge windows. "Time for you to make the tea," he said with a grin.

"Ok." I said. Matching his grin. I turned away quickly so I could stop grin matching and get back to frowning and more appropriate facial expressions. Like shock and awe for example.

I staggered past Captain McHale in his chair. At which point, without averting his gaze from right ahead and without so much as a flicker of emotion showing on his face, he dropped his left shoulder and shied slightly away from me. Making it obvious he did not want me using him as a handrail again. I started to look in his direction, but his hat waved its bobble at me aggressively, warning me off.

I found myself suddenly back in the chartroom, propelled through the heavy curtain, no doubt by the same wave that had caused Captain McHale's hat to flap its bobble.

"Remember you're making tea, young man," he said. His voice raised over the hubbub from the North Atlantic.

"Yes sir." *'Silly old goat.'* I thought. *'Still thinks it's funny, even now.'* The very thought of my coffee making debacle when we left London made me cringe.

"I heard that!" His clipped tones penetrated the curtain.

For a moment I thought I had said *'Silly old goat'* out loud. "Didn't say anything sir." I wailed.

"You were thinking loud thoughts."

"No sir." I lied.

"Hurry up with tea...."

"Yes sir."

"...and don't break anything."

"Yes sir."
"What!"
"No… err…Yes… I mean No sir."

The *New Zealand Star* continued to pound its way through the ocean. One-minute rearing up, the next plummeting and tilting downward until, once again, it shuddered and shook as it met the next mighty green wall.

Letting go of the chart table I took a pace towards the daybed at the back where the cups, pots, milk, sugar, tea, and coffee were all stacked on a large tray put there earlier by the steward. The ships movement forced me to grab hold of the shelf above the cups.

'Bobble hatted maniac thinks I'm an idiot.' I stopped myself thinking suddenly and grimaced, imagining my thoughts flying through the curtain and becoming words. As I tensed, my hand shifted on the shelf. A book of nautical tables that had become separated from the others, fell off the shelf onto the tray, knocking several cups and a teapot crashing, banging, and tinkling onto the floor. Now, I could actually hear the raised eyebrows and the shaking heads. Now I could hear the thoughts coming through the curtain.

'Boy's an idiot.'

CHAPTER 17

SEEING TO

The sun glinted off the wave tops. A gentle breeze ruffled my hair. The morning warmth caressed my suntanned limbs as I reflected on the experiences, disasters and adventures that had come my way since I had stood at the bottom of the gangway in London looking up at the 'Looming Thing.'

Actually, I had just clattered my shin on the ironwork as I clambered clumsily into the starboard lifeboat and all the adventures, experiences and disasters that had come my way since I had stood at the bottom of the gangway in London were washed away in a sea of pain! The 'suntanned limbs' thing wasn't really accurate either. Yes, the sun was glinting off wave tops, but it wasn't caressing suntanned limbs. The limbs it was caressing were more, milky white, spotty, thin, stringy looking objects that dangled beneath oversized shorts.

Various appropriate expletives that should not be uttered in the presence of the clergy escaped my cracked lips, which also hurt due to the severe blistering they had received from the 'Glinting sun' and the 'Gentle breezes' which had conspired to target themselves on my mouth during my previous days final bridge watch. I was understandably annoyed at the fact that it had taken only a few hours of Atlantic sun to blister my mouth. I was sure it was the fault of the 'Hair Gods.' Not content with giving me silly hair, they had conspired with the 'Sun Gods' to make me look even more ridiculous.

Anyway, I had been sent to said lifeboat to clean, scrub, check and otherwise 'see to.'

Down To The Sea. A Cadet's Tale

"What do you mean 'see to'?" I had asked Albert, the Chief Officer.

"See to...! You know...See to...! See to...!" He waved his arms in a windmilling, flapping motion.

Our Chief Officer was, I had come to learn, prone to windmilling and flapping. Especially when exasperated by cadets with stupid questions. The fact that this was my first trip and having had nothing whatsoever to do with lifeboats, let alone 'seeing to' them before, had obviously escaped him.

This was my first ever morning of deck work on board my first ever ship.

The horrendous weather had finally abated, the sun had come out and a warm, light southerly breeze had sprung up from the...erm...well... south, I suppose.

Normally, Steven, being the Senior Cadet, would trot up to the bridge at six o'clock each morning to see the Chief Officer and receive a list of jobs to be completed that day. However, he had taken me with him these first couple of times because, I think, he didn't like to tell me I couldn't come in case he hurt my feelings.

Having spent a further day of conducting watches after the weather had become more co-operative. (I with the third mate and Steven with the second mate), we had trudged dutifully to the bridge for our six am... or, oh six hundred hours to be more exact.... or even better, six a bloody clock in the bloody morning, appointment.... on the fourth day of our voyage from London to Auckland. We were, as I said, to go and 'see to' the lifeboats.

I decided that as the Chief Officer was in danger of doing himself a mischief if he continued windmilling, I would feign understanding and both Steven and I had beat a hasty retreat. *'Anyway'* I thought, *'Steven will know what... See To... meant. 'What with him being an old salt of one trip.'*

"What did he mean 'see to'?" said Steven when we reached the relative calm of the boat deck.

I stared at him.

"Don't you know?!"

"No" Steven looked forlorn.

"But... but... you have done a...before... you know last trip... What did you do last trip?" I finally managed.

"I wasn't on lifeboats last trip!" he wailed. "The other two cadets did that" … "I was on flags."

A wave of sympathy and understanding for Albert swept over me. I had to work hard not to windmill….

"Stop dawdling you two!!" The Mate was standing at the top of the ladder leading to the starboard bridge wing. The one we had just clattered down.

"Get moving!" he shouted. His voice at full bellow so as to be audible above the engine noise emanating from the huge Blue Star funnel.

Panicked by his sudden appearance, Steven and I took off in different directions. I bolted aft along the boat deck heading for the ladder down to the next deck, Steven, showing remarkable presence of mind, ran round the funnel heading for the port lifeboat which meant he was almost immediately out of sight of the Chief Officer on the starboard bridge wing.

Albert watched my panicked retreat. "Where are you going now?" he roared.

I glanced back whilst in full flight down the steps.

"Going to get the stuff" I shouted, not having the faintest idea what 'stuff' I would need.

"What stu…!" Albert's voice became lost in the engine and wind noise…

I stood on the narrow aft accommodation deck at the bottom of the starboard ladder thinking, not for the first time, that qualifying as a salty sea dog was not going to be as straightforward as I had thought.

"Brian!" Steven was leaning over the rail on the boat deck.

"What did he say?" … "the Mate, I mean," he said, eyes wide. I could see the sunlight through his ears as I squinted up at him. "He wanted to know where I was going. So, I told him I was going to get the stuff".

"What stuff?" said Steven looking puzzled.

"Don't know" I said. "Stuff to do lifeboats with I suppose."

His shoulders sagged. "We will have to ask … erm … someone."

"Who do you suggest?" I said, still squinting.

He thought for a moment then a light dawned. His face brightened. "I know … Third mate … yes … he's in charge of lifeboats!"

Steven was, actually, speaking as he clattered down the steps and headed for the starboard alleyway.

'Of course,' I thought. *'It was the Third mate's responsibility to keep the lifeboats cleaned, stored and ready for use.'*

Then another thought leapt into my head. ... Its six a bloody clock in the bloody morning! The third mate, being on the eight to twelve watch would probably still be in the land of nod.

"Stev...!" I started to shout as I took off after him. But by now the heavy alleyway door had slammed shut.

It is well known amongst experienced seamen, that all ... I repeat ... all, doors on ships built since Ben Hur was a trainee oarsman, don't open ... or shut ... with ease. Every single one of them has some sort of loose handle, wonky hinge, rusted lock, or it's just a plain old pain in the posterior to open. This one was no exception, and I was no experienced sailor. Tug as hard as I might I could not open the thing.

Not until, that is, Steven came crashing through it from the other way sending me flying backwards.

I just had time before I crashed to the deck to register the sight of Steven, followed by a large (at least size twelve) working boot hurtle through the door. ... The heavy metal door that then crashed against the bulkhead with a sound like Thor's Hammer striking Big Ben.

"I think he was asleep," my senior looked forlorn again.

"Really?" I muttered, sarcastically as I scrambled to my feet.

"Yeah ... so were we!" said a voice.

We both turned slowly. Standing by the other alleyway door ... the one leading to the Engineers cabins, were three sleepy looking engineers. Well to be exact, three very, very annoyed, sleepy looking engineers clad only in a collection of different coloured Y Fronts.

"Err ... ah ... um ... lifeboats" muttered Steven, pointing upward.

"Yes" said Barry, who was the largest of the group. He exaggerated the middle of the word elongating it menacingly. His thick scouse accent adding a large dollop of threat to his menace. "Yes ... we heard, couldn't not hear really, being woke up by you two fairy elephants running around the boat deck at six o' bloody clock in the bloody morning!"

They all scowled.

"Yeah ... bloody elephants!" another voice joined in. Dave, the

Third Mate was standing by the other door leading to the Mate's cabins, scowling, and scratching his ample stomach. A fourth colour of Y front on display. *'Must be some sort of secret clan uniform'* I thought. *'Or perhaps they're Masons.'*

"Did you send them up there?" Said Barry jutting his chin in Dave's direction.

"…Course not," Dave was indignant. "Must have been the Mate," he said, stooping down to retrieve his boot. Then he turned on his heel, stepped over the storm sill and disappeared into the alleyway.

"Well tell him not to," shouted Barry after him.

"You tell him!" floated back.

All three engineers turned to look at Steven. They would have looked at me, but I had managed to bravely sidle my way to a position placing Steven between me and the angry mob.

"Sorry about that, "he muttered. "Won't happen again."

"No," I said, peering over Steven's shoulder "Ever!"

"Better not!" said Barry doing the jaw jutting thing, this time in our direction.

"Yeah," said one of the others.

They trooped back into the alleyway. Each one glaring over their shoulder as they stepped over the storm sill. All muttering things about stupid, thoughtless cadets and the medieval tortures that would have been visited upon themselves if they had done anything so stupid when they were cadets.

The door slammed shut. *'That's probably woken the rest of the alleyway,'* I thought.

Heaving a collective sigh of relief, we galloped off down the next set of stairs.

"Where are we going?" I asked landing with a jolt on the deck behind Steven.

"I don't know" he said, frowning. "Third Mate wasn't much help."

"Well, we'd better think of something quick or The Mate will be after us"

Steven's face contorted while he thought, then he suddenly brightened, and a smile lit up his face.

"I know." He took off heading down the starboard side of the ship towards the forward main deck. I trotted dutifully behind.

"We'll ask the Bosun."

Another wave of horror washed over me. The Bosun. The Boatswain. The huge muscled, grizzled, short tempered hard case that ate dragons for breakfast.

We trotted up the main deck towards the foc'sle where the Bosun had his lair. I managed a quick look behind and up towards the Bridge. Good. No sign of the Mate. He must be busy.

"Bosun?" said Steven in a questioning tone as we entered the forbidden zone.

"Gerroot!" roared the Bosun.

"Pardon" said Steven. We both remained rooted to the spot.

"Gerroot, GERROOT!" ... Fire leapt from his eyeballs "Dinea Kimineer!" He pointed at the door.

We became entangled with each other trying to get out of the door at the same time.

"STAY OOOT!" he roared.

"What was all that about," I said when we had recovered from the shock. "What language was he speaking?"

"I forgot," said Steven looking forlorn again. "We are not allowed in there without asking him first."

I frowned at him "Now? ... Now! You remember. He probably has us marked for death now!"

"Anyway, we can't ask him to let us in until we know what language to use!" I said.

"I think he's Scottish," said Stephen.

"Scottish? ... Scottish?!" I squawked ... "Sounded like a cross between Norwegian and Mongolian to me!"

Steven's forlornness went up another couple of notches.

"Well, we'll have to do something" I looked at my watch. "It's nearly twenty to seven and we haven't done anything yet!"

"What we're best doing, I think, is going back up to the boat deck" Steven was starting to panic now. He was, after all, the senior bod, and as such would take the brunt of any rollockings that might come in our direction.

We scampered off back along the foredeck, up the ladder to the accommodation, along the starboard companionway and back up the ladders to the boat deck. I nearly cannoned into the back of Steven when stopped suddenly just as his eyes became level with the deck. His head moved slowly back and forth as he scanned the area for predatory Chief Officers and lurking engineers. From my view further down the ladder … meerkats came to mind.

The area was, apparently, clear. He leapt up onto the deck and headed for the port boat. I followed closely.

"Where? …Where? … have you two been!?" The Chief Officer shouted from the bridge wing, glaring. Well, when I say glaring, he might not have actually been glaring, but his aggressive body position with hands on hips and head jutting forward, strongly suggested a glare of some sort.

Steven came to an abrupt halt. This time I couldn't stop and cannoned into the back of him. We both sprawled on deck, Steven banging his nose on the wooden planking. I looked up and scrambled back to my feet stepping on his ankle in the process. He yelped and heaved himself up, clutching at his ankle, then realizing, with horror, that blood had started dribbling from his nose.

"Ahh… urgh… oof… doze!" Steven stared at his blood covered hands and then appealingly first at me then at the distant Mate.

"Doze..." he said again.

Our boss stared down at us, a look of utter incredulity on his face. His shoulders sagged, he shook his head and with the gait of a thoroughly beaten man walked slowly away towards the wheelhouse shaking his head as he went.

CHAPTER 18

Caribbean

The fine weather continued, and Steven and I settled into a routine, that was, to me, extremely comfortable. Steven would head up to the bridge after our slumbers were shattered by whoever The Mate had sent down to get us up. I usually, well, always, had to get up first, jump down from the top bunk, then start kicking him and jabbing at him until there was some sort of response. Ever since he arrived on the ship Steven had shown a remarkable lack of 'awakening' ability. The Mate would then give Steven a list of jobs that needed to be done and he would duly trot back down to the cabin and tell me which ones I would have to do. We would then set about these tasks until breakfast time when both of us would go through the quick-change routine so as to be fully uniformed when entering the Saloon for our bacon and eggs. Well, my bacon and eggs, Steven's healthy nonsense. He had cereal, or something equally silly. In fact, he had even brought, with him, some 'muesli'! *'Muesli'?* Who, I ask you, who, eats 'muesli'? What's even stranger is, not that I had never heard of it, but it was nineteen seventy-one, so I don't think it had even been invented then!

Anyway, after breakfast it was back to the cabin, quick change back to our rompers and then continue with our allotted tasks. Same quick-change routine at lunchtime followed by more 'allotted tasks' until five o'clock when, inevitably, it was, yet again the quick-change routine before dinner.

The weather was good all the way across the Atlantic. Every day was much the same. Blue skies, small fluffy white clouds, continuous sunshine with a fairly stiff breeze to cool things down, which made working on deck fairly pleasant.

I say 'fairly pleasant' because the main tasks given to us by the Mate, throughout the voyage, seemed to be chipping old rusty paint off things and believe me, there were endless 'things' off which the rusty paint had to be chipped!

We chipped old rusty paint off bulwarks, hatch coamings, hatch tops, booby hatch covers, booby hatch coamings, bulkheads, decks, derricks, winches, doors, railings (the thought of chipping railings still causes a feeling of futile horror to creep down my spine even now) ... What else? Oh yes, cranes, masts, bollards, bitts, dodgers, and navigation light housings. Chipping, chipping, and more chipping. Why the Mate didn't say, at the start of the voyage, "Go and chip stuff until we get back to England," I do not know.

It wasn't until I had done a couple of trips as cadet that I realised that Chief Officers usually sent cadets to 'chip things' because they didn't really know what else to do with them. All cadets had a 'Task Book', a big blue flimsy thing stuffed with pages and pages of seamanshipy type jobs, all of which had to be 'signed off' as being completed. However, Chief Officers had enough to do without having to scan through big blue books and organise suitable tasks for cadets. Much easier, and far less time consuming to say, "Go and chip things."

Sometime later, my last couple of trips as a Senior Cadet doing day work, were much more pleasant as I discovered that, in addition to Chief Officers not knowing what to do with cadets, they also did not like to admit this fact to the Bosun. Therefore, one could say to the Chief Officer... "The Bosun wants us to do... x," and to the Bosun "The Mate wants us to do... y," knowing that both x and y had already been done some months before. Both would agree to these tasks being 'done' because it got them out of having to decide what to do with us. So, after the Senior Cadet had been to the bridge at six a bloody clock in the bloody morning to 'get' the jobs, it was back to bed for an hour before breakfast!

Anyway, as Steven and I were only on our first and second trips, we had not yet worked out any of these, 'dodges,' so... chipping it was.

Of course, in reality, Chief Officers, surprising though it may have seemed to first trip cadets, had, actually, been cadets themselves. So, any dodges or skives were mostly perpetrated with the cadets feeling delightfully smug at being so clever and Chief Officers looking on with amusement at the shenanigans of his charges.

Several days went by with us going through the same routine. Evenings were spent either chatting in cabins or in the bar, drinking and listening to long stories about what happened on the 'Something Star' twenty years before, or, what happened on the Kiwi coast last trip. Occasionally, even, what happened to someone else on an entirely different ship from an entirely different shipping company.

I have to admit, though, all the tales were extremely funny in the telling and I didn't care whether they were all completely factual or not. I just couldn't wait until I had my own stories to tell. I did have some, what I thought, were quite funny tales, but as they were about things that happened in Slough, Woking or maybe even the dens of iniquity in, say, Ruislip or Little Wold Under Marshes, I decided to say nothing as these tales didn't quite match up to Rio de Janeiro, Yokohama, and Bangkok.

Six of the evenings, however, were right up my street. Film nights. It was, you will remember me saying earlier, the cadet's duty to show the films. Each film twice. Once to the officers and once to the crew. There were generally three films to each box, so that meant six showings.

Now then, that, you may say to yourselves, sounds fine, and it was fine. To me, that is. However, it was not fine to poor Steven. The horrors he went through when we were in London where he had to show one of the films, 'Ned Kelly,' a film he had shown four times on his previous ship, were akin to those suffered by victims of… of… well… something horrible! So now, to add horrible insult to horrible injury he was forced to show that very film twice more. Not to mention the other two films… twice more! He did try and persuade the Mate that it would be an innovative idea to allow me, the junior cadet, to show the films to 'gain experience.' Albert was having none of it though and insisted that it was far too important a duty to be left in the inexperienced hands of a first tripper. I did notice, though, a smirk play around his mouth as he turned away from delivering his final decision to Steven.

So, that was that Steven had to show the films and I had to assist. As far as I was concerned this was ideal and I carefully watched each time he put a new reel of the film on and laced it up to the projector. The main thing, I discovered, to having a peaceful showing, was speed. You needed to have deft fingers to lace the film through gates, around wheels, passed lenses and arrange the holes in the film so they matched the tiny spigots on the little drive shafts.

In cinemas of old there was apparently two projectors, so when one reel ran out the other projector would be turned on and a seamless transition would be made from one reel to the next. Projectionists would know precisely when to turn on the next projector because exactly six seconds before the final frame of the reel went past the lens a little circle would appear, very briefly, in the top right-hand corner of the screen. When that little circle appeared fingers would scrabble at switches. Get it wrong, there would be a gap in the film and audiences would become annoyed, agitated, then soon after, angry and would begin displaying their displeasure by hurling things - ice cream, nuts, seats etc, at the screen, or sometimes, at each other.

In our case we only had one projector, but speed was still of the essence. The gap in the film caused by this changing of reels was actually quite handy as it gave the audience time to visit the conveniences, stretch legs and get an alcohol top up. The need for deft fingers and speedy reel changing on behalf of the projectionists was still necessary so that said projectionists could change a reel and use conveniences, get beer, stretch legs etc., before becoming the target of unkind comments, nuts, crisps and so on.

So, life drifted along for us very pleasantly. Steven plied me with 'interesting' facts and 'fascinating' information about a vast range of subjects. All to do with the ships, and the sea, but mostly about engines, which was something I became a little worried about as time went on. He seemed to be slowly but surely morphing (heaven help us) into an engineer. Unfortunately for him, even that fine body of mechanical wizards became a little tired of his continual statements about engine bits. I could tell this by the amount of times he was told to "Fuck Off!" by one of them. On one occasion by several of them at once!

To be fair, though, by the time we entered the Caribbean he had calmed down a bit and was able to go into the bar without everybody leaving in a hurry.

The Caribbean... the sea of tales and legend, of pirates and buccaneers, of men o' war and sailor's taverns, of mysterious triangles and... and... other erm... mysterious stuff.

Actually, I can't say I noticed any difference between this sea and the Atlantic which we had just left by way of the Mona Passage which lies between the Dominican Republic and Puerto Rico.

... "In fact," said Steven to the assembled masses, "there was a naval battle here on the nineteenth of April seventeen eighty-two between a British fleet led by Admiral Hood and a French fleet."

Barry, JoJo, and I had been standing on the after deck with mugs of tea discussing the injustice of the bollocking they had just had from the Second Engineer.

"It wasn't our fault." Barry had had a pained, hurt expression on his face when he arrived spilling tea all over the deck. JoJo had followed after him, frowning and also slopping tea about the place.

"Yeah!" he said. "Not our fault!" his voice rising with indignation.

"What wasn't?" I said looking from one to the other.

Barry opened his mouth to speak.

"We are in the Mona Passage!" said Steven excitedly, his face beaming as he came up behind us and placed his mug of tea carefully down on the bulwark.

Barry's mouth shut suddenly as all three of us turned quickly towards him. Steven, completely oblivious to the fact that he had interrupted Barry in mid flow, prattled on about the naval engagement.

... "Yeah, and most of the French fleet was captured." He nodded his head vigorously, while looking at each of us in turn, emphasising the importance of his information.

"Oh." Said Barry who constituted exactly one third of the assembled masses.

"And... and..." continued Steven. His excitement growing. "There was an earthquake and a massive tidal wave here as well!"

"Oh," said Barry, raising his eyebrows.

JoJo grinned. "Didn't that make things a bit difficult?"

"Make what difficult?" said Steven obviously confused.

"The battle," said JoJo, pulling an exasperated looking face.

"Eh?" Steven's frown deepened. If it could have done, it would have reached the end of his nose.

"Yeah," said JoJo, "the battle."

"Yeah," said Barry, joining in. "The battle."

"The one with French ships," said JoJo.

Steven's head flew back and forth as he stared uncomprehendingly at each of them.

JoJo rolled his eyes and said. "Well, think about it. It must be difficult trying to fight battles and ride massive tidal waves at the same time."

There was a short pause while JoJo's observations sunk in, then, shoulders sagging and eyes raised heavenwards, Steven became irritated.

"No! No! No! He was nearly shouting now. "The tidal wave was later."

"What? ... Like... in the afternoon?" said JoJo.

Steven stared at him. "Eh? ... No! Later! Later!" His face was becoming purple with frustrated incredulity at the stupidity of his audience.

"Evening, then?" enquired Barry.

I thought Steven was going to stamp his foot.

"NO!" He roared. "Later! Later!" His face was a perfect picture of purple rage and frustration. He took a breath. "Later," he said. "Around nineteen ten."

Barry 'tutted' and rolled his eyes. "That's what I've just said. In the evening."

Steven stared while his brain tried desperately to comprehend.

"Ten past seven," said Barry in clarification.

"NO!" he shouted again, "Not the time! ... The year! The year!"

Now Steven completely lost the plot and did stamp his foot. He tried to speak but the apoplectic nature of his temper wouldn't let him, so he flung his arms in the air and spun round, intending, to stomp off. Unfortunately, one of his arms connected with his mug of tea which was still resting on the bulwark and propelled it into the Caribbean.

"Aagh!" He screamed in frustration. The other three of us leaned over and looked over the rail, heads slowly turning towards the stern as we hunted for his mug. Nowhere to be seen. We all turned slowly back to look at Steven, who was still staring into the ocean.

He looked up. "My tea's gone." He whispered sadly.

"Aye, gone," said Barry nodding.

Down To The Sea. A Cadet's Tale

"Lost," said JoJo shaking his head.

Steven turned slowly and wandered away towards the duty mess.

"Well," JoJo turned and looked at Barry, "that went well."

"Yep. Saved us from a long lecture about Mona's passage."

"Even better for me," I said.

They looked puzzled. "Why's that?" they said in unison.

"Saved me from a long lecture about Mona's Passage from him and a long lecture about your bollocking's from you two."

There was a pause while they thought.

"Fuck off," said Barry.

The next few days drifted by with a regular mix of chipping, eating, drinking, film showing, chipping, chipping, pleasant weather, blue sea, gentle low swells, chipping, and a warm south westerly breeze. I knew it was from the southwest because Steven had told me. There was no hint of rain and life was very pleasant. The only blots on our landscape, mine and Steven's that is, was some discomfort due to sunburn and the homework situation.

We had several 'modules' of work to complete. Tasks involving navigation, chart work, ship stability, ship construction etc. which, I didn't mind really. It was the maths, physics and electronics that bugged me. For example, 'maths'. Now then, who? I ask you? Who, actually needs to use the quadratic formulae? Who?

In all my sixty-five years on the planet I have never, ever had the remotest of opportunities to leap to my feet and exclaim "I know how to solve that problem, yes, minus b plus or minus the square root of four a c over two a should cover it, dontcha know!"

Hah! Complete tosh!

Actually, that first trip, I was lucky. I had a 'Steven' to help me do it. Well, when I say, *'help me do it'* I mean *'do it for me.'* He was marvellous. He was actually interested in it all.

So really, the sunburn was more of a problem. Steven went a bit pinkish but I, (because as usual I didn't listen to more experienced people), went a deep pink all over. Every inch of exposed skin was, after a while red and then, of course, started to peel. I couldn't make a fuss over it though because sunburn was considered to be a sort of self-inflicted wound and therefore could not be used as an excuse for not turning to for work. In fact, several people took great delight in telling me that it was a flogging offence. Now, I am fairly sure that flogging had been stopped as a punishment at least a couple of years before I joined the Merchant Navy. So, I assumed what they meant was, I would be in deep doo-doo if I tried to take a day off due to sunburn. I appeared, though, to be one of those lucky few 'pale skins' that don't suffer from sunburn too much and I have been ever since. I go a bit pinkish to begin with then gradually go a deep brown colour. This, of course, makes me really, really annoying to many, many people. Particularly English folk, who have to go through the agonies of sunburn and/or the time consuming, but necessary creaming up routines with the factor fifty.

We were at sea for about twelve days, if you count the day we left London and the day at anchor outside the port of Cristobal where we were due to refuel for the long haul across the Pacific Ocean.

Those twelve days seemed to fly by and I found I had become settled into the routines of life on board a ship at sea very quickly and I actually felt quite disappointed when life changed again and Steven and I found ourselves back on watch (me, with Dave, the Third Mate and Steven with John, the Second Mate), albeit only for the last twenty four hours before approaching Panama.

We were due to take on more fuel in Cristobal which is the port on the eastern side of the Panama Canal and according to all the knowledgeable old salts we would be there for about twelve hours, at the most, whilst 'bunkering'.

It was about noon on that twelfth day of our passage when Captain McHale arrived on the bridge wearing full uniform including his cap with full gold oak leaf on the peak, having been called by Dave when we sighted the tower on the breakwater at Fuerte Sherman which marks the entrance to Limon Bay.

The wheelhouse was full of people all talking at once as our leader marched through the chartroom door. Apart from the four of us, there was the Able Seaman who had been on lookout duty and had been called in to man the wheel and the Bosun who had stomped in with a scowl on his face looking for the Mate, who he had apparently been called to see but couldn't find. Captain McHale had to cough loudly to make his presence known at which point all talking stopped, the Bosun stomped off none the wiser and the wheelman grabbed the wheel while Dave busied himself with turning off the autopilot.

"Ahh," said Captain McHale, adjusting his peaked cap as he stepped onto the bridge and looked up and down. His eyes alighted on Steven who wasn't quite quick enough in looking busy.

"Young man," he bellowed, "nip down and get me a mug of coffee."

"Yes Sir," said Steven but remained rooted to the spot.

… "Today" snarled the captain, a quizzical expression on his face, as he looked at Steven. Obviously wondering why he was still there.

There was a loud clattering noise as Steven galloped down the bridge wing ladder which his lanky six-foot two-inch frame reached in three huge steps. I watched him go, after which there was a short pause while everybody else, who had also watched his panicky departure, arrived at the same question.

"Why did he go down the bridge wing ladder?" said Dave. "What's the matter with going inside? It's quicker."

Everybody shook their heads and muttered stuff about 'cadets these days etc.,' only I alone understood the panic, which bought on an inability to think, suffered by cadets when Captains barked at them.

"Anyway." Said Captain McHale, barking at everyone else. "Let's get this vessel into Cristobal, shall we?"

It was about half an hour later as the ship drifted serenely towards the anchorage in Limon Bay that Captain McHale shouted from the port bridge wing.

"SOMEBODY!"

"That's you," said Dave quietly, without removing his eyes from his binoculars which were pointed towards a beach area outside Colon, the city that the port of Cristobal belonged to.

"Ooohhh," he continued, "some lovely looking women there."

I had no interest. I was busy hurtling towards the bridge wing door, hoping to get there before the second 'Somebody!' came my way.

"SOME...! Ahh, there you are." I just made it in time and skidded to a stop a few inches from his advancing presence.

"Go down and see where Mr. Waddington has gone with my coffee."

I raced off and reached the accommodation deck in about ten seconds where almost crashed into 'Debbie' coming up the stairs from the deck below.

"Have you seen Steven?" I asked, panting.

"Ooh," he said, pouting, "you never chase me like that."

I grimaced at him.

"No need to pull faces," he said. "I have just seen him carrying a cup of coffee up these stairs. He was heading toward your alleyway.

I galloped off again, wondering why on earth he would be going down the alleyway with the coffee. I reached the forward end of our alleyway in time to see Steven disappearing out of the door at the far end. *'He must be going up the ladder to the boat deck'*. I thought as I, yet again, skidded to a halt, turned one hundred and eighty degrees and headed back up the stairs.

"He's just coming now Sir." I said passing Captain McHale by the chartroom door.

"But where's...?" I didn't hear the rest and I reached the starboard wheelhouse door before he could take another breath to continue his questioning.

I went out onto the bridge wing in time to see Steven coming across the boat deck with the coffee. His progress was hampered by a long slow swell that had appeared from nowhere which caused the vessel to role a bit which, in turn, caused him to zigzag across the deck and practice his *'Coffee mug balancing and walking while the ground shifts'* act.

"Well, where is he then?" bellowed our leader coming up behind me.

"Here sir." I said pointing down the ladder at Steven who had made it across the deck and was now a couple of rungs up the ladder.

The Captain pushed passed me and stood at the top of the steps.

"Where have you been boy?" he shouted.

Steven, taken completely by surprise, looked up suddenly to see the horrifying sight of his leader peering down at him from on high.

Now... if one is on a fairly steep set of steps and one tries to look up, balance coffee, deal with shock, deal with horror, answer a question, take step and continue in an upwards direction... something has to give. In

Steven's case several things gave. Firstly, the question answering thing became a squeaky wail, secondly the coffee balancing act suffered greatly and finally the step and upward movement proved to be far too many elements to co-ordinate at the same time. The result was his arms made it to the bridge wing, but his body tipped forward due to his missing the step. This meant his chin came into sharp contact with the top step which caused him some acute discomfort in that area naturally leading to a heart-rending cry.

"Ahhgarooff!" Wailed Steven.

"Bloody Hell!" roared Captain McHale who, showing remarkable athletic abilities, leapt backwards as the mug escaped Steven's fingers and crashed onto the deck of the bridge. Unfortunately, he wasn't quick enough to avoid the contents of the mug which were deposited on the sparkly white tropical shoe and sock on his left leg.

"Pilot boat approaching Sir." Said the Third Mate appearing in the wheelhouse doorway.

Captain McHale looked up slowly from studying his brown and white speckled footwear. From the expression on his face, he was obviously wondering why oh why would a company he had worked for and been loyal to for all his working life, force upon him such morons who were obviously under instruction to make his life a living hell.

He shook his head slowly, took a deep breath and headed towards the wheelhouse, then stopped as his speckled foot inadvertently kicked the coffee mug across the deck. Stopping, he looked down at it then turned slightly and peered at Steven's head, which was the only part showing above deck level.

"You've chipped the mug." He said with a quiet voice, and then continued into the wheelhouse.

CHAPTER 19

CROCS...

... "Well, I think we should," hissed Barry looking fiercely at all of us in turn.

"Shhhhhhh" whispered JoJo. His finger pressed to his lips. "It'll hear ush." The four or so exceptionally large 'Cuba Libres' and six beers he had consumed during the previous four hours were starting to have an effect.

Steven was staring ahead his eyes like saucers.

The road stretched into the darkness beyond the harsh bright white street lighting. Except… you couldn't really call it a street. What ramshackle buildings there were we had left behind about half an hour ago. Half an hour of running, walking, stumbling, and sweating in the tropical heat. The bright neon and noise of 'The Strip' seemed a world away. Now all that was left on either side of the road was jungle. Black impenetrable jungle. Black impenetrable loud jungle. Very loud in fact. A constant cacophony of noise assailed the senses. Crickets, bugs, crawly things, and animals of every type competed with each other to make the loudest sounds. The road stretched ahead of us. Well made. Tarmacked. Newly painted markings in the centre. A road strangely at odds with the dense jungle on either side. More light created by the huge working lights at the port somewhere ahead created a strange white glow overhead blotting out the tropical night sky. It all made the way ahead and the surrounding jungle so much blacker.

To make matters worse foliage rustled and moved in the darkness beyond the road. Huge flying insects buzzed and circled the lights. The lights themselves made buzzing crackling noises.

Down To The Sea. A Cadet's Tale

It was, to a first trip cadet, truly, truly frightening. *'Only my second port ashore,'* I thought, *'and I am in all kinds of strife again! The first time it's blonde women and Austin Minis with punctures, now its bloody crocodiles!'*

Well, a crocodile, to be exact.

For that, with his saucery eyes, was what Steven was staring at. A huge twenty-foot-long, dark, crocodile shaped erm… shape, covered half the width of the road ahead.

It had been Barry, striding out in front, who had spotted it. He had come to a sudden stop in the middle of the road. We were all trailing behind, trying to keep up, sweating profusely. Our trendy seventies clothes entirely unsuitable for the jungles of Central America.

"Fookin 'ell!" He had said in a panic-stricken stage whisper. Whenever Barry became stressed over anything his scouse accent became positively intense. "Look at the size of that!" His voice had risen to a squeak.

Coming to a sudden halt we had all peered ahead. All of us leaning forward.

All, that is, except JoJo, who had continued walking, completely oblivious to the death dealing, sharp toothed monster that blocked our route to safety.

"Don't go up there!" Barry had grabbed him by the arm as he strolled past. His stage whisper becoming a stage shout.

JoJo had all but fallen over. His left foot becoming tangled up with his right foot.

"I think it's looking at us" said Steven slowly. Not moving his head, or mouth, at all.

JoJo turned his head and leaned forward at the same time causing him to wobble a few steps in the direction of the beast.

"Ahhh… no, no!" whispered a panic-stricken Steven loudly, again without moving a single facial muscle.

"Don't move!"

Everybody froze. We stood still. As though engaged in a bizarre game of statues when the music had stopped.

"Well, we can't just stand here all night," I said, after we'd stared at the thing without moving for what seemed like an hour.

"Like I said, I think we should go back to the bar," said Barry.

I looked at him "We can't do that. That doesn't get us back to the ship!" I flapped my arms in frustration. "Does it?"

"Well, I'm not going past it. Those things are bloody fast. Have your leg off in a second," said Barry also flapping his arms.

"Stop flapping," squeaked Steven urgently, waving his arms.

"You stop flapping!" said Barry, flapping.

"I don't think it has sheen us," slurred JoJo spinning his head in Steven's direction, which caused another wobble. Towards us this time. "It's looking the wrong way."

Steven had still not moved a facial muscle despite all the arm movements. "Its eyes are on the side of its head …so… one eye is pointing in our direction." He, again, managed this entire sentence without as much as a twitch.

We all turned and stared at the beast. JoJo's head spinning back and causing yet another wobble towards the black shape.

There was silence for some time while we all stared at the shape. Trying to make out the position of its eyes.

"Perhaps we could go through the jungle and round the crocodile" I said.

There was a pause while they all looked from the beast to the jungle, back to the beast, then to the jungle then at me. In an amazing feat of timing both JoJo and Barry said the same thing in unison.

"Fuck off!"

"Well, someone else come up with an idea then," I said, waving my arms again.

"You're bloody deranged you are," said Barry pointing his chin at me. "Go through the jungle!?" He turned his head and peered into the blackness. "There are things worse than crocodiles in there!"

"Like what?"

"You know…. Animals and things!"

"What?" I said. "Things worse than a twenty-foot speedy monster with big teeth"

"Yes… and crawly things and flying things… so… no thank you!" He thought for a second, looking at the shape in the road. "Snakes!" he exclaimed.

"Where?" squeaked Steven finally moving all his muscles as he jumped in the air and spun round, eyes bulging.

Barry and I stared at him. JoJo continued to stare at the crocodile.

"No," said Barry rolling his eyes. "I mean there are snakes in the jungle. You idiot!"

"I think it moved," said JoJo leaning forward at a ridiculous angle to get a closer look.

Steven squeaked again as we all stared back at the shape in the road.

After what seemed like ages. JoJo sighed and spun his head round peering closely at Barry's left ear.

"Nope!" he exclaimed. "Musht have meen bushtaken".

We all sighed. Barry rolled his eyes again and started to say something, but then thought better of it and shut his mouth quickly.

"I think..." JoJo started to say loudly.

We looked at him, waiting. He continued to gaze at the crocodile.

Well?" said Barry frowning. "Well?"

JoJo turned slowly and stared at Barry for a few seconds while a puzzled expression began to pass over his face.

"Well, what?" he said.

Barry's face began to turn purple. I couldn't actually see his face turn purple because it was too dark. I could just, sort of, feel the purpleness in the air. Anyway, this was not a good sign.

"Quickly JoJo," I hissed. "tell us what you were thinking, or Barry is going to hit you!"

"Nah," said JoJo, grinning.

"Yes," said I. "He might."

"Naaahh... he won't hit me... I'm his mate" said JoJo grinning and swaying at the same time.

"Sssshhhh!" hissed a distraught Steven. We all froze and turned slowly to look up the road. Nobody breathed for a few seconds, then exhaled noisily when nothing happened.

"Well, what I was going to say was..." JoJo stopped and peered at each of us in turn before continuing. "I think we should just wait here until a car comes." He nodded his head emphatically as though agreeing with himself.

There was a pause while we all took this in.

"Why?" said Barry, rolling his eyes and flapping his arms again in exasperation.

"Wants a lift somewhere, does it?"

Dealing with sleeping crocodiles was the very last thing any of us had expected.

The evening before all this happened had started so well. Even Albert, the Chief Officer had been in a good mood. Everybody on the ship had been in a good mood. We had, effectively been given the night off! May not sound a big deal, but believe me, it was an unusual event. It didn't feel all that unusual to me of course because I just assumed everything that happened was normal procedure.

But getting a day off during a bunkering stopover was extremely, and I mean, extremely, rare.

We had completed the bunkering by the time the sun had come up the morning after we had arrived at the berth in midnight. Cristobal. All the engineers had worked tirelessly through the night taking on fuel for our trip across the Pacific. Hardly a drop was spilt, even at the latter stages when extreme caution was needed as tanks were 'topped off'.

Steven and I had stayed on watch until midnight, when in a rare fit of compassion the Chief Officer had allowed us to go and get some sleep.

"No going in the bar though," he had said sternly. "We should be sailing early in the morning, so you'll be needed at silly o'clock to get ready."

He was partly right. We were called at 'silly' o'clock, well, four am to be precise.

Then everything changed abruptly.

Officials with briefcases had been and gone, paperwork had been signed and everybody was in full preparation mode when the ships agent had breathlessly galloped up the gangway and disappeared into the accommodation to find the Captain.

Minutes' later word had spread around the ship like wildfire. Something was afoot. Rumours ranged from 'We have got the wrong fuel' to 'We are all flying home. The company's been bought by Arabs'!

Actually, I never did find out why we had to stay. But then I can't really remember being overly curious. I was far too caught up in the excitement of it all.

An hour after the agent had left, the Mate appeared on the deck by number two hatch where I had been melting in the heat, excitement rapidly waning, whilst half-heartedly chipping some rust off the hatch coaming.

"Now then young man," he said grinning.

Initially my heart sank. I prepared myself to receive another epically meaningless, tedious, muck covered task.

"Now then…. Get changed into your uniform then get up to the bridge. You can help Dave get the gear ready. We have to shift ship in about an hour."

"Where to?" I asked standing up and clanking my chipping hammer down on the hatch top.

Shifting ship meant exactly what it said. Moving the ship from one berth to another, or across a dock. Sometimes, it meant only moving it along the dock by a hundred or so yards. But of course, a ship is a fairly large and heavy item, so moving the thing anywhere takes a bit of organizing.

"We are going," he was grinning even more now, "over there" He pointed across the dock. "Away from the bunkering berth". The grin widened … "And what is more" he said, "we are not sailing until tomorrow noon." His joyous face was a sight to behold.

With that he turned on his heel and trotted away. He did actually say something more, over his shoulder, possibly telling me why we were staying so long in Cristobal. Whatever it was I didn't hear. Which is why I can't remember, probably.

So, of I galloped across the deck, up the steps, into the accommodation.

"Going ashore later?" It was JoJo. He was leaning against the Duty Mess door, his boilersuit covered in black oil. The same black oil that streaked his face, matted his hair and adorned his hands that were clenched around a mug of coffee.

"Err… yeah. 'Spose so" That was the first time it occurred to me that I would be able to actually set foot on dry land since leaving London.

I raced up to our accommodation deck.

"Going ashore later?" Barry, this time, ambling down the stairs, also covered in the same black oily stuff as JoJo.

"Err... yeah... yes... think so" I said heading for the starboard alleyway.

I could feel the buzz of excitement filling the ship by the minute. This was a strange phenomenon that, over the years, I found happened on board all merchant vessels. The minute there was a hint of something out of the ordinary that same buzz would manifest itself. Then spread like wildfire. Infesting everything it came into contact with. Humans, machinery, captains... Anything. This was probably because anything out of the ordinary nearly always meant extra time ashore.

As I reached the cabin, I heard heavy footsteps behind me approaching at speed.

"We're shifting ship." It was Steven at a full canter. He skidded to a halt watching me as I felt around the trunking above the door.

"I know," I said. Feeling further along trying to locate the key.

"Dave says we can go ashore." Steven continued watching while I rummaged.

"I know," I said. One arm became tired, so I changed hands and went on tip toe trying to reach further back.

"JoJo's going as well," said Steven.

"I know, I know" I said, volume and exasperation entering my voice.

"Even the Mate's going" he chortled. A hint of water buffalo creeping in.

"I know," I shouted, using both hands now as far as I could reach at the back of the trunking.

"The bloody keys' not here!"

"I know," said Steven.

I stopped and stared at him. My arms still above my head, hands at the back of the trunking. "You know... You know... What do you mean you know? ...Where is it? He looked at me, a genuine look of surprise and hurt on his face.

"It's here," he said, pulling the key from his pocket. "I had it from before."

My jaw clamped shut. The words hissed out "In your pocket... In your pocket....in your pocket," was all I could manage.

"Erm... yes," he said.

"Oi!" It was The Mate standing at the end of the alleyway arms akimbo.

Down To The Sea. A Cadet's Tale

Our heads swivelled in unison. Me on tip toe, arms above the trunking. Steven looking hurt holding the key aloft.

"Hurry up… get a move on!" roared the Mate. "We're ready to shift" He disappeared. His feet making loud thumping noises as he bounded up the stairs to the bridge.

Steven looked at me. I looked at Steven.

"Well?" I said.

"Well, what?" said Steven.

"Aagh… open the fuckin' door!" I hissed.

"I can't," said Steven.

My eyes widened. "Why n …?" I started to say.

"You're in the way" he said. "And your hands are still on the trunking."

I had managed to calm down by the time I reached the bridge and pottered about getting flags ready, testing handheld radios, changing batteries and various other small tasks Dave had assigned me. Even though we weren't actually sailing anywhere and 'across the dock' is hardly an epic voyage, everything had to be prepared as though it was. I found out, as my sea going career progressed, that where ships were concerned 'plans' could change at the drop of a hat. So, everything had to be ready.

The Dock Pilot, an American, appeared on the bridge having been shown the way by Steven who, as soon as he had left the gentleman to the tender mercies of Captain McHale, disappeared back into the accommodation and hot footed it to his station 'down aft' with John, the Second Mate.

Radios crackled into life, orders were issued and repeated. One of the AB's appeared and took hold of the wheel. Tugs were 'made fast' at either end. Lines were cast off and within ten minutes of the pilot appearing we were off on our voyage of discovery 'across the dock'.

In fact, the whole thing took about half an hour after which I was told to take the pilot down to the gangway which had touched our new bit of parking space within seconds of the ship arriving.

After depositing 'Chief Pilot Captain Walter Standing'…. that was what was printed on his name badge… by the gangway, I galloped back to the Bridge. "Pilot's away sir," I declared to Cap'n McHale, who, as usual, stared at me for few seconds.

"Ok, young man you can go."

I spun on my heel and headed quickly for the door "Yes sir… thank you sir".

"Just a minute!" bellowed the captain. I skidded to a stop. "Come here."

"Sir?" I said approaching cautiously.

"Are you going ashore young man?"

"Yes sir." I said. A moment of panic entering my mind. Was he going to stop me from going?

He looked at me closely for several seconds by which time I had convinced myself he was going to ban me from going ashore. To make matters worse my face was beginning to redden.

"Mmmm" he said. "Well… well… you be careful my boy… you be careful," and with that he stalked off to the bridge wing. That moment was to stick in my mind. Why, I could not think. It was not until I was much older and in a position of responsibility and in a comparable situation that I realized what it was I had spotted. As he turned, for second, just a brief second, I had seen the face of a man who cared. He was concerned about me. Of course, at the age I was then, I was too young and stupid to recognise it.

My main concern was getting into the trendy seventies trousers and getting ashore.

CHAPTER 20

THE NEW YORK BAR

We all stood staring at the doorway to the New York bar. Barry and JoJo slightly in front, Steven and myself leaning to left and right looking over their shoulders. Well compared to us, they were salty seadogs of experience. At least two more trips anyway. So, it was only natural that they should lead the way. There was also the culture shock effect. For a seventeen-year-old youth from the leafy lanes of Surrey, whose only foreign adventures thus far consisted of a couple of holiday hops across the channel in the family caravanette, standing in front of a rough bar full of darkness, big hard case drunken tough seaman and even tougher women, is, believe me, a tad daunting. The earlier eager expectancy and bravado had disappeared with the taxi.

The reason we had turned away from the cab that had delivered us to the door of the New York Bar and was now hurtling down the road with the driver celebrating collecting a huge tip which was, in fact JoJo's change and were staring, was because Dave, our Third of All Navigating Officers had just exited the establishment. The swing doors had crashed open, and he was now swaying in front of us. A huge, ear to ear, face splitting grin appearing as he saw us.

"Ah," he said, "Ahah, ha." His voice became louder as he thrust his face towards us. Waves of alcohol laced air wafted over us. He would have fallen over had it not been for the girl holding him up. She gave a little squeal as they both tottered forwards. Our attention was, as one, taken from Dave's leering smile to the girl, who was probably the cutest, most beautiful creature any of us had seen. Well, since London anyway.

The thing that was most awe inspiring about her was not her perfectly formed, dusky, racially indeterminate features. Not her long straight shining blonde hair. Not her lithe, superbly proportioned torso, the top half of which threatened to overwhelm an extremely skimpy, sky blue bikini top. Not even her long dark legs and very, very sexy hips which also tussled with tiny clothing, this time, short, and I do mean short, spray on hot pants. The single most awe-inspiring thing was the superhuman strength and balance she displayed, considering she could not have been more than five foot five tall, in holding up eighteen stone of very inebriated Merchant Navy Officer, whilst perched on a pair of white high heeled toeless shoes. (The girl, that is…. Not the Merchant Navy Officer…. Although…since then I have seen… No… tell that story in the next book!)

"Ahah, hahahaha." Burbled Dave again, still grinning, his right arm wrapped round her shoulders.

The girl pouted at us, smiled sweetly, looked up at Dave, looked back at us, grinned widely displaying a row of what were once teeth but were now mostly crooked tarred fangs and then swept her left hand in front of her, reached across and grabbed Dave firmly by the crotch.

"Ooohhh… ah… haha… hoohoo!" said Dave.

The girl grinned even wider showing a few more stumps. All four of us, as one, flinched slightly and stepped back.

"We go fooorrrk now," she growled, sounding remarkably like Jack Nicholson with a cold.

"Ooohhh… ooohhh…hmmm," breathed Dave.

Steven looked puzzled. "Fork?" JoJo and Barry turned slightly and looked at him, both with raised eyebrows. The penny dropped after a short silence. "Oh, ah, yes. I see." All three of them turned to look at me. I raised my eyebrows, grinned, and set my face in, what I hoped was a knowing 'I'm a salty seadog and knew what she meant' type of look. Actually, my penny had dropped just after Stevens. Luckily, he gave a short nervous burst of his water buffalo laughs so everybody was looking at him and hadn't noticed my equally puzzled expression.

The girl frowned at Steven for a second, then turned abruptly and led Dave away by his trousers.

We had left the ship half an hour earlier, the four of us, rattling down the gangway four steps at a time. I had been surprised that it was only us going ashore at that time. It wasn't the scenario I had envisaged. My mind had led me to believe that almost the entire ships company would all trot off together. That idea had been scotched earlier when Steven and I had walked into the bar having rushed around the cabin getting ready after the 'Shift Ship.'

Dave and three of the engineers had already gone. As had the 'Sparky' and the Chief 'Fridge' Officer. The rest of the officers were all staying aboard, either through duty, preferring to catch up on sleep or just not bothered.

Albert was behind the bar. "Quick beer before the evening's adventures?"

"Yeah, why not?" said JoJo rubbing his hands together. The rest of us mumbled or nodded our agreement.

Albert disappeared as he ducked down to the fridge. "Any of you lot been here before?" his voice floated up at the same time as his hands appeared thumping four well shaken cans on the bar top.

"No." We all said in unison amid fizzing noises as we all tried to open beer cans without spraying the furniture.

He reappeared grinning and kneeing the fridge door shut with a practiced flick of his right leg.

"Fuck me!" he said. "You sound like a barbers shop quartet. Perhaps the women will give you a free one if you sing nicely!"

Barry scowled. "Yeah, right."

"Free what?" said Steven. Everybody stared at him. A short silence ensued while Steven's brain engaged.

"Oh yes… Ah… Oh… I see."

Albert's shoulders dropped and his face started to take on the beaten look that began to appear when Steven planted his nose on the boat deck a week ago.

"So," I said. "Nobody's been here before?"

Silence. Everybody looked at everybody else.

"Dave has." said the Mate.

More silence while everybody looked over their shoulders and around the room in a brief visual hunt for Dave. Which, really, was stupid because everybody there knew that Dave had already gone ashore.

"He's already gone," said John, the Second Mate as he lowered his head back to his magazine after also scanning the room for the departed Dave, "but he did say he was going to the New York Bar."

There was another silence while cans of beer were quaffed noisily.

"Ooh," said Albert, shaking his head, "rough place that." There was another elongated silence broken by the odd, mumbled, "yeah, rough place." I looked round the room to see everybody nodding sagely.

"Remember that bloke on the Newcastle Star got his ear cut off," said Geoff from the far corner. Both Steven and I stared at him. Our eyes widening.

"Yeah, that's right." Said Albert. "Big bloke… what was his name?"

"Crusher," said Geoff.

"Oh yeah, that's right." Albert looked off into the middle distance while he thought.

"What?" said Steven. "Actually, cut off?"

"Yeah… sliced."

"In a fight?"

"Yeah." Said Albert, wiping the bar and looking directly at Steven. "And she broke his nose. He was in a bit of state when he got back to the ship."

We both stared at him, eyes like those of frightened rabbits. There was a short pause while the information filtered through.

"She!?" We said in unison again.

"You two really should be a double act." Said Albert, laughing.

"She!?" We said again. More laughter. This time from everyone.

"Yeah." This from Geoff in the corner. "The girls in that place are a bit rough." He put down his book. "I remember one trip when…"

"Yes… well… anyway, we'd best be off," interrupted JoJo, tossing his can into the bin. Barry did the same. Steven and I were still staring at Geoff.

"Right!" said JoJo pushing me in front of him. "New York Bar it is!"

There was a gurgling noise from Steven as he tried to get off his stool and finish his beer at the same time. The result was the gurgling noise and a beer stain down the front of his shirt.

"Beer…! He managed to say as Barry dragged him off his stool by his shoulder and shoved him towards the door. "Bring it with you," he said.

Down To The Sea. A Cadet's Tale

The taxi ride hadn't taken long. The ship was tied up at a 'Lay By' berth so there wasn't much of anything between the ship and a well-made road that disappeared round a sharp bend into what looked suspiciously like dense jungle to me. The traffic was light but there were plenty of yellow cabs, like the ones you see on films dashing around New York with bad tempered drivers shouting obscenities at Dustin Hoffman.

One squealed to a stop alongside us and a sleepy looking moustachioed driver glanced in our direction without speaking. We all piled in. I followed JoJo and Barry into the back seat leaving poor Steven to sit in the front with the driver. No sooner had Steven shut the door then the cab shot forward forcing us all into the backs of our seats and more beer to be spilled from his can.

The driver looked at Steven while the cab continued to accelerate towards the sharp bend. He was still looking at him as he wrenched the wheel to port and took the vehicle at full tilt around the corner. Both Steven and I banged our heads on the window. More beer was spilt down Steven's shirt.

It took a mere five minutes at the speed of light to reach 'The Strip'. We screeched to a stop on a corner, and we all leapt out. JoJo handed over some money and the cab instantly sped away leaving him staring after it with his hand still out. "Bastard!" he said. Looking at me.

"What did I do?" I wailed.

"No, not you, you pillock!" he said, "him! He's gone off without giving me any change!"

"Bastard." We all said staring after the cab. All except Steven, that is. Steven never swore. However, we didn't stare long because that was when Dave came crashing out with his lady friend on their way to 'foorrhhhk'

"Well," said JoJo, squaring his shoulders once we had all finished staring after Dave. "Let's have a look." He started forward.

"Ooohhh yes," breathed Barry. I squared my shoulders also and followed, wishing I had opted for a quiet night in with an informative book. Thinking back, this was, actually, quite brave of me. After all, I was about to enter, for the first time, a foreign bar where large tough men called 'Crusher' had their ears cut off! By women!

Just before he went in ahead of me, I had a glimpse, over JoJo's shoulder, of faces peering out of the round windows that were about head height in the blue swing doors. Girls faces. About five in all. Each of them breaking into excited smiles as they spotted our approach.

JoJo went through the door first, followed by Barry, both of them disappearing into the darkness beyond. Shrieks of delight went up from the window, girls and both men were instantly swallowed up by the darkness, the noise, the loud music, and the cigarette smoke. Steven went in just ahead of me and the last thing I saw as I too was swallowed up, was a bright light illuminating his ears as one of several spotlights that pierced the darkness swung back and forth across the mass of humanity that thronged the place.

I was allowed no time to linger on Steven's illuminated ears. As I passed through the doors, I was set about by at least three women. What they looked like I had no idea. One threw herself on my back her arms round my chest. Another grabbed an arm and snuggled her head into my neck and a third stood in front of me, placed one hand gently on my cheek and planted a kiss squarely on my mouth.

All this would have been really nice, particularly as I had never experienced a popularity with opposite sex such as this! However, it was all a bit nullified by the shooting pain between my legs as the girl kissing me was a tad rough with her other hand in grabbing me by the crotch at the same time.

I did a passable imitation of Dave a few minutes earlier. "Ooohhh… oooffmm!"

These tactics on her part obviously won whatever battle was being fought and the other two girls released their grips and walked away hips swinging. They both looked over their shoulders, giving me sultry looks and pouting, presumably so I would know what I was missing. Unfortunately for them I was too occupied with the sultry looks from the girl who had just detached herself from my mouth. Not to mention the pain from the vice like grip that she maintained on my underneaths.

"My boy," she said into my ear, "you, my boy."

I agreed.

When you have an assertive woman of an aggressive nature leading you around by the trouser front then, believe me, the best option is compliance. It matters not your religious convictions, your political persuasion, your

Down To The Sea. A Cadet's Tale

sexual orientation, or your present state of mind or even your upbringing. You will, I say again, you will…. comply!

I was led to a booth. The place was absolute bedlam. There were seamen in there of every nationality under the sun. Or so it seemed. Some of them having just finished work, in shorts and T shirts. Some, even, in boiler suits. Others were dressed to the nines. Suits and ties! The only common denominator was the trendy seventies hairdos. Then there were the women! There seemed to be hundreds of them. Every shape, every size, and every colour imaginable. Every single one of them beautiful in their own way. All working girls, and all of them ready to extract money from the men who rushed ashore from a multitude of ships that passed that way.

Again, I was learning a life lesson. Luckily, I had been brought up properly. Brought up to respect all professions. Even the iffy ones! So, I was prepared to be polite. Prepared to pay serious attention to the likes, dislikes, and vulnerabilities of these girls.

Actually, that had nothing to do with it. What was more on my mind was that I had been seriously frightened by the lecture on venereal diseases my class had been given just before leaving the school of Navigation in Southampton and I didn't want to catch anything!

There was serious conflict going on in my head. Although they would never admit it, that same conflict went on in the minds of most… no… all first trippers who entered such a place. The women looked lovely. Temptation filled the air. But the real conflict, the real worry, the uppermost thing in their minds and mine was, 'what will everybody think if I *don't* go off with one of them?'

Anyone who tells you otherwise is a liar or a fool.

So, there I was at a booth against the far wall. Really it was a curved seat, about six people long with a table. So, unless you sat on the end you could not look cool while sitting down. The table was far too close to the seats. You had to do the sitting shuffle. This meant an initial sitting manouvre followed by a bouncy shuffle along the seat to let your lady into the same area. Uncool. All those visions you have of yourself looking like James Bond in the presence of stunning looking women go immediately out of the window. If, of course, there are any windows.

The booths were situated all around the room from near the door, which was by the start of the bar, right round the room to the other end of the same bar. Except at that end there was a door which, I found out later, was the toilet. (When I say later, I mean much later. Several voyages later, actually. I was never there long enough to need the toilet). There were several other loose tables around with an assortment of chairs. All of them, booths and tables, sort of 'pointed' towards a small patch of floor with little blue lights around it, which, judging by the tired looking woman of substantial proportions and indeterminate age range (But definitely past the forty mark) who was slowly gyrating around on her own, served as a dance floor.

My lady friend shuffled onto the seat next to me, careful to maintain bodily contact. I assume this was because, having claimed her prize, she had a fear that if contact were lost then some unworthy interloper would steal me away.

The spotlights continued to swing back and forth, the light passing over our booth every few seconds. This gave me a chance to actually see, in five second bursts, my kidnapper. She was actually very pretty with long straight black hair with a round face and a cute button nose. She leant in closer, stoked my face gently with one hand and whispered in my ear. "You buy me one drink?" She said it with real heart felt passion, as though she was declaring undying love. Even drawing away slightly and staring at me with imploring eyes and her head tilted to one side like a puppy asking to be stroked. She almost sobbed the last word breathing out heavily, so it sounded more like "Drinkehhh".

"Yes, of course," I said, not wanting to appear ungentlemanly.

For some reason, a vision of my mother drifted across my mind. "Always be polite," she said, "you haven't got enough vests!" I squeezed my eyes shut to make the image go away.

"Eh... My Boy... Wassi you name?" said the new love of my life.

"Brian." I said, opening my eyes quickly.

"Eh?"

"Brian."

"Eh?"

"Brian, Brian." I shouted.

"Ahh." She nodded her head, an understanding smile spread across her face. "I much Likeh you name." Her hand came up and she started stroking my cheek again. "Eees strong man name." Her hand let go of cheek and dived between my legs causing this 'strong man' to yelp like a one of those miniature poodles when you step on them.

"I lorve you." She suddenly announced. "I lorve you ver mucho. You ver strong down here." Her face went into the doleful puppy dog look again, with a pout for good measure, while her hand squeezed. "You my Iyaniyan."

It took me a while to understand what she was saying. Then I realised I had made the mistake of saying my name twice. So, that was that. My name was now Iyaniyan. Pronounced, apparently, Eye-an-eye-an. I deduced it was just not worth the effort of trying to explain to her the subtle nuances of English pronunciation.

A large moustachioed man appeared at the table looking stern. This bought an alarmed look to the face of my loved one. She spoke to him in rapid Spanish. He snarled a "Si." At her and left. She immediately turned her attention back to me, but my attention was suddenly taken by a familiar sound from the next booth. A sort of Water Buffalo type noise. I looked over my shoulder. Sure enough, there was Steven with two women. Two women, mind, one either side of him, both kissing him and manhandling him in a, shall we say, rough manner. Two thoughts briefly crossed my mind. The first was one of jealousy. How come he got two women and I only got one, (that thought quickly turned to one of sympathy when my beloved's left hand squeezed tighter). The second thought was more of alarm than anything else when I realised, we had all been separated at the door as we came in.

I tried to say to Steven "Where's Barry and JoJo?" but my date for the evening suddenly let go of my trousers and grabbed me by the chin, trying to wrench my attention back to her. The result was my chin going one way and my eyes the other, so all my mouth could manage was "Ayer ee Arar a Oo, Oo!"

"Whah?" said Steven as he disappeared under the scantily clad females.

I had no time to continue the conversation as my attention was again diverted by a loud crash, louder even than the music that was thumping from hidden speakers somewhere. The moustachioed one, who had just that second left the table was busy upending some unfortunate customer onto one of the tables nearer the bar. Glasses crashed, oaths were shouted, and the customer was hauled off the table and unceremoniously pitched through the swing doors.

I felt very alone.

There and then I learned a valuable life lesson. If one of the great Greek philosophers had been standing there in his white sheet thing, I have no doubt he would have leant towards me, looking grave and said in quiet philosopher tones. "Cometh ashore, young Iyaniyan and no matter how many kindred spirits cometh with you, thou shalt be on thine own, pal!"

Another thought suddenly hit me. I had no clue whatsoever as to the name of the future Mrs. George now alternating between nuzzling my neck and chewing on one ear lobe.

"What's your name?" I said when she came up for air.

She suddenly sat bolt upright and stared at me, gasped and then fell into my arms and laid her head on my chest. I waited. Nothing happened for a few seconds then she slowly lifted her head, gazed lovingly into my eyes, cupped my face in her hands and said. "Jane."

I stared at her. That was not what I expected.

Anyway 'Jane' kissed me, wiped away an imaginary tear, and said, her voice cracking with emotion. "My Iyaniyan, my Iyaniyan, you want name of me. I lorve you."

I was beginning to think that perhaps I had inadvertently proposed marriage or something when she suddenly pulled herself together and said. "Men not want name of me."

Just for an instant I felt sorry for her. What she had said was probably true. All the men she met, night in, night out, didn't give hoot what her name was. Anyway, that brief thoughtful moment was interrupted when the Moustachioed one reappeared suddenly and plonked a glass full of a black liquid with ice floating in it down in front of me and a thimble sized glass of a pinkish liquid down in front of 'Jane'.

"Seven." He said.

"What's in it?" I asked.

He leant on the table and pushed his moustache in my direction.

"Seven." He said again.

I untangled one arm from 'Jane' and fished in a pocket. I had come ashore with the princely sum of twenty dollars all in one-dollar notes. The actual currency of Panama is the 'Balboa' but it is now and always has been since the Americans built the canal, closely allied to the Dollar which is also used alongside the Panamanian stuff. I only knew that because Steven had loftily told me all about it when I made the mistake of asking him about going ashore and getting spending money one evening in mid-Atlantic. That was when, in an obvious weak moment, his attention to 'Steam Reciprocating Engines' had briefly wavered. As he had never been ashore in Panama before I don't know how he knew about it, but… he was right.

"Seven." Said the moustache again. Obviously, I wasn't fishing fast enough. I finally unearthed my money and went to count out the seven.

"I make help." Said 'Jane' and grabbed all of it. She deftly counted out the notes which our waiter snatched from her and walked away. I grabbed the remains from 'Jane' instantly seeing that she had given him eight. She could see that I could see that there was a dollar missing and immediately threw herself at me and started the ear nibbling thing again. "He like beeeg tip." She said between mouthfuls of lobe.

In view of the treatment meted out to the unfortunate customer a few minutes previously, I decided against complaining about my missing dollar. I took an exploratory sip of my drink. It appeared to be coca cola. A little disappointed I stirred it with the long green swizzle stick that had come with it and took a long swig of it. Different drink altogether! It was Bacardi and coke! A Cuba Libre! I could feel it going all the way to my boots. I coughed and spluttered, then gasped in air, my eyes widening and beginning to water.

In the meantime, 'Jane' had lost interest in my ear. Probably found it too difficult to catch during all the coughing and gasping.

"Eh, my Iyaniyan, you gots more dollar?" She said stroking my face.

"More dollars?" I said.

She smiled coyly. "You gots more dollar…" She paused. "I lorrrrve you long time" and ran a finger down my shirt front until it reached my trousers where she hooked it under my belt.

Her eyelids lowered.

"…We go foorrhhhk."

CHAPTER 21

Homeward Bound

"Where have you been?" JoJo peered at me with bleary wide eyes as I joined him at the bar. He hiccupped and then returned his gaze to his drink.

"Over there at that table… the one next to Steven." I shouted over the throbbing disco music. He paid no attention for a while, preferring instead to watch over his drink.

"Oh," he said at last. "Thought you'd gone off with that black-haired bird."

I had battled through the throng to join him at the bar where I had spotted him sitting through a gap in the now crowded dance floor. My love interest 'Jane' had departed for pastures new when she discovered IyanIyan was skint, apart from his measly twelve dollars (So that had eased my troubled mind. Simple economics had saved the day. No more worrying.

"This is Bill," said JoJo, still staring at his drink.

I looked at his drink as well. It looked similar to the one I had just finished at the table whilst apologising for my lack of funds to 'Jane'. "I've just had a Cuba Libre." I said.

JoJo looked puzzled, then said again "This is Bill."

"Gudday!" said another voice. "Yeah, Bill's the name." The Australian twang was unmistakable. A huge beast of a man levered himself off the stool the other side of JoJo and stuck out a hand the size of a shovel. "You off that Big Pommy Meat Boat on the layby berth?"

"Oh… Hi," I said, offering my dainty little digits which were immediately crushed to a pulp as soon as Bill got within range. "Yeah, the *New Zealand Star*."

"Christ!" He exclaimed, "you're not bloody Kiwis are yah?"

"No… no. We're all British."

"Ah right." He took along swig of a bottle of beer with Spanish writing on it. "Say, that Shelagh you were with looked alright." Another long swig. "Seems to have given you the elbow though. She's just gone off with a big Scandywegian bloke." He sounded quite hurt and indignant on my behalf.

"Yeah, I didn't have enough money." I said glumly. "Bloody drink cost me seven dollars!"

"No," said Bill. "It didn't."

I looked at him puzzled.

He said, "Your drink… your Cuba Libre, cost you two dollars fifty." He stabbed a huge finger at me. "Your Shelagh's drink cost you FOUR dollars fifty!" he all but leapt of his stool as he told me.

"Four fifty!" I said, shocked, "for that little pink drink?"

"That's right… Four fifty!" He took another pull at his beer. "Ya see…" He leaned towards me, one hand on JoJo's shoulder. "It's only coloured water. The girls get a dollar of that money every time they get one you blokes to buy them a drink." He nodded his head at me several times to reinforce his revelation. "I've just told ya mate here the same thing. He just bought some tart TWO of them!" He nodded again. "She's just buggared off with a big Scandywegian as well! That's why he looks so angry."

JoJo nodded slowly. "Yeah," he mumbled, "skint again."

"Anyway," said Bill, "Gotta go. Things to do." He hopped off his stool. "Hey, Miguel!" He shouted to the moustachioed one who had just that minute reappeared behind the bar. "Give these fellas a beer each will ya." He threw a five dollar note on the bar top.

Miguel stooped down and came up with two bottles which he wrenched the tops off with two conveniently placed bottle openers that were fixed to the rail inside the bar, slammed them down in front of us, grabbed the five dollars and walked off without smiling.

"Cheerful eh," said JoJo, frowning.

"Oh… he's alright," declared Bill, "queer as a nine-bob note, lives with a Tranny over this place. Used to be a boxer once." JoJo and I stared after Miguel. "Nice bloke though."

He grabbed a white hard hat that had been sitting on the bar top in front of him, with ENGINEER stamped across the front in dark blue military style letters. "Anyway, I'm off. See ya 'round fellas!" He shouted over his shoulder and headed towards the door.

I stared after him for a while, trying to process all the information he had just fired at me.

"Who...?" I said after a while. "... Was that?"

"Bill." Said JoJo returning his gaze to his drink.

"Yes, I know that." I rolled my eyes. "What I mean is... you know, well... well... who?"

JoJo sighed, "He's an engineer at the canning factory down the road apparently."

We both stared at our drinks while music, lights and humanity throbbed around us.

"Hello," said Steven clambering onto a stool next to me. He looked glum as well.

JoJo lifted his head and looked at him.

We stared at him for a bit then JoJo said. "Let me guess, those women have got all your money and they have both taken off with big Scandywegians?"

Steven's shoulders dropped, he looked at both of us in turn, then sighed and said "Yeah. Exactly right." He frowned, "How did you know?"

"Because" I said. "That is exactly what has happened to us."

Shoulders dropping even further, Steven said, still frowning, "very expensive in here."

We both nodded in agreement staring at our beers.

"Costs the earth for a drink."

We both nodded staring at our beers.

"Bit of a rip off if you ask me."

We both nodded.

"I mean... bit much... ten dollars a time!" his voice went up a couple of octaves as the indignity of being ripped off hit home.

We both started to nod, stopped when we realised what he had just said, then turned to look at him.

"Ten dollars!?" I said. "Ten dollars!?"

"Yes, one Cooboo Loobie, or whatever they are and one of those little pink things for the girls." He thought for a second, his frown becoming deeper. "Well fifteen actually. I had to by two pink things." Now the frown became really deep causing his eyebrows to meet in the middle. "Why, what did you pay?"

Both JoJo and I made blowing noises, went "tsk" a couple of times, shook our heads, then both of us replied at the same time. "Seven," said I. "Six," said JoJo. Then, realizing he had the best deal, grinned. "Mind you, I did have to pay two dollars in tips." His grin disappeared.

"I had to pay one dollar," I said.

"Didn't know you had to tip as well. I didn't pay anything." Steven looked pleased with himself.

"I've still got twelve dollars left." I said. "Shall we have another beer?"

"Good thinking," said JoJo quickly. Steven nodded.

I managed to attract Miguel's attention by sticking my arm in the air and making drinking shapes with my fist then pointing at each of us in turn. I'd seen people do that in films and was quite surprised that it actually worked. Miguel came over almost immediately, ducked down and produced three bottles of beer, opened them and plonked them down in front of us, all in one smooth movement. I started to wonder how he opened three bottles with only two openers, but my thoughts were interrupted when he stuck an open hand close to my chin, pointed his moustache at me again and shouted "Ten!"

"I thought…" I started to question his arithmetic skills when tot-ting up prices but stopped when the moustache bristled at me.

"Ten!" It said.

I handed over ten notes. Miguel's hand remained open. The moustache came closer. I handed over another note. He gave me a dismissive glare, turned on his heel and stomped off down the bar. We all watched him go and then grabbed our bottles. It was as though it was some form custom, some type of etiquette, not to touch the bottle until the barman was at a safe distance.

We sat there for a while sipping beer and watching the goings on. Men continued to flood in the bar. Men continued to flood out of the bar. Usually attached to women. I actually saw 'Jane' twice. Occasionally a girl would wander over, run a finger up my back, or JoJo's back, or Steven's back, then insert herself between two of us, facing whichever 'My Boy' she thought the most likely to buy a pink drink or maybe to pay up and 'Foorrhhhk'.

A thought suddenly forced its way past the women and the loud music and into my befuddled brain.

"Where's Barry?" I said.

JoJo and Steven both sat up and did that stupid thing that people do. Exactly the same as in the bar on the ship when everybody looked round for Dave when they all new that Dave wasn't there. They both looked over their shoulders. They had me doing it. I even looked over my shoulder!

"Don't know," said Steven.

"He went to the Zanzibar, around the corner." Said JoJo.

"When was that?" I asked.

"When Miguel Moustache over there threw him out."

"Was that him being tossed out before, just after we came in?"

"Yep, that was Barry."

I looked at him sideways, an aura of disbelief over my face. "Nah, don't believe it." I kept looking at JoJo expecting him to burst out laughing any second and tell me he was only kidding.

He didn't. "You don't know Barry very well, do you?" He raised his eyebrows slightly. "He is always… always being thrown out of places."

"But… but we'd only just walked in."

"I know," sighed JoJo. "But he upset Moustache somehow and he just tipped Barry up and heaved him out the door." He paused while he drank out of his bottle. "I did go out after him. He was ok though. Some woman had a grip of him and dragged him off to the Zanzibar." He grinned. "Anyway, I had other things to do."

"Pity we didn't meet Bill when we first got here." I said. "We'd still have some money."

"Who's Bill?" Said Steven.

I ignored the question. Another thought had just struck me. "Apart from the two dollars I have got left, has anybody got any taxi money to get back?"

JoJo slowly shook his head, continuing to stare at his drink. Steven stared at me with a horrified expression on his face.

"No." he said. "What will we do?"

Down To The Sea. A Cadet's Tale

"Walk." Said JoJo, climbing clumsily off his stool. "Oof!" he declared tripping over his own feet. "Those Cuba Libre's were strong!"

"Who's Bill?" said Steven.

JoJo looked at him, swaying. "Engineer from the canning factory."

"Oh."

"Come on, let's go," I said, heading for the door.

"Canning factory?" Steven looked bewildered but followed after me. Just before we reached the doors, which were continually swinging as people jostled to get in and out at the same time, I noticed, in the corner booth by the door, Derek, one of our able seamen sitting in the centre with his arms stretched out along the back of the seat. He had the widest grin imaginable across his face. "Awright Brian?" he managed to say without removing the grin. His unmistakable cockney twang sounding strangely out of place. given the surroundings. I wasn't going to, but if I did wonder why he was grinning, my wondering was answered almost immediately when a small female head appeared, rising from his lap, then dipped down again, slowly rose up then began pumping up and down furiously.

JoJo and Steven had obviously seen this as well and all three of us, unable to take our eyes off the spectacle, cannoned into each other as the left-hand swing door hit me squarely in the side of the head on its inward journey!

We all stood on the road outside the New York Bar. Steven rubbing his chin where it had hit the back of JoJo's head, JoJo rubbing the back of his head with one hand and his nose, which had hit my head, with the other. I was rubbing both ears. One, where the door had hit it and the other where it had suffered the nose strike from JoJo.

"Which way?" Said Steven, who, for once had avoided any nose trauma.

"Well, we came down that street and the got dropped off just here. But I can't remember whether we turned left into this street or right."

We walked to the end of the road and peered left and right. The 'Strip' was behind us. The short road we had come down had no lights at all in it and seemed to be unmade and the buildings derelict. The road we were looking into was entirely different though. This one was well made, well-lit with various shops and restaurants, all of which were open and busy.

"Ooohhh," said Steven, "I'm hungry."

"Go on then," I said. "I'll have a fillet steak, chips and peas."

His face lit up briefly, then his shoulders dropped as he stuck his hands in his pockets.

"Oh, forgot… haven't got any money,"

"Exactly." I said.

I was about to say something sarcastic, but the sound of heavy, hurrying footsteps took our attention suddenly. We all turned quickly to look back up the road we had just come down.

There was Barry, sort of half walking, half running and continually turning to look back towards the bars. "Wait for me!" He wailed. "Were you leaving without me.?" He looked hurt.

"Thought you were… erm… busy," said JoJo, swaying with the 'Cuba Libre Effect'.

"Not anymore. Which way's home?" He looked up and down the street.

"We were just trying to decide." I joined him looking first right then left then back again. "There's bright lights in both directions. The brightest ones seem to be to the left, away from the town. Look you can see over the treetops.

"That'll do us then." He said. "Let's go." With that he took off down the road."

"If you've got some money, we could get a cab." I shouted after him.

"No!"

I was about to say, "Why not?" When I heard angry shouting coming from the area of the strip. The loud rock music blasted out of doorways and then suddenly subsided as doors were thrown open and swung shut. I could see people running. Sharp, hoarse, high pitched, female voices mingled with deep, staccato, Latin American voices.

"Quick run!" Shouted Barry, already several paces down the road and leaping forward into a full gallop.

That galvanized us all into a full speed retreat towards the jungle.

"Why are we running?" I panted as I clumped along in my trendy platform shoes

"Forgot to pay," wheezed Barry over his shoulder.

The voices got louder. Steven made a whimpering noise and put on a remarkable turn of speed, racing past all three of us with genuine panic in his eyes. This burst of speed was easy for him because he was wearing more sensible footwear than the rest of us. We, of course were wearing trendy seventies clothes. If you have seen, or can remember platform shoes from that era, you will understand the difficulty there would be in escaping angry Latinos at speed!

Steven, by now, a good twenty yards ahead, disappeared round a bend in the road. We got there a few seconds later. The voices behind us were louder, then, suddenly they began to fade. I risked a look over my shoulder as I followed Barry round the bend. Whoever was after us was running up the opposite road, past all the restaurants and shops.

"Whoa!" I said. "They've gone the other way."

"Keep going 'til we get to the next bend," panted Barry.

Steven was already out of view.

"Alright, alright, that'll do," puffed JoJo as we reached the corner. He stopped, swayed, looked round and asked the obvious question.

"Where are we?"

"Dunno," said Barry. "Brian said the Port was this way."

"Err… Hang on!" I frowned at him. "I said the brightest lights are down this way, so I am assuming the Port's this way." I waved a finger at the lights. "Assuming, only assuming."

Barry looked up the road, the way we were going. "Where's…?" He started to say. "Oh, here he is."

I followed his gaze to see Steven cautiously appearing from around the next corner and walking slowly back towards us. "Have they gone?" he looked passed us down the road.

"They went the other way." I told him. Turning to Barry I said "Anyway, what was that all about? What did you mean 'forgot to pay'? How can you forget to pay?"

"Well…" he said waving his arms. "It was her fault."

"Who?"

"That silly tart I was with. If she hadn't have taken all my money for drinks, there would have been some left for her and the hotel room!"

"What hotel room?" said Steven looking from Barry to me and back again. We stared at him for a few seconds until the light dawned.

"Oh… Yeah… I see."

"As it was," continued Barry. "I only had five dollars left. Just enough for the room."

JoJo was still swaying and looking down the road. His head turned and he looked at us.

"What room?" He said.

"Oh, fucks sake!" Barry flapped his arms in frustration. "It doesn't matter. Let's get walking or we'll never get back." He stomped off. "How far is it? Anybody know?"

"No," said everybody.

We followed Barry along the road towards the bright lights that loomed over the trees.

It was about ten minutes later that Barry saw the crocodile.

CHAPTER 22

CROCODILE

It must have been nearly an hour we stood there, waiting for the that bloody crocodile to move. Steven was still giggling occasionally over Barry's sarcastic response to JoJo's suggestion about waiting until a car came.

"I still think we should go back." Said Barry after a long silence.

"Well," I said, "that might have been an option if you'd paid the woman instead of doing a runner."

"Her fault," he muttered sulkily.

"No… No, it wasn't her fault at all. It was your fault; you shouldn't have gone anywhere near a hotel if you didn't have the money."

Barry looked away towards the crocodile, which still refused to move a muscle.

"Was her fault," he said.

"Wasn't," I said.

JoJo turned around and peered at us. "You two give me a headache." He swayed slightly, taking a step to regain his balance. "You're like a couple of kids. Friggin' arguing all the time."

"Not me," said Barry, looking away again. "It's 'im," he tossed his head in my direction.

"… 'Tisn't," I muttered. "it's 'im."

"Shut up!" said JoJo holding his head.

"I think it moved," Steven whispered.

"Eh?" said Barry loudly.

"Shhh!" Steven put his finger to his lips. "Shhh! I think it moved.

Look." He stuck his head forward, frowning in his effort to see if the thing was actually moving.

We all did the same. Standing as still as possible. Except JoJo, that is, who had some balance issues when he moved his head forward. He was forced to take a couple of steps again.

"Ahhh... Don't move, don't move!" Said Steven, with a hint of panic in his voice.

We all stood still. So did the crocodile.

After what seemed yet another age, we all started to relax slightly and the panicky breathing noises we were making began to calm and I could hear the jungle around us starting to rustle. A breeze had sprung up from nowhere and had begun to stir the tree branches into life. The noise became louder. Then, quite quickly became louder again sounding more like... well... more like an engine really.

Steven suddenly jolted beside me, his whole body becoming tense as he flung his arms out.

"Shhh!" he hissed.

"Oh, not again!" wailed Barry. "Look! It hasn't fuckin' moved!" He looked at Steven but flung his arm out and pointed at the beast.

"No... No!" said Steven in a whispering shout. "Listen..." he cocked his head on one side. "There's a car coming!"

We all engaged in head cocking, eardrums straining for sounds of car engines. Sure enough, over the sounds of the rustling trees and the huge sighs of relief, there was, in the distance, a car engine.

The four of us quickly realized, more or less at the same time that the car was coming from the direction from which we had come. We all turned and stared back down the road. There, in the distance, the last bend we had walked round was beginning to light up as a vehicle approached it.

"All we have to do now..." I said looking at the back of Barry's head, "... is hope it's not a car full of Miguel-the-Moustache and his merry gang of cut throats after Mr. Stud here!"

"Told you, it was her fault," he said turning around to glare at me.

I glared back "Well... I don't think they..."

"Shut up!" shouted JoJo.

"Shhhhhhh!" shouted Steven.

War was averted when a vehicle rocketed around the corner. It was a

Jeep of some sort. Steven immediately jumped into the middle of the road and started flapping his arms up and down. "Quick," he said. "Make it stop. It'll wake the crocodile!"

"Oh..." Barry looked at him. "Oh... and you shouting and jumping about in the road flapping like turkey won't wake it up?" He shook his head.

The Jeep slowed down and came to a stop a little down the road and we walked towards it. The driver stuck his head round the windshield and peered at us.

"What the fuck are you four Gullahs doing here?" said a familiar voice.

"Bill!" I said, relief causing my voice to go up several decibels. "We can't get past this bloody crocodile."

Bill stared at me.

"Shhhhhhh!" said Steven. It's sleeping.

Bill shifted his gaze to Steven who still had his finger to his lips. "Who's he?"

"That's Steven," I said, "he's with us."

He peered up the road, "what crocodile?"

"The one up there." said Steven going back to his stage whisper. "In the road."

Bill squinted and stared up the road again. "Well..." he said. "I can't actually see a crocodile." He frowned and moved his head forward a bit. "Unless it's hiding behind that piece of tree trunk in the road."

We all turned and looked towards the beast. Bill started to chuckle. There, a few yards up the road was a tree trunk. A tree trunk about the size of a large crocodile.

Daylight had chosen that moment, that precise moment, to shed more light on the scene. All it needed was a heavenly Charlton Heston type voice to go "Ta Da!... Fooled ya!"

Instead the heavens were filled with Bill laughing.

"Ha! How long of you Bozos' been standing here frightened of a tree trunk?"

Nobody said anything.

"Didn't even know we had any crocs around here." He said. "Or alligators, for that matter"

Steven stared at the log. "It does look a bit like a crocodile." He said defensively.

"Barry's fault." I said gleefully. "Again."

"Yeah, well, like he said, it looks like one," said Barry defensively.

JoJo sighed, "Anyway, we can at least get to the ship now." He turned to Bill, "Thanks for that, mate."

"No probs. Do you want a lift, it's a bit of a trek?"

We all turned and looked up the road. "Can't be too far," said Steven. "Those lights are pretty bright now." He waved an arm in the general direction of the glow over the trees.

Bill puffed his cheeks out and sighed a long sigh, a resigned look on his face. His shoulders sagged. "Get in the Jeep," he said, "you'll need a lift."

We all muttered thanks and climbed in. JoJo in the front, the rest of us squashed in the back seat. As soon as we sat down Bill rammed the gear stick into reverse and wrenched the wheel hard over to the left while the Jeep shot backwards. The headlights swept the jungle as we swung round.

"Where are we going?" wailed Steven, grabbing hold of the door frame.

"To your ship," said Bill. "You bunch of lemons were walking the wrong way! Those lights are from the Canning Factory." He rammed his foot on the accelerator. "That's where I was going. On me way to work! I'm on earlies.

JoJo groaned and so did Steven. Bill couldn't stop laughing.

Barry's face lit up. "Hah!" He exclaimed. "It was 'im!" A large finger was jabbed in my direction, "he said it was this way."

"No, I didn't. What I said was...."

"SHUT UP!" said JoJo and Steven together.

It did not take us long to get to the ship. Barry and I sat in grumpy silence. JoJo started to nod off and Steven plied Bill with questions about crocodiles. None of which he knew the answers to.

The Jeep slithered and crunched to a halt by the gangway and after a brief round of goodbyes Bill raced away into the night. Never to be seen by the four of us again.

Going up the gangway I thought how strange the shapes and sizes that guardian angels came in.

The ship was quiet. No sign of life save a watchman on the gangway. At least until we went in the door to the gangway deck. There was still music and noise coming from the smoke room. I looked at my watch. Two thirty in the a.m. I, for one, had had enough adventure for one night. Crocodiles, Cuba Libre's, women of doubtful virtue and of course being chased by El Toro and his gang of cut throats had all taken their toll. Bed for me.

Barry and JoJo headed straight for the bar. I took the stairs. Steven hesitated, then chose the stairs, following close behind me.

"Oi!" It was Barry. "Where d'ya think youse two are going?" he was at the bottom of the stairs looking up.

"Bed." I looked down at him and waved an arm in the general direction of the cadet cabin.

"No," said Barry.

"Yes."

"No, you can't," he spread his arms wide. "Anyway, we haven't had the debrief yet."

"What debrief? There isn't a debrief!" Exasperation creeping into my voice.

"There is," he said.

"You don't have a debrief after a run ashore! What are you talking about?" I thought for a second. "In fact, we don't have debriefs about anything…. Ever!" I said, flapping my arms to highlight the ridiculousness of his statement. "That's Royal Navy nonsense… this, in case you have forgotten is the Merchant Navy!"

"There is… still… a debrief," he said in an infuriatingly calm and superior voice.

"Ok… Ok…Ok! I said, starting back down the stairs.

Steven tutted in annoyance and came after me.

We trooped into the smoke room to be greeted by several grinning faces all of which enquired immediately after our sexual exploits. Nothing else interested them. It was obvious that as soon as Barry and JoJo had entered the room, they had been verbally accosted by the people therein, all asking about their run ashore, demanding a detailed account and also demanding an appearance before the committee of the two other lowlifes that had been seen to go ashore with them.

"So… none of you got any women then?" asked Whiskers, after Barry had recounted his tale of woe. Minus the crocodile episode, of course.

Minus, also, the bit about the woman in the Zanzibar and about being chased. In fact, the only bit he did talk about was being thrown out of the New York Bar which he seemed quite proud of! I began to suspect that being thrown out of pubs, clubs and bars was the norm for Mr. Barry Johnson.

The four men by the bar: Whiskers, the Fourth Engineer, Jimmy, the Third Engineer; John, the Second mate and, of course, Ian the Chief Engineer back in his usual position behind the bar were all leaning in, waiting for Barry to answer. There was a long silence.

"Well… well he did!" blurted out Steven suddenly and pointing at Barry. "But he didn't pay because he didn't have any money left, only for the hotel though and that's when we were chased by gangs of blokes and couldn't get passed the crocodile!"

Everybody leaned away from Barry, turned, and looked at Steven for several long seconds. Steven could always, I discovered, sometimes to my extreme annoyance, be relied upon to end a lull in any conversation. He was completely unable to cope with long silences. Having satisfied his instincts, he now, fell silent. A panicked look on his face as his head swivelled around the room staring at each of us in turn.

Ian tipped his head on one side, a quizzical look on his face. He frowned. "Crocodile?"

Barry glared at Steven. There was another long silence and Steven again opened his mouth to speak.

"Fucking big crocogate… err… dile!" slurred a voice from one of the chairs at the other end of the room. It was JoJo. I hadn't even noticed he was missing from the group around the bar. He must have walked straight in, sat down and nodded off. Obviously, the Cuba Libre's were having more of an effect now. Steven's mouth snapped shut.

"You're 'avin us all on," said Whiskers. "Don't believe a word of it!"

Then it began. The inevitable…. "I remember… on the 'Whatever Star' we…."

Whiskers sniffed, pulled out his pipe and began scraping the bowl with a biro. "I remember, on the old Timaru Star," He paused while he did a bit more vigorous scraping and then peered closely at his handiwork. "That's the old Timaru Star, not the new one." He stabbed the stem of pipe at the room in general to reinforce which ship he was talking about.

'Time to go' I thought. "Just going to the toilet." I said. Making a dash for the door.

There was silence from the smoke room as I made it into the alleyway. I just reached the stairs when I heard Steven say, "Me too!" In an over loud agitated voice. This was followed by a sound of pounding feet as Steven's size elevens carried him out of the immediate danger of an "I remember" session.

We both galloped up the stairs and into the starboard alleyway, only stopping when we arrived panting outside the cabin door.

"Phew," puffed Steven. "That was close, I thought Whiskers was going to tell one of those never-ending tales!" He reached up on top of the trunking for his key, found it and unlocked the door.

"He was." I said, walking in and throwing myself on the daybed.

Steven sat on the bottom bunk and started taking off his shoes. I found I had no energy left, nothing. My shoes stayed where they were. I couldn't even raise enough energy to look at them, never mind take them off. However, with a supreme effort I managed to look at my watch. The dial shouted at me "It's three! … that's three!… yes, three o'clock in the morning!"

I groaned. We had to be up in less than three hours.

"What's the matter?" said Steven.

"We've got to be up at six a bloody clock in the bloody morning!"

"Wish I'd stayed on the ship now," he sounded glum.

I was beginning to drift off when a picture of sleeping crocodiles drifted into my mind. I smiled, then chortled a bit. *"Well, it was all a bit ridiculous… Wasn't it? Well, I mean, crocodiles?"* I chortled again.

"What are you sniggering at?" said Steven. That made me laugh out loud. "Well?" He started to giggle. Then he snorted and the water Buffalo made an appearance. That set me off properly, tears began to roll down my cheeks and I laughed louder. Within a minute we both could hardly draw breath. Loud guffaws and water Buffalo noises could be heard over half of Panama.

The silly thing was Steven had no idea whatsoever what I was laughing about.

CHAPTER 23

OVER EASY

The American Canal Pilot wanted eggs. Not just any eggs, he wanted eggs, over easy.

"What does that actually mean?" said 'Debbie', the steward.

"Dunno," I said grumpily. The area over my right eye was throbbing. One of the 'Cuba Libre's' from last night seemed to be lodged there permanently.

"I thought you'd know."

He tossed his head and pouted at me. "Haven't the faintest idea dearie." He shifted his weight to one leg, stuck out a hip and gave me the 'I don't know and I don't care so you'd better find out' look.

"Haven't you *any* idea?" I looked at him with a pleading sort of look. He shook his head slowly, still pouting. The hip went out another inch. I sighed and looked back towards the bridge wing. Captain McHale had ambled... well... limped over and was in deep discussion with the American. A pained expression found its way on to my face. "I am going to have to go and ask, aren't I?" Debbie raised his eyebrows to full 'Of course' height and tilted his head to one side to complete the look.

I sighed again. "But...." I started to say a final pleading 'but' sentence. Debbie's eyebrows became angry eyebrows and his head tilted even further sharply.

Glowering I turned on my heel and headed towards the bridge wing.

We hadn't had the three hours I had expected to sleep off the night's adventures and booze. I had been wrong. We only had two. Well… one and half actually. By the time I we had stopped giggling like schoolgirls, it had been approaching three thirty. Then we were both awoken by Martin, one of the Able Seamen, crashing through the door at five o'clock and shouting "Get up, we're leaving!"

Steven, as usual, hadn't moved a muscle. I, as usual, had leapt off the top bunk, landed heavily and fell over. Then, I had woken up properly. As usual.

Well, when I say woken up properly, I don't mean really properly. Only properly in that my eyes were open and things like arms and legs, were able to function without conscious connection to any thinking processes, and I could manage some erratic flapping motions. Steven still hadn't moved a muscle.

I allowed my legs to take me to the bathroom where my hands did something with shower controls and some sort of washing procedure took place. A huge effort and a burst of tremendous will power meant I was able to dry myself and go back into the cabin, dragging a clean uniform shirt and shorts from the wardrobe on the way.

Steven hadn't moved a muscle.

The door had crashed open at that point and the Mate had appeared. "Come on, hurry up!" He said grinning and throwing a small blue notebook on the table "…Better get round everybody quick and get the 'All Aboard' book signed."

About to leave, he had spotted the large lump that was Steven, cocooned in a sheet, still in his bunk, not moving.

"What's the matter with him?" He said frowning. He raised his foot and jabbed a boot at the mummified form "GET UP!" He roared.

For a second or two nothing happened. Then the lump began to unwind and slowly morph into human shape. Steven's head popped from underneath the sheet and he stared uncomprehendingly first at me then at Albert. We stood and stared for another second then all at once as Albert started to repeat his polite request, Steven realised that the Chief Officer, in full uniform, was staring down at him wearing a very deep frown. Panic had obviously set in and he attempted to leap out of the bunk. Unfortunately, the upper bunk is not far, in terms of height, from the lower bunk and a solid half inch thick piece of wood runs along the entire length of the structure. This is purely for decorative purposes and hangs down about two inches below the top bunk. There was loud thump as the top of Steven's forehead connected with this decorative wooden thing with some force.

"Ooohhh!" said Albert and I in unison. A sympathetic grimace on both our faces as our heads moved back an inch in tandem. Steven, wearing an expression which was somewhere between a startled impala and an angry pussycat, fell back until his head hit the bulkhead behind the bunk. This caused him to rocket forward until, again, his forehead connected with the decorative thing.

"Ow! …Ooofff! … Aagh! Noises escaped from his mouth each time his head connected with something.

"Ooohhh!" said Albert and I again, recoiling further.

Steven toppled sideways. "Ohhooomfff!" He moaned; his head buried in the pillow.

Albert turned slowly and looked at me. I turned and looked at Albert. Albert shook his head.

"Why is it……?" He had started to say… but then stopped, unable to find the right words. He left at that point still shaking his head. Once again, a beaten man. He shouted over his shoulder as he reached the door. "When soft lad there gets his act together, tell him to go down aft for stations. You get the book done and then up to the bridge." There was no time for me to answer. He had gone, pounding up the alleyway. Still trying to comprehend the pantomime he had just witnessed.

Dressing quickly, I had left Steven to make his own way in the world. I had galloped out into the alley in search of people to sign 'The Book'. It had not taken long. I managed to find all the Chiefs of things fairly quickly this time. Except for the Chief Engineer who was, for some inexplicable reason, in the engine room! Much to my horror this meant I had to go down there as well. I had gathered all my courage in one sock, gritted my teeth and entered the nightmarish place through the door in the port alleyway on the gangway deck. The usual loud generator buzzing, humming diesel sound, mixed with other grinding, banging, thumping, whirring noises had assailed my delicate ears. My nostrils had filled with the unmistakable smell of engine rooms. Anybody who has spent even a short spell on a ship and has been unfortunate enough to have to visit an engine room will know to what I refer. But then, engineers seemed to like it. I had clambered down approximately five thousand very steep steps artfully arranged in batches of a thousand each, only to find that the man had recently left by an alternative route to go to the bridge.

"Oh," I had said to JoJo who happened to be in the control room when I reached it, having watched my descent from the top and was consequently grinning like a demented cartoon cat. "Fuck!"

So off I had gone, back up the five thousand steps, in the heat, in a temper. The main reason for my grumpiness was the state of my uniform shirt which was now covered in sweat and grubby marks which I couldn't touch due to my hands being covered in oil and other black greasy substances that engines in rooms seem to produce out of thin air.

After some stomping around and muttering to myself I had tracked the errant chief down and got him to sign my book. I then headed for the bridge and helped Dave, who was looking as though he had been up all night, check over the bridge equipment and get it ready for leaving. In fact, Dave *had* been up all night. He had only arrived back on the ship about ten minutes before and was now wandering the bridge in a dishevelled state clutching a mug of black coffee.

Captain McHale arrived on the bridge just as we had finished checking things and were waiting for the radar to warm up. He stood in front of us, immaculately dressed in sparkling whites and stared at us. I in my, now, grubby white shirt and Dave in his un-ironed white shirt with lumps of his un-combed seventies hair sticking out at random angles from beneath his cap. Our leader started to frown. Both our shoulders started to sag, convinced that a severe bollocking was imminent.

"Good morning." A loud voice boomed across the bridge. It was a loud American accented voice, so it sounded more like, "Guuurd Moorrnin'."

We all swivelled our heads in the direction of the chartroom door from where the booming had come and stared like three startled rabbits caught in headlights. Captain McHale, with his eyes wide and his mouth in a sort of startled 'O' shape. Dave with his sticky-out hair and a vacant wide-eyed expression and me wearing both their expressions at once.

He looked at us, moving his eyes from one to the other slowly.

"Hi," he boomed. "Captain J.T. Buckman…" He continued to peer at us. "…Your pilot today. We ready to depart?"

Captain J.T. Buckman was an impressive figure. He must have been all of seven feet tall with huge shoulders and a vast, and I do mean vast, mid-section that overhung his belt buckle by a good foot at least!

I and Captain McHale came to at the same time. Dave just stared.

"Ah, yes good morning Captain," said the captain taking a step forward.

Unfortunately, I took a step forward too. Ships bridges are fairly confined spaces and the bridge on the *New Zealand Star* was no exception, so my step forward meant I had to move closer to Captain McHale who was to my left. I stepped forward with my left foot as he stepped forward with his right foot. My stride was bigger than his. My left foot moved in front of his right leg. This caused my left foot to land on his right foot rather heavily, at the same time… sort of barging in front of him, obscuring his view of the American, who could see nothing of Captain McHale who was completely hidden by my gangly grinning frame. To make matters worse, my leader had not finished his sentence when the collision occurred so his "Good Morning Captain," instead of sounding imperiously British, finished in a high-pitched squeak as the pain shot up his ankle.

Dave continued to stare.

"Get out of the way boy!" roared Captain McHale pushing me and hopping on one foot at the same time.

I became confused, turned towards him, and said "Sorry Sir" but he had already hopped passed me, so my "Sorry" became directed at Dave who was still staring. It was then I noticed that Dave's shirt was buttoned up the wrong way and he was missing one epaulette. Also, there was what looked like baked bean sauce on the left pocket. I spun back towards the pilot and started to say "Sorry" again, but he was still looking at the other two. One immaculately dressed and hopping, the other dishevelled, wearing half a can of baked beans, one epaulette and still staring like a four-year-old meeting Father Christmas for the first time. (Not to mention the sticky out seventies hairdo.)

Debbie, the steward appeared in the doorway at that point and took command of the situation.

"Would you like me to bring you some breakfast sir?" He said, in a perfect deeply toned voice. In fact, sounding nothing like his usual effeminate self.

"Eh?... Oh... Ah... Yes," said the American. "Erm... can I have bacon, crispy, with eggs over easy and coffee?" It wasn't really a question. It was more a statement of intent to eat. He didn't say please either. But I came to understand over the years that Americans sort of imply please when asking for something... rather than actually say it.

So, there we were, nobody except the American knowing what "Over easy" meant.

"Erm... excuse me sir," I said. This was after I had stood for a while at a respectful distance from the conversing captains having given in to Debbie after her bullying stare had worn me down.

They both turned and peered in my direction. "Yes?" They both said at once. It would, I thought, have been obvious who I was addressing as my gaze was centred on a point some seven foot above the deck.

"Erm... Well." I took the coward's way out. "The steward was wondering about the eggs, sir. He was just wanting to confirm what you meant by ...erm... over easy, sir."

Our Captain made a 'tsk' noise and raised his eyebrows, the American captain looked at me with a pitying expression and drawled "Waaaallll son. I reckon over easy means cook 'em... but kinda easy... ya know. ...Then ya kinda flip 'em over... but, also, kinda easy like."

"Of course." I said.

"You just cook 'em as normal." I said to Debbie when I got back to the chartroom where he was lurking. "Then turn 'em over."

He raised his eyes heavenwards, stuck out a hip again and flapped a hand at me. "Pfff... just fried eggs then!" He puffed, turned on his heel and went off down the stairs.

"Yeah," I shouted after him in an American accent. "But kinda easy." Debbie shouted back instructions as to what I should do next. I didn't follow them because the act described in the instructions was completely impossible. Instead, I went back to the bridge. Dave hadn't moved. He was still staring.

"Dave... Dave... Dave... wake up!" I said in a loud whisper, pushing his shoulder.

"Wha... What?" He breathed.

"We're leaving in a minute... shall I turn the radar on? It must be warmed up by now!"

"Yeah... yeah... warmed up." He ambled off towards the bridge wing.

I sighed, went over to the radar, and pushed the required buttons and twiddled the appropriate knobs in the necessary sequence to make the thing work.

The tugs had arrived at either end of the ship and were being attached to the ship. 'Made fast' in nautical speak. Everybody seemed ready to depart.

Captain McHale appeared in the bridge wing door. "Engines to Standby." He said, still frowning at me.

"Engines to standby." I repeated and moved the Engine Room Telegraph forward one notch and then realised I didn't have the movement book to hand... or a pen for that matter. This meant I had to commit the heinous crime of leaving my post at the telegraph in order to get the book from the chartroom. It took me approximately naught point naught, naught two of a second to get there and back as Captain McHale turned to go back on the bridge wing. He didn't notice. Neither did Dave who had come back inside and was hovering near the centre of the bridge consul brandishing a radio. But then Dave wasn't noticing much of anything at that point

There was another clatter and an Able Seaman appeared in the bridge wing door. It was Derek. He was the bloke whose nether regions were enjoying the attentions of the oral cavity of a lady of dubious virtue that we had seen as we left the New York Bar. He was still grinning as he marched in and took up his position at the wheel.

"Single up fore and aft!" shouted our leader.

"Aye sir," shouted Dave back and repeated the order into the radio twice, once to the Mate on the foc'sle and again to the Second Mate down at the aft end of the ship. Unfortunately, although Dave had no trouble speaking into the radio, shouting was another matter. His throat, obviously suffering after the night's shenanigans, wouldn't allow shouting. So, what came out of his mouth instead of a nice clear "Aye sir," was a loud "Arse!" The two captains turned their heads in his direction, frowning. Dave went red and turned away to cover his embarrassment while he spoke into the radio. Derek and I had extreme, and I do mean extreme, difficulty in keeping straight faces.

In fact, that one minor incident became one of those major, life defining moments. I sailed with that same Able Seaman on several voyages later in my sea going career, and that was always the way we greeted each other whenever we met. By shouting "Arse!" then falling about in fits of laughter! Childish, I know, but that's the Merchant Navy for you.

The rest of the un-berthing and leaving the port went smoothly. Lines were cleared, orders were shouted, engine movements were relayed, and radios squawked clicked and hissed. Moments later Tugs pulled and pushed, Dave managed not to throw up over the captains and Derek and I managed not to break into giggling fits.

Overall, very efficient.

We headed out through the port entrance passed the breakwaters and into the bay. The vessel hissed through the flat calm water and the engines rumbled gently. During all this the sun had come up and the heat had increased rapidly, a haze had begun to form making the sun look vague and the water started to look dull and grey.

"Port five" Ordered the pilot.

"Port Five." Repeated Derek and turned the wheel.

"Steady on one nine five." Drawled the pilot as he sauntered past the wheel.

"One nine five." Said Derek. The ship steadied on its new heading and we headed towards the Panama Canal entrance. I could feel the anticipation rising. My first Panama Canal Transit. I actually felt good that fine sunny tropical morning.

Ah yes, the tropics. Panama. The heat. The jungle clad hills. Dusky maidens. The mighty merchant ship thundering across the bay. Officers stalking the bridge in sparkly white uniforms, peaked hats at jaunty angles. The sheer romance of it all.

Dave was sick over the port side just then but not before getting some of it down his sweat stained, incorrectly buttoned up shirt. At the same time there was a crash as Debbie returned and a tray was plonked down on the chartroom table.

"Yoo-hoo dearies!" he said sticking his head out of the chartroom door. "The pilot's easy overed eggs are here!"

CHAPTER 24

INTO THE BIG DITCH

The Panama Canal. An excessively big ditch dug a long time ago to connect the Atlantic Ocean to the Pacific Ocean. Or to be more precise the Caribbean to the Pacific, thus enabling large boats full of people's stuff to get said stuff to other people quicker than taking it all the way round the bottom of South America. Or vice-versa.

Sounds simple. But actually, a monumental feat of engineering that cost thousands of lives over the many years of its construction. Was it worth it? In monetary terms it has probably earned its keep over the hundred or so years of its operating life. In terms of human suffering? Don't know. In terms of lives bettered or saved? Have to weigh that against the suffering, trauma and death endured by the thousands and thousands of workers used to build it. So, again, don't know.

Apparently, the King of Spain wanted to have a go at hacking his way from one ocean to the other in the fifteen hundred's and ordered a survey of the area. I don't think he personally wanted to dig it of course, he had a few chaps lined up to do it for him. That was way back in fifteen thirty-four. The idea of building of a canal in those parts continued to crop up over the years with various suggestions and even one or two false starts. Even we Brits had a go around eighteen forty-three and entered into deal with the Grenadians to complete a canal in five years. That never got past the planning stage. There was a small disagreement over funds, I think.

Three years later the Americans started nosing around and a crossing was completed, but a rail crossing, not a canal. Not surprising really.

Americans were always good railways. Canals were not really their thing, although they had done quite well in that field with the building of the Erie Canal and a couple of others. But still, railroads were the order of the day. I can think of hundreds of 'Iron Horse' stories in books and films. But precious few 'Watery Ditch' tales.

The first proper attempt at digging the canal didn't start until eighteen eighty-one. Actually, on the first of January eighteen eighty-one, and it was inspired by some French bloke called Ferdinand de Lesseps. This guy apparently knew his onions because it was him that had, not long before, caused the Suez Canal to happen.

Unfortunately, old Lesseps cocked things up a bit because of his lack of local knowledge. He only visited the place during the dry season and then only the coastal bits which were relatively easy canal digging areas. He failed to listen to local folk who told him about the dense jungle that clad the interior hills... hills mind... not conducive to large ditch digging by any stretch of the imagination. Nor did he listen to the warnings of the raging torrents that the nice little rivers became during the wet season. Nor, even, was any notice taken of the very large poisonous snakes and spiders that infested the jungle or the horrendous diseases dished out by combat boot wearing mosquitos the size of small family motor car.

As a result, the whole project went bankrupt in eighteen eighty-nine but not before killing some twenty-two thousand people and causing some eight hundred thousand investors to lose their savings. Perhaps if he had got the investors to dig the bloody thing, they, the investors, could have protected their investment. It would certainly have been better for the local folk who died in their thousands and anyway what's a few hundred thousand investors... plenty more where they came from.

The Americans bought the rights from the French in nineteen hundred and four (after encouraging some Columbians to revolt, the outcome of which was the creation of a new breakaway country called Panama) and started digging a little while later and so, finally, in nineteen fourteen, some four hundred years after the Spanish King guy ordered a survey and several thousand more deaths, the cargo ship, S.S. Ancon, made the first ever Panama Canal passage.

During that first year nearly one thousand ships made the journey between the oceans and a whole new era of trade between the nations opened up. That trade would probably have been greater but for a bit of tiff going on in Europe at the time. A tiff that caused a death toll and a scale of destruction that made the building of the canal seem like a flea bite on the rump of the planet.

The other thing was that the Chileans became a touch miffed as the canal caused a huge reduction in their trading wealth. But… you can't please everybody… and the canal, over the years, was used increasingly. By the time young George was clinging to his engine room telegraph handle in nineteen-seventy-one a lot more ships per year were passing the through the canal until by two thousand and eight nearly fifteen thousand ships per annum made the transit. That's millions of tons of people's stuff passing through what was once impenetrable jungle.

I, as the *New Zealand Star* approached the entrance to the canal, new none of this. Even if I had have known I would not have cared. Being a British, seventeen year old, first trip sailor at the time, I can speak with the authority of experience. British, seventeen year old, first trip sailors do not now and never have been, overly concerned with the details of Panamanian history.

Except one.

Yes, of course, Steven. It was he who told me all this stuff during our transit of the canal.

Steven, I had come to realise, had a remarkable ability. He could come upon something, an object, a place, a person, even a big ditch in a jungle and within a remarkably short space of time, know everything about it. He had, I think, a sort of superpower. Perhaps he was bitten by radio-active earwigs whilst playing in the rectory garden when he was a four-year-old or something. Anyway, he should, at least, have had some sort of Superhero uniform, perhaps with a large 'K' on his chest… 'Knowledge Man'. One with a cape fluttering behind him and his underpants on outside his trousers.

Anyway, a combination of good pilotage, swift execution of orders, good seamanship… and a couple of tugs… saw us in to the first set of locks. I spent my time gripping the engine room telegraph and moving it to the correct position when told to, then writing the action in the movement book. All the same as leaving London, arriving in Cristobal, shifting ship, and leaving Cristobal. By now I was feeling quite the expert in nautical matters. Actually, I was only experienced in writing things in a book and moving a lever forward and back a few inches, but, nevertheless, it was on a ship and therefore nautical.

"Stop engines." The pilot's voice drifted in from the bridge wing. "Stop engines," whispered Dave, trying desperately to keep his head still. "Stop Engines," I repeated and moved the lever to the upright position.

Just then, Dave's Walkie Talkie burst into life. In fact, it burst very loudly into life causing Dave an agonising few seconds of intense, searing pain over his eyes. You could actually see the agony racing around his Cuba Libre filled brain.

The loud, static filled noise sounded something like… "Shshshshsht… mool…shhhhshsht…fashtarft…shshsht... Over…shtck."

It echoed and crashed around the bridge at about a thousand decibels.

"Roger," whispered Dave into the machine, clamping his eyes shut against the pain.

The ship moved smoothly into the lock. Dave opened one eye, turned towards the starboard bridge wing where the Pilot and Captain McHale were standing in the far corner of peering intently over the side at the rapidly decreasing distance between ship and concrete wall. "Mule fast forward," he croaked.

"Eh?" frowned Captain McHale, turning to look at him.

"Mule's fast forward, sir." Dave made a valiant attempt at shouting the information, but it still came out as a croak, louder, but still a croak and the effort caused his voice box to fail at the last syllable, so the "Sir," came out as a high-pitched girly squeak. Our Leader and the American stared at him. Captain McHale's expression one of glaring annoyance. The Pilots' one of grinning understanding.

"Think yer boy there… is…ah… kinda… suffering." He growled, pausing every few words which made him sound remarkably like John Wayne.

Dave returned to resting his head on the bridge window, I wrote everything down in the movement book and all the Captains and Pilots went back to staring at the concrete.

That was until the same noise from Dave's radio crashed around the bridge again and his head jolted off the window…

"Owww!" He yelped as his neck muscles tweaked into life as they took the full force of his head rocketing backwards off the window. "Ooofff!" He cried as those same muscles sent his head back into the window with a thump.

He held his forehead and with an expression on his face like a distressed four-year-old started to gasp out the information he had just heard "Mule secured aft." Actually, he only got as far as the word 'mule' when both Captain McHale and the pilot, having already been alerted to the possibility of information coming their way by the static filled cacophony issuing from the radio and the accompanying series of yelps that followed, shouted "We heard!" Dave then went back to his original position, gently laying his forehead on the window. I continued scribbling in the book.

The 'Mules,' which everyone was talking about, were not, of course real live donkey like animals. They were in fact huge electric locomotives of immense power that ran either side of the lock and were secured to the ship by steel hawsers. So once in the lock system a vessel was completely under the control of the actual lock. All movement, up, down, forward, back, and even sideways was dictated by the lock itself… Clever really.

The ship drifted further in and began to slow as it approached the huge, looming lock gates ahead. These lock gates were, in themselves, a mighty piece of engineering. They were over twenty metres high, each of the two sections was nineteen and a half metres long and two metres thick.

The whole radio, static, shouting thing started again a short while later when the ship came to a stop in the correct position in the lock.

"Ship secured," mumbled Dave as Captain and Pilot strolled into the wheelhouse out of the sun.

I wrote it down.

So, there we were, in the Gatun Lock system, the first set of locks in the Panama Canal. Quite amazing really. Not the incredible engineering that allowed ships of umpteen thousand tonnes to be lifted up twenty-six metres, over eighty feet in old money, from sea level to the same elevation as Gatun Lake, without pumps, purely by gravity. Nor the incredibly sad, violent history of the canal's construction. The really amazing thing was that Dave wasn't sick down his shirt again. He looked truly awful. However, he soldiered manfully on and carried out every one of his traditional, Third Officer, tasks without hesitation or complaint. But it was a struggle.

Down To The Sea. A Cadet's Tale

In fact, sitting here now, writing this, and thinking back over my time in the Merchant Navy, I can count on one hand the number of times a crew member, of any rank, let everybody down by not doing their job. It never seemed to matter how they were feeling, how desperately they needed to sleep, how much pain they were suffering, how bruised and battered they were from the previous night's exertions, they would always turn up, turn to and be there when required. One of the things that British seamen can be proud of, I think. Reliability. Particularly in the face of adversity. By adversity I mean things like dangerous situations, violent storms, difficult and challenging vessels, the New York Bar etc. etc.

Anyway, getting into the lock didn't seem, by any means, easy, to me. The walls seemed awfully close. Nearly every muscle in my body remained taut with anxiety all the way in, waiting for the loud crunching noise as we crashed into the towering concrete. It never happened of course and if it had of done it wouldn't have been my responsibility anyway. But it was still worrying nevertheless, and I was glad when the whole thing was done and the ship had come to a stop.

Actually, that was another 'life defining' moment in my career. Not in my Merchant Navy career, but my career as a person, as a human. For the first time I found myself wondering what it would be like to be responsible for all this. Well, all of anything really. The enormity of that responsibility began to infiltrate my thinking.

Of course, this thought didn't last long. It rattled around my enquiring adult mind for a few seconds but was soon chased away by the much more powerful adolescent mind. Crowded out by stronger images and thoughts such as crocodiles, Cuba Libres, and 'Jane'. I did, however, decide there and then, I would forgive Captain McHale his frowning grumpiness, which, I concluded, must be as a result of all this worry.

Staring out of the window, to me, the ship felt vast one minute then tiny and insignificant the next as the walls, towering above the main deck seemed to close around us. Then even tinier as the huge lock gates closed slowly behind us.

There are three sections to the Gatun Lock system. Well, six, really, I suppose. If you count the parallel system alongside the locks for us south bound vessels. Ships heading north towards the Atlantic were being lowered down to sea level at the same time as we were being raised to the Gatun Lake level, but, apparently, according to the Encyclopaedia Stevenia, both sets of locks could be used in any direction. So, if there was a bit of a rush on for, the Atlantic, say, then two ships could go in that direction at the same time. This, to my mind, made the whole thing even more impressive and it briefly crossed my mind to learn more about it. But that quickly passed when I remembered I wasn't very studious.

"Get out of the way!" roared Captain McHale.

I jumped, and quickly moved back to the consul. I had been daydreaming and had drifted into the doorway to the chartroom. Our leader instantly lost my sympathy for his immense responsibility and any intention I had to forgive his grumpiness drifted away on the warm Panamanian breeze as he stomped past and went towards the chartroom.

As luck or strange happenstance would have it, Steven, wearing an expression somewhere between and excited schoolboy and an awestruck koala Bear, appeared in the doorway just as Captain McHale was trying to go out. I could see the back of our leader's neck and his ears start to turn purple with rage at being impeded twice in the same minute by gangly, clumsy, idiot cadets.

"Get out of...!" he started to roar again. His voice rising in pitch as his frustration and anger became unbearable and altogether too much for his larynx to cope.

Captain, Senior Pilot Walter Buckman came to our rescue.

"Yeah, say, Cap." He drawled calmly. "Can I get a cup o' cawffee?"

I briefly had the impression that Captain McHale's head was about to explode as he whipped round and looked at the pilot, but he seemed to regain control of his temper and satisfied himself by turning on poor Steven. At first staring at him, then lowering his voice to a sort of strangled shout.

"Waddington!" His beard bristled ominously. "Coffee for the Pilot!"

Steven stared at him, his grin disappearing rapidly, along with the koala expression. Memories of his last coffee making mission not two days earlier obviously entering thoughts.

"Now boy! Now!"

There was a bang as the bridge door slammed shut and Steven's size twelves could be heard thumping down the stairs.

"If you'd like to follow me Captain." Our leader carefully opened the door that had just slammed shut in his face and followed by the Pilot, left the bridge, and headed for his cabin.

I was left in the wheelhouse with Dave, who was still cooling his forehead on the window and Derek the wheelman who had, throughout the entire process remained quiet and calm, taking notice only of whatever helm orders were given him.

"Bit bad tempered this morning, isn't he?" I said.

Dave slowly turned his head towards me so that at least some small part of it maintained contact with the cool glass of the bridge window.

"Yeah." He said, stared at me for a while, then slowly turned his head back again and closed his eyes.

Derek, on the wheel said, "I've sailed with him before and he's always like this when it's hot."

"Yugh." Said Dave, without moving his head.

"Great," I said. "So, he's going to be grumpy all the time the weather's hot?"

"Yugh," Sighed Dave, without moving his head.

Derek grinned, "Not me. I don't come up here much." His grin widened, "That's for all you lot to deal with." He was still smiling but there was a hint of smug satisfaction in his voice.

"Yugh," breathed Dave, without moving his head.

The door from the alleyway to the chartroom burst open and a mug of coffee appeared followed by a harassed looking Steven.

"Where's the Pilot?" he said quickly, his eyes darting back and forth below a deeply furrowed, sweaty brow.

Dave opened an eye but shut again quickly.

"With the Old Man." I said.

Steven turned on his heel and headed out the door.

"…Erm… hang on!" I shouted.

"What!" Steven stopped abruptly and turned back slopping several millilitres of coffee on the deck.

"Don't want to upset you or anything but that mug looks familiar."

Steven joined me in looking down at the coffee mug. Derek looked at it and even Dave dragged his head off the window and peered down at it.

"It's got a chip in it." I said. "It's the same one as the other day."

There was a noise like an out of sorts rusty steam whistle that slowly got louder. A keening type of noise. Dave, myself, and Derek looked round and up and down to see where the sound was coming from. It was several seconds before we all realised, at much the same time, that it was Steven. His panic-stricken face was turning white, and his eyes were beginning to leave their sockets. The keening began to become a low wail as the memory of his nightmare over the very same coffee cup came racing into his already harassed brain.

He hurried away. Again, his feet pounded down the stairs and he landed with a thump on the next deck down.

"Ah, Waddington!... There you are... Is that the Pilots coffee?" Captain McHale and our Pilot had at that very second, emerged from the cabin.

The bridge door, at that point slammed shut. But not before we heard one of Steven's plaintiff, heart rending, whimpers.

We all looked at each other. Then Dave put his head back on the window.

CHAPTER 25

PACIFIC

The sun was glinting. Off the wave tops again, and with a gentle, long, low, slow swell accompanying the Pacific breeze that made the sub-tropical heat nicely bearable, the weather could not have been more idyllic.

It was the morning of the day after we had left the canal and the ship was swishing its way through the azure blue water. Rising and falling slowly, rhythmically, as the swell passed beneath. Even the engines seemed to bask in the gentleness of it all. They throbbed quietly with just the occasional loud rattle as some obscure part of the structure became stressed and complained briefly.

The generators, which normally buzzed with loud urgency reminding everybody of their importance, were on mute mode, or so it appeared. No urgency today.

All was at peace.

"SOMEBODY!" "SOMEBODY!" Captain McHale stood at the top of the steps leading from the starboard bridge wing to the boat deck, hands on his hips, looking down at me.

I had actually seen him come out of the wheelhouse and march onto the bridge wing but had not been quick enough in dodging behind the funnel. If I didn't know better, I would have sworn the bloody thing was also looking down at me, laughing. I made a mental note to improve my 'Keeping out of sight' skills.

"Ah, young man, come up here at once!" He bellowed. Then he turned on his heel and stomped back into the wheelhouse.

We had completed our transit of the Panama Canal after what had been a delay ridden, apparently much longer, passage than was usual.

Technical problems with the huge electric powered 'Mules' in Pedro Miguel Locks had caused some of it, but, prior to that there had been a long wait, at anchor, in Gatun Lake, followed by a slow passage through the Gamboa Reach, the longest of the 'Reaches' or buoyed channels at the southern end of the lake. Then, before reaching the Pacific side of Panama we had passed through the Gilliard Cut, which was really a huge trench dug through the jungle clad hills that overlooked Panama City and the port of Balboa. When I say 'Trench' I should say narrow trench... or better still, very narrow trench. It was, obviously, wide enough, but it still seemed very narrow to me and several times we squeezed past much larger ships on their way north towards the Atlantic. However, Captains, Pilots, Officers of Watches and even Wheelmen seemed perfectly at ease with the idea of thousands of tonnes of stuff squeezing past and missing each other by a whisker. So, I concluded, after heaving sighs of relief, and checking underwear, that all this was normal, and everything was under control.

After the final delay in Pedro Miguel, the last step down to the level of the Pacific Ocean in Mira Flores Locks went smoothly and we were finally on our way out of the canal. Under the Bridge of the Americas, (Which, Steven insisted on telling me, was built in nineteen sixty-two, was five thousand four hundred and twenty-five feet long and there was two hundred and one foot of space from the bridge to the water for us to pass underneath) then out into the Bay of Panama. We slowed down for some ten minutes or so while Captain Buckman shook hands with Captain McHale, left the wheelhouse, galloped down the stairs, (hotly pursued by Steven, who was supposed to be accompanying him to make sure he reached the main deck safely) heaved his ample frame over the side and on to the pilot ladder and dropped nimbly on to the deck of the pilot launch which whisked him away towards the port of Balboa. He had looked back at the ship once when he was about fifty yards away and waved at a panting, sweat soaked Steven who had just arrived at the ladder position.

Then he was gone. His powerful little boat powering its way through the rippled waters of the Bay of Panama towards the port of Balboa.

The Pacific part of the voyage started. I had written in the movement book 09:34 Pilot away. 09:42 C.O.P. 'Commencement of Passage.' We had been in the canal for just over twenty-four hours. The 'Mates', Chief, Second and Third had maintained their own watches with Steven and I doing six-hour shifts on the bridge as 'gofors' and 'fetchits' … and we did, continually. "Cadet! Go for that! Cadet! Fetch this!"

I put my pot of white paint in the shade and rested the brush I had been lazily slapping across the engine room skylight mountings, made my way across the boat deck, up the ladder to the starboard bridge wing and went into the wheelhouse. The tension mounting in my head as I wondered what I done wrong this time. *'I knew it was too good to last'* I thought. *'Perfectly good morning painting in the sun ruined by Bobble Hat'.*

My powers of persuasion had been on top form earlier that morning, persuading Steven, when he appeared back in the cabin with the list of jobs handed to him by the Mate during his daily trip to the bridge, that I should do the menial painting job by the funnel while he did the infinitely more important and crucial task of chipping the rust patches off the after deck. What with him being an expert on such matters, etcetera.

"Ah! … Young man, there you are." Captain McHale peered at me through his nineteen sixties style sunglasses, all oversized frame and real glass.

"That was very good work you did during the canal transit." The glasses came off and he produced a large red handkerchief from somewhere and began to clean them. I stood staring at him completely dumbfounded. 'A compliment? For me? Me? Me!' My brain was becoming obsessed with the word 'Me'.

"Erm thank me Sir." I said. As usual, in his presence, the ability to form coherent sentences deserted me. He frowned and stopped cleaning. "No, erm, I mean you, Sir."

The frown deepened. "Me what?"

"No, err… Sir. Not you, sir. I meant 'you', erm, Sir."

His brain seemed to becoming as confused as my brain and I could

Brian George

see a purplish tinge start to appear around the edges of his reddening, frowning visage.

Dave, it was his watch, stood behind him trying desperately not to burst into laughter. His face performing acrobatic contortions while his lips disappeared as he squeezed his mouth shut.

Captain McHale closed his eyes, breathed deeply and with what must have been a remarkable effort in the face of such provocation, calmed his inflamed nervous system.

"Anyway," he said through gritted teeth, "as I said, good work, very efficient." He turned away coming face to face with Dave who stiffened suddenly clamping his teeth together in an attempt to contain the wild giggles that were threatening burst out. This unfortunately gave him the appearance of someone suffering severe constipation, not helped by the squeaking noise that escaped from his lips.

"...And what's the matter with you?"

"Nothing…. Nothing…" Dave managed, his face turning a dark red with the effort.

"Mmmm." Captain McHale looked at him with suspicion for a moment then headed for the chartroom door, paused briefly and said, without turning his head, "Send Mr. Waddington to see me, I'll be in my cabin."

"Yes Sir." I said to the open-door space. He had already gone, disappearing in an instant into the darkness of the shaded room.

I looked at Dave who had finally let go and was laughing hysterically. Silently, but hysterically none the less.

"It's not funny." I said frowning at him. "He makes me nervous."

That really set him off and he staggered off to the port bridge wing guffawing loudly.

I trotted off out into the sunlight and back down the steps to the boat deck, where I met a frowning Steven advancing towards me with my paintbrush in one hand and my paint pot in the other.

"Where have you been?" He said, waving my brush at me. "This has gone all stiff and the paint's started to go hard."

"All right, all right! Keep your hair on," I said, frowning back at him. "I was summoned to the bridge by the Old Man." My nose moved half an inch skywards and my chest puffed out a millimetre or two. "He actually complimented me on my work during the canal trip."

"Transit," said Steven, handing me my stiff brush and hardening paint.

"Eh?" That was not what I expected him to say.

"Transit…" His nose went up higher than mine. He was much taller than me so it was obviously higher, but it actually moved upwards more than mine. "…Transit, it is called a transit."

"Err, yes well, anyway…" He always had the ability to verbally flummox me. "…He wants to see you now." I pointed at the bridge. "He's in his cabin."

Steven looked towards where I was pointing. "If he's in his cabin, why are you pointing at the bridge?"

That really confused me. My arm stayed where it was, abandoned by my brain which was trying desperately to keep up with Steven's usual verbal acrobatics.

"Err… Erm… because, because, because… that's where I was!" I blurted out.

"Ok." He said calmly and walked off back towards the steps down to the next deck. I was left standing, wild eyed, watching him walk off in one direction with my left arm still pointing in the other direction.

"Oh yes," Steven had stopped and turned back, "the mate says we both have to paint the after deck now, the bit I've been chipping anyway."

"What about my painting?" I said.

"Well, hurry up and finish it while I'm with the Old Man." He said flapping a dismissive hand in my direction as he trotted off towards the steps again.

I shook my head and my shoulders drooped. *Just as I thought, a gentle quiet day in the sun, ruined!'*

The rest of that day passed much like many others. Much like any of the days of fine weather when we crossed the Atlantic really. It was hot and sunny with a few scudding fluffy clouds, occasionally a darker one could be seen in the distance. One of them actually had some rain coming out of it. You could see a grey, see through, narrow sort of sheet between cloud and sea. That was the first time I had seen an actual patch of rain. I didn't know it then, but I was to see many, many more. Not only would

I see them, but they would cause me some considerable headaches in later years, and some hilarity. But that's for another book.

The ship swished on, morning smoko came and went. I finished what I was doing on the boat deck and managed to get the paint pot back to the shelf in the bosun's locker and the brush in a tin of cleaning stuff without encountering the man himself, who still frightened me near to death every time he snarled in my direction. I had, in fact, been extremely lucky throughout the trip. My 'Bosun avoidance' techniques had worked well and I had hardly come into contact with him at all. The 'Technique' actually consisted, mainly, of hiding behind Steven (who was much taller than me) every time the Bosun appeared. I did, however, on occasion, have to engage in some spirited argument to persuade Steven to go and see him about jobs or equipment, when it was clearly my place to go.

As far as I can remember it took us about fifteen days to cross the Pacific. It was an excellent time. Day after day after day of lovely weather, extraordinarily little rain, and endless sunshine. Not too hot with that nice breeze all day.

At one stage, not long after leaving the canal, it may have been one or two days or it may have been longer, I really can't remember we passed the Galapagos Islands. The Islands of Darwin fame.

I probably wouldn't have noticed, (after all, they were just distant smudges on the horizon) but Steven came rushing up to the foc'sle, where I was lazily slapping yet more paint on something vital.

"Look! Look!" He shouted, in a state of extreme excitement, his flapping hand describing an arc over a great swathe of ocean.

I leapt up expecting at least to see a giant super tanker bearing down on us.

"What! What! I shouted back, my head swivelling back and forth at the same time as his hand.

Nothing. I could see, nothing, save… well… sea, really. I looked at Steven who was still staring out into the oggin with his arm sticking out.

"What!" The annoyance was obvious in my tone. It went with the deep frown and red face.

"Islands!" he breathed, his voice suddenly becoming reverential and church like.

I still couldn't see anything, even though I was squinting like a myopic bulldog with my hand shading my eyes as I scanned the horizon.

"Where?"

"There! ... There!" There was an increased urgency in his voice, as though his discovery was going to disappear.

I looked at him. He was pointing in a completely different direction to where I was looking, I realised then I was looking at the wrong end of his described arc.

"There!... There! He said again becoming even more excited.

"Alright, alright." I was beginning to get a headache. "Keep your wig on!" I scanned in the direction of his trembling hand. "Ah, yes, I can see it! I can see it!"

The excitement was infectious. I could hear it creeping into my voice. It was, after all, a mere smudge on the horizon. A slightly darker bit of sky that could, really, have been a cloud.

"Them," said Steven.

"What?"

"Them," he said again. "Not it, them. There are several islands."

I scanned some more. "No," I said, "no, sorry, only one."

He looked at me. A note of smug pity crept into his voice.

"Those..." I thought for one terrible moment he was going to add 'Young man' to his sentence, his voice seemed to be heading in that direction.

"Those... are the Galapagos Islands."

I looked again. "Could be Shangri-fucking-La mate. I can still only see one."

"Yes," he rolled his eyes, "but there are several of them, so therefore they are a 'them,' not an 'it'.

"But" I countered. If I can only see one island, then I will say "I can see it....it.... not... them" as I was speaking I could feel my voice getting louder.

"No..." He began.

"Oi!" We both jumped and looked round. It was the Chief Officer's gentle tones. "Oi!" he bellowed again.

Both of us spun round in different directions trying to locate him.

"What… Yes?" said Steven, a note of desperation in his voice. We were still turning in circles…

"Down here you idiots." The Mate had come up the ladder to the foc'sle, but only far enough that he could see us. As a result, when we had finally located the source of the noise, all we could see was his head, at deck level. The rest of him was halfway down the ladder.

"How about a bit more painting and less chat?"

"Sorry Sir," said Steven, glowering at me.

"…Mmmm, well, anyway the Old Man wants to see your record, workbook thingy… erm… things, so I hope they are up to date." He disappeared, his feet clattering on the ladder until he reached the deck.

We looked at each other, horror spreading across our faces.

"Have you done yours?" Steven's voice betrayed his brain's frantic mental search for a solution to the problem. The problem that was growing, ever larger, ever more insurmountable. Namely, the 'I haven't done it' problem!

I couldn't laugh at the comic contortions his face was going through because the plain answer to his question was 'No!'

"No." I said.

"Oi!" … It was the Mate again. We both stared down at him as his disembodied head again appeared atop the ladder.

"Meant to say, you, Waddington, bring them both up to the bridge when you come for the jobs in the morning."

"Yes Sir." Said Steven to the space where the Chief Officer's head had been. He had gone so he swivelled round to look at me.

"What time is it?"

"Don't know." I said grumpily. "Haven't got a watch on."

"We'll get this job clued up and then we had better make a start on the workbooks." He leaped into action and slowly picked up my paint pot. He was obviously formulating a plan of action. His face took on a sudden calm expression.

I waited for the lifesaving formula to be revealed.

Nothing happened. He stared out to sea, the paint tin dangling from his fingers,

"Well?" I said.

"Well, what?" He looked puzzled.

I flapped my arms in frustration. "Well, what are you thinking?"

He continued to gaze out to sea, then spoke in his reverential voice.

"Did you know? ..." I leant forward slightly in anticipation. "... The Galapagos Islands were discovered by accident in fifteen thirty-five."

My mouth dropped open.

"There are..." His nose lifted slightly again "As I was saying... actually, twenty-one Islands in the group." He glanced in my direction and nodded knowingly.

My mouth was now at full extension and incapable of any further jaw dropping. I couldn't speak at all. The surprise change from workbooks and painting to a full history stroke geography lesson, was too great.

Emboldened by what, he presumably thought, was my astonished interest in all things 'Galapagos', Steven carried on.

"Yes," he said with renewed vigour. "The first person to live there was an Irish sailor called Patrick Watkins, who was marooned there in eighteen hundred and seven. He stayed there for two years."

"Two years." I said.

"Two years." Repeated Steven, nodding. ... "And... nowadays there are well over three thousand people living there!" The nodding became somewhat vigorous as he revealed this startling piece of information.

"Three thousand." I said.

"Over, three thousand." He took a breath. ... "And..."

"Oi!" ... A tinny but loud Chief Officer voice drifted over us. Actually, an angry, tinny, but loud, Chief Officer's voice drifted over us. "What did I say about chat and painting?" He bellowed.

We both looked back towards the bridge where our boss stood holding a megaphone to his face.

"I'd get on with the painting afore yon mon oop there gives me the instruction." Growled another voice close by.

"Our heads swivelled back and forth, a mixture of horror and bewilderment on our faces.

"Doon here, ye pair o' numties."

We looked down in unison. Horror turned to sheer abject terror, our eyes, in unison, widened.

The Bosun! As the Mate had done earlier, he had come part way up the ladder to the foc'sle so only his head was showing.

We stood rooted to the spot. The Bosun stared at us "Well?" His voice was full of menace. Mind you, he could ask you if you would like a cup of tea and make it sound like an invite to a satanic ritual!

Steven made a sort of, short, breathless, low wailing noise. Well one of us did. It might even have been me.

"Wha… wha… wha… what instruction?" Managed Steven bravely.

The Bosun advanced at speed up the remaining ladder. His huge barrel chest being pulled up by his even bigger arms. The ones with the vast muscles in them.

"The instruction tay skelp the hide o' the pair o' ye!" He roared. "Noo… get yeh paint puts an' fahk away af tae yon after deck 'an slap sem paint an yon nimber five hatch coaming."

We both stood staring at him. Neither of us had understood a word, however, once he had reached the top of the ladder and began to advance towards us, we understood enough to retreat and grab paint pots and brushes and manouvre ourselves round him towards the ladder he had just ascended. Steven was a little way in front of me as I clattered down the ladder and begun running along the main deck towards the accommodation deck ladder. He turned his head slightly, fear still etched into his face.

"What did he say we were to do?" he panted.

"Fucked if I know," I said.

"Oh." Steven looked even more worried if that was possible.

"What…?" He said, puffing harder now, … "Did he mean… 'Skelp us?"

"Don't like to think about it," I said, as I overtook him.

CHAPTER 26

PAINT

We weren't 'skelped', flogged or keelhauled that day. Although we came close to getting a 'damned good wigging' over our tardy approach to all things big blue floppy workbook and college related. Me because I was too bone idle and to disinterested in mathematics etc. Steven because his knowledge was far in advance of any floppy workbooks the Merchant Navy Training Board could offer, and he was bored with the (to him) simple sums and straightforward ship stability equations his Nautical College could come up with.

However, we were forced into a period of study by the weather.

It rained. In fact, it kept raining for nearly two days. Not hard, bounce off the deck type rain, but a constant very heavy, very dense type drizzle. It was still hot, in fact hotter than when the weather was clear. But then, it was nearly always like this around the equator, Steven had told me over his muesli the morning after we had been painting in the sun. The Galapagos Islands now distant smudges on the horizon.

Steven had continued his lecture on 'Popular Weather Patterns of Equatorial Areas' for a while until he realised no one was listening. The first clue he got was when he noticed that Barry and JoJo had left the breakfast table. Undeterred, he continued until the second clue arrived, which was me departing.

The rain continued for a full forty-eight hours, by which time we were far away from the equator, just as Steven had said it would.

I discovered, over the course of my seagoing career, that he was completely right. I never once crossed the equator without there being rain involved, usually a lot of it.

Any stories you read about 'Crossing the Line' ceremonies involving people being covered in goop and getting permission from 'King Poseidon', forget it! It always rains. As I say, I 'crossed the line' many times and not once was there any ceremonies. Rain? Yes. Ceremonies? No.

So, studying it was. We spent some of our time finding out details about our ship and putting this information in our big floppy blue books and the rest of it tackling problems set by our respective Nautical Colleges. As a lot of the questions seemed to be the same, I began to suspect a degree of collusion between these seats of learning. They seemed to be determined to come up with preposterous problems that had little to do with real thinking. I mean, if your ship has difficulty getting under a bridge, up some river or other because it's too tall, then you have no business taking it there in the first place! Go somewhere else where the bridges are higher! Seems simple enough to me. That saves all that mathematics involving water density, weights of ships and heights and arcs of spans etc.

Anyway, the more important thing for us to concentrate on (to my mind at least) was, of course, film night.

These nights had to be spread out a bit because the passage was longer, but much to Steven's delight the Mate decided suddenly one evening that even though I was a complete idiot, I should be able to handle 'film showing' on my own. A daunting responsibility I know, but I was sure I could cope with it. Promoted again! To Chief Projectionist! Definitely a step up from my last promotion. Barman on a strange ship!

Thankfully the box of films had been changed in Cristobal. Our ships agent had organised a swop with another British ship whilst JoJo, Barry, Steven and myself were busy escaping non-existent crocodiles.

Once we cleared the equatorial area the weather changed drastically and returned to clear skies and a warm breeze that sometimes became quite strong but remained balmy and pleasant.

Steven and I went back to chipping things and then painting the chipped things exactly as we had before the enforced studying period, but not before a dressing down from Captain McHale over our somewhat lacksidaisical efforts at the academic stuff. We stood in his cabin one morning, (having been summoned to appear before him at 'oh nine

Down To The Sea. A Cadet's Tale

hundred hours sharp!') with our heads bowed, while our leader, with the Chief Officer present, went on and on, for what seemed like a week, about the importance of studying and passing exams. I could see from the expression on Steven's face that this was somewhat painful for him. He was academic enough and could do most of it standing on his head, so to be told off for not doing his homework like a naughty schoolboy must have been galling to him to say the least. But full credit to him, he took his telling off without a murmur and even managed to sound grateful when we were ushered out after an uncomfortable fifteen minutes.

"Yes sir, thank you sir." He muttered.

I only managed a quick, sullen "…Sir." Steven was more grown up than me. I didn't get out of naughty schoolboy mode until my late forties.

Despite that ticking off I found life in the Pacific was just as relaxed and pleasant as it had been in the Atlantic and I slipped easily into the routines of day to day living. Even my projectionist duties went off without a hitch and I showed "Bullit" "A Fist Full of Dollars" and "The New One-Armed Swordsman" to officers and crew alike. I did become the target for some orange peel and peanut based missiles along with some unkind observations during the showing of the last film on the list, a particularly awfull, overlong, badly dubbed Kung Fu epic, but I received apologies afterwards from the officers concerned.

Steven didn't appear in the bar for any of them. I think his Mick Jagger experiences had destroyed his film watching abilities for good, or maybe the delights of steam reciprocating engines were too good to put down.

So, life continued. Steven and I chipped and painted, the ship rumbled its way across the Pacific, the weather remained hot and clear, the ocean remained blue and there was a constant gentle swell that made our home move with gentle pitching and rolling motion that just became part of life itself. There was always something to see. Most days schools of dolphins would appear and dart in and out of the white foaming bow wave created by the large bulbous nose just under the waterline. Flying fish could be seen skimming over the surface of the constantly changing ocean. Occasionally a ship could be seen passing in the distance and once, even another Blue Star vessel passed us heading back towards Panama. It came close enough for me to read the name… Newcastle Star … There was a bit of hooter blowing and from my position up near the bow where I was busy with my chipping hammer, I could see the Chief Officer, John the Second Mate and Dave the Third all waving at people they knew well on the bridge of the other vessel.

The name Newcastle Star meant nothing to me at that moment standing there with my chipping hammer in hand, other than it was a ship in the same company with the same huge blue star symbol on the funnel. It never entered my head that in exactly four years' time, to the day, I would be standing on that same bridge, on that very ship as the Third Mate. Different ocean, but nevertheless, same ship.

The next day Steven and I caused some merriment amongst the entire ships company by getting ourselves into a classic 'cadet' situation.

We had been sent to paint the after deck on the port side. In fact, it was the very after end, right at the back or, in technical terms, at the arse end, of the vessel. (The 'arse end' was what everybody called it, though, as much as I searched the seamanship manuals, I could not find this term mentioned anywhere.)

A large pot of red paint, well barrel really and two large trays to tip the paint in were given to us that afternoon by the Bosun, along with two rollers, one each, attached to four-foot poles. This, after we had spent the morning 'cutting in,' going around the edges with a paintbrush painting the bits where the rollers couldn't get at.

So, off we went 'rollering' away happily in the sun, chatting about this and that, finally shouting to each other as we moved further apart and it became more difficult to hear what each of us was saying over the noises from engines, oceans and various bits clanking, thumping, rattling, squeaking bits ships' equipment and tortured metal that filled the air. I occasionally looked up and admired our handiwork and once waved lazily at a couple of boilersuited engineers that had appeared, leaning on the rail outside the door to the accommodation on the deck above the main deck which we were painting. They waved back and I could see even at that distance they were smiling. *'A perfect day'* I thought. *'All's right with the world'* and went back to rollering. In fact, I was feeling particularly good. All was right with the world and after a few more energetic rolls I looked up again, smiling towards the people on the deck above and noticing that

Down To The Sea. A Cadet's Tale

there seemed to be a lot more of them there, all smiling in our direction. One or two of the newcomers waving. I waved back and glanced over at Steven to see if he had noticed our audience. My partner in crime, my immediate superior had a look of horror on his face and was looking around about himself wildly. Something was wrong. He had the same expression on his face I had seen in the Panama Canal when he had hurled coffee over Captain McHale's shoes. I looked around Steven's painting area, then at Steven, then back at the accommodation deck. Now there were even more people there. Not only were there more people but Captain McHale was on the boat deck above with the Chief Officer. All the people below them were looking at us and laughing, some of them hysterically, but our two leaders were just sadly shaking their heads. I looked over at Steven and found him looking at me with the same expression on his face. His gaze lowered slowly to the deck and looked about him. My eyes slowly followed his and I immediately saw what had happened. Steven had painted himself into a corner! He was completely surrounded by paint. He couldn't get out of his position without tramping all over the area he had just painted. I couldn't help it. I started to laugh as well. How stupid a thing to do! Hah! Painting yourself into a corner! Laughing, I looked up again at the audience, they were all now looking at me and laughing even louder. Barry was actually kneeling and doubled over. I raised my eyes heaven wards and turned away towards my tray of paint.

Real horror flooded over me, making my face blush and my legs feel like jelly.

I had been too busy talking and waving to notice... I had been separated from my tray. I couldn't reach it. A sea of paint stretched before me. Turning towards Steven I could see he was looking at the paint 'barrel,' that also stood surrounded by its own sea of paint. Even louder laughter came from the audience as they watched me become aware of my situation.

To complete the horror, I realised that not only had I separated myself from the barrel and the tray, but, like Steven, I had separated myself from the rest of the world by paint as well! The laughter continued to assail my very red ears as my realisation of the consequences of my stupidity manifested and turned my brain to embarrassed mush.

It took a while, but I finally managed a look towards the accommodation. I could feel my face burning like an out of control sun. The audience was dispersing still giggling to themselves and Captain McHale and the Chief Officer were pacing purposefully away towards the bridge. All of them, without exception were shaking their heads. Once again, I could imagine the speech bubbles above their heads. 'Stupid boys.'

After that incident and of course the 'Walking in the wrong direction and being frightened by lump of tree' debacle, life in the bar became interesting. Well, interesting for most people, more a mild horror for Steven and I. Endless comments about crocodiles, trees, paint and cadets were made. They were a bit of a pain, to be honest, but, I must admit, some were extremely ingenious and though I hate to admit it, very funny and not entirely undeserved.

We did attract and audience the next day while we were painting… or … I should say … repainting our allocated bit of after deck. All hoping for some more entertaining faux pas,' from Blue Star's very own version of Laurel and Hardy!

Despite all this, life continued pleasantly enough, and it wasn't too many days later we were put back on watches and my excitement level increased along with the nervousness. The unknown was approaching again, and I realised how quickly life at sea, actually sailing between ports that is, had become normal to me. In fact, underneath the nervousness and the excitement there was a hint of regret that the passage and the daily routines were coming to an end. On the other hand, I was relieved that that particular two weeks was over, and I would be able to start afresh and never make any more stupid mistakes.

Hah! No chance! More mistakes were on the way, even worse than painting errors. But I was, of course, blissfully unaware of what was to come as I galloped up to the bridge one warm, cloudless star filled evening some fourteen days after watching the jungle clad hills over the Panama Canal disappear over the horizon, to start an 'eight to twelve' watch with Dave.

"Evenin' kiddo." Said Dave jovially without taking his eyes away from his binoculars. "Nip out and take a bearing of that ship over there on the starboard bow for us." He took one hand off his instrument and flapped it the general direction of a tiny cluster of lights between our bow and the green glow from the starboard navigation light nestling in its housing on the outside of the bridge wing.

"Two seven five." I said importantly as I strode back into the wheelhouse after fiddling with the compass repeater on the starboard bridge wing.

Dave repeated what I said then went to the wheel and clicked the autopilot pointer round ten degrees to starboard. "Better get out of his way." He said.

"Yes" I agreed feeling even more important. It may sound trivial but a little thing like taking a bearing of another vessel on a collision course with our own ship and then having a decision made about the direction and safety of fourteen thousand odd tons of that very ship, based entirely on the information I had obtained and had relayed to the Officer of the Watch was a huge boost to my confidence and made me feel much more part of the bridge watch 'team.'

Albert, The Mate, came in from the other bridge wing.

"That's' everything Dave, nothing more to tell you."

"Aye." Dave lowered his binoculars and looked at Albert as he strode past, heading for the chartroom. "Ashore tomorrow night?"

"Ooohhh Yesss!" said Albert grinning. "We should be tied up by the afternoon and I've heard nothing about starting discharging, so we should get a break." He stopped, half in and half out of the doorway. "You going ashore?"

"Hope so." Said Dave. "Just got to persuade John to do night aboard."

"Good luck!" Said Albert, grinning as went through the door.

"You going ashore?" Dave was looking at me.

"Erm... I think so, not really sure." I hadn't thought about it.

Dave peered through his binoculars again, then walked back to the wheel and clicked the auto pilot pointer back to the original course.

"Should get some mail as soon as we arrive." He muttered, partly to himself.

"Mail?" I queried... then "Oh yes." Another thing that had been crowded out of my brain by the million other new thoughts and experiences. Then that thought was suddenly replaced by a guilty feeling. 'Cathy! I hadn't thought about Cathy for a long time. I should have. I was really upset when I watched her car disappearing in the rain outside the docks in London.'

Dave was speaking again.

"Hope our address lists were ok, eh?"

I came back to the present suddenly.

"Oh, yes." I frowned and immediately went back to the past again, remembering the time, a day before sailing from London.

"Go and see the Third Mate." Albert, the Mate had said that evening. "Before you go ashore. See if he wants hand with the address lists."

I had galloped along the alleyway to Dave's cabin, frowning and in a mild panic because I was frightened that this extra task might interfere with my love life.

"Ah yes." He had said as I appeared in his doorway. "You can help."

Dave was standing in the middle of his cabin with strange blue streaks on his once white shirt that matched the blue marks on his hands, face and arms. On the floor in front of him had stood a strange looking metal machine, also covered in blue streaks… well… when I say blue… it was more of a deep purple really… Anyway, this machine was only about two feet high, covered an area of about three-square feet and had a large upright handle on the side that was obviously meant to turn some sort of machinery inside. On the side of the contraption the word GESTETNER was displayed in white letters.

I had been too pre-occupied with 'Cathy thoughts' on my way to his cabin so the sight that greeted me had come as complete surprise.

"We have to print these address lists." Dave had said.

"Address lists?" I had been completely perplexed.

He had explained. "Everybody has to have the addresses of the ships agents in each port we're going to so their nearest and dearest can write to them." A sad, sort of resigned expression had appeared on his face as he had transferred his gaze to the object on the floor "And this… thing… machine… is how we print out enough address lists."

A shudder ran through me as I continued to remember the blue/mauve ink filled hour I had spent holding on to the insides of the obviously broken machine while Dave cranked the handle a few thousand times to produce a hundred or so 'address lists.' In unison we both looked down at our hands. We still had faded mauve fingers now, weeks later!

CHAPTER 27

LAND OF THE LONG WHITE CLOUD

If you walk down Queens Street in Auckland towards the sea and keep walking after you cross Quay Street you will walk directly onto Queens Wharf. So, if one's ship is parked right up as far as you can get it on Queens Wharf, then the bow of said ship points directly up Queens Street and it is but a short stagger for all aboard to the fleshpots and delights of the city.

This simple fact explained the grins on the faces of officers and crew of the M.V. New Zealand Star when they found out that the allocated berth for their vessel was, indeed, Queens Wharf.

I had come back up to the bridge the next morning after almost colliding with Dave as he galloped out of his cabin. Both of us, not late, but heading for work a little later than we would have liked. We had, as usual, had our breakfast before going up, in fact Dave had had two breakfasts. Two full fried egg feasts, one after the other. That was why it took us a little longer. I had finished mine quite quickly but felt I had to stay until he had finished his. This, mainly, because he had launched into a 'Last trip, in Auckland…' story and I had listened intently, wanting to gain as much insight to what might happen in our next port of call as possible.

So, it was with no little haste we had hurried from the saloon that morning, dived into our respective cabins, (with me trying not to make any noise so as not to wake Steven who had been on the twelve til four watch and was snoring loudly. Although, judging by my experiences previously in trying to wake him, I could probably have performed a full tap dance routine to the music of Led Zeppelin for all the difference it would have made) and then rushed out and headed for the bridge.

Our leader was in his chair by the chartroom door when I arrived on the bridge. He seemed to have got over his fear of me grabbing him by the shoulder now and there was no involuntary flinch as I passed him. It was me that flinched as I caught sight of the view through the bridge windows. I hadn't taken any notice when people had referred to New Zealand as the 'Land of the Long White Cloud', just thinking of it a name, a romantic name, dreamed up by some poet or explorer from the dim and distant past. But there it was… the 'Long White Cloud' stretched out before me, low down on the horizon. A long strip of white stretching from one edge of my vision to the other, only broken by another ship, some distance off. 'So, I thought. 'The description is accurate.'

Impressed, I said with a degree of excitement entering my voice. "So, that's New Zealand then."

Dave, who had been ahead of me entering the wheelhouse and was now peering into the radar, looked up and turned his head towards me, a puzzled expression on his face.

"Eh?" He said.

I nodded towards the cloud ahead of us. "There." I nodded again. "There. New Zealand."

He looked out of the window, still puzzled. Then that expression disappeared, and a smile appeared. At the same time, I heard a strangled chortling noise from behind me and I turned to see Captain McHale trying not let his amusement show and the Mate going into the chartroom in a hurry bent over, as though he had a sudden attack of the stomach cramps.

I turned back to Dave who said, with some difficulty.

"No… No… No… That, kiddo, is a long white chunk of cloud. We are heading towards it because… because…" He was having a tough time suppressing the laughter by now. "Because, at this very moment, we are going around the vessel you can see, also ahead of us. If you would care to look through the port bridge wing door you will see a large lump of land covered in grey clouds… That, my lad, is New Zealand."

At that point Albert, the Mate lost control and loud guffaws issued from the Chartroom.

"Oh." I said.

"A little control, Mr. Harris, if you please." Captain McHale came to my rescue, though I could see the smile he was trying to hide plainly. "An easy mistake to make." He added as he hopped off his chair and stood beside me.

"Do you know why it is called 'The land of the Long White Cloud'?"

"Erm, no Sir." My face was back to its traffic light red again by now.

He walked towards the port bridge wing. I followed behind, scowling at Dave who was making faces at me and trying not to laugh at the same time.

"It's a Maori name." Said the Captain coming to a stop just outside the door.

"Aotearoa, in their language." He looked at me, I think he was deciding whether I was paying attention, then continued. "'Ao' means cloud, 'tea' means white and 'roa' means long. The actual 'New Zealand' name is Dutch in origin. It comes from the word Zeeland, which is actually spelt with two e's, not 'e' and 'a' like we spell it now. Zeeland means Sealand in Dutch and is the name of a coastal province in Holland. Apparently, the Dutch explorer Abel Tasman named it when he spotted it, way back in the seventeen hundreds."

I nodded, saying nothing but wanting to show I was listening.

"Anyway, young man, you will, I am sure, have learned a lot about New Zealand by the time we leave the coast."

"I bet he will as well." Muttered Dave, grinning, as he came out on to the bridge wing.

Captain McHale scowled slightly. "Yes, thank you Mr. Spiggot… I trust you will look after our two young cadets and make sure no harm comes to them?" His tone was questioning, and Dave's face lost its grin. He changed the subject quickly.

"Back on course, Sir." He said loudly. "Our ETA at the pilot station is oh nine twenty."

Captain McHale watched him retreat hurriedly into the wheelhouse, then turned to me.

"I think it's about time you made me a cup of tea." He said.

Exactly four hours later the ship was tied up on Queens Wharf with the bow pointing directly up Queens Street.

The launch carrying our pilot had arrived a few minutes after we had approached the pilot station with engines stopped, drifting towards the designated pick up point. I was sent down to stand by the pilot ladder that was hanging over the port side, put there about half an hour earlier by the crew after a brief radio conversation between Captain McHale and the pilot launch. Our pilot had scrambled up the ladder and leapt down on to the deck without making use of the steps and stantions put there for his safety and galloped off towards the accommodation deck door giving me a cheery "Gudday" as he passed. I chased after him, feeling as though I should be ahead of him, opening doors and showing him the way. Actually, I discovered that that was the way of things and pilots usually went straight to ships bridges quickly and efficiently all by themselves very often followed by a sweat stained panting cadet who they had left behind three floors down.

Thinking back now, I can remember one particular nightmare in New Plymouth, New Zealand. Still only a cadet, I had joined a ship there, having flown out from the UK. After a hellish, near thirty-eight-hour flight via various Middle Eastern and Indonesian airports, followed by a bone jarring, nerve jangling flight from Auckland in horrendous weather aboard an ancient Fokker. I had arrived in time for the vessel to sail and had about twenty minutes to get to my cabin, unearth suitable uniform and then locate the bridge on a ship I had never even heard of before, let alone seen. Although the actual 'leaving the port' went reasonably well, when it came time for the pilot to disembark, young George found himself touring alleyways and peering round corners hoping to find some clue as to the way out with the irate pilot in tow. Not a good start to the voyage.

Anyway, the tugs Tihawina and Aucklander had pushed and nudged us into the first berth on the wharf then Captain McHale had rung the engine room telegraph to indicate 'Finish With Engines.' and disappeared below with the pilot leaving the Third Mate and myself to finish things off and close down all the bridge equipment.

So, there we were, parked in Auckland.

I trotted down from the bridge and went to the cabin where Steven had just arrived ahead of me and was peeling off his uniform.

"The Mate says we have got to get changed into our boiler suits and report to him." He said, hopping on one foot and trying to get the other leg free of his trousers. "Probably have to open all the booby hatches and get ready for the dockers to come. Should start discharging cargo straight away." He had a lofty 'I've been here before and know about these things' tone to his voice and would have said more if he hadn't toppled over and banged his face on the table. He said nothing further while he sat on the floor and pinched his nose to stop the bleeding. I felt, briefly. Sorry for him. His nose seemed to be a target for everything. Floors, tables, heads, bunk boards… everything.

'At least it's saved me from a lecture on fascinating facts about New Zealand. Of which he is bound to know plenty.' I thought.

I changed into my boilersuit while Steven administered to his injury which, had stopped bleeding almost as soon as it started.

'His nose must be getting tougher.'

"Did you know …?" He said, getting to his feet. "That the Māori's call New Zealand the…"

I interrupted him quickly. "…Land of the Long White Cloud and it was named by Tabel Masman and its Maori name is Aotor… rori …aer or something and Zealand was spelt wrong because it was a coastal pronouncement…" There was a note of triumph in my voice as I finished my monologue. I took a breath, feeling pleased with myself.

Steven stared at me. "How did you know all that? Actually, it was all wrong but who told you." He sounded quite indignant.

"Captain McHale, actually." I said, matching Steven's loftiness. "We had a conversation on the bridge earlier." My nose went a bit further in the air. "Anyway, it's not wrong, he…"

The door crashed open.

"Come on hurry up!" It was the Mate. "Number three hatch needs opening; they're taking that bloody great lorry out." We followed him out into the alley way in a hurry.

"Here." He shouted over his shoulder. "Booby hatch keys." A set of Yale lock keys sailed over his head, bounced off Steven's shoulder and landed on the alleyway floor in time for me to stand on them. I did a sort of pas de deux, flapping my hands and bending in a camp fashion to reach down and retrieve them without stopping. There was a loud guffaw from behind me from Barry who had just come in the after-alleyway door.

"Ooh lovely." He said. "Very Dame Margot!"

'Again' I thought. *'Bloody, again... Every time I do something embarrassing, there's an audience.'*

I consoled myself by directing his attention as to where he should go, and in what manner... and galloped after Steven and the Mate who were, by this time, gone from sight.

Out on deck there was, what can only be described as, organised bedlam. The three of us arrived at number three hatch and joined both the other two Mates, the Bosun and a few suited folks who looked as though they were important. I immediately trotted off and opened the booby hatch, allowing three riggers to disappear down the ladder.

The ship shook just then as the hatch covers started to squeak shudder and rumble their way along the coaming and, section by section, drop into the space forward of the hatch.

I looked over the coaming down into the hatch and could see the riggers had already started to open the lower deck hatch covers to reveal the 'Bloody Great Lorry'. That was the time that my understanding of loading a ship began to sink in. A great deal of planning must go into it to make sure the right cargo is positioned in the right place so as to be accessible at the right time in the right port. My respect for senior officers both ashore and on the ship went up a notch or two.

We spent the next few hours watching while the lorry, that Dave had tried so valiantly to park all those weeks ago in London, was readied for lifting and riggers swarmed over our 'Stulken' heavy lift derrick at the forward end of number three hatch to get that ready to connect to the lorry. I again found myself with the 'Cargo Times' book and jotted down the times of various stages of the operation. There was an air of something risky going on that made me feel as though I should make sure that I recorded everything accurately. So that's what I did, furiously scribbling in the book every time some piece of equipment was ready, something was attached to something else or there was some sort of movement.

The whole 'Getting Things Ready' part of the operation took quite a while and there was even time for Steven and I to get a quick lunch break. One at a time, of course. We galloped off in turn, up to the cabin, out of boiler suit, into uniform, along to the saloon, ate lunch (at speed), back to the cabin, out of uniform, into boilersuit and back onto the deck. Half an hour tops! All fed and watered! It was one of the major skills of Merchant Navy cadets, eating and working at the same time.

So, we were both there when the 'Bloody Great Lorry' was finally lifted out of the hatch and onto the dock. Our huge heavy-lift derrick purchase wires, as thick as a baby's arm and covered in grease, lifting the huge truck slowly up and clear of the hatch coaming. Then the span wires, not quite as thick but just as impressive as the others, hauled the thing across the ship and over the dock. The ship, big as it was, took on a marked list to starboard as the thing was lowered slowly onto the dock. This took some skill by the riggers on the controls as they had to speed up the purchase wires as the weight came off. If they stopped lowering the purchase wires too soon then as the ship came back upright the truck would have been dragged back towards the hull. Everybody held their breath at this point. You couldn't see anybody holding their breath, but the collective sighs once the truck was securely on the ground was audible enough to give the game away.

Albert, the Mate turned away from the spectacle and looked at us. He laughed.

"Ok," He chortled. "You can both close your mouths now."

My teeth snapped together at exactly same time as Steven's as we looked at each other, both realising that we had been staring with childlike awe, mouths wide open, as the truck was transferred to the dock side. I hastily wrote '13.52 Truck Landed' in my book.

"Right, you two can knock off now. There is no more cargo work today. Just make sure the hatch is closed and the booby hatch locked then you can bugger off." He turned on his heel and started talking to the suited gentlemen that were hovering near him.

We stood and stared. Time off! No more work today! Dave tapped me on the shoulder, and I turned to look at him.

"I'd do what he says Kiddo."

My mouth was open again. Steven's also as he stared at Dave.

"Eh?" I said.

Dave rolled his eyes. "When you are told to bugger off by the mate then it is always an innovative idea to do that very thing, very quickly. If you don't, then further work will come your way, also very quickly." He stuck his head further forward, so it was only a few inches from our faces. "So, fuck off!"

We did. At speed.

"Leave me the Cargo Times book!" Dave shouted after us as we went up the steps towards the accommodation deck.

"Shall we go ashore?" said Steven.

We had reached our cabin in record time, then come to stop when we both realised that we didn't know what to do next.

"Erm… well… yes I suppose so." I said slowly, thinking while I spoke. A thought came to me. "Didn't you say you were here last trip?"

"Ah… yes… well… I was." Steven was starting to look forlorn again, so I was not filled with hope that he was going to come up with something interesting to do.

So, it came as no surprise when he said. "I wasn't actually here. We went to Wellington then Timaru then Bluff." His forlornness was completed with shoulder sag.

"Well let's go for a wander then, shall we?" I started to get out of my boilersuit. "If we hang around here too long the Mate will turn up and give us another job."

Half an hour later we were in our 'Going Ashore' rig and trotting down the stairs having seen the Chief Steward and got the Kiwi dollars we had asked for, which wasn't much. Cadets pay in nineteen seventy-one was not a lot. I had the princely sum of forty dollars which was about twenty pounds worth while Steven, who was better off than me and on a couple of pounds more a month, had fifty dollars. We both hoped that was going to be enough to see us through the stay in Auckland, but somehow, I had my doubts.

We just reached the door to the deck when I was startled by a very loud ringing. It came from a telephone that, just like in London, had been installed in the alleyway. This time the wire must have been shorter because the set, complete with slots for coins, was right by the outside door and not opposite the Saloon as it had been in London.

Steven stopped abruptly and stared at it. I, as usual, wasn't quick enough in breaking and ran into the back off him. He, his hand already pushing the door, had to do a nifty leap to clear the storm sill and reach the outside deck without landing on his nose. Unfortunately, Steven wasn't capable of nifty leaps. His gangly six-foot frame wasn't built for it and so, one leg went out, one leg stayed in. I stood on the foot attached to the leg that had stayed in. Steven yelped as his trailing leg, now minus a shoe yet again, crashed into the sill and was then dragged across it as his body fell to the deck on the far side.

I remained on the inside, with Steven's shoe.

Loud prolonged laughing came from behind me, and I turned to see Barry and JoJo doubled up with mirth.

I scowled at them.

"You had better answer the telephone." Said JoJo, wiping the tears from his eyes.

"Me?" I said. "Why me?"

"Because you, you dipstick, are standing next to it." Said Barry, also wiping tears.

I gingerly picked up the handset.

"Hello." I said quietly.

"Gudday!" bellowed a high octave female voice. "Is that the Kiwi Star?" It sounded as though she was bellowing down a megaphone and the sound could be heard all over the alleyway as I snatched the phone away from my ear.

"Erm… Yes, it is." I said, still holding the handset six inches away from my ear.

"Ah great!" she shouted. What times the party?"

CHAPTER 28

PARTY

Ship's gangways, circa nineteen seventies, rattled. A distinct loud aluminium rattle. In fact, they had a sound that could be heard even above all the other 'ship' noises. They would bounce as you walked up or down them… well… clatter is probably a better description. This clattering would mix with the scraping noise the bottom of it made as it moved, only a few inches, along the concrete of the dock. If you add to that the sound of high heels crashing down on to the steps as their owners try desperately to stay upright, cope with the bounce and look ladylike all at the same time, then you will have the even more distinct sound of guests arriving at a ship's party.

That was the sound Steven and I heard through several closed doors, even above the hum of the generators, as we sat, nursing cans of beer, by ourselves, on stools in the bar.

We had managed to find our way ashore once Steven had stopped hopping around clutching his shin. It would be safe to say that I was not his favourite person at that point in time. I think he was a tad fed up with me either standing on his feet or causing his nose to bleed. To my mind it was his own fault for having a large nose and even bigger feet. Nothing to do with me.

Anyway, the phone had been snatched out of my hand by Barry as soon as he heard me say "What party?" in response to the question from the loud female New Zealander on the other end. He had scowled at me and then smiled sweetly as he said "Seven Thirty" into the handset.

I hadn't heard much else because an angry Steven had wrenched open the door and leapt back into the alleyway in search, yet again of an errant shoe.

"My shoe! Again?" he spluttered.

"Well, sorry, but you stopped suddenly… again!" I swung round in a circle hunting for it. "Here it is." I retrieved it from the corner where it had somehow ended up.

"Shut up!" shouted Barry. He was scowling at both of us, caught in the middle between a loud female in one ear and arguing cadets in the other ear. If he put the handset close to his head a shattered eardrum from the ultra-loud lady was likely. If he held it away from his ear he couldn't hear because of the drama over the escaped footwear.

I heaved open the door and we both hustled out into the afternoon heat leaving Barry talking sweetly into the phone.

Once Steven had hopped about putting shoe back on we clattered down the gangway, along the dockside, the ship towering over us on one side and huge warehouses on the other side, then through the gates, Steven striding in front wearing his usual dark trousers, plain shirt (with tie), sensible shoes and his tweed jacket with elbow patches. *You look ridiculous… I mean… who wears elbow patches nowadays! Hah!'* I thought as I thumped along behind him in my platform shoes and trendy seventies blue loons flapping beneath my yellow, big collared, shirt.

Auckland is a beautiful city. I went back there recently for the first time in forty odd years and it still just as good as it was on that warm, sunny southern hemisphere summers day in February of nineteen seventy-one.

Apparently, it used to be the capital back in eighteen forty. In fact, in the very same month, February, of eighteen forty, the new governor of New Zealand, William Hobson, chose the area and named it after George Eden the Earl of Auckland, who was the Viceroy of India at the time. All this information came my way via Steven, of course, as he and I crossed over the dock road and marched up Queens Street.

"Of course, the Capital before that was Russell, which is in the Bay of Islands" he said as we passed the grey Post Office building. Crossing the next street an irate motorist, who had to brake a tad quickly to avoid us, hooted angrily as we scuttled across the road. Actually, it was me he hooted at, but it was Stevens fault. I was just trying to keep up with the lanky git as he just took off, loping across the road without looking, still waffling away. "… Wellington became the Capital in eighteen sixty-five." He said. At least I think that was what he said, I was busy skipping round the bonnet of the braking car. He came to a stop outside the South Pacific hotel. "Did you know…" He continued as I jolted to a stop on the kerb. "Did you know… That Wellington was once called Port Nicholson."

"Whoopee-fucking-doo!" I muttered under my breath.

"Pardon?" Said Steven.

"Nothing, nothing." I said. "…But why name a city in New Zealand after a bloke who is something to do with India?"

"Ah, well, you see it wasn't named after the Earl of Auckland, it was named *for* the Earl of Auckland."

I frowned. "What's the difference?"

"Erm, oh, erm… well… erm I don't really know." He said. His turn to frown.

"Perhaps old Billy Hobson and George the Viceroy were mates and called cities after each other." I theorized. "Perhaps there's a city called Hobson somewhere." Steven's frown deepened. He was obviously trying to decide whether I was being serious or my usual flippant annoying self. He paused for a while then turned on his heel and strode on into the depths of the city.

We didn't have a particular place to go, we were just walking. In those days, the drinking age in New Zealand was twenty-one so we couldn't go for a beer or anything. Not because it was against the law particularly, just that we didn't look twenty one. In fact, I didn't feel a day over twelve actually. Coffee shops hadn't been invented back then and cafes where we could get a cup of tea and a sticky bun seemed to be non-existent as well.

So that's how my first run ashore in New Zealand went. An exceptionally long walk, no alcohol and not even a cup of tea and sticky bun. We arrived back at the ship about two hours after leaving it, hot, tired and thirsty but we had, at least seen some of the city.

I couldn't have known it then, but I was destined to return to Auckland a number of times over the following fifteen years. There were many adventures, some good, some not so good to come for me in that city.

"Think some ones arriving." Announced Steven.

Our heads turned in unison towards the bar door which was propped open by a chair.

The fact that we were actually alone in the bar waiting for party guests, female party guests at that, to arrive, may seem odd, but I discovered over the years that there was a certain protocol to attending such functions.

The routine was as follows; firstly, on arrival at a particular port, if the public phone supplied to a ship didn't ring immediately and a conversation with a female of the opposite sex about the timing of a party that very same evening didn't take place, then there was always someone in the officer's quarters (usually an engineer) who had a book full of phone numbers of places where partygoers might reside. Nurses' homes, student houses, dens of iniquity… that sort thing. These would be contacted, and a time arranged when said partygoers should arrive.

Secondly, cadets would be tasked to make the Smoke Room look like a party place. This usually meant closing the curtains and turning some of the lights off.

Thirdly, whoever was running the bar that particular trip would get in a copious amount of extra beer and one or two bottles of martini… 'For the Sheila's'.

Then, precisely thirty minutes before anyone was due to arrive everybody would disappear and leave the deck cadet or cadets to meet the guests either in the bar, at the top of the gangway or even, in cases where the guests were inexperienced ships party goers, at the dock gates.

There would, occasionally, be an appearance by a junior engineer, but it would be brief and fleeting as they wandered past the bar door pretending to be on the way somewhere to do something important. They would glance in to see if anybody was there yet and hurry on their way. Everybody wanted to 'smooth in' later and make an entrance rather than initiate first contact and have to engage in conversation and awkward introductions.

"I'll go and look." I said, jumping off my stool and heading for the open door. Anything was better than sitting there waiting.

I reached the door to the deck just as it burst open.

Brian George

"Jesus Christ!" Yelped a large, dark haired woman of some thirty odd years as she virtually leapt into the alleyway. She was wearing a dark mini skirt that was a tad too mini which almost met a white blouse somewhere near her ample midriff. Said blouse matched her white high heeled shoes that she carried in her right hand and a white handbag, once again, ample, which was in her left.

She stumbled forward.

"Jesus Christ! She exclaimed again.

'Ah' I thought. *'She has high heels, she's not a regular ship's party goer. If she were a regular ship's party goer, she would have easier to control shoes. High heels and gangways are not a good combination.'* (Nowadays it would be considered dangerous to have high heels anywhere near a ship and there is probably a book full of European laws covering the subject. But this was the seventies and Health, and Safety hadn't been invented.)

"Watch out for the storm sills on this alleyway door, girls!" She roared over her shoulder. "They're nearly as high as the bloody hatch coamings!"

I changed my mind. *'A regular ships party goer'.*

"Hi mate!" She turned her attention to me. "…Name's Mylene… was it you I spoke to on the phone?"

"No." I said. "That was Barry."

"Barry?" Said Mylene. "Is he here?"

"…Err… No." I stuttered. "He's getting ready… He's from Liverpool." Quite why I said 'He's from Liverpool' I don't know. I think I felt that Barry needed some sort of explaining. It might lessen the shock when meeting him.

Mylene frowned and then bent down to put on her high heels, grabbing the shoulder of a much smaller girl that had stumbled in behind her.

"I'm Jasmine." She said through gritted teeth as Mylene's fingers dug into her flesh. "Who are you?"

Jasmine was altogether the opposite of Mylene, she was petite, with long brown hair, fringed at the front and waist length at the back. Her choice of party frock was different too, she was dressed in tight jeans that finished mid-calf, a good six or seven inches from a pair of plain black slip on shoes. A pink t-shirt completed the ensemble. No sign of a handbag.

"…Are you the captain?" She continued, tipping her head to one side.

'Cathy does that.' I thought and immediately blushed.

The door crashed shut behind them and was immediately opened again to the sound of loud giggling as three more females stumbled over the sill and into the alleyway. All of them dressed like Mylene. All wearing different coloured miniskirts and blouses. All of them requiring bigger miniskirts and blouses and all wearing white high heeled shoes. (None of them having the sense to take them off whilst negotiating the perils of ships gangway ascending… hence all the clattering before).

There was a sudden silence as we all looked at each other. This was followed by more giggling from the last three girls to arrive, who were all turned away in a huddle, going through that young female group ritual that happens when they're meeting people. The one where they look sideways at each other for a few seconds, then giggle and bend at the waist until their heads nearly bang together while they mutter and giggle (again). A bit like a rugby scrum but without muscles and gum shields. This is usually followed by an upright haughty posture of defiance. What they are actually defiant about, or of, I have no idea. I discovered later in life that it was just a 'thing' that they did.

None of this, however, applied to Mylene and Jasmine. They stood, confidently staring at me with an expectant expression on their faces.

"Well?" Said Mylene, rolling her eyes.

I looked from one to the other. "Well, what?"

"The bar. Where's the bar?" This from Jasmine who had taken a step forward and was now only six inches from my face. "Are you the captain?" She repeated her first question.

"Oh… erm… of course… yes… it's this way!" I stuttered, turning on my heel and heading towards the bar door. "Follow me."

Jasmine turned and faced the gigglers. "This way girls, the captain here is takin' us to the bar."

Like Mylene, she had a strong nasal New Zealand accent, so 'bar' sounded more like a long drawn out 'baaarre' when you hold your nose.

I had taken a few steps but stopped and turned back.

"No, no, no, I am not the…!" I started to explain who I was, but the words wouldn't come out quick enough.

"Hi girls!" said a deep voice behind me. I stopped explaining and turned around. It was Barry. Not only was it Barry… It was Barry with a deep voice… In fact, it was Barry with a deep voice and a sort of Yugoslavian accent, or, at least, a hint of Russian or something.

"I am… Barry." He announced this as though we had all been waiting a week for his appearance on stage.

I stared at him. Steven appeared in the doorway wearing a deeply puzzled expression and also stared at him. The gigglers giggled a bit more but walked towards him.

Mylene and Jasmine smiled, and the older woman said. "Hi I'm Mylene. Was that you on the phone earlier?"

"Yes." Said Barry. But with his new accent it sounded more like "Yais."

"Yais." He said again. "Iss wassa me."

"Ya sound a bit different in real life mate." Said Mylene. "Thought yer mate 'ere said you were from Liverpool."

'Hah, rumbled!' I thought. A grin appearing. Barry glared at me.

"Ahh. Yais. Eet issa possibool… many, many peoples say zis to me. On de telephonic, in zer day, I ama sound Eengerleesh!"

Stephen and I stared. More giggling came from the bar as, by this time the gigglers had moved ahead of everyone else and were busy scanning the area.

I nudged Steven out of his trance and pushed him back into the room. He looked at me uncomprehendingly and whispered.

"Why is he talking with a deep voice and a funny accent?"

I probably looked equally uncomprehending.

"I don't know!" I hissed back shoving him towards the bar stools. "We'd better get these girls a drink or something."

However, I needn't have worried. The 'Female Arrival Detection Radar' that seemed to be fitted as standard to most engineers was obviously fully operational as several of them appeared in the area at precisely that moment. Remarkably, Ian, the Chief Engineer, had materialized from nowhere and taken up his usual station behind the bar.

"Barry's talking in a funny accent." Steven told Ian as soon as the latter popped up from retrieving an errant beer bottle that escaped his clutches and had rolled noisily to the corner of his narrow area.

"What? … Oh! … Again?" Said Ian frowning. "He tried that routine when I was with him on the Rockhampton Star, didn't work then, don't suppose it will work now." He ducked down behind the bar and reappeared with two bottles of beer and plonked them down on the bar top in front of us.

He explained further.

"… He pretends to have some sort of European ancestry, thinks it makes him interesting to women for some reason."

Steven and I turned to watch Barry, his arm firmly around Jasmine's waist, walk across the room and deposit her on the long, hardback seat near the far corner of the smoke room. We turned back and resumed leaning on the bar. Ian was slowly shaking his head with a pitying look on his face.

"Right!" We all jumped in shock. It was Mylene. Ian's eyes opened wide, and his head rocked back in shock and both Steven and I received a jolt as she slapped us both hard on the back. "Right… Let's get this party started! Where's the music?" She shouted. "… And I want a gin!"

There it was. The start of my first 'Kiwi Coast'.

We had arrived in Auckland that morning, it was now eight o'clock in the evening and already I had seen a vast lorry unloaded, set foot on land as far as possible from home as I could get, was at a party and been thumped on the back by the lovely Mylene. All in the space of a few hours. I thought back to that first few hours on the ship in King George the Fifth Dock in London on a cold, damp, misty afternoon. I had had more new experiences in the space of a few weeks than in my entire sixteen or so years of life. What else could possibly happen?

CHAPTER 29

SCOUSULA

That first party had gone quite well, I thought. Music and dancing there were plenty of, as was there beer and spirits. Several people, both guests and hosts imbibed greatly and collapsed in untidy heaps in chairs looking extremely uncomfortable but snoring loudly, nonetheless.

Others, again hosts and guests, made apparent rapid friendships and disappeared to quiet corners, or cabins to further these international relations. Tiptoeing out quietly and furtively so as not to disturb the soring heaps or get in the way of the few couples slow dancing to the high tempo, very loud rock music issuing from the speakers at either end of the bar with their faces stuck together.

Steven and I were sent out a couple of times each, to meet more young ladies... well... ladies, young and not so young actually. Each time this happened it was just after Mylene had availed herself of the ship's telephone.

"Yeah!" I heard her saying. "It's great... they've got gin!"

Barry, to everyone's amazement managed to keep up his Mid-European accent all night, sounding increasingly like Count Dracula with a nasty case of tonsillitis as the night wore on.

At one point he wobbled over to where Steven and I were sitting at the bar. He was clutching a shy looking blonde girl round the shoulders. Jasmine had long since abandoned him and was now enjoying an inebriated snooze on the lap of 'Whiskers' in the far corner of the room.

Down To The Sea. A Cadet's Tale

"Ahhh, Brian, (he pronounced it Bri-oon) Theese ees my petit poi, ze looverly Arena."

The Little Pea Arena scowled at him. "Ariana." She said.

"Eh?" said Barry.

"Ariana… the name is 'Ariana'!" She was looking annoyed.

Barry grinned. "S'wot I said… Anyway, Araneena here…" He stopped to take a breath at that point, nodding in her direction and began to continue the sentence but realised his Dracula accent had slipped back to Liverpuddlian. His eyes looked furtively at all three of us in turn as he tried, in a split second, to determine whether anyone had noticed.

"Err…Yais," He seemed satisfied that he had got away with it. "Yais… my Ariareena ees inviting me to ride ze 'orse with 'er at ze weekend."

Steven and I stared at him. The very last thing you expect to hear in a ship's bar, at a party, over loud rock music was a Liverpuddlian engineer talking about riding horses in a Transylvanian accent.

Ariana was losing her shyness. "Yeah," she said enthusiastically. "You can come too if you want."

This was not what Barry had in mind. His eyes widened in shock, and he tried to make his mouth protest and stay in character at the same time, but nothing came out.

"Great! … me too!" It was JoJo. He had come up behind Barry and draped his arms around him and Ariana at the same time.

"Yeah." Said Ariana again, "We've got a riding stables up towards Browns Bay. In fact, …" she thought for a moment. "…The more the merrier. Why don't you ask the rest of the lads if they want to come to? … You could get a minibus…won't cost much between you." Her shyness had disappeared completely, and she looked back and forth between us eagerly. She actually reminded me of Cathy, she had the same sort of enthusiasm. That thought immediately gave me the glums and reminded me that I had not had a letter from her despite her promises in that café in London two million years ago.

There was a sort of, anguished whining noise coming from Count Dracula. We all turned to look at him.

"Something wrong Baz?" said JoJo smirking wickedly.

Barry was scowling at him "Naaahh." He said. (I assumed that was 'no' in Transylvanian). "Naaahh, I am… how you say? … forget me… I 'ave leave ze 'orse riding trousers at my 'ome." He smiled suddenly, obviously delighted at his inventiveness.

"No, no, it's ok, jeans will do, but if you want, I can get you some jodhpurs." Ariana came to the rescue.

"Yeah mate, there you are, see, all sorted!" Said JoJo slapping Barry on the back. He looked at us then. "What about you two, you up for this? Can you ride?"

"Yes." We said, again in unison.

It was actually true, we could both ride horses. I had spent nearly every weekend from the age of ten right up to the time I went to the nautical collage riding horses at a stables on the edge of Chobham Common, a few miles from our house near Chertsey in Surrey.

Steven, it turned out, had also been riding, with his father apparently and a local Member of Parliament. In fact, he had, at one time, actually owned one… a horse that is… not a Member of Parliament.

All this came out in a rush of conversation that left poor old Count Barry Dracula standing outside the group looking on bewildered. However, after a while plans were made for the next weekend, JoJo seemed to be the keenest and took over the arranging. Both Steven and I were enthusiastic and promised to come if we had the time off and Barry, well, Barry just looked bewildered and angry in turns but agreed in the end to come. He could do nothing else really, he was clearly besotted with the lovely Ariana.

Not long after that, the party sort of fizzled out. Most people, officers, and guests alike, had gone. Some of the girls had left alone ordering taxis to take them home. This included Ariana, who gave poor bewildered Barry a peck on his Transylvanian cheek and left with Marlene who had been manning the Bar after Ian had gone to bed, but not before, I discovered later, she had given JoJo her phone number. (Ariana that is, not Marlene.) Those attendee's that had… erm… gone off on pairs to cement international relations… were still cementing and 'Whiskers' and Jasmine were still snoring in the corner.

'All in all,' I thought, *'A good night!'*

The next day was all go. We were both up early, Steven and I, helping to open hatches, rig lighting and filling in the cargo times book. As usual Steven woke up properly about an hour later.

"Oi!" The mate shouted at me as I raced past his cabin on my way to get changed back into my boilersuit after breakfast. "What are you up to?"

I skidded to a halt. "Just going to get changed and let Steven go for his breakfast." I said warily, wondering what was coming next.

"Right, well," he said without looking at me, "You two can work as normal the rest of the week, then, as there is no cargo work on Saturday or Sunday you can have that time off." He pushed his chair back, put his feet on his desk and turned his head towards me, grinning. "I suggest you both make the most of it."

"Right yes we will." I said. "Thank you… erm sir… thank you."

He picked up a newspaper and disappeared behind it. "Tell Waddington I want see him before he has his breakfast, will you?"

"Yes sir." I said tripping over the ever-present door sill as I turned and ran off down the alleyway.

The rest of the week was, actually, only that day, which was Thursday and then Friday. Both days were hectic for us, we ran back and forth at the behest of our superiors, going for things, finding people, helping to clear up things, helping mend things, holding tools and stuff for people while they mended other, more technical things and of course making sure flags were put up and taken down at the right times and that all the deck and accommodation lights were turned on before it got dark and were turned off before breakfast in the morning.

All the stuff that had been put in the ship in London now came out of the ship. Boxes and crates of everything from car parts to stockings, from toys to refrigerators. Barrels of washing up liquids to dangerous chemicals. Everything you could think of seemed to have been loaded and was now on its way to new owners. Well, into the giant sheds that lined the dock, anyway.

As in London, it was quite a sight, organised bedlam with a background orchestral movement of squeaking, rattling cranes, loud shouts, revving lorry engines and clanging hatch covers. The gangway bounced constantly and made its own particular clanging noise as people raced up and down it either looking for someone or bringing information and pieces of paper to sign.

In the evenings, the bar filled with people, Engineers, Mates, cadets, and some of the girls from the party who had become attached to various ... erm...members of staff..were there as well, so it was quite lively at night.

On the Thursday evening JoJo came to our cabin and announced that Ariana would arrive on Saturday morning in her brother's station wagon, early, to pick up the four us budding cavalrymen and take us to her parents riding and pony trekking establishment for a day on horseback and a bar-be-que, which would cost us five Kiwi dollars each. Sounded good to me. 'At last,' I thought, 'a chance to show off at something I know I can do.'

"Barry's crapping himself." Chortled JoJo. "Not only has he never been on a horse, but he also thinks he's got keep up that ridiculous accent all day in order to impress Ariana!"

And so, it came to pass. Ariana duly arrived at seven o'clock that Saturday morning with the promised station wagon, and we all piled in. Barry leapt in the front so he could sit next to his beloved. "I 'ave waiting for yuieu mon cher." He said with a serious frown. "Yuieu 'ave been in my 'art." His accent was gradually moving west, and Transylvania had moved a couple of countries closer to France. There was a definite Gallic feel to it now.

"Err yeah… right." Said Ariana frowning back at him, then she let the clutch out a tad too quick and we rocketed away, out of the dock area and off up Queen Street.

From that point on the only person to speak was Ariana as she talked non-stop about anything and everything but mostly about Auckland and the surrounding area. She was, obviously, proud of her city. The other reason nobody else spoke was sheer terror. The car had only two speeds; very, very, very, fast or stop and Ariana seemed to have learned to drive at the Ayrton Senna School of Motoring. I actually felt sorry for Barry sitting in the front.

It took about an hour to get to the stables, and we were all, I think, relieved when we pulled of a tree lined country road onto a gravel track that curved off into the woods. Ariana continued to talk as she waved when we passed several riders coming in the opposite direction.

"That was my mother taking a bunch kids on an early lesson." She explained.

We came out of the woods and I could see the road gently arcing away to our right with grass fields stretching to low hills on either side. At the end of arced drive was an open gate which seemed to lead into a courtyard of some sort surrounded by a collection of low buildings and by the time a minute had passed we were shuddering to a stop outside a large wooden shed just inside the gate.

"Right, this is the tack room." Said Ariana leaping out of the car. "Let's get you sorted.

"Sorted?" Said Barry looking even more terrified than he did before.

JoJo slapped him on the shoulder as he unwound himself from back seat.

"Yeah mate, sorted!" He elongated the last word making it sound menacing.

We were ushered into the tack room which was deceptively large with rows of saddles on brackets on one wall and bridles on hooks on the far wall. Ariana was already seated at the small wooden desk opposite the door.

"Brian you're on 'Tramp', Barry you're on 'Hiawatha', Steven you're on 'Popeye' and JoJo you're on 'Midnight'. She reeled off the horse's names and ticked something off each name in a large stiff-backed notebook after each name. We duly handed over five dollars each and she then led us over to a long row of stalls, each one with a horse's head sticking out over the closed half of the stable door. Each one, that is except for one at the end.

"Right, Barry, that one on the end is yours." Said Ariana pointing.

"But there's no one in it!" wailed Barry.

Ariana turned and looked at him, a huge grin slowly forming on her mouth. We all looked him.

"Ahhh!" she exclaimed. "You 'ave forget you zee accent of ze Transylvania?"

Barry's shoulders dropped and his face turned red as he realised his last sentence had been broadcast in pure Liverpuddlian.

"Shit!" He breathed eloquently.

Everybody burst into hysterical laughter and all the horses retreated into their stables in one movement.

I felt sorry for Barry, he had put so much work into his Count Dracula pick up technique but all to no avail.

"Anyway," Ariana was still giggling, "let's get moving. You blokes have ridden before so you can sort yourselves out...Barry, you come with me." She was all efficiency and in command. I began to wonder what had happened to the shy girl that had been following Count Dracula around in our bar only a few days earlier and how she had come to be at a ship's party in the first place.

The three of us that had ridden horses before took our mounts from their stables and led them to the centre of the courtyard while Ariana helped Barry who was looking thoroughly dejected by now. She helped him mount up and gave him instructions while she tightened the girth and made sure his feet were in the stirrups properly, placing each one in the correct position like she would with a child novice. Barry just sat, shoulders slumped and looked exactly that; a small child on his first riding lesson. He let out a small whimper as a grinning Ariana led him to join us.

We sat in a row looking at each other.

The Kiwi Star Cavalry was ready. Barry whimpered again.

CHAPTER 30

KIWI STAR CAVALRY

We rode slowly out of the courtyard and back down the driveway to the woods and then turned off onto a narrow track that wound its way into the trees.

Ariana was in front, attached to Barry's horse by a novices leading reign, while Barry himself was slumped on his mount, gripping the front of his saddle and the reigns with white knuckled hands. Every time there was a slight change in direction there was a sudden tension in his shoulders, a stiffening of his arms, an even tighter grip on the saddle and another small whimper would escape his lips.

He was not having a fun time. Occasionally he would try and turn his head and glance back towards the rest of us, but that just caused an instant loss of balance and he would suddenly stiffen and jerk his head back to a forward looking position. After a while it became obvious that he had decided to keep his head rigidly still and facing forward, which transmitted to the rest of his body. So, from behind it looked as though he was sitting to attention with his head thrust forward, his previous slump gone. We couldn't see it, but it was easy to imagine the wild eyed, panic stricken look on his face.

JoJo had picked up on all this immediately.

"All ok up there Barry?"

Barry said something, a couple of words only, but I could only hear the last one which was "Off."

"Sorry Barry," said JoJo. "Didn't quite catch that, you'll have to turn your head round."

Silence.

"Oh Baa…ree." Sang JoJo, grinning.

Silence.

"We still can't here you." JoJo extended the last two words and warbled them at Barry's back.

Silence.

"Baa…" he started again.

You could feel Barry's temper emanating from his rigid skull. It was too much for him, he spun round in the saddle in a spine snapping twisting movement, his eyes blazing, and his face all screwed up.

"Fuh … Ahh … Heehahoo!" he shouted, the last syllable an octave higher. I am fairly sure he meant to say, "Fuck Off," but the sudden movement when he twisted round caused his left hand to retract towards his body suddenly. Now, as his left hand was attached to the left rein and as said left rein was attached to the bit in his horse's mouth, the head of the horse moved sharply to the left. Therefor the horse, quite naturally, thought it was being instructed to turn to the left and obligingly did so. It took several paces to the left and stopped. Meanwhile, Barry, taken completely by surprise and trying to turn around, lost his balance completely and slid slowly off the saddle to the right. Too add to his problems, whereas his left foot slid out of his stirrup, his right foot did not.

"Ooff!" The noise from his mouth came immediately his back hit the ground. He lay there for a second stunned before the panic-stricken look returned. The horse, feeling the lightening of the load and the noise slowly looked round, lowered its head, stared at him inquisitively, flicked one ear as a sort of question and then instantly lost interest, turning back to apply full concentration to a tasty looking tuft of grass.

JoJo laughed out loud. Unfortunately, this startled his horse which leapt forward with a remarkably rabbit like hop, causing JoJo to become unseated and shoot upward, his feet losing contact with his stirrups. Well, lose contact with everything, really. The horse took another bound sideways, ensuring that it was not in the same place when JoJo came back down again.

"Ooff!" exclaimed Barry, again, as JoJo landed on top of him.

"Ow! …Ow! …Oowoo! Shouted JoJo.

All this ow…ing and ooff…ing now further startled all the horses. Mine in particular, which copied JoJo's horse in its rabbit imitation routine, depositing me on the ground in short order.

In the meantime, Barry's horse, being again startled, quickly lost interest in the tasty tuft and took off after the other two riderless nags dragging Barry, with JoJo on top along the path. Fortunately, the stirrup strap on Barry's saddle came loose from its retainer after a few yards leaving him and JoJo cuddling each other on the ground while all three horses cantered off round the bend and out of sight.

I sat up, rubbing my shoulder which had taken the brunt of the meeting with the ground, and looked around. Arianna was calming her horse down which was prancing around looking angry, the other girl from the stables who had come with us was doing much the same, and Barry was busy trying to heave JoJo, who was still laughing, off him. My gaze moved slowly over the scene until I was looking back up the path. There was Steven and his horse looking remarkably similar with fixed sad looking expressions, staring at us without moving.

"Shut up!" I said.

Steven raised one eyebrow and the horse twitched one ear.

JoJo was still laughing.

"It's not funny!" scowled Barry. "I could have been killed! Trampled to death by this bloody herd of wild animals!"

"Yeah!" shouted Arianna looking directly at JoJo. "That was all your fault! Why do you always have to be so juvenile" She was really angry. "Now we've got to catch three bloody horses!"

JoJo was still laughing as the two girls trotted off to start the search.

"Yeah, juvenile." Barry was checking his entire body for injuries.

"Yeah juvenile." I echoed. Truth was I was feeling silly having fell off a horse and was glad of someone to blame.

JoJo continued to chortle to himself, while Steven and his horse continued their mournful staring.

"Does this mean we won't get our bar-b-que?" He said.

We all looked at him and all said something different at the same time.

"Shut up!"

"Fuck off!"

"Dunno!"

We did get our bar-b-que.

In fact, it didn't take long for the girls to capture the horses. Apparently, horses don't gallop away for miles. They soon lose interest in escape, preferring to seek out something tasty to eat, so Arianna soon appeared round the bend leading JoJo's horse.

"Mandy's bringing your horse." she said, looking down at a blank faced Barry who said nothing. "Here's yours." She held out the rein to JoJo who was still grinning like Cheshire cat.

"Thank you kindly, ma'am." He said, bowing deeply with mock courtesy. Arianna grinned back and I saw something in their eyes that passed between them. That made me think. Arianna had said to JoJo, when he was laughing about the horses running off, "Why do you always have to be so juvenile?" ... My mind raced a little. *'Always?'* ... *She had said 'Always'*.

"Hey mate, here's your horse." I was still busy working out this JoJo-stroke-Ariana relationship and hadn't heard Mandy come up behind me. Also, I found I was still sitting on the ground. Mandy held out the reins towards me and I held out my hand to take them, but she deftly grabbed it with her other hand and helped me to my feet. She smiled at me and held on to my hand for a little longer than necessary. I smiled back. There is something about the first physical contact with a female of the opposite sex that is like nothing else. Particularly when there is a realisation that that particular female, at the very least, likes you. There is a sort of electric charge that passes between you. Unfortunately, I didn't notice any of this electric charge stuff, I was far too immature and naïve to cotton on to anything like that straight away.

"Thanks." I muttered as she released me and used the same hand to reach round and start brushing the mud and twigs from my back. I, as usual, went bright red.

"You're blushing!" Announced Steven loudly. Cathy, immediately and inconveniently popped into my head. I could see her standing in my cabin, head tilted on one side. Immediate mental anguish rushed into my head, but then also crowding in came the thought that I had not had a letter from her since we left London. Nothing at all.

"I'm not." I hissed at him, busying myself with saddle and stirrup arrangements as everybody else looked at me.

"Are!" said Steven.

"Not!" I said. I went around the other side away from staring eyes. My horse turned his head and peered at me, flicking an ear towards me at the same time. I scowled back it him, convinced he was grinning at me.

I climbed aboard, adjusted the girth, and turned my horse in circle to keep my traffic light red face away from everybody else and realised, in that instant, that Mandy was a fit, young, pretty girl with long brown hair. Why had I not noticed her before? Now I was angry! Angry because I had not had a letter from Cathy. Angry because she had dared to pop, uninvited, into my head. Angry because I had not noticed Mandy and angry because both these girls, together had teamed up to... to... well... make me angry and make me red in the face! Mandy was already back on her horse and she winked at me as my eye line passed hers. I frowned at myself, then tried to change expression and wink back at the same time which made me look like a bulldog chewing a wasp. Mandy's expression became inquisitive but, luckily, she had no time to dwell on it.

"Come on you two!" Arianna already had her horse walking brusquely along the path and the others had followed. Mandy, me, and my newly anguished mind followed.

The ride to the bar-b-que place was uneventful. Arianna and JoJo led the way, chatting and laughing, followed by an extremely hacked off Barry with Steven close behind looking all stooped in the saddle. I was next with Mandy bringing up the rear and we all sauntered along at a sedate pace until the path began to rise and a bit more effort from the horses was required.

At the top of the rise the trees suddenly gave way to a broad open grassy hillock with one solitary small tree halfway up. Larger green rolling hills stretched further beyond the one our mounts took us up. When I say green, I mean, green, very green. The New Zealand version of green hills is entirely different to the English version. It is difficult to describe. You have to see it to believe it. If you have been there and seen it you will know what I mean. If not, take my word for it, it is worth the trip.

I could see smoke rising just beyond the hillock and as we crested the top, a long low wooden building appeared, the roof extending further down at the front to form a cover for a paved area on which stood a large stone bar-b-que which was the source of the smoke. Next to it was a long table with bowls of something arranged down the middle and cutlery all laid out. Chairs were scattered each side of the table. It was a beautiful setting made perfect by the aroma of cooking meat from the bar-b-que.

Mandy rode up beside me. "Hungry?"

"Very!" I answered her query with some enthusiasm, and she laughed.

"Me too!" She said and spurred her horse to a trot, overtaking the rest of the column which would have been ok, however, one of our mounts took exception to being passed and suddenly leapt forward in order to keep up with Mandy. It was, of course, Hiawatha, Barry's horse. Ears flat, eyes rolling, the animal shot forward suddenly, causing a terrified squealing noise to escape from Barry's mouth as he bounced around, legs flailing, while both hands flew straight between his legs and grabbed the front of his saddle in a white knuckled death grip. Mandy pulled her horse up and watched as Barry rocketed passed her heading for the long table with the bowls of something on it.

At that moment, an older woman appeared at the door of the building, it was the woman we had seen when we were driving up the track to the stables, Arianna's Mother.

"Strewth!" She exclaimed. Mind the table!"

I can only assume that Hiawatha recognised the voice of someone in authority, without hesitation she changed direction ninety degrees and stopped. Barry did not. For the second time inside an hour, he parted company with his transport, again his body continued the line of original motion. This time, though his right knee did not clear the saddle, so, although his body wanted to carry on in a straight line it was prevented from doing so by that inconvenient knee. The horse turned sharp right and stopped, Barry left the saddle and carried straight on for a couple of feet until the knee engaged, this caused him then to follow his horse. However, as the horse stopped suddenly and unlike the last unseating incident, this time raised her head, Barry's nether regions collided with the area just behind her ears, leaving him, just for a second or two perched on top of Hiawatha's head. This, of course, was not to the animals liking, nor was the way Barry's hands, having been forced to relinquish their death grip on the saddle and desperately seeking something to grab hold of, were gripping her ears. She dropped her head suddenly. This had the desired effect. His hands left the ear grip and he finally contacted the ground, fingers first, in a sort of handstand with his feet still in the stirrups. Hiawatha then raised her head, so it was now topside of all of Barry with her nose close to his buttocks, which she sniffed gently and then started to back away. Barry's fingers scrabbled desperately in the dirt.

"Help!" he wailed.

The Kiwi Star Cavalry looked on in stunned silence. We had all come to a stop while this spectacle unfolded.

Steven, looking mournful, was the first to speak.

"Barry's fallen off again." He said.

It was a pity Barry missed the bar-b-que. It was wonderful. There were steaks the size of a small hippopotamus, lumps of lamb, burgers, sausages, potatoes of all types, crusty bread, five different salads and endless sauces, pickles, and dips.

'Magnificent!' I thought. 'These people really know how to eat.'

I had a brief attack of feeling sorry for Barry, but it went away halfway through my first sausage and it wasn't until we'd nearly scoffed the entire contents of the table that Steven mentioned him.

"I wonder how far Barry's got?" he said wiping lumps of grease and lamb chop off his face. He didn't get much response. Everybody was too busy finishing off their own lumps of meat and it was Aryanna's mother who finally said.

"Hope your friend made it back to the stables ok."

JoJo looked up and replied. "Yeah, he'll be alright, he's just got a bit of a paddy on, that's all. Once he's calmed down, he'll see the funny side of it."

"Dunno about that," said Steven in between nibbles of his last chop bone. "He was pretty steamed up about it!"

"It'll take him a while, walking." Said Arianna's Mum.

"Mmmm." JoJo was non-committal, being still engrossed in picking meat off bones.

Arianna's Mum continued.

"Particularly as he is walking the wrong way."

"The wrong way?" I said frowning.

Barry, or... poor Barry as I should probably now refer to him... had, finally snapped. With superhuman strength he had managed to dig his hands into the dirt and stop Hiawatha dragging him further backwards and Arianna's Mum then came to the rescue, caught hold of the horse and untangled Barry from the stirrups,

"That's it!" He roared as he got his feet "No more Fu...!" He stopped and looked at Arianna's Mum who was still holding his arm and frowning at him. "No more friggin' horses!" He glared at each one of us, daring someone to argue with him.

Nobody spoke. He finished glaring and said.

"I'm walking back. You can stick your bar-b-friggin-que and your friggin horses!" With that he turned on his heel and stomped off back down the track we had just come along. The Kiwi Star cavalry had silently watched him march away over the hill.

"Yeah." Arianna took over from her mother. "We've been riding in a big... erm... sort of circle. If he wants to walk to the stables all he had to do was go over that hill." She pointed to another low hillock just past the building. "The riding centre is about two hundred yards that way. Once we get cleared up, if we get moving in... say... about fifteen minutes, we'll be back well before him."

Steven looked in the direction Barry had gone, then looked back the way Arianna was pointing, frowned and looked worried.

"He was a bit cross when he left," he said, shaking his head. "He's going to be really, really cross when he walks into the stables and finds us already there!"

"Mmmm." Said JoJo. He had found more meat clinging to the underside of a chop.

As it turned out we did get back before Barry even after more riding around the countryside. Arianna's Mother, whose name was Mary, took us on a tour of the valleys and hills. As I have said before it's a beautiful country and I wish I had appreciated it more at the time. But, of course, at that age, appreciation of local beauty spots was not at the top my agenda.

During our tour around the area JoJo, Arianna and her mother, Mary had stayed together mostly, Steven trotted along behind them in a world of his own, which left me to chat and get to know Mandy. She was extremely easy to talk to, funny, highly intelligent (way above my intellect) and very inquisitive about England and all things English. She was at collage and intended training to be a vet and... well, I rather liked her, which gave me some guilty feelings over Cathy, who kept popping into my head every so often, but... *'She hasn't written to me!'* I thought to myself indignantly. *'She said she would!'* The trouble was, I could remember saying to her I would write, but I couldn't actually recall her saying she would write to me. *'She must have done... I'm sure she did... yes, I am absolutely positive she said she'd write... I think.'* Of course, it still hadn't occurred to me that I hadn't been anywhere near a writing pad or a pen all trip.

We arrived back at the stables after about an hour having gone past the bar-b-que place again. Arianna had been right, it took us exactly five minutes to ride, slowly, from there to courtyard. Barry arrived, limping, and looking murderous, about five minutes later. However, he said nothing and neither did we although Steven opened his mouth and seemed to be about to speak to him, but JoJo gave him a withering stare.

"Enjoy that, Stevey boy?"

"Erm yes, very good, but..."

"Good, good." JoJo cut him off mid-sentence and continued glaring at him. Steven got the picture and shut up.

The drive back to the ship was uneventful, but I got a real boost to my ego when Mandy gave me a hug and kissed me on the cheek before I got into the car. I went red again, of course but managed, what I hoped sounded like a casual question.

"Do you get into Auckland much?"

She looked directly at me "No," she said. My hopes plummeted to my boots which was a strange feeling as up to that moment I didn't realise I had hopes.

"But I can get there easily." She grinned. "I have a car."

CHAPTER 31

THE LETTER

It was when I got back to the ship that the letter arrived. I was shocked, excited, horrified and felt guilty all at once.

Shocked that someone had actually sent a letter, excited because I wanted to read it, horrified when I found it was from Cathy, horrified and guilty because I had just a couple of hours before arranged to meet Mandy on the steps of the Post Office in Queens Street the very next day. (Anybody reading this who has been to Auckland on a ship will remember this meeting place.) Girlfriends of seaman down through the ages have uttered the immortal words.

"Yip, Ahl meet you at tin t tin on the powst offiss stips"

I had snatched the letter from the Chief Stewards hand as he held it out. Then felt guilty for snatching.

"Sorry." I said far too loudly and scurried off like a ferret that has taken a chunk out of the hand that has just fed it. Of course I had ripped the thing open by the time I reached the cabin, but unfortunately it was one of those airmail letters, you know, the blue things that you needed a degree in origami to open. So by the time I had finished ripping it to shreds trying to find the writing, it was in four separate pieces and I had to lay it out on the table and fit it back together in an arrangement that made the scribble readable.

Steven, who had already wearily staggered into the cabin ahead of me, watched with interest from his position stretched out on the daybed, his eyes peering over the edge of the table.

"Letter from Mum and Dad?" he enquired.

"No!" I said, again a little too sharply. Stevens question had engendered yet more guilt because I hadn't written home yet and I knew I should have done. He flopped his head back down on the cushion and lost interest in me.

I started reading.

Dear Bryan,

'Well that hurt for a start. She can't even spell my name right!'

Haven't heard from you so I thought I would write to you. I had expected you to send me a letter from Panama.

'More guilt!'

Anyway, nothing much happening here, been to a couple of good parties and got really drunk at one of them.

'Parties! Parties? Weddings off! How can this woman of mine even THINK of going to parties when I am sailing the seven seas, risking life and limb ...? What's more she's getting drunk to boot.'

My disappointment and righteous indignation knew no bounds and I stopped reading and paced up and down. Well, as there wasn't much room for pacing I went round in an exceedingly small circle and made as much noise as possible while doing it to wake Steven who had, annoyingly drifted off to sleep during my world ending trauma.

"What! What! Wha..? He spluttered as he came to suddenly. Raising himself to table-top level.

"Nothing!" I said, but at the same time was thinking

'That'll teach him to sleep through such a ... such a... such a ... thing!'

There was a knock on the open cabin door and the Chief Steward marched in.

"Ah, there you are." He frowned. "You grabbed one letter out of my hand and didn't give me a chance to give you the other one." He said.

He thrust another blue origami kit in my direction which made me feel even worse as even more guilt flooded over me. I could see my mother's handwriting on it. I took the letter and he left, still frowning.

By now I was in a totally confused state, convinced that the entire world was conspiring to make my life a misery. My face was all gathered together in a kind of, 'whole face' frown with my eyebrows that close they were in danger of knitting themselves together.

"Your frowning." Said Steven. I opened my mouth to answer but he continued speaking. "Don't know what you have to be upset about." He looked up at me. "Nobody writes to me."

That one simple sentence bought about an epiphany! A realisation! A boy to man moment!

I felt instantly guilty at being such a selfish, unthinking arsehole.

"What?... not even your Mum and Dad!"

He flopped back down on the daybed.

"Erm, well... apart from them." He sighed a wistful sigh and closed his eyes. "But even then my mother writes the letter and my father just signs it."

I didn't know what to say to that. Luckily Steven kept his eyes closed and appeared to be on the point of nodding off again.

I smoothed out my letter which had become a crumpled, squashed ball in my clenched, angry, indignant fist, and read on...

> **Met some really funny guys at one party, they were all student dentists. You would have liked them.**
> *No I wouldn't... and b. Don't want to know any more!'*

I read on.

> **One of them, Miles, was very nice and took me to a concert in Hyde Park the other day.**
> *'Miles! Miles the dentist!'*

I leapt (again) to my feet and paced in a circle (again). Murderous thoughts concerning anyone remotely connected with dentistry invaded my tiny brain. I vowed there and then never, ever to visit a dentist again... ever! That would teach her and the... the...Guild of Better Dentistry.. Hah!... and what's more she would have my rotting gums on her conscience!

The letter, scrunched into a ball shape by my white knuckled grip, bounced around the inside of our small rubbish bin.

Gentle snoring came from Stevens direction. I glared at him...

'And you can fuck off as well!' I thought loudly and sat back down on the chair with a thump.

Steven snored on. I sulked for a few seconds and then JoJo appeared in the cabin.

He stared at me for a while then said, "You two fancy a walk up the road after?"

I looked at my watch. Ten past five.

"Yeah, why not." I muttered sulkily. Steven snored on.

"Fuckin' 'ell!" said JoJo. "Maybe a little enthusiasm might not go amiss." He stuck his head forward and raised his eyebrows to emphasise his point. Then he noticed my other airmail letter on the table.

"Ah hah!" he said, smiling a knowing smile. "The mail." He tilted his head to one side and his face took on an annoying sympathetic look. "Been dumped, have we? You definitely need a run up the road then."

I frowned an angry frown at him and opened my mouth to tell him that the letter he was looking at was from my parents, but I didn't actually get that far.

"Horses!" shouted Steven suddenly sitting bolt upright on the daybed, his eyes wide and staring. A tuft of hair sticking strait up from the top of his head.

Both JoJo and I stared at him in silence. There isn't really much you can say to a shout of 'Horses!' Steven stared back in an obviously confused state.

"Oh... Oh... erm... sorry... dreaming." He flopped back down on the daybed. Well, he would have flopped back down but during its upward trajectory his upper body had caused a slight movement of his lower body backwards... towards the bulkhead at the end of the daybed... so... he only got three quarters of his flop towards his previous prone position when his head connected with the aforementioned bulkhead with a resounding crack.

"OW, HOOHOO HAFF!" he bellowed sitting back up again and clutching his head with both hands.

We continued to stare at him.

"JoJo wants to know if we want to go up the road later." I said gently.

"Oooh." Said Steven quietly.

JoJo shook his head, turned and headed for the door.

"I'll stick me head in about seven on the way out... be in the bar til then."

"Oooh." Repeated Steven.

I sat and sulked some more.

"Where's Barry?"

JoJo had, as promised stuck his head in the door of the cabin on his way ashore. I had leapt to my feet and hurried out, hair still wet from the shower, trendy flares flapping, silly big-collared shirt far too yellow and platform shoes sounding like a battalion of Dutch clog dancers.

"Erm.... he's not coming." Said JoJo a bit sheepishly. "He's still mad at me over Arianna." He looked over my shoulder. "Where's Steven?"

"On his bunk snoring again... said his head was hurting so he lay dawn with his book on Steam Reciprocating Engines."

"Would have thought 'Steam Reciprocating Engines' would have made it worse!" said JoJo frowning and looking me up and down, his face taking on a pained expression. He opened his mouth to say something but closed it suddenly, shook his head, turned and strode off down the alleyway "Anyway, just us then... we'll go and get a beer." He said after a few steps.

"I'm not old enough." I said, stopping.

"Don't worry about it." JoJo strode on. So I followed.

We rattled our way down the gangway and along the wharf towards the gate.

Curiosity got the better of me even before we got out of the dock gate and onto Queens Street.

"So erm, wha.. what's with Arianna and Barry?" I stuttered as I made valiant efforts to keep up with JoJo's giant strides.

"Ahh, well... It's my fault I suppose." He said. "I have known Ariana for a couple of years now. I met her on my first trip here. In fact I had to change ships here last year. Some bloke on the **Rockhampton Star** broke his leg and they were shorthanded anyway so I changed over from the **Timaru Star** and ended up spending an entire month here.

One week of it in a hotel... with Ariana." He paused and grinned. "Best trip to sea ever!"

We scurried over to the other side of the street and continued apace past what appeared to be Woolworths.

"So Barry didn't know any of this?"

"Nah." He looked sheepish for the second time that evening. "Should have told him really... but it was just so funny watching him do his Count Dracula act."

He fell silent then and concentrated on looking for a suitable watering hole.

I felt sorry for Barry. It wasn't actually turning out to be a good trip so far for him. What with being flung out of the New York Bar, chased by a collection of angry Panamanian prostitutes, bouncers and other ne'er do wells, being held at bay by a tree trunk, falling off horses, having his powers of seduction ridiculed and then finding out he was trying to get off with the wrong woman, he must be wondering what next!

"Here we are, this'll do." JoJo disappeared through an open door. I galloped after him, trendy flares still flapping.

"So.. Brian... you've been dumped."

We had found a corner of a wooden shelf to lean on. The place I had followed JoJo into was long and thin with a bar down one side and this 'leaning shelf' sort of thing down the other side. Not a chair or table in sight! JoJo had ordered a jug of beer and brought it over with two glasses while I remained at the shelf guarding our claimed territory. The barman looked suspiciously over at me, but he was obviously busy so his attention was quickly taken by more demands for service.

"Erm... well... I don't know." I answered him and felt immediately stupid. Not for being dumped by Cathy but for sounding so pitiful.

"Anyway, I'm seeing Mandy from the stables tomorrow if she can come to Auckland." I paused for dramatic affect and took a swig of my beer. "She has a car."

"Yes, I know." He looked at me over his beer. "She's a nice girl, and... what's more she's a cousin of the lovely Ariana."

Another revelation! All this was becoming a bit of a soap opera.. sort of nautical Coronation Street... sea going Payton Place!

"Anyway," continued JoJo, "What did Cathy have to say, I mean, how did she finish the letter.

"Why do you want to know?"

He shrugged. "Just making conversation. We all get letters like that. There was a bloke on my last ship got three. Three!. All at the same time!"

I looked at him disbelievingly.

"True!" He exclaimed, laughing. "He had three girlfriends, one in Los Angeles one in Singapore and one in Chipping Norton."

"Chipping Norton!" I laughed. "So she was his regular girlfriend I suppose.

JoJo stopped laughing and looked puzzled.

"No." he said.

We continued to lean in silence for a while.

"Well?" he said.

"Well what?" I stood up straight. Why I don't know, it just seemed the appropriate thing to do.

"How did she tell you?"

"She said she met a dentist at a party."

"And...?"

"She said he was really funny."

"And...?"

"He took her to a concert."

JoJo thought for a while with a frown on his face.

"That doesn't mean he's shagging her does it?" He said in a really annoying matter of fact sort of tone.

I gaped at him.

"Just means she went to a concert. So... how did she finish the letter?"

"Well... well she ..erm ...erm." I ran out of things to say.

"Erm.. I haven't actually read the end of it."

He turned and looked at me.

"Yet." I added, feeling not a little stupid.

"You haven't read...!" He raised his eyes to the heavens.

"So how do you know you've been dumped?"
"Well... it's obvious isn't it. She's going out with a dentist!" I shouted.
"I suggest, you idiot, you go and read the end of the bloody letter!"
I had no answer to that. Mainly because he was right, of course.
"What now?" was all I could think of saying.
"Yes, now! You won't rest until you have, now, will you?"
He drained his glass. "You go back, I'm going further up Queens Street."

I smoothed the crumpled letter out on the desk while I listened to Stevens' rattling snores. As soon as JoJo had left the bar I had virtually ran all the way back and crashed into the cabin. Steven hadn't moved from his opened mouthed prone position I had left him in. I did fleetingly wonder if he had succumbed to his head wound and rigor mortis had set in, but my crashing through the door filtered, after a few seconds, through to his brain and after an initial explosive snort and a very loud fart he began his usual rhythmic snoring. I raced over to the waste bin, pulled out the letter and proceeded to, again, smooth it out.

I read on.

> *Anyway it wasn't a very good concert and he turned out to be a bit of a prick. He tried to grab me so I left him there and drove home!*

I now felt totally and utterly bereft for the opposite reason from my earlier bereftness. It wasn't him that was the prick... (Well... he was a prick for trying to grab her) ... but I was just as much of a prick for jumping to conclusions and thinking she had gone off with a dentist!

> *Nothing much else has happened here, weather has been awfull of course. Oh, I got the puncture fixed, it made me think of you...*

'Not sure that's meant as a statement of endearment!'

> *...and that last night we were together.*

'Ahh, I see... there I go again, conclusion jumping!'

So, no more news from here. Hope you write soon and hope to see you when you get back.

Love...

She had signed it... **Kathy xxxxxx.**
'Kathy! With a K!'
I tried to think back. Why did I think her name began with a 'C'? I gave up in short order... too difficult for my shallow mind. Anyway, it was too busy dealing with my monumental stupidity. Why would you not read the whole letter? Idiot! Still. It meant that I wasn't dumped. A grin began to play around the corners of my mouth and threatened to become a full smile. But not for long. Guilt appeared again in the form of Mandy. I had promised to meet her tomorrow night.

Women! I frowned and paced for a while and then attempted to ease my guilt by reading the other letter I had been given, the one from my Mother. But of course that didn't help. By the time I had heard all about how deep the snow had been, the problems with the car, my sisters triumphs and disasters at school, fathers failed attempts at buying a new car, not to mention the trauma caused to Mr. and Mrs Greenfield next door when their main water pipe burst, flooding the entire ground floor and ruining the brand new three piece suite, I was beyond suicidal and approaching serial killer mode. So I gave in and decided that Steven had the right idea, grabbed the paperback I had been trying to start since we left London, scrambled up into my top bunk, switched on the reading light, battled momentarily with an uncooperative pillow and opened the book. I then read the same page I had read five times before and nodded off.

Our stay in Auckland lasted nearly three weeks. All the cargo that had been loaded in London was for this one port, There were huge crates of machine parts, large, thin crates of sheet glass, cardboard boxes full of metal containers of something and metal containers probably full of cardboard boxes of something. All of this was labelled as general cargo on the cargo plan. It all came whizzing out at some speed via the shoreside cranes and our own deck cranes and derricks. Our heavy lift forty ton

Down To The Sea. A Cadet's Tale

Stulken was only used for that huge lorry that had been removed from one of the lower holds when we first arrived. It was never used again that trip.

For the next two weeks after our horse riding episode Steven, JoJo, Barry and myself settled into our own routines. JoJo and Barry worked a normal daily routine in the engine room but didn't socialise much. JoJo disappeared ashore to meet Ariana most evenings while Barry, apart from a couple of brief shopping trips 'up the road' stayed in the bar after work. Steven and I galloped around the ship fetching and finding out, delivering information to chief officers, second officers, third officers and on one or two occasions to Captain McHale himself. This was usually after a brief argument as to whose turn it was to go up the Stairs of Doom to his cabin. Somehow it always seemed to be me.... something to do with my rank apparently.

As usual flags were hoisted and lowered at the right times. Likewise, deck lights were turned on and off, also at the right times. To begin with this was done by both of us but later it seemed to be just me.... something to do with my rank apparently.

One of the jobs I was assigned to was to "Guard" a consignment of several tons of cartons of whiskey. I was left on my own in a lower hold to watch the dockers and drive forklift trucks into the darkest corners of the hold then return with pallets containing several dozen cartons, all wobbling precariously on the forks of the truck. It was then plonked onto a larger pallet, hooked up to wire strops and whisked away out of the hatch. All that precarious wobbling led to some ... erm ... spillage and breakage leading to some interesting, shall we say, situations. and.... well... I was the only form of security down there..... something to do with my rank, apparently... But they are stories for another book.

Loading had started after a few days alongside, which really made the ship rattle and thump. Once a hold had been emptied the entire space was scrubbed, cleaned and fumigated, then dunnage was laid, (strips of two by two wood laid in one direction with strips laid diagonally on top. This provided an airflow underneath the stacks of frozen lamb carcasses that were about to be placed in the hold. The freezing cold air that would flow under and around the carcasses was provided by a refrigeration plant lovingly cared for by our Chief Refrigeration Engineer. A huge fierce Scotsman called Alistair who hailed from the same part of the world as our bosun. (Hewn from the same piece of rock I shouldn't wonder.) He was helped by Michael, the 2nd refrigeration Engineer who was the complete opposite of his fierce boss, being a quiet unassuming young man. Tall and gangly with a shock of ginger hair he could usually be found, when not in the engine room, in his cabin reading books on the great steam railway engines of the world. This, of course, meant that he was Steven's hero and the pair had spent a lot of time together whilst we were at sea going into raptures over pictures of the Flying Scotsman and the like.

Anyway, as I said, the loading had started. Large rope slings full of frozen carcasses came flying across the deck and disappeared into the first hold ready, landing with a ship shuddering thump on the dunnaged floor of the space where each carcass was manually carried to its space.

All this meat arriving led to one of the age old cadet tasks on this type of vessel... 'marking off'. As the meat was loaded and stacked, we had to run around with reels of coloured tape and wind it up and down stacks of cargo to denote which meat belonged to which shipper. A task that became more difficult as the amount of cargo increased.

All these frozen dead things had to be loaded in the right order and marked for the various owners. We would race around the hold with our reels of tape wrapping the different colours around the stiff, solid frozen limbs of the lamb carcasses, reporting everything to the second Mate, John, who was responsible for drawing up the plan of the cargo which would be used at the ports of discharge to plan the efficient removal of said frozen things.

It had been the day after "The Letter" had arrived, my social calendar suddenly became empty. Mandy rang to say that our evening meeting in Auckland was off as she had to work late. We didn't make any further arrangements during that call and I had the feeling that her initial enthusiasm for seeing me had waned somewhat and I never actually saw her again. Feelings of rejection and devastation set in briefly but I had guilt running rampant in my head over Cathy and the fact that I hadn't written to her, so that very night I girded my loins, stiffened my resolve, banished my fears, straightened my spine, sat down and put pen to paper. One hour later I had written.... nothing! It actually took until late in the night that

I managed to cobble together a two page missive of whining, apologetic, inane paragraphs that I considered suitable enough to send to my beloved.

There was one moment of panic when I realised that I didn't know her surname and a bit more guilt slipped through for a brief moment when I thought she might have told me, and I had forgotten it. So, I just had to address the letter to 'Katy' and then the address she had given me during our last hour together in that café in London… After the… erm… 'puncture incident'. My face defaulted to its normal traffic light red as I scribbled the address.

My parents got a one page missive. I never was much of a letter writer. I can hear, even now, my Mother's voice every time I returned from a voyage.

"You could have written a bit more often you know!"

Our last day in Auckland was a Wednesday. Loading was completed during the afternoon, well before five o'clock. I had been sent that morning to put up the 'Blue Peter' flag, indicating the ship would be sailing and everybody better get back on board or else, as we had been told we would be sailing at four o'clock.

Four o'clock came and went with us still alongside. Five past four there was a flurry of activity as the ships agent galloped up the gangway and disappeared into Captain McHale's cabin. Shortly after the Mate appeared at our cabin.

"Change of plan." He puffed. "Not leaving until tomorrow morning so flags and lights as normal but leave the Blue Peter up." … and off he went, only to return exactly fifteen seconds later. "…And we are definitely going to Bluff after Gisborne."

Steven looked at me as soon as the Mate was out of the door.

He grinned, then started to chortle. "So… you will get to find out where 'Buff' is. He exaggerated the word to make sure I remembered my asking where 'Buff' was all those decades ago in London.

Very annoying!

CHAPTER 32

GISBORNE

Leaving Auckland was another first for me. Leaving my first proper foreign port. There were even people on the quayside to see us off and I looked down at them from the bridge wing while Dave and I waited for things to get moving after we had prepared the bridge equipment for leaving.

It was a beautiful southern hemisphere summers morning, with not a cloud in sight. There was a gentle breeze blowing directly down a Queen Street immersed in cool, dark shadow, in sharp contrast to the vivid blue sky above. That same breeze gave a perfect lazy feel to the morning. The ship was quiet. There was, of course, the usual hum and buzz from generators and the sounds of the crew from all departments going about their preparations for leaving, but apart from that… peace.

My gaze moved up from the quayside and I turned around. The bright red and blue of the huge Blue Star funnel stood out against the background of the harbour and the New Zealand flag fluttered gently at our mast head. Underneath, the red and white pilot flag did its best to keep up with its bigger neighbour but kept getting one corner caught in the halyard so only half of it could be seen. It denoted that the pilot that would take us out of the confines of Auckland harbour was on board. He had arrived earlier and was in Captain McHale's cabin. Steven had met him at the top of the gangway an hour ago and taken him up, closely followed by a steward bearing a tray laden with tea and biscuits.

John, the Second mate, white tropical shirt gleaming, wandered out of the wheelhouse and joined me on the bridge wing.

"So…" He said, grinning. "What did you think of Auckland?"

"Brilliant!" I exclaimed. Which was exactly what I thought of the place and I could feel a longing to come back building in the back of my mind. That longing jostled for space with the hope of being on a ship the very next voyage that came here.

"Actually…" I started to explain my thoughts to John but was interrupted.

"Tugs are here!" It was Dave walking swiftly across the wheelhouse. "Better ring stations and call the Old Man and the Pilot."

"I'll do that on my way down." Said John. "Where's Steven? He's supposed to be with me down aft when we leave."

"Dunno." Dave and I spoke in unison.

"Last I saw of him he was showing the pilot into the Old Man's cabin." I continued.

John disappeared into the chartroom muttering to himself, something about cadets and places they should be but weren't.

"So," said Dave, grinning just as John had done a few minutes earlier, "what did you think of Auckland?"

"Brilliant!" I said again. "Actually, it…" The tug 'Aucklander' announced its arrival with a deafening blast on its whistle.

"Better press the button for stations," said Dave, "I'll talk to these tugs." He picked up the radio, that he had just that minute put down, from the consul and started speaking while he ambled back out to the port bridge wing.

"Aucklander, Aucklander… New Zealand Star, New Zealand Star… over."

The tug captain replied almost immediately in a broad Kiwi accent. "Yeah… this is Aucklander… Where d'ya want us mate?"

I didn't hear the response; I was busy ringing bells to let everyone know to go to their assigned station for leaving. At the same time the door burst open and Captain McHale and the Pilot swept through the chartroom and into the wheelhouse.

"Ah, young man.," said the captain as he brushed passed. "All ready?"

"Erm... yes Sir, Third Mate is talking to the tugs and stations has been rung."

"Good, good... well," He peered at me and grinned. "What did you think of Auckland laddie?"

"Oh... erm... Brilliant!" I exclaimed for the third time. "It was really..."

"Tugs fast fore and aft sir!" It was Dave shouting through from the bridge wing.

"Thank you, Third Mate." (He did actually say thank you, but I don't actually think Captains ever meant 'thank you' when they said, 'thank you,' It was just a habit. A sort of Master/servant bonding thing.)

He looked at me and raised an eyebrow. I looked back. "Well?" He said.

"Oh... erm... yes," I said, "I think Auckland..." Captain McHale raised his eyes heavenwards and tutted. "No..." He continued. "Have you put all this in the book?"

My brain was forced to change gear rapidly. *'The book? ... ah... of course... yes... the book!'* I had forgotten the movement book. I rushed into the chartroom, grabbed said book and galloped back out. Then galloped back into the chartroom to get a pen.

I didn't look at him, but I could feel the captain's eyes heading heavenwards again and hear his thought. *'Stupid Boy'.*

It appeared, anyway, that nobody was really interested in my opinion of Auckland after all.

Our stay there had, of course been memorable to me. My first proper foreign port. My first ships party. My first experience of unloading. Lots of firsts in fact.

"Let go aft!" Captain McHale shouted from the bridge wing.

"Let go aft." Said Dave into the Walkie Talkie. At the same time the pilot walked into the wheelhouse and spoke into the V.H.F.

"Standby Aucklander."

"Righto!" said a tinny voice from the box.

I scribbled furiously in the movement book.

"Let go for'wd!" Captain McHale again and Dave repeated the command into his radio.

I could see the taut bow line go suddenly slack as the tension was released by the Able Seamen controlling the winch on the foc'sle. Our stern had begun to move slowly away from the quay as soon as the after line had been released. Now the forward rope had been released the bow began to move out as well.

"Gently Aucklander." Said the Pilot.

"Righto." The tug attached to our back end thumped and rattled gently as its engines burst into life and then almost immediately went silent again. It was enough force on the tugs line to give us a bit more momentum, so the stern moved a little faster into the centre of the dock.

"Slow astern!" shouted the captain.

This was my big moment! I had been called into the wheelhouse suddenly while I was reminiscing in my mind about the 'Kiwi Star Cavalry' and told that today I would be on the engine room telegraph. A great honour indeed! Of course, I had to do the movement book as well and I was slightly worried about having two important tasks to perform at the same time, but I was determined to get it right and had been listening carefully for the first command.

"Slow astern!" I shouted back and moved the telegraph handle to the right position.

"Slow astern!" I shouted again, grinning like an idiot once I had completed my task. The ship shuddered and shook as the engine rumbled into life. I stared hard out towards the captain waiting for the next order. This came about thirty seconds later.

"Stop engines!"

"Stop engines!" my repetition of the order had escaped my mouth almost before Captain McHale had finished speaking. He didn't look at me, but I could see him frowning slightly. I vowed to leave a small gap between command and repetition next time as I moved the handle back to 'STOP'.

"Book!" Hissed a voice behind me. I turned; it was Dave.

"Eh?"

"Book!" He hissed again. I looked blankly at him for a second. Raising his eyes heavenwards he said, still hissing but louder now. "Write it in the fu...!"

"Oh yes… about to… erm… doing it now!" I interrupted him, grabbing the pen and blushing furiously at the same time.

'Nearly got it right!' I thought.

The ship drifted serenely and quietly backwards out of the dock and into the bay. A few more orders were shouted and in no time at all we were shuddering our way past Rangitoto Island on one side and the much smaller Brown's Island on the other.

By this time, it was getting on for ten o'clock in the morning. I had 'taken' the pilot to the pilot ladder and seen him leap onto the pilot boat and be whisked away back to Auckland. As usual he had been way ahead of me on the way down, having, probably, spent more time on the vessel over the years than I had in half a voyage.

Once again, I was on watch with Dave doing the 'eight til twelve'. No day work for us cadets this time, the passage from Auckland to Gisborne was only seventeen hours so we were to stick to watches which meant poor old Steven had to endure another 'twelve til four' night watch.

Coffee arrived at half past ten and Captain McHale went off to his cabin. Not long after I was surprised to see Barry limp on to the bridge.

"Where's the Old Man?"

"He's in his cabin." I answered. I was tempted to ask about his injuries, but I knew from JoJo that the horse-riding stroke Ariana stroke Count Dracula episode was still a very sore point with him. Coupled with the fact that all the whole thing had earned him was a new nickname of 'Scousula',

(Just in case anyone from foreign lands is reading this, the nickname is a combination of 'Scouse'

Which is a slang term for anybody or anything from Liverpool and, obviously, Dracula after his mock mid-European accent)

"Got some paperwork for him." He muttered as he hobbled away.

I was pacing up and down the starboard bridge wing when Barry re-appeared, still limping.

"Where's Dave?"

"Other wing." I said flapping a hand towards the port side. "How are your wounds?"

"Still limping, aren't I?" he muttered, scowling. "Bloody horses."

I decided it was best not to pursue my enquiry due to the murderous look on his face. Dave agreed, he had asked the same question after giving him a hearty "Hi Scousula!" when Barry had appeared on the port wing and received a short sharp answer for his trouble.

"I think it is going to take til, at least, Panama before he gets over it." He said, grinning from ear to ear.

I went back to pacing and watching the New Zealand coast drift past. By this time, we had just come out of the Hauraki Gulf and passed the Great Barrier Island on our port side and Fletcher Bay on the Starboard, the weather was simply perfect and there was a gentle southerly swell that set up a nice lazy pitching movement. All was right with the world. All was at peace.

"Oi!" It was Dave who startled me out of my reverie, I turned, too quickly, back towards the wheelhouse door and tripped over my own feet, stumbling into the doorway.

"Yes, very elegant." he said, "Now pirouette yourself back out to the compass, get some bearings and put a position on the chart."

That was the trouble, you see. I was beginning to discover that this 'Going to sea' lark was, really, the perfect job, so it was sometimes difficult to remember that it was just that, a job. Actual work. What's more, I was being paid for it!

The next morning found us anchored in Poverty Bay, a couple of miles off Gisborne, awaiting the arrival of a pilot and 'riggers'. We had arrived in the early hours of the morning on the 3rd of March 1971, anchored and then waited an hour for information from the port authorities, which finally arrived by V.H.F. radio at twenty past four, just as a faint glow of light was appearing in the east.

A tinny, disembodied voice told us we would be entering the port at about eight o'clock and the riggers would be on board fifteen minutes before.

The ship moved up and down gently to a fairly hefty northerly swell as I clattered down the stairs leading from the bridge, having been sent away by the Chief officer to get a couple of hours sleep before we entered the port.

'Riggers' were apparently being sent out to us by boat with the pilot and a tug was on standby to assist us alongside. The riggers were necessary, because the gentle swell we were experiencing could become very, very un-gentle very, very quickly. Special mooring ropes with a quick release mechanism attached were necessary so the ship could get away from the dockside in a hurry. Thousands of tons of ship caught in large South Pacific swell, bashing against a wood and concrete dock was not considered a good state of affairs by the people responsible for the upkeep these things, so, should such a swell appear the ship could be manoeuvred away in hurry after the large metal pins in the release mechanisms on the mooring ropes had been given a mighty thump with large maul wielded by a suitably large 'rigger'.

A sleepy looking Barry was hunched over a mug of coffee as I bounced into the duty mess.

"We're here." I said cheerily.

"Gathered that." He didn't smile. His face remained completely impassive.

"How's …?" I started to enquire about his equestrian injuries, not that I was particularly interested, more as a sort of conversation starter really.

"Don't ask!" He interrupted suddenly and loudly.

"Ok." I busied myself with making tea and then sat down opposite him. "Been here before?"

"Yeah, came here last year on the 'Rocky'." He was referring to the **Rockhampton Star** and I remembered the Chief Engineer saying that Barry had tried his 'Count Dracula' accent without success on that ship as well.

"Any good?" I enquired, tentatively.

"Yeah, not bad. We had a couple of good parties last time." He brightened up a bit. "Met this Maori girl, Marama her name was."

"Oh." I said. I was tempted to ask if this was the girl he had tried out his Transylvanian routine on, but I thought perhaps not just now. "Can she arrange a party for us?"

He grinned. "Mate," he said, "You don't need any party arrangers here. Once we get alongside and they put the phone on it'll ri… well, you know, you were there, you were in Auckland, you saw what happened, phone rang when we were walking past it!" He stopped suddenly and became interested in his coffee. I think he realised he was straying dangerously close to having to talk about Count Scousula.

"Sounds good." I said, stirring my tea.

He was saved by the bell, literally. An alarm sounded and he leapt up and did the sideways bent over shuffle bounce that's necessary to get out from those bench arrangements, where the table sort of covers half the seat so you can't stand up without leaning most of the way over the table, which, in turn means that as soon as you move one leg, the laws of gravitational physics mean that you have to sit down again. You then have to repeat the procedure at least four times before you reach the end of the seat. If there is four of you sitting in a row, you all end up bobbing up and down like demented pistons until everyone has bounced themselves out of the seat.

I finished making my tea, picked up the mug and headed towards the cadet's cabin. Sleep time.

Barry was right. The phone did start ringing. In fact, it started ringing as the phone man was plugging the thing in.

I had had a whole one and a half hours sleep before being awoken by the Able Seaman on watch hammering on the cabin door, flinging it open and shouting "Get up!" Then I had spent a couple of hours on the bridge assisting in manoeuvring the ship onto her berth. (I use the term 'assisting' lightly. The correct term would probably be 'hindering'. But nobody shouted at me, so I must have done something right.)

A shower and breakfast had followed, then both Steven and I had been sent out on deck to help open the hatches and prepare the ship for loading. We were due to be in Gisborne for about a week taking on wool and frozen lamb.

It was nearly eleven o'clock by the time I was allowed to get back into the accommodation and head for the duty mess again to give myself a mid-morning boost of coffee. The phone had begun ringing as I walked past it on my way to the duty mess. The phone man was still actually attached to it, touching it, and Barry was right there, next to him. I think he had been there since the poor bloke had arrived, watching him install it.

He snatched the phone up the instant it began its ear piercing, shrill, ring tone.

"Strewth! He's keen!" said the phone man as he staggered into me having been pushed aside by a salivating Barry.

"Hullo." His Transylvanian accent was gone and actually so was his Liverpudlian accent. He was all politeness and... well... niceness! "Yeh,

Yeh, Oh, Yeh, Great, Seven o'clock then." He turned away suddenly so his back was to us, cupped his hand around the mouthpiece and muttered something mostly inaudible about love, replaced the instrument on its cradle, then turned, blushing profusely, and walked off towards the stairs grinning.

"Party tonight, seven o'clock." He said over his shoulder as he bounded up the steps.

CHAPTER 33

ANOTHER PARTY

Loading had begun that morning at about half past nine. Once again it was a beautiful day with a clear blue sky and warm, gentle, northerly breeze carrying all the sounds that were now becoming so familiar. Cranes rattled into position and their cables twanged and hissed as nets full of frozen meat were lowered into the depths of our vessel. The ships winches whined and clattered as they also dragged the wires for her own derricks as they lowered cargo into different hatches. Wool here, meat there, and in number two hatch, carboard covered single blocks of butter weighing fifty- six pounds each. The ship itself shuddered and shook as all this stuff landed in the lower holds. The stuttering, banging noise from diesel engined forklift trucks on the quayside racing back and forth with yet more loads mingled with the shouts, laughter and occasional angry cries from the myriad of dock workers, foremen, riggers and drivers added to the frantic atmosphere.

Steven and I were again kept busy 'marking off'. As in Auckland the meat was loaded and stacked but this time all the hatches were taking lamb carcasses

After witnessing Barry's phone call shenanigans, I had grabbed some coffee from the duty mess and taken it to our cabin and sat down with a thump on the chair. Almost immediately Steven clattered into the cabin.

"Need my jumper." He announced opening the wardrobe with one hand while thrusting the other one into the depths to hold the luggage in. (We had, by this time, long since become adept at opening the door, holding in the luggage, and extracting clothes all at the same time.)

"Cold down there." He said, shivering to make his point.

"What are you both doing in here!?" It was the Mate. He filled the doorway and had a thunderous look on his face. "One of you should be on deck all the time!" He roared.

I leapt to my feet in a guilty fashion spilling coffee. Steven, equally startled, took a pace back and pointed in the general direction of the front of the ship.

"I was just...!" We both said at once.

"Coffee, Second Mate said...!"

"Jumper...cold...!"

We continued talking at the same time. Our excuses for both being off the deck at the same time were all to no avail, however, due to them being drowned out by the clattering of suitcases. Steven had used his luggage holding hand to point with.

There was a second or two of silence while our senior manager joined us in staring at the heap of suitcases on the floor. That silence was broken by Steven who made a sort of frightened squeaking noise and leapt over the baggage, sidled past the Mate, and ran down the alleyway. He didn't have his jumper. That was still in the wardrobe.

Over my time as cadet, I discovered that Chief Officers had the unerring knack of being able to turn up at the wrong place at the wrong time. They would always...but always, arrive at the door of the cadet's cabin precisely ten seconds after both cadets had gone in it. Even when, as in this case, there was a perfectly reasonable explanation for the gathering of cadets in one place.

Albert watched him go then turned his gaze to me.

"You having a break?" He asked quietly.

"Erm... yes." I answered slowly.

"Wrong!" He said, smiling. "Third Mate wants you at number five hatch."

I thought about explaining that Steven was getting his jumper and maybe I would go to do the third mate's bidding in, perhaps, a few minutes, after finishing whatever coffee was left in my mug. But decided that, on reflection, that was not a good idea. Not that it mattered anyway because

Down To The Sea. A Cadet's Tale

the Chief of all Officers had gone, stomping off in the same direction as the fleeing Steven.

The rest of that working day went by the same way as the morning had passed. Lots of running up and down ladders for both of us. Down to the icy cold of the lower holds, up to the summer heat of the deck. Backwards and forwards from one end of the ship to the other, until, at around five o'clock, there was a sudden rush of people off the ship, hatches were closed and sealed, cooling fans became active in the right places to keep frozen cargo frozen, and Steven and I went about our usual end of day routines. Routines we had become quick at and had down to a fine art. Lowering flags, turning lights on and locking up all the hatch access points in time to get changed and go and eat.

(Merchant Navy cadets throughout history could easily be taught many diverse and quite complicated routines with ease. All you had to do was stick the possibility of access to food on the end and leave it to them.)

Dinner time arrived, uniforms came out and all four of us cadets found ourselves, for the first time in a while, at the dinner table together where Barry was questioned about his woman friend and who she was bringing to the party.

"She lives with her sister, Morella." He said from behind his soup spoon. "They have a house about a mile or so out of town."

"Is it a wooden house?" Asked Steven, suddenly.

Barry stared at him. So did both JoJo and I, all of us eager to find out what could possibly be of interest about what a house, occupied by two sisters, was constructed from.

"How would I know?" He said frowning. "Anyway, what difference does it make whether it's bloody wooden or not?"

We all continued to stare. Steven continued slurping soup.

"Well," he said, between spoonfuls. "It's interesting because bricks are very expensive here so most houses are wooden."

There was a silence while we all digested this stunning piece of information. Barry was still frowning and then he drew breath to speak. JoJo interrupted him.

"No... no... no... leave it!" He said waving his spoon first in Barry's direction, then in Stevens'.

"I don't think I can cope with the responsibility of knowing and retaining the mind blowing, globally important, environmentally challenging answer to that."

Everybody fell silent, while Steven continued to slurp soup, oblivious to the mental torture and social stress his random thoughts could cause.

There was no cargo being worked overnight. In fact, I can't remember doing one single round of night cargo work at any port on the Kiwi coast. Not once! Ever!

Everything was extremely civilised in those days. Nine to five...ish and no weekends. Wonderful. So Steven and I decided to go for a walk 'up the road'. It was always called that, going ashore, I mean. It was very rarely called 'Going ashore,'. Everybody would ask "Are you going up the road?" In fact, the only time I can remember it being called 'going ashore' was at the Nautical collage at Warsash, during my years pre-sea training. There you HAD to call it 'going ashore' otherwise people with stripes and hats would shout at you for not being... 'nautical'... enough. Which was all very well, but the bloody place was about half a mile away from any water!

Anyway, six thirty in the evening found Steven and I plodding 'up the road' and into town where we wandered about aimlessly in our usual going ashore rig. Him in his jacket and tie, me in the flappy loons and yellow shirt. A drink was out of the question as we were both under twenty- one and neither of us would be able to pass as that age if we tried. So, we passed several pubs and bars without attempting to enter, along the Esplanade, then over a bridge which spanned the Taranganui River up to Fitzherbert Street. Then we came upon another river. Place seemed to be full of rivers!

Our navigating skills deserted us then and we ended up lost, but the one thing that the crew of a Blue Star ship had going for them was the funnel. That large blue star in a white circle, surrounded by that huge red funnel acted like a beacon to lost souls, and sure enough, once we found ourselves on some slightly higher ground, we could see it poking above the rooftops.

It was getting on for seven thirty by the time we got back to the ship. I could hear, even as we climbed up the gangway, that classic song from the early seventies, the one with the deep meaningful lyrics... "Ooo... oo... eee... chirpy-chirpy cheep-cheep, chirpy-chirpy cheap-cheep, chirp!" It's one of those super annoying tunes that gets into your head and won't go away until... well... forever, apparently. I can hear it now! Aargh!

A few moments later I followed Steven into the bar to find it deserted. Not a soul around. The bar cassette player had been put on and left to play by itself. Whoever had got the bar 'ready' had obviously run off to prepare himself for his own grand entrance. This was also very annoying, one of the reasons we had decided to go for a walk was to try and escape being the designated 'Kiwi Star Party Welcoming Committee', all to no avail it seemed. Even as we stood there, I heard the outside door to the accommodation open and a female voice drifted along the alleyway.

"Jesus! Will ya look at the size of theses storm sills, girls? Ya have to get ya knees up by your bloody ears to get over them!"

Steven looked at me and raised his eyes heavenwards.

"Looks like we're 'it' again." He said, gloomily.

It didn't take long for the party to get going. The F.D.R. (Female Detection Radar) was on full, so all the engineers did their... 'smoothing in fashionably late'... routines, soon after. Plus, our three bosses, Dave, John, and Albert appeared as well. Dave, the Third Mate was usually there but it was unusual to see the Second and Chief Mates at the bar during a party. Both were married and had large families and were not really party people, however, stories of their exploits in times gone by did, frequently, reach my ears, but then, that was the case with most people I met and worked with during my time at sea. Come to think of it, every single person I met... ever... has had some tale to tell or had some tale told about them. I think most people have probably got a book of stories inside them.

About half an hour went by during which several female guests arrived. Steven was swept away to the bar by Felicity, who turned out to be the loud woman complaining about the storm sills. She was a tall good-looking woman, but loud... very loud. I can't remember seeing Steven get a word in edgeways during their initial conversation, but they must have got on well. Judging, that is, by their faces being continually stuck together a little later in the proceedings. "Conduct most unbecoming for a clergyman's son!" said the Second mate to me some days later.

'Everybody has a story in them, and everybody has conduct most unbecoming in them as well.' I thought.

It was then that Barry appeared with two women, one on each arm. Both had jet black hair, beautiful dark olive skin, looked extremely fit, lithe and were each in possession of smiles that lit up the room.

This was Marama and Morella.

CHAPTER 34

Driving Lesson

Barry was grinning. But then, if I had walked into the bar with a beautiful woman on each arm, I would be grinning as well. This was Barry's moment. He must have been waiting for this all trip.

The two girls hung on to his arms as he walked to the bar and said, in a voice that showed not a hint of Liverpool, nor Transylvania, but a touch of James Bond.

"Vodka Martini... and two Gin and tonics for my friends."

Everybody fell silent and looked at him.

"A what?" said Ian from behind the bar.

It was, actually, Felicity 'Storm Sills' who ruined the moment for Barry. Her strident tones rang out from the corner of the room where she was engaged in conversation with 'Whiskers' (this was before she became face-welded to Steven).

"Hey!" Marama! How ya goin girl!"

I saw Barry's shoulders drop. This intrusion into his big moment was bad enough but unfortunately the obviously oblivious Felicity continued.

"Didn't 'know ya were coming to this shindig, ya could've give me a lift."

Down went Barry's shoulders another notch. But there was more, Marama and her sister turned round and squealed with delight.

"Fel!... Didn't know yous was comin' neither!" Her voice was harsh and rasping and didn't go with her looks at all.

'Fel' bounded over, hurdling a coffee table without breaking her stride.

"We just saw this boat in the port and thought we'd 'ave a look. Ya know, me and the girls."

"Oh... right... yeah." Marama was nodding enthusiastically, then she threw in a sideways head flick in Barry's direction. "We came with Barry." She paused, then recalled. "You remember Barry, Fel, he was on that other Star boat."

Felicity thought for bit and leant over the bar to get a better look at Barry's face, which, by this time, was in full, 'eyes closed, maximum distress, bright red, mode.

"Nah," she said thoughtfully. "Never met him."

Morella grabbed her sisters' arm and whispered something in her ear, at which Marama frowned, obviously thinking hard.

"Oh! Of course! That was Bjorn!" She cackled.

"Hah! Yeah! Screeched Felicity and slapped Marama on the back. "But that wasn't a Star boat. That was that Swedish ship."

They both fell about, cackling.

Everybody else in the bar had watched all this in silent amusement. Their heads moving back and forth as the conversation flowed between the two women.

Ian looked at Barry across the bar.

"What was it you wanted Barry?"

Barry grimaced and kept his eyes closed.

"Beer." He muttered.

I had already noticed, on several occasions previously, that when things started to go wrong for Barry, the hits just kept on coming. Tonight, was no exception. He was about to take the first sip of his drink when the bar door opened and in walked JoJo and with him, holding his arm and looking lovely in short black dress, was Ariana.

Barry's drink stopped a few millimetres from his lips as his head turned towards the door and remained there while his face went through more emotional gymnastics. His eyes, his wide, staring, horrified eyes, followed the pair as they walked towards the bar.

At that point I suddenly lost interest in the Barry and JoJo show due to the delicate touch of a female arm slipping itself around one of mine. I jumped slightly at the suddenness of the touch and looked around and down to find Marama's sister, Morella, staring up at me with wide, innocent, dark, sultry eyes. I know that may sound odd, that someone could have eyes that were sultry and innocent at the same time, but, believe me, it is possible. This was my first encounter with such eyes, and I was somewhat bewitched.

"Hubo, by dames Boreba." She said.

"Pardon?" I bent down slightly so I could hear better and was immediately aware of her subtle perfume that wafted up at me. She was dressed in a simple white blouse and blue tight jeans that showed off her perfect, petit figure.

"Boreba." She repeated slowly and then sniffed loudly. "I'be god a gold."

"A gold?"

"Yeb... a gold."

I frowned a puzzled frown at her.

She frowned back. "A gold..." My frown remained. "A gold." You dough... a gold... ib by doze!"

"Oh." I said, straightening up and nodding as the light dawned. "You have a cold."

"Yeb." She smiled then suddenly doubled over and sneezed over my shoes.

"Dorry." She said. "I shouldn't ab cub."

I quickly translated this into English and agreed with her, she shouldn't really have come out at all. I felt sorry for her. But she did look lovely and I remained bewitched. Not only that, but I could also feel a slight panicky feeling. (You must remember I was noticeably young and had only just started the beginners course on "Woman and Survival. Part 1: Approach.) I was still at the stage where I assumed that all woman, of any age, shape, and form, would, at first encounter, run away screaming at the prospect of spending even another minute in my company and was therefore amazed when a woman of the opposite sex even spoke in my direction!

"But... anyway, you're here now, come and have a drink." I said, leading her to the bar. "What will you have?"

"Din ad donic, beeze." She sniffed.

"Gin and Tonic?" Thought I'd better make sure.

"Yeb." She was looking at me and nodding, confirming my translation.

Ian was watching her.

"Din ab Donic coming up." He said chuckling.

Morella tried to chuckle too, but you know what it's like when you suddenly find something funny and you give an inadvertent, sort of, nasal, air blowing sound? A small laugh through your nose, so to speak. Not a problem, normally, but in Morella's case a bit of a disaster. Her small, polite 'nose laugh' turned into a loud snotty snort of epic proportions as a large yellow globule rocketed out of her left nasal passage and hit the bar top with a sound like a large jellyfish being squished by a small Volkswagen.

A silence descended around the bar area while we all stared at the mucusy mess.

"Jeez Morella!" Felicity's quiet subtleness filled the room. "Great snotter girl!" He eyes were fixed on the offending blob, her face a picture of awestruck admiration.

"Dorry." Said Morella.

By this time JoJo had reached the bar and was standing by a forlorn looking Barry who was staring into his beer. (I don't think he had even noticed the nose missile that had missed his beer by inches.)

"Alright Baz?"

Barry took a deep breath and nodded.

"Yeah, 'spose."

Arianna stepped around JoJo and laid her hand on Barry's shoulder.

"Good to see you, Barry." She smiled as he looked round and nodded at her.

"Yeah, good to see you too. All ok?" He was smiling too, although it looked a little forced.

I felt a strange relief come over me. I think I had been subconsciously worrying that the situation would get out of hand and JoJo and Barry would end up coming to blows, given Barry's penchant for solving relationship problems with his fists. In fact, I had been greatly relieved when everything had appeared normal at the dinner table earlier. Arianna's presence had racked up the tension a tad, but all seemed ok now.

JoJo wandered away from the bar with Arianna once they got their drinks, Marama draped herself over Barry once they got theirs and Steven... Well!... Steven, our son of a clergyman, our gangly, gawky, walking encyclopaedia, became the star attraction. He danced furiously to the loud seventies rock music blasting out from the eight-track cassette deck that the Chief Engineer was jealously guarding behind the bar. Felicity gamely gyrated, twisted and bobbed her head up and down, flinging herself about the place in an effort to keep up with him, while I sat next to Morella, in the corner, discussing the disadvantages of having a cold at a party on a ship. At least that's what I think we were discussing. Couldn't really be sure though. Music was too loud.

At one point we managed a half-hearted dance, a slow one, during which Morella clung to me with her head on my chest sniffing loud, clogged nose, type sniffs while I manoeuvred us around the postage stamp sized 'dance area' occasionally having to avoid the waving tentacles of Steven and Jasmine who were, still, it seemed, gyrating at the same speed as they were when fast rock music was playing.

The party continued into the night, some people left early only to be replaced by others who had been ashore first and had recently wobbled back aboard. One or two strangers arrived at various times, both male and female, but everybody was affable, friendly, and smiling and there was no trouble.

Around about one in the morning Barry rushed across to our corner.

"We're going now." He announced, his grin even wider than when he had walked into the bar earlier. "You two coming?"

"Yed dob course." Said Morella.

"Yes!" I said. probably a bit too quickly...and loudly.

"Bit to pissed to drive..." Marama had appeared behind Barry and she leant on him, also grinning as she spoke.

"They came in her car." Explained Barry, looking at me.

"Yeah, we drove... in the car." Marama confirmed so no one was in any doubt.

"No problem!" Exclaimed Barry "We'll drive!"

"Yeah!" I nodded enthusiastically, hoping Barry hadn't had too much either.

We all headed for the smoke room door, Morella sniffing, Marama wobbling, with Barry and I trotting along behind like expectant puppies. The alleyway was no problem, wide enough to accommodate trips, bumps and drunken weaving, but the door to the deck with its storm sill caused a bit of a pile up. Poor Marama came off worst as she was the one who fell over it, ending up sprawled across the sill, half in and half out. Barry tried to stop but ended up doing a sort of hurdle over her in an effort to avoid kicking her in the backside. His landing was not elegant and he thumped down on one foot on the far side of Marama, who, unfortunately, was trying to bounce up, so, whereas he achieved his objective of not kicking his girlfriend in her posterior, his trailing knee thudded into the back of her head.

"Ow! Fuck!" She roared demurely.

Both Morella and I came to a halt but not before I clattered into the back of her and had to grab her round the waist to stop us both from joining the crashed and injured.

"Oi!" The gentle husky female tones that could only come from Felicity echoed along the cross alleyway. She was standing by the door to the smoke room, right hand on her hip and her left arm straight out from her shoulder disappearing into the room itself. "Where are yous' all goin'" she twanged.

"Marama's place." Said Barry, sticking his head back in the door and catching the very same Marama a glancing blow to the nose with his knee as she struggled to get to her feet".

"Ooff!" said Marama.

"Great, you can give us a lift!" Felicity bellowed and turned her head to look in towards the bar. "Stevo! Come on, we got a ride home!"

With that she started to walk forward, and I saw then what was on the end of her left arm. It was, of course, 'Stevo', Steven, looking worse for wear, bleary eyed and decidedly unwell.

"Where're we going...ing to off to now?" Slurred Steven as he shuffled along on the end of Felicity's fist.

"Home, mate!... Home" she said, deftly releasing her grip and swinging her arm down and then round his back in one smooth movement before he fell over.

Once everybody had finished tending their wounds, we all made our way precariously down to the dockside. Things got a bit hairy when the gangway started to bounce around a bit as we clattered our way along it, but we arrived safely enough on the shore and walked over to Marama's red car. I should say Marama's small red car. Marama's exceedingly small red car! I can't now remember what sort it was. I just remember it being ridiculously small and very red.

Barry opened the passenger side door (there were only front doors) and stood aside, I assumed for the three girls to get in, but, obviously, the gentleman in him was pushed aside by more basic thoughts because once Marama had tipped the front seat forward, he leapt in first and she fell in after him. Felicity was next and she somehow dragged Steven in with her. He ended up spread across all three laps with his size elevens sticking out the door and his head buried in Barry's crotch at which point Barry grabbed Steven's hair and held his head in the air as though it had been severed from its shoulders by an axe in a Pagan ritual of some sort. Steven didn't utter a word but blinked like owl, with his mouth making a perfect round shape which completed the look of bewilderment.

"Get off!" Squealed Barry. Stephen was incapable of any reply and stared straight ahead while, at his other end, Felicity was heaving and tugging his legs into the car. The result of all this was Barry, Felicity and Marama squished tight on the back seat with Steven folded on top in the middle, sitting on at least two laps and his head rammed at a neck snapping angle against the roof.

The seat thudded back in the upright position and Morella, still sniffing loudly, got in the front seat. I watched all this, thinking myself smart to stay away from the mayhem. However, my smart thinking brain slowly began to realise that there was nowhere for me. Apart from the driver's seat, the car was full. I bent down and peered into the back.

"Erm... What about me?" I enquired.

"You're driving!" It was Barry who answered. I couldn't see him, he was buried under part of Steven, but his scouse accent was back, piercing the night air.

"Me?" I exclaimed. "Me!"

"Yeah You!"

Everybody stared at me. Everybody, that is, except Steven, who had, somehow, extracted his right cheek from the roof, twisted round and was staring at Felicity.

"You." He said.

"Nah!" She bellowed, "Not me... Him!" Unable to use her hands because they were trapped under her, she nodded her head in my direction. Steven twisted back and looked at me.

"Him." He said, blinking.

I stared straight back at him but decided, as there was obviously no one home, not to reply. Instead, I ran round the front of the car, opened the driver's door and leaned in.

"Barry!" I could feel the panic rising. "Listen carefully! I can't drive! I only ever had one lesson!"

Even on that side of the car I couldn't see where he was, Steven was, somehow, still obscuring him.

"Well, that's one more than me pal!" He said. "I haven't had any!"

"But... but... but... you're an engineer! You can do engines and stuff!" desperation was setting in now.

"Engines, yes. Driving, no!" He flapped a hand in the general direction of 'Ahead'. Anyway, it'll be alright, they drive on the same side of the road as us and, and look, the steering wheel is on the same side as our cars."

"Are we going... or what?" It was Felicity. Her strident Kiwi tones echoing around the dock, even though she, too, was buried beneath six foot of folded Steven.

"Yes... yes...yes....in a minute!" I said.

"Well hurry up mate." She screeched. "Dyin' for a wee here!"

"Bee doo." Said Morella from the front passenger seat.

I gave up. *'Oh God'!* I thought. *I'm going to get arrested! I'll run over someone and kill them! I'll crash and wipe us all out!'* Imagining all sorts of hideous scenarios of carnage and mayhem, I squeezed in, sat behind the wheel, and slammed the door.

"Where do you start it?" I said sulkily.

"You just turn the key." Said Marama from somewhere in the back. She sounded remarkably calm for someone who's car was about to be driven by a novice.

"What key?" I was scrabbling about around the steering column with sweaty fingers.

"This one." She said. A hand appeared from behind Steven dangling a huge set of various keys attached to an even bigger pink plastic heart. I opened my mouth to ask the obvious.

Whi...?"

"The biggest one... and hurry up I need a wee too!"

"Okay, okay." I muttered scrabbling again, this time with a whole jailer's chain of keys in my hands.

By pure luck, the key slipped easily into the hole it was designed for and I wrenched it forward.

The car made a 'whuh' noise and jumped forward, Steven made a similar sound as his right ear and cheek scraped across the roof.

"It's in gear!" wailed Marama, sounding less confident now.

"Push the clutch in!" shouted Barry.

"Hurry up!" Advised Felicity.

I flapped my hands in several directions at once then managed to connect my left foot with clutch and pressed it. (Not easy when you are rammed up against the steering wheel in a seat positioned for a small slim woman.) My left hand grabbed the gear lever and took it out of gear, then put it straight back in again while my right hand wrenched the key forward. The engine burst into life, lots of life in fact. It screeched as the revs built suddenly.

"Whoa!" shouted everybody at once, including me.

"Foot! Gas pedal! Clutch!" Everybody was suddenly full of good ideas related to car driving. I let the clutch up and took my foot off the accelerator (how it had got there in the first place, I have no idea.) then pressed it down again, then took it off again as the clutch engaged and the car leapt forward. My passengers were simultaneously rammed back in their seats then rocketed forward as I took my feet off everything. *'Don't stall!'* My mind commanded the car as a confused looking Steven appeared briefly next to me then immediately retreated, at speed, into the rear compartment. My feet attacked all the pedals again and the right foot must have got to the accelerator first, but then it took fright and jumped off just as the car suddenly leapt forward and raced away from my control for several yards. That fast forward movement caused the same foot to increase its fright ratio and head for the brake. The car stopped suddenly, very suddenly and my passengers, again in perfect unison were flung back, then forward violently, then back with a thump into their seats.

Steven appeared next to me again. I had brief glimpse of his bewildered, wide eyed face looking at me, before he turned his head forward in time for his nose and forehead to hit the windscreen with loud 'donk', which brought a collective sharp intake of breath from the others.

"Wow! That'll hurt!" exclaimed Felicity.

Steven remained glued to the windscreen as a small whimper escaped from his mouth.

Felicity reached over and hauled him back upright which meant his head was returned to its position rammed against the roof.

"Ow, woo, oopff!"

There was silence. The car had stalled.

After a short, shocked silence Barry spoke.

"You've stalled it."

CHAPTER 35

A Normal Night of Passion

"I beel orbal." Morella was sitting on the end of her bed looking thoroughly dejected. I was standing by the door and I genuinely felt sorry for her. The poor girl obviously had a heavy cold and should have stayed in bed. Cavorting at a ships party was, after all, not the best remedy for the flu. And she did look truly 'orbal'.

I was, actually, still having a little trouble understanding what she was saying, and I started to say, *'Do you mean you feel awful, or do you mean you feel horrible?'* but I only got as far as...

"Do you feel....?" When I was stopped by an icy glare topped with a truly epic frown.

"Yeb!" she said.

I tried another manly, 'Man handling a crisis' approach.

"Can I get you a hot water bottle?" I was cringing before I got to "hot" *'God! I sound like her mother. Worse! I sound like her grandmother!'*

She, of course, snorted her contempt and managed to inform me that a much better idea would be to get the whiskey bottle that was on the dining room table. This I did and poured a glass for her, which she necked in short order.

"Dads bedder," she said.

Ship's parties never ever go as you expect them to. This was a sort of 'fact of life', I was to discover. They are a beast of unknown ways and wiles. Once set in motion there is no stopping them. They tear through one's life taking one's very soul with them. My very first party had resulted in me riding horses, this one had me taking an illegal driving lesson in small, overloaded car designed for hobbits, and then playing nurse to a beautiful woman with the flu. In her bedroom!

Our journey from the ship to Marama and Morella's house had taken about 15 minutes.

After my kangaroo hopping style of driving had bounced us out of the immediate vicinity of our ship, I had taken the decision to remain in first gear. Gear changing was a far too complicated procedure for that time of night, so I piloted us at a good four miles a fortnight, engine screaming, towards the main road. It was then, as we approached what passed for a gate but was actually a space in the grassy area between the road and the car park, it occurred to me that I had not a clue where to go.

"Where are we going?" I had to shout over the screaming of the vastly over revved engine.

It was Marama who answered, also shouting over the noise,

"See that road right opposite the gate?"

"Yes." I said, squinting through the windscreen against the glare from the floodlights that were turning night into day.

"Well, it's the second house on the right, the white one."

I turned in my seat and looked at her.

"What? ... What? ... "Wha..! We could have bloody walked!" I wailed.

"Should have done," mumbled Barry. "It would have been quicker than Speedy Gonzales here!"

"Yeah, and mine is three houses further along, you can drop me and Stevo off there first." Felicity's dulcet tones came from behind 'Stevo' who's head was still rammed at an impossible angle against the roof.

"I'm desperate for a wee." Said Morella.

I sulked in my pilots seat while we dribbled, engine still at full volume, passed the security hut, across the main road and up into the opposite street.

The houses were all bungalows, detached, with lawns in front of each. (I didn't actually notice this at the time, of course, I had other things on my mind, like driving! But I can remember later thinking the houses were quite posh even though they were opposite the docks. A bit different from London!) I rattled to a stop at Felicity's house by means of a spectacular stall that, once again rocketed everybody forward and Barry actually head butted me in the left shoulder. Everyone, that is, except Felicity and 'Stevo' who was, by now firmly wedged against the roof, his head still at an impossible angle with his right ear firmly against his shoulder.

Barry, Marama and Morella all hoped out of the car and began running back towards the house we had just passed on the way to Felicity's. This involved a particularly spectacular piece of athleticism from Barry, as you will remember, the vehicle had only front doors, so he had to go headfirst past Jasmine and Steven, who were in the middle, to get to the passenger door. To this day neither of us can fathom out how he managed it. But manage it he did, even somehow, overtaking the two women.

"Where are you going?" I shouted after them.

"Desperate!" Shouted Marama.

"Wee!" That was Barry who was way ahead.

"But... but... the car! What about the car?"

"Leave it!"

I grabbed the keys, slammed the door and took off after them.

"OI!" I came to a sudden stop and looked back. It was Felicity who had shouted.

"Get this fucking great gangly lump off me!"

I wrenched open the door and peered in.

A gentle snoring noise came from the senior cadet.

"He's asleep." I explained.

"Don't fucking care! She roared. "Get him off!"

I pulled him towards me and he became unwedged suddenly, causing me to fall back into the road with Steven on top of me. Felicity immediately scrambled out of the other door and I heard her feet pounding up the path towards her front door. Steven came to at that point, leapt to his feet and did a sort of three sixty spin while he worked out where he was, gazed at me lying in the road for a second, frowned, spun again and then took off after his lady friend.

Reflecting on the fact that, through all this, even when he was out of the car, Steven's head was still stuck to his left shoulder, I got slowly to my feet and walked back towards the white bungalow that Barry and the girls had disappeared into.

"Goda dleep dow," Morella was wriggling out of her jeans. "Gib be a dand."

Gently easing the jeans of a beautiful, petit, sexy woman while she lies alluringly on the bed, hips thrust upwards, is, of course every seventeen year old boy's dream.

AAAAASCHOOO! Morella sneezed spraying nasal content in several directions at once.

End of dream!

"Dorry," she rasped.

Once I had got her jeans off she turned and crawled under the duvet.

"Ged in." she said, flapping a hand at the other side of the bed. She fell silent then apart from her rasping flu-breathing.

I moved round and sat on the bed, took my shoes off and then my watch and put it on the bed side cabinet. Fortunately, my aim wasn't that good and it fell on the floor. I say 'fortunately' because having to pick it up made me look at it and notice the time. Ten to five. This took a good three minutes of furious brain action to realise it was... ten to five.... *'Yes... ten... to...five...'* My brain plodded through its realisation process. *'Ten minutes before the hour of five' ...little hand on the five... big hand on the ten to......'* This was followed by a wave of horror and self-pity as I finally understood what that meant. It meant that I had to be back on the ship and ready for work in two hours.

'No point in getting in the bed' I sulked. I had a horror of being late for work, well, late for anything really, so I set my mind on the fact that I would have to stay awake until probably lunch time at the earliest. So, I decided the best thing to do was to go back to the ship now. This very minute.

Morella snored and snuffled while I put my shoes back on and tiptoed out of the bedroom, turned left and headed down the short passage towards the living room. Two things occurred to me at that point, one; I needed the toilet and two; would Barry need to be woken so he wouldn't be late for work? That then set off another thought; what about Steven?

My mind working overtime, I headed for the bathroom which, I knew was the first door in the alleyway by the living room entrance because I had seen Barry disappearing into it as I arrived after abandoning Marama's car outside Felicity's house.

I could still hear Morella snoring, and a similar noise coming from the other bedroom as I opened the bathroom door. I stopped, and my jaw dropped. My poor brain, as if it hadn't had enough work to do over the past few hours went into processing overdrive again as it tried to cope with the site of Barry, sitting, fully clothed, on the toilet, fast asleep. His head slumped onto his chest.

"Barry!" I whisper-shouted. You know, when you whisper so loud it becomes, what you think is a quiet shout but is actually louder than talking normally.

He lifted his head and stared uncomprehendingly at me.

"Fahh off!" He muttered dribbling delicately from the corner of his mouth.

"I'm going back." I said. "Everybody's asleep, snoring and got colds." I paused. Nothing. No response.

"Barry!"

"Fahh off!"

"Barry!"

"Fahh off!"

"You'll be late for work!"

"Fahh oooffow!" Barry fell off the toilet.

Steven was standing at the top of the gangway, still dressed in his going ashore outfit as I clattered my way up closely followed by a pale distressed looking Barry. It had taken us five minutes to walk inward bound the fifteen minute outward bound car journey and you could easily see that we were both suffering from the effects. Barry in particular. Falling off the toilet had caused several gallons of undigested beer to flow from his mouth into the bowl, and judging by the colour of his face, there was another couple on the way.

"You look awful!" said Steven.

We looked at him from our position three quarters of the way up.

"Yeah, well," shouted a bad tempered, frowning Barry. "You look like a bag o' shite yourself." Which he instantly regretted. Not saying what he said, it was the shouting that was the problem. It obviously hurt his drink mutilated brain.

"How come you're back already?" I asked, taking care to keep my head still and calm.

"Oh, you know, erm, just felt like it. Sun was coming up and that."

Barry and I looked at each other and then looked up towards Steven again, both of us starting to say in unison "The sun was coming up?" but then finding that Steven had already disappeared, which left us looking silly standing on a swaying gangway talking to no one.

"Hah!" said Barry. "Bet he never got anywhere with... with...that loud woman."

"Don't know... Don't care!" I muttered. "Need breakfast!" and stumbled after Steven into the accommodation.

CHAPTER 36

BRIEFLY BLUFF

The rest of that morning ground slowly along. I dare not go anywhere near my bunk for fear of succumbing to temptation, getting in it and falling asleep. Not waking up in time for work was a cardinal sin.

Steven seemed to not suffer from such fears and was snoring loudly by the time I had made my way up as far as the alleyway to our cabin. It was the snoring, in part, that drove me back down the stairs and towards the duty mess on the other side of the cross-alley where I made myself a mug of tea and sat, still resplendent in my trendy 'party/going ashore' rig, on the oily plastic bench.

After a period of staring blankly at the table sipping tea, I was brought back to reality by indeterminate noises from indeterminate parts of the ship. She was beginning her morning wake up routine. Doors were beginning to open; humans were starting to move; machinery was buzzing louder. You could almost feel her stretching and yawning into full awakeness.

"Ah! You made it back then." It was the Mate. He had appeared in the doorway and leant on the frame while I was busy table staring.

"Good night last night?" He said, grinning.

"Well, erm, yes, sort of." I realised then that I had not had enough 'Good Nights' to be able to judge. Not enough bad nights either, come to that!

"Mmm," he pursed his lips. "I won't enquire further."

He pushed himself upright. "Anyway you had better go and get your mate up. It sounds as though you have got a walrus and several sealions in your cabin. Young Waddington is out for the count."

With that he left suddenly leaving me to heave my aching body and sore head off the bench.

Steven was indeed 'Out for the count' and it took a good half an hour to get him awake and up... well up anyway. I knew "awake" would arrive at about midday.

Showering and dressing made me feel a little more alive and after a few minutes of urging Steven to get dressed and switched on I ventured out on deck and into the frantic world of loading a ship and the rest of our stay in Gisborne. A place that, until that afternoon, on another planet, in the chartroom with the second mate, just after my promotion to barman on another ship, I had never heard of.

"We are going to Auckland, Gisborne and Bluff." He had said.

After Steven had annoyingly corrected me about my thinking the second Mate had said Buff rather than Bluff, I had taken no further notice. Terrible thing for a Navigating Cadet to admit I know, but, well, I did have far more important things on my mind at the time. What to wear when I went to meet Cathy and other urgent problems of the same nature!

So, the week continued, as in Auckland Steven and I ran back and forth, helping to do this, messing up that, writing things in the cargo times book. (Making it up if we found we had missed something.) Clambering down a ladder into a cargo space with reels of different coloured tape, marking off acres of frozen lamb carcasses that looked exactly the same as the other acres of frozen lamb. Clambering back up the ladder and down another one with reels of different coloured tape, marking off acres of frozen lamb that looked exactly the same as the other acres of frozen lamb. Smoko at ten, lunch at one, knock off at five and dinner at six. In and out of uniform and back into boilersuits three times a day.

After dinner in the evening, as in Auckland, the bar was the centre of the universe. Ian, the Chief Engineer took his place behind the bar. (I discovered, as my sea going career progressed that this was not a normal state of affairs. Generally Chief Engineers stayed on the other side of the bar. I also found that Captains hardly ever came in the officers bar, unless it was after lunch or they were asked.)

Barry, Steven and I saw Marama, Felicity and Morella the evening after the party. They, and several other girls that had... erm... formed a connection with various members of staff, used the smokeroom as their 'local' for our entire stay in Gisborne, which ended up being ten days.

Poor Morella heroically staggered to the ship every evening still full of flu bugs and I fussed and tended to her and we managed a run ashore at the cinema and a night at her place, with Barry and Marama, towards the end of our stay.

We didn't see much of JoJo and Ariana. They were off doing their own thing every evening until three nights before we were due to leave when she, Ariana had to head back to Auckland. Tearful goodbyes ensued on the quayside followed by a three days of grumpy JoJo.

Exactly ten days after we arrived we departed for 'Buff.'

More tearful goodbyes on the quayside followed by a couple of days of grumpy Brian, Steven and Barry.

"Well?" ....

It was Barry asked the question. We were all sitting at our table in the saloon waiting for breakfast. JoJo and I looked at Barry, then followed his gaze towards Steven. Steven also looked at Barry, then at us, then at Barry again.

"Well what?"

Barry rolled his eyes. "We are waiting." He said. JoJo and I looked at each other, both wondering what it was we were waiting for.

"Waiting for what?" said a bewildered Steven.

"We...ell," Barry waggled his head then tipped it on its side and smiled as though indulging a small child.

"You usually give us all a full lecture about a place when we arrive on everything from the geography to the favoured colour of the populations socks!" His Liverpool accent lent a extra edge of hilarity to his statement. Unfortunately Steven didn't notice it stared moodily at the tablecloth.

"Oh ... Shut up!" was the only quickfire witty response he could come up with. There was silence after that while we all joined Steven in tablecloth staring.

We had arrived in Bluff earlier that morning after a three day passage down the coast past Portland Island and across the bay that houses Napier and Hamilton. On down past Castle Point then across the wide expanse of water that is the entrance to the windy gap between the North Island and South Island. Past Christchurch, Timaru and Dunedin, round the corner and on into Bluff. All of those places I had either vaguely heard of or were completely new to me. I knew absolutely nothing about them. Little did I know that all of them would play a great part in my future... But they are stories for another book.

All in all it had been a pleasant eight hundred odd nautical mile trip. A bit of rough, windy weather passing the gap between the islands but mostly warm and sunny. However, there was a distinct chill in the air when we sailed into Bluff.

After breakfast Steven and I had changed into deck gear and met the Mate by number three hatch to get our instructions for the day. Steven was in raptures because the ship was parked under the "Meat Loaders" and they were about to be lowered into position.

Whereas he hadn't given us lectures on the history of Bluff, he had, despite never being here before managed to give me a short lesson in how these giant dinosaur looking machines worked.

"They are a mechanical marvel!" He enthused while hopping around the cabin trying to get his other leg into his boiler suit. "The loaders were first used in nineteen sixty four on April the fourth and they are really good, they can load tons of frozen lamb into all five hatches at once." His head was nodding up and down to emphasize the amazing ability of these things.

"The first ever ship to use them was a Kiwi ship called the 'Hauraki.' He informed me as we hurried across the deck towards our boss.

They were weird looking things. Five of them seemed to grow out of the roof of the huge dockside shed that went the length of the dock. Towering above the roof they were enclosed metal rectangular 'tubes'. The first part stuck straight up high above the roof of the shed and the second part which was almost as long as the first part was bent at an angle of about forty degrees forward with a larger bit on the end. So...as I said... sort of dinosaur shaped.

"Ah there you are," said Albert as we skidded to stop at his side. "Normal stuff," he continued. "But you will have to be on your toes to keep track of things." He frowned and stuck his face forward, looking intently at each of us in turn. "Make sure you don't miss any marking off. The lamb comes in pretty fast here." His face came even further forward. "In several hatches at once!" With that he turned on his heel and sped off towards the accommodation block.

Steven, his mouth open and eyes filled with awe, immediately turned his attention to the loaders which were being lowered into position over the hatches, their mouths dipping into the hatch just below the coaming. We both went and peered down number two hatch in time to see the beast lower its tongue deep into the hold.

Poetic eh! Actually they were really one long conveyor system that started in the shed where loaders put the carcasses on to a belt which transported it a point underneath the vertical part of the rectangular tube thingy. There, some sort of mechanical shenanigans went on which turned the belt into a series of slings. The carcasses were then automatically carried upwards in said slings up, out and over the roof of the shed until they found themselves over the ship. Then the belt whatsit, after further mechanical wizardry became slings again, which lowered the carcasses into the hold where they were deposited onto slide which whizzed them onto a table for the very large, fierce looking Kiwi blokes to grab and take to wherever they were to be put. So the tongue thing I poetically described was just the other end of the belt/sling arrangement.

All very interesting to Steven who even managed to slip away that afternoon and go and look at the other end of the loader, the end in the shed.

I was about to head up the steps to the accommodation to get a cup of tea when an even more excited Steven returned and skidded down the same steps.

"It's even better in there!" He exclaimed. "You see, what happens is..."

"Oi!" The Chief of all Officers, Albert was standing at the top of the steps looking down at us. "Number five hatch, pronto, new load starting, hurry up!"

Steven made a face and galloped back up the steps and rushed off.

I looked quizzically at the Mate.

"The head Stevedore just told me that there no more new loads coming today.",

Albert grinned. "Yeah, I lied," he said. "Just saved you from a lecture on meat loaders though." His grin widened. "You owe me and John a beer."

We spent only four days in Bluff, so I got to see very little of it. The weather turned bad on us and it rained almost constantly for three of the days but because the lamb was undercover throughout the whole process, the weather had little bearing on the loading. The only things that got wet were Steven and I rushing from one hatch to the other to mark it all off.

That first time in the far south of New Zealand wasn't overly memorable. Little did I know, however, that I would be back there that same year and eight times more thereafter. After which I would have some wonderful stories to tell. Actually, a ship nearly left me there once, but, again, a story for another book.

I did manage to get ashore briefly one afternoon with Steven during a lull in loading while everybody was waiting for more frozen lambs to arrive.

We went to the signpost at Sterling Point which is quiet a tourist attraction. The signs on the post point to major places on the globe The South Pole, New York etc with distances.

Steven spent the whole trip telling me all about the place. How the first ship there was the 'Perseverance' which arrived in 1813. The place was settled in 1823 and was originally called Campbelltown. All interesting stuff but lost on me really, what with me being a shallow youth and all.

Anyway our four days at 'The Bluff' (as it is often referred to) soon came to an end. The ship was low in the water now. Fully laden with frozen lamb, frozen mutton, frozen butter and hopefully not frozen bales of wool.

Apparently that actually happened once on a refrigerated cargo vessel in a nameless company. The wrong stuff became frozen. The story goes that the Chief Refrigeration Engineer on that particular vessel was not the usual refrigeration engineer and was not au fait with his equipment. This resulted in him misusing his equipment and not paying it enough attention. In turn, this misuse and lack of attention caused a bit of an upset. All the lamb in Number two lower hold on that nameless vessel was kept nice and warm while the wool in number two lower tween deck was frozen solid!

This caused consternation in head office and vast sums in compensation had to be paid to the people who had hoped to receive frozen meat and warm wool. Not to mention the extra wages that had to be paid to the dockers who had dig out a whole hold full of rotting meat through clouds of bluebottle flies and dispose of it. Apparently, when the hold was first opened in Victoria dock in London's East End, you could smell it in the nicer suburbs of Staines.

I believe there was some shouting and one or to people left the employ of that particular company.

The blue Peter flag was hoisted, hatches were battened down, derricks and crane jibs were stowed. Dave and I prepared the bridge equipment, the ships agent scurried about with bits of paper until all was ready.

On the evening of our fourth day in Bluff we were ready to head for home. Back to Blighty. Avonmouth to be precise.

CHAPTER 37

Oops!

"Just nip down and check on the pilot ladder young man."

"Sir?" I couldn't help the questioning sound in my voice. The lights of Bluff could still be seen behind us and we were thundering out of the bay... well... it felt like thundering, but really, we were only doing about six or seven knots. There was a headwind blowing steadily and our speed through the water, albeit fairly slow, added to the wind, that made it feel as though we were going much faster.

"Pilot ladder! Pilot ladder!" Captain McHale was frowning at me.

"Erm... yes Sir." I left my position by the centre consul in the wheelhouse and departed rapidly via the chartroom, thinking furiously. 'What?... what was I supposed to do with the bloody pilot ladder? Check on it? What did that mean? Just look at it? Measure it? Ask it if it was ok and did it want a cup of tea? What? What?'

I reached the accommodation deck and nearly collided with Derek, one of the Able seamen, coming out of the starboard alleyway.

"Where're you going in such a hurry?" He said, nimbly hopping to one side.

"Pilot ladder." I said.

"Pilot ladder?"

"Yes, bloody pilot ladder." I raised my eyes heavenwards hoping to look as though I knew what I was talking about and was sharing the information with him.

"Oh yes," he said. "It had to be changed over didn't it."

Ah… a clue!

"Yes… erm… changed over." I said, nodding.

"Keep changing their minds." He was scowling now. "First they said the pilot would disembark on the starboard side, so rig the ladder there." (I continued nodding, eyes and eyebrows going up and down furiously as he spoke, hopefully giving my face one of those agreeing, sympathetic looks.) "Then they said, oh… change of plan… it will be the port side… so we put one out on that side and took in the starboard one. . . now I think they want it on the bloody starboard side!" (My face really hurt by this time from all the eyebrow boogieing.)

"There is one on this side anyway." He started to wander off. "I think some-one was sent to put it back over." I heaved a sigh of relief. All I had to do was stick my head over the side and see if the ladder was the right distance from the water and check that wooden portable steps up to the bulwark was fixed in place so the pilot could easily get over the side, on to the ladder and down to the pilot boat that would be careering alongside the ship through waves, that to us, in a ship of some seventeen thousand tons, were mere ripples, but to a small twenty foot pilot boat were much, much bigger. *'Courageous people, these pilots. Flinging themselves on to a wood and rope ladder and in the dark, dangling over dark churning water. Then leaping on to a tiny heaving boat.'*

My thoughts drifted away and were replaced by a feeling of horror as I reached the main deck and discovered there was no ladder. No steps. Nothing there. I looked up the bridge windows and along the edge of the bridge wing fronts for signs of someone watching me. Nothing there either. *'Good'*, I thought.

But then, a new dilemma presented itself. Next to the steps down to the main deck, tucked neatly away, was a nice shiny, white painted pilot ladder, some wooden steps and a set of single metal poles that bolted onto the bulwark for the pilot to hold on to while he climbed onto the ladder. My shoulders dropped. *'Shit'* I thought. *'Now what do I do. Do I go back to the bridge and say, "I have checked on the pilot ladder Sir and it is not there." Or do I go back to the bridge and say, "I have checked on the pilot ladder Sir and it is not there, but there is one nearby." Or do I put the bloody pilot ladder over the side myself, saunter back up to the bridge and say, "It's ok Cap… sorted it myself!" Or do I jump in the water, swim back to Bluff, phone Morella,* declare undying love, beg to come and live with her for ever and get a job in the local supermarket.'

These were my options.

'Ugh… life is so bloody complicated' I thought. … and it was starting to rain! Did I mention that? Well, it was. As soon as I stepped out of the door to the accommodation, I felt it. It wasn't raining when I left the bridge, so why does it have to rain now? I stood there seething; fists clenched. A bit like a five-year-old after being told he can't have any sweets. I took a deep breath and considered the situation.

The last option had great appeal, but the jumping in the water and swimming back bit might have caused me some suffering so I discarded that idea fairly quickly.

'So, really, I thought, 'the best option is to put the bloody thing over myself.' I had seen the crew doing it and it didn't look that difficult. I took a breath, grabbed hold of the rolled-up ladder, and started to heave it in the direction of the ships side. At that point, I remembered why it didn't look difficult when the crew did it. There was always more than one of them doing the job! A simple fact, but extremely relevant at this point in time because the bloody thing was heavy! However, I managed, after some eye bulging, red faced, muscle straining heaving, to get the thing over to the bulwark, at which point I risked another glance upwards to the bridge. No one looking, 'Must all be busy navigating.'

Now came the tricky bit. Getting the thing to dangle over the side. When anybody from the deck crew did it, they just flung it over the side bit by bit, controlling it with a well place foot to stop it all disappearing at once and floating away.

I started heaving. My efforts were rewarded by a whack up the backside from the first 'spreader.'

I had forgotten about the 'spreaders.'

A pilot ladder is a rope ladder with wooden rungs. Now then… If you have just rope with wooden rungs, when you try to climb up, or down, the stupid thing starts to turn round. Once it has turned round then it is no longer square on to the ship, therefore, as one's feet push against the rung, it goes away. As it goes away, your hands are gripping the rope sides like billy-o and in a natural reaction, pulling in towards one's chest. So, you can imagine the result. One ends up lying almost horizontal with one's elbows sticking out, looking really silly and unable to move up or down. (There is, of course, the thing about the likelihood of falling off, resulting in death by drowning, being smashed on the deck of the pilot boat, or getting squished between the two vessels, but believe me, to young seaman, looking silly is far, far worse than any sort of body squishing death plunges.) There is, of course, a proper, safe way to climb such a ladder to stop all that ungainly, dangerous, feet in the air, stuff. You actually climb up it as though it was a piece if rope. So, you only use one side, and your feet use the rungs while they point away from you. However, in order to take out the 'silly look' someone invented spreaders. Every few rungs, say, every tenth one, or so, the next rung would be longer. This is the 'spreader', it sticks out about three feet either side and keeps the ladder square on to the ship's side. Ingenious! I am sure there is a law, edict, decree, rule, or Act of Parliament of some kind in an official looking document that says how long these things were supposed to be and how many rungs apart, but I had forgotten about them… probably wasn't listening during a lecture at the Academy of Better Seagoing at Warsash whilst on my years pre sea course.

Anyway, I stepped over this thing and continued to heave the ladder over the side, deftly stepping over the spreaders as they came round, and occasionally peering down to see how far away from the water the ladder was.

Then, it all went wrong.

During my last peering session, I had decided that two more rungs should go over the side and that would mean that the ladder was just above the wavetops rushing past the ship's side. I let one rung go over. My calculations were wrong, and I felt a sharp tug on the ladder. *'Oops,'* I thought. 'Too much, better pull some back'.

You will, of course, be way ahead of me here and know what was bound to happen.

I tried to heave the ladder back up but most of the ladder… most of the very heavy ladder was over the side, therefore the very heavy ladder would not budge. The very heavy gravity assisted ladder gave a couple of huge jerks as one or two of the larger waves caught the end of it. I knew this was happening because I could feel it through my foot that was standing on one of the end pieces of the rope sides that were conveniently long enough to tie to something to stop the ladder from falling in the water. *'Ah!'* Said my panicky brain. "Shit!" Exclaimed my mouth. I hadn't tied the bloody thing off before I started lobbing it over the side. 'Better do it now, quick!' I thought as I took my foot off the end of the ladder and went to grab one of the ends.

There were about five rungs left on my side of the bulwark, plus, of course, the ends of the rope. So, therefore there were five rapid clunks and a couple of swishing noises as the they all escaped my outstretched hand and followed the rest of the ladder into the Southern Ocean.

This time my brain didn't say anything. It had gone numb.

"Shit!" Said my mouth, which seemed be becoming its standard, stand-alone response when abandoned by brain control. I turned and slowly looked up at the bridge. Still no sign of anyone looking down for which I was grateful, but I could feel the panic rising.

"What are you up to?" I whirled round to see John, the Second Mate standing at the top of the steps from the accommodation deck.

"Oh …erm …. ladder …erm …pilot …lost it!" I blurted out. *'Had he seen me lose it?'*

"No." he said.

"Eh?" My brain was starting to hurt again.

"No… No, you haven't lost it."

"Eh?"

He raised his eyes to the heavens. "It's over there, on the port side I can see it from here, you dope!"

A strange feeling of guilty relief flooded over me at that point as I realised, he didn't know anything about the ladder I had just flung in the ocean.

"Ah! … Yes! …. Of course! … Hah! Silly me." I attempted to look as stupid as possible, which wasn't really difficult. Much better to be thought of as a dope that couldn't find the ladder, than the idiot who flung one over the side! That was my thinking at that point if you can call it thinking. Panicky waffle would probably be a more apt description.

"Anyway, what do you want it for?"

"It has to be moved to this side."

"Well then," he said, sticking his head forward. "It's a good job those AB's over there, the ones by the pilot ladder, are engaged in that very task. As in, moving it over to this side."

I frowned and climbed up the steps towards him, stopping halfway and peering across the top of number four hatch. Now I really felt stupid, there they were, four of them, dismantling the steps and stantions and rolling up the ladder.

"What's occurin' by yer?" Taffy, one the older AB's, with a Welsh accent deeper than the South Wales valleys he was from, had come out of the accommodation door.

"They're moving the pilot ladder over to this side." Said John.

Taffy frowned. "Don't need to, there's one here." He said, leaning past me and looking down at the main deck. "Oh, it's gone!"

"Yes." Said John, exasperation creeping into his voice. "That's what I have been saying, it is now over there and will shortly be back over here." He pointed specifically at the main-deck bulwark where the ladder should be.

"Strange." Said taffy. "The steps and stantions are here."

We all looked down at the steps and stantions.

John shook his head. "Anyway," he said. "Not my problem." And with that he strode off back along the alleyway.

"Erm … yes … I'd better go back to the bridge." I said quickly and followed John through the door, leaving Taffy looking down, in a bewildered manner, at the empty space where the pilot ladder should have been.

It took all of thirty seconds for me to gallop back up to the bridge where I arrived panting to be confronted by captain McHale and the Pilot in the wheelhouse.

"Ah, young man, there you are!" He frowned at me, pointing his chin in my direction. "Pilot ladder secure, I hope?" His beard gave me an angry bristling.

"Yes Sir, crew are just rigging it back on the starboard side Sir."

"Mmmm." He peered at me for a second. "Right, well, take the pilot down now."

I managed to keep my face straight and stop my shoulders from drooping… just. I gritted my teeth and smiled.

"Yes Sir,"

By the time I galloped back to the bridge the ship was ploughing into a substantial swell. The pilot had just made it off in time and I had watched, holding my breath, as he descended the ladder and dropped onto the deck of the plunging pilot boat. The little craft had peeled away from the ships side and headed back towards the harbour, soon disappearing into the rain which was now getting heavy and felt horizontal. It had quickly become that 'In your face' rain that hurts. The wind had increased rapidly and was made worse by our increased speed as the ship cleared the land and started the voyage back to England.

Everybody was on the bridge when I got there. John, the Second Mate, the Navigator, was checking the charts, Albert, the Chief Officer was deep in conversation with Captain McHale, Dave, the Third Mate was there because it was his watch. I was there because I was on watch with Dave and Steven was there because… well… I don't know really, just because… he was.

"Right! You two!" The Mate shouted from the wheelhouse. Steven and I wobbled towards him from the chartroom. Captain McHale was already in his tall chair by the door, and he made a distinct movement away from me as I passed him. He was obviously suffering flashbacks to when I grabbed his shoulder the last time, we encountered severe weather.

"You two are on watches for the next few days until the weather calms down. Usual arrangement." He looked at me. "You're with Dave… now, and Steven, you're with me. So, go get some sleep, see at you at four."

Steven grumbled to himself and wandered off.

"Don't forget the book!" shouted John from the depths of the chartroom. I looked blankly at The Mate. He stared back.

"Yes, don't forget the book."

"The book?"

"Yes! The book… clocks remember?"

I remembered. It was me that took the book round to all the heads of departments, deck, engine room, catering etc. for them to sign to say that they knew the clocks would be moved backwards or forwards by an hour or half an hour to keep up with the daylight. It was all about time zones and stuff to do with the sun at noon… navigational things. All the way out the clocks had to be put back half an hour at midnight as we progressed westwards until we reached the International Dateline. Once we crossed that then we were no longer in the west, we were then in the east. Which meant we had to get used to the idea that because we had put the clocks back and were behind Greenwich Mean Time, we then had to put the clocks forward twenty-four hours because we were suddenly in the east, which is ahead of Greenwich Mean Time. So… the day before we arrived on the Kiwi coast the clocks went forward meaning that that particular day, which was a Tuesday, I had had to go round with the book for everybody to sign to say they agreed that the next day would be Thursday! Missing out Wednesday altogether. So… now, I had to go round with the book again and get everybody to sign to say they agreed that although today was Friday… we were crossing the Dateline thingy again, going the other way, so the clocks were going back, because we were going into the western bit of the planet so tomorrow would be Friday!... again!

It was about then the ship started to move significantly. When I say move, I mean in a movement extra to the forward movement created by the seriously large engines we had down below. Over the next hour the weather was much the same as it had been, overcast and cold, but the wind increased dramatically and with it, the sea. It became mountainous! It was the most dramatic change in sea conditions I was to see in all my time in the Merchant Navy. Huge rolling white topped waves came rolling in from the Southeast making our, by comparison, puny little ship climb up on side of these monsters, then tip and head down towards the bottom of a vast green and black looking cliff of water, burying the entire front end under a foaming maelstrom of angry Southern Pacific Ocean. Quite what we had done to upset it I don't know, but it was severely ticked off and sent row upon row of these huge waves at us. Just in case we didn't get the message, torrential rain carried at speed by the deafening howling wind battered against the bridge front windows making it almost impossible to talk without bellowing at each other.

This was an entirely different monster to the little blow we had encountered when leaving the English Channel and entering the Bay of Biscay at the start of the voyage. There was no point in trying to master the bad weather boogie in this ocean! It was more a case of hang on to something and don't break any limbs until a three second window of level ship opportunity came round, then make a dash for the next holding on point. That last time this happened, in the Bay of Biscay, we could see where we were going. There had been a lot of moonlight breaking through fast moving clouds and the rows of waves glinted and frothed in that white ethereal light as they approached us. This time there was no moonlight, just sheets of driving rain accompanied by a wind that shrieked around the wheelhouse rattling the windows and howling through the rigging on the derricks. The waves just suddenly appeared, higher than the vessels superstructure, hurling themselves at us from our starboard bow causing, not only that terrible, rollercoaster like, stomach churning, rising, and plunging movement, but a frightening rolling motion at the same time. We were now much lower in the water, being full of cargo, so, whereas the pitching was similar to the last time (although much steeper) the rolling was much more pronounced and there was a worrying delay when the ship reached the point where it should start to roll back before it did actually start to roll back!

I staggered back into the wheelhouse and clung on to the radar, closing my eyes and praying quietly as the ship reached one of those worrying points, positioned myself between the main bridge consul and the radar so I had plenty of things to hold on to and stared out of the window. Nothing but wet, rain lashed window filled my vision. Turning my body round without letting go of anything proved somewhat difficult. Turning my body round without letting go of anything and looking cool and nonchalant like everybody else was nigh on impossible, but I thought I had managed it as I looked back towards the captain's chair.

"You look a little worried, young man." Captain McHale looked his usual calm implacable self.

"No Sir." I lied and then watched in awe as he slowly fished out his tobacco pouch and did the 'John Wayne one handed cigarette rolling thing.' Even his bobble hat looked somehow cool when he did that.

The sound of smashing crockery drifted through the open chartroom door as the Mate wrenched it open, let go of the handle and let it shut again. A momentum arresting water mountain had arrived at the same time as his hand pulled at the door handle causing him to topple backwards and fetch up against the chart table with an angry yelp. He had another, this time successful, go and the door swung shut behind him again.

The weather remained like that for a full three days.

CHAPTER 38

ROPES

The sea calmed, the ship calmed, the crew calmed, and all was back to normal in no time. The weather very quickly became very 'South Pacific like' once the wind went away. The sort of South Pacific weather you see on films about… erm… well… the South Pacific, I suppose. All blue skies, scudding, small, fluffimus cumulus clouds and gentle breezes.

"Perfect weather for more painting." Said the Mate.

Steven and I had arrived on the bridge at the usual time, six o' bloody clock in the bloody morning, expecting nothing else. However, that morning was different.

"But" continued our leader, "today is different." He paused again for dramatic effect. "Today, you will be working in the lifeboats."

We looked at each other, Steven was frowning again.

"We did those on the way out." He said.

"Ahh… I know you did young Waddington, but you didn't finish doing them." Albert was smiling a sort of mirthless grin. "You will, no doubt, remember when we were in Auckland, a truck… well… several trucks actually… arriving with stores?"

We both nodded and Steven's frown disappeared and was replaced by a scowl as we both realised what was coming.

"Manropes." He muttered.

"Precisely," said the Mate, "Dave's brand new, premade, factory spliced, shiny lifeboat manropes arrived and now require putting on the spans between the davits."

"I was hoping we could go and work in the engine room." Said Steven hurriedly. The Second Engineer said he had jobs for us."

My jaw dropped and I stared at him. "We?" I squeaked. The very last place on the planet I would want to be in was an engine room. "We?"

"Yes," said Steven, "he said we could help with one of the generators.

"No, he didn't." I said. Panic creeping up my spine.

"He did." Steven was frowning again, his eyebrows looked angry.

"Didn't." I said.

"Will you two schoolboys shut the fuck up?" The Chief Officers head was on a swivel, his eyes darting from Steven to me and back again. His face a picture of indignant incredulity.

"Just go away and do as you're told."

"Yes sir." I said childishly loudly and turned away quickly before Steven could say anymore. The important thing, I realised, was not the engine room thing itself, horrible though it might be, it was making sure the Mate didn't remember Steven's statement later. There was still a long way to go before we reached Avonmouth so I would have to make sure Steven didn't go anywhere near our Chief Officer without me there to head off any further ridiculous ideas of getting young George in an engine room.

I didn't have anything against engine rooms themselves. I am sure they are wonderful fascinating places for those people who like engines. I, however, did not like engines then and I do not like engines now. What's more I am absolutely sure that I will not like them in the future. Noisy, dirty, oily things, in my opinion, that work on some sort of magic that involves hot things and explosions. I have nothing but awe and respect for those people that somehow understand such machines. But… not for me, not in this lifetime. Maybe next time round…

We left the bridge in a hurry and galloped off to find the new manropes. Steven didn't speak to me all the way to the forecastle, where we went, looking for the Bosun. This could have been because he was angry with me for shoving a spanner in his 'engine room working' scheme, or, of course, it could have been that he was, like me, busy having kittens over having to hunt down the Bosun and ask him for something.

"Whaat fer?" He scowled up at us from his seat outside the store when Steven timidly approached him and asked for the manropes.

"We… we…we…" stuttered Steven.

"Stip yer stutterin' laddie aan spek yer mind!" the Bosun stood up and deepened his scowl, his voice going from a deep rumble, up through several gears and settling on a loud boom.

I took a step backwards and half a pace to one side, so I was bravely positioned slightly behind Steven.

"Ahh, err, ropes... man... I mean man ropes...!" Steven's fright was beginning to overwhelm him.

"Lifeboats!" I heard a voice say and then realised it was me. I was too shocked by my own bravery to say anything else but peered out from behind Steven's right shoulder.

The Bosun leant sideways slightly and tilted his head so he could see who was speaking. I shifted my feet and leant the other way to get back behind Steven, who, uncooperatively moved further away, whereupon a huge bosun sized hand shot forward and grabbed me by the shoulder while another hand of matching size and power pushed Steven to one side.

The grizzled old sailor stared into me. "Eh?"

"Lifeboats, lifeboats, manropes, new ones!" I squeaked in rush of words that went up three octaves in the sentence, my eyes widening with each word.

"In yon store." He said releasing me suddenly and tossing his head in the general direction of the door behind him. Steven leapt forward and headed towards the door with me following closely behind.

"Wait!" Bellowed the Bosun.

Steven stopped suddenly and whirled round so he was facing me. I was not so quick and carried on a whole pace. Of course, the inevitable happened. My still advancing head connected, once again, with Steven's stationary nose.

"Ow. Owww. Hahoowoo!" His anguished cry was cut short as he grabbed his nostrils. "By doze! By doze! He wailed, then stopped and scowled the mother of scowls at me. "Ah-ged!" There was a tangible heartfelt anger in his voice.

"Pardon?" I said stepping back and rubbing my forehead.

"By doze!" He let go of the damaged piece of his anatomy briefly and blood flowed down over his lips.

"My nose! Again!" He hissed angrily before re-grabbing it and stopping the blood flow.

"Sorry," I muttered, "but you stopped suddenly again."

"Feck me!" The Bosun was looking at us with a sad incredulous expression which reminded me of... well... the look everybody else we encountered gave us after a few minutes.

"Feck me!" He said again shaking his head. He looked back along the main deck and raised his gaze to the starboard bridge wing. The Chief Officer was standing on the raised compass binnacle platform at the outside edge of the bridge wing deck. He also was shaking his head. (We seemed to induce a lot of head shaking in people wherever we went.)

"I will get yer ropes laddie." The Bosun disappeared into the store as I watched the Chief Officer, head bowed, walk towards the wheelhouse. 'That,' I thought, 'was the third time he's seen me cause damage to Steven's nose.'

"Here's yeh ropes, now dinnea feck em up!" He said, emerging after a few seconds and flinging four huge coils of rope on the deck. Whereupon Steven, obviously keen to get away, let go his still bleeding nose and bent down to pick up the nearest two coils. I, even keener to get away, did likewise with the other two coils.

"Ye'll no be able to carry 'em." Said the Bosun as we both, unable to move them never mind lift them, fell into our respective piles of rope. Cue more head shaking from the Bosun.

"Would ye like soom help maybe?" He said softly. Which was all very well, but, although it sounded fine to me, to Steven it sounded not so fine. He had explained one evening in the bar during the outward-bound passage, not long after we had left the Panama Canal.

"Have you noticed," he had said, "how the bosun's voice sounds the most threatening and sinister when he is speaking quietly and being nice?"

I could remember agreeing with him enthusiastically and right now I could feel the menace that came with his kindly offer of help.

"It's ok," I said quickly, "we'll manage." I summoned superhuman strength from somewhere and grabbed a coil of rope, lifted it and staggered off down the deck, not stopping until I got to the bottom of the steps leading up to the accommodation deck.

"This is stupid." Announced Steven as he arrived, puffing and panting at the bottom of steps also.

Down To The Sea. A Cadet's Tale

"Well I can't see any other way of getting these bloody ropes up to the boat deck." I said frowning at him.

"No… No… No," he said, looking frustrated. "I don't mean that, I mean us being so frightened of the bosun. In fact, I am going to stop being frightened." His face took on a angry determined look.

"Very good." I said. "You do that." I looked at him directly. "What are you going to do? Challenge him to a duel perhaps? Cutlasses at dawn?" I shook my head as I bent down and grabbed my rope.

"No, I am just going to be more assertive and not run a mile whenever I see him." He was gazing out to sea and nodding his head wisely while all this life changing, 'boy becoming a man' nonsense was flowing from him. "You should do the same." He said suddenly after a brief pause.

I looked at him, horrified. "No thank you. I am quite happy to remain frightened to death." I said.

"But I will come and visit you in whatever High Dependency, Brain Trauma ward you end up in."

He wrinkled his forehead again. "Oh, don't be such a…."

"What the feck are you two ladies gossiping aboot the noo? Bellowed the Bosun. He had come up behind us and was standing with a coil of rope in each arm. "Get a move on!"

Steven and his new assertiveness squeaked in fright and fled up the steps.

"Take some fecking rope with yeh!" The bosun's face was beginning to turn purple and his biceps seemed to be growing by the second.

There was a loud clattering as Steven turned and came back down the steps two at a time. He reached the deck with a thump and grabbed at the nearest coil, which, unfortunately I had just started to pick up.

"Not that one!" I shouted. "That's mine!" He dropped it and grabbed the other one, his eyes wide, staring and panic stricken. There followed a demonstration of the power a human being can summon when motivated by fear and panic. Steven, using what must have been every ounce of strength in his beanpole like structure, took two paces up the steps and hurled the coil of rope that he previously been barely able to carry, up towards the accommodation deck. I watched open mouthed as the large coil sailed through the air towards the outside alleyway some six feet above our level. I was completely awestruck! My senses were totally flummoxed by this incredible strength. A strength and power that caused a very, very heavy coil of rope to cut through the tropical air like a discus. Approximately one second later my brain was reprocessing due to a second phenomenon. The coil, during its initial upward movement seemed to be heading for the alleyway, however, for some aerodynamic reason, halfway up, it began to arc to the left. There followed one of those moments that are, at the time of happening, sudden, shocking and mind numbing, but when recalled later always seem to have happened in slow motion. Instead of landing on the deck, the flying coil hit the top of the bulwark, at the point where it began its dip down towards the main deck, whereupon it then seemed to stop, suspend itself upright somehow, standing on its edge. It then spun slightly until it was side on to us lower deck observers and we could see right through the hole in the middle. Two forces came into play at that point. Firstly, Steven began to run up the steps, secondly the Pacific Ocean chose that moment to cause a slight swell. Enough swell to make the New Zealand Star roll slightly to starboard. The coil turned its outside edge a little towards us and toppled gently over the side.

There was a silence for what seemed like an exceedingly long time.

That's not quite true. About the silence I mean. There was an agonised low-pitched wailing noise that issued from Steven's gaping mouth as both his hands flew to his face and he turned away from the horror and looked at us. I went to the side and joined the Bosun in peering along the length of the ship. There was no sign of the coil whatsoever. It had gone. Disappeared.

'Again?' I thought. *'That's the second thing that's been lost from this precise point on the ship.'*

Steven was distraught. He couldn't speak.

I continued to think of pilot ladders.

"Oh God!" Breathed Steven into his hands.

The Bosun and I slowly turned to look at him.

"Oh God!" He said again louder this time with degree of… of… well… 'Panicky horror' I suppose you could call it.

"Oh God! Oh God! Oh God!"

"It doesnae matter how many times ye call to Him," Said the Bosun quietly, "Ye'll get nay help there." With that he turned on his heal and walked away.

I did briefly think that, maybe, with Steven's father being a vicar and all, what the bosun said might not be entirely true. But I dismissed it almost immediately as being ridiculous. I mean vicars, excellent folk that they are, probably aren't far enough up the ecclesiastical food chain to warrant heavenly assistance for their offspring. Maybe if his father had been a Saint or a Pope or something then perhaps something could have been organised. Winged chariots full of… full of… well, whatever winged chariots come full of… might have been dispatched to rescue the errant manropes from the oggin. Anyway, Steven, it appeared, was on his own! Not even a cherub!

"We'll have to tell the Mate." He said quietly after a moment or two trying to get his mouth to say what his horrified brain was telling it.

"What?" I exclaimed, frowning deeply. "We? … WE! … What are you talking about… WE?" I paused, but only to take a breath, "I didn't throw the bloody thing over the side. You did that, all on your own!"

All the 'Team… help each other… look after your mate… always back each other up' thing left me the instant the thought of standing in front of the Chief Officer and telling him 'We' had hurled his equipment over the side in mid pacific. Very cowardly of me I know, but in my defence I was only seventeen and a petulant youth. Petulant youths are supposed to be like that.

Steven looked distraught. Again.

We now had three heavy coils of rope to get to the boat deck. Which, I suppose, was better than four. Less weight to carry, which was good, unfortunately that weight had now been transferred to Steven's shoulders. The weight of responsibility can, at times, be heavier than the weight of a manrope or two.

"I'll have to go and tell the Mate." He said suddenly, turning and then running up the steps. I think he was in a rush to get to the bridge before his courage failed him altogether.

I felt a little bad that I didn't go after him but then realised I was left with all this bloody rope to get up two sets of steps and across the boat deck. *'Yes,'* I consoled myself, *'that was fair enough. I do the heavy lifting, Steven gets the bollocking."*

It was about fifteen minutes later that a very sweaty George arrived at the port lifeboat and threw the first coil of rope on the deck.

"Where have you been?" Steven was standing by the forward boat davit (that's the thing at either end of the boat that holds up it up and stops it falling in the water) looking pleased with himself.

"What do you mean … Where have you been?" I was panting. "Lugging these stupid ropes up the stupid ladders… and …erm, while we're on the subject… where have you been? I thought you were going to be keelhauled for destroying ships equipment or something."

"So, did I!" said Steven with feeling. "But the Mate was exceptionally good about it actually. He said not to worry and that he would tell the Third Mate for me because that's who is responsible for boats and stuff." He smiled brightly, His face a picture of calm, hopeful innocence.

"Mmmm…" I wasn't sure about this. "So, Dave doesn't know yet?" I said quietly. Steven shook his head, his calm expression beginning to disappear. "So, Dave doesn't know yet that you threw his brand new, unused, still coiled manropes over the side? The very manropes he was boasting about finally getting hold of after three trips of trying to persuade the powers that be that they were necessary.

He doesn't know that HIS Lovely new manropes, that were to adorn His lifeboats, are now minus one. The third officer, whose actual job it is to look after the lifeboats does not know…" I stopped talking because of the whimpering noise that began to come from Steven.

"Do you think he'll mind?" He said.

It took us about twenty minutes to heave the remaining coils of rope up the ladders, across the boat deck to the port side and over to the boat. I brought the last one up and by the time I got there Steven had cut the cords holding the ropes in a coil and was trying to unravel the very new, very stiff, exceptionally long lifeboat manropes. I can't remember how long they were supposed to be but there was some 'Board of Trade' regulation or other that demanded these things were three times the height of the deck above the water multiplied by the square root of the wind direction on Easter day or something. Anyway, they were long and causing Steven a great deal of trouble.

"These things are very stiff, how are we going to get them up into the boats and to hang properly from the span?"

I looked at the problem with my rapier-like mind and natural, problem solving nature.

"Dunno." I said.

"Steven frowned and was obviously thinking hard. "I remember someone telling me about this." He said, his face brightening. "Ah yes!" He was nodding his head furiously as the solution to the problem raced into his mind. He smiled a knowing smile. "All we have to do is stretch the rope out on the deck and unstiffen it." He was smiling and nodding at me as he spoke, ending on a note of triumph.

I sighed. "How is that going to make it unstiff? What piece of physics is your solution based on?"

Steven's smile faded again. "Erm… Well." He elongated the word 'well' to give himself thinking time. A few seconds went by in silence until Steven's brain decided it had had enough scientific thought and moved on to 'what to do next'.

"What we'll do," he said brightly, "is… we'll tie one end to the railings over there," he pointed to the edge of the boat deck where the white painted railings edged the boat deck. Stanchion posts every few feet supported three horizontal railings which went right around the boat deck. The top rail was for leaning on and the conveniently placed bottom railing was for putting one foot on whilst leaning in a seamanlike manner. I don't know what the middle one was for. Some sort of support structure probably.

"Yes." I said slowly wondering what was coming next.

"Then we'll throw the whole coil over the side and the weight of it will take out all the kinks." His face was now full of triumph and delight.

"Erm… right I see." I wasn't so sure. It sounded feasible but I had that feeling that there was something not quite right with his thinking. However, I helped him cut the rest of cords and get the thing over to the rail where he, I stress the word 'HE', tied the end of the manrope to the top rail.

"Right, lift! He shouted as we both heaved the thing upwards.

Now then… I should have cottoned on to the problem as soon as we started to lift. As we had discovered these things are heavy and awkward to move. The manropes were premade, which means throughout the length of the bloody things, every few feet or so, as per yet another Board of Trade regulation, a knot was tied so people in an emergency could control their descent from the deck to the lifeboat when it reached the water. So… they are long, very lumpy, difficult coils of rope to manage... and oh so very heavy.

'*That's it!*' I thought. '*That's the problem... weight! Heavy! When it uncoils and reaches all the way down, we won't be able to pull it back up! Some of it'll hit the water and get wet and be even heavier!*'

"Stop!" I screamed out in panic.

"Stop!" Screamed Steven at the same time as me. "It's too heavy!" He had realised, at precisely the same time, that the thing was too heavy. As I said, fortune favoured us. The rope Gods smiled briefly down and stopped a disaster.

Just for that one brief moment.

"WADDINGTON! YOU FUCKING IDIOT!"

Fortune, the Gods and everybody else deserted us and ran for cover. It was Dave. He was descending the ladder from the Bridge with a murderous scowl where he had just arrived to take over from the Mate, who had obviously told him about Steven's unfortunate mishap with the other coil.

We both turned to face this new menace. Unfortunately, in my panic, I let go of my side of the coil. The disaster that the Gods had tried so hard to stop happening... happened. The coil started to topple over the side. Steven tried manfully to stop it going, but away it went, sent on its way with an ear-piercing shriek which could have come from anyone of us.

"Oh God." Steven looked over the side. Dave, who was still halfway down the ladder, stopped and stared.

At the same time, the part of the rope that was still in coil form plummeted into the water at high speed with a resounding slap that could easily be heard over the sound of the ship's engines. The rope jerked and yanked hard at the railing to which it was still tied as the ropes end finally uncoiled and streamed out along the side of the ship. It hit the water again, this time it hit so hard that the end flew into the air, so it was almost level with the afterdeck, before descending, faster now, into the sea. The process was repeated, another loud slap and the end of the rope flew back into the air. This time, though, it was different.

Steven, you see, was not good at knots and remember it was he who tied the manrope to the rail. There was, just as the ropes end reached its maximum altitude, a horrible grinding noise. Steven and I looked at the rail. It was bending, only slightly, but it was, definitely, bending.

Steven stared. I stared. Dave, who was advancing now from the ladder towards us, stared.

"That rails going to break! Shouted Dave. "Get out the way QUICK!" He screamed. We needed no further invitation. We ran. Dave ran. The rail began to make a twanging noise and bent further, and Steven's knot… well Steven's knot… came undone. The rope, its entire length airborne, sailed away behind us, finally hitting the water astern of the ship.

There was a silence you could cut with a knife.

"Well, the rail didn't break." Said Steven.

Dave turned slowly towards Steven and lifted his head so he was looking directly up the nose of the much taller cadet. The third of all the officers tried to speak. Rage and fury were evident. His face was a purple colour, and his mouth was moving and contorting but no words would come out. His hands began to come up and were making, first, fist shapes, then finger wagging shapes then open palm shapes and back to fists, still no words would come out. Steven began to cower away. Dave's head began to shake and became an even darker shade of purple as he continued to stare up Steven's nose. Finally, a word made it past his furious lips.

"Ropes." He whispered.

Neither of us dare to move.

"Ropes." He said again, a little louder. His head stopped shaking and settled on a less frightening quiver but that just gave the rest of him a more menacing look, particularly as his mouth forced itself into a demonic smile. If you have ever seen one of those horror films where an evil demon possesses someone… well… That was Dave!

"Ropes." He growled again still staring and quivering at poor Steven. He managed then, with an extraordinary effort to control his face and he turned away, slowly moving in a shocked shuffling motion towards the bridge.

He was angry because he had lost his prized manropes.

Steven was angry because we had done it all wrong again and lost Dave's prized manropes.

Me? … well I was angry because I had just realised, we had missed breakfast!

Three days later we entered the Panama Canal again.

CHAPTER 39

LAST LEG

The breakwater marking the outer limits of the harbour at Colon disappeared over the horizon. The sea was flat calm, the sun was setting, and the evening gloom was descending. There was not a cloud in the sky and the ship thumped its way towards the gathering darkness... and home. The pilot had disembarked after the usual chase down to the pilot ladder. I had helped put the ladder over the side earlier so was quite proud of myself because we still had it! I was standing in the wheelhouse feeling pleased with myself.

The Panama Canal and bunkering in Cristobal had come and gone in a flash. I quite enjoyed coming into Cristobal. It was my first return port! The first time I had come back to a port I had been to before! A proper 'Salty Seadog'.

The Mate arrived on the bridge as soon as he was released from his station on the forecastle.

"What are you looking so smug about?" He said as soon as he saw me.

The salty seadog fled the scene. "Nothing." I mumbled, blushing furiously yet again.

"Mmmm... yes... well.. you can go down now." He said. "Back to day-work for you two, tell Steven to be up here, six thirty tomorrow morning, as usual."

"Will do." I shouted over my shoulder as I hurtled through the door and aimed myself at the stairs.

I didn't get far.

Down To The Sea. A Cadet's Tale

"Just a moment young man." Captain McHale was in the chartroom doing his one-handed cigarette rolling thing.

"I will need to see the both of you soon and review your workbooks and your collage correspondence work." He said, peering over the top of his sunglasses.

"Oh… erm… yes Sir." I said. Immediately thinking of how long it would take me to get it all up to date. *'About two months.'* Was the answer.

Something in my face must have given away my thoughts. He stopped rolling.

"I trust everything is up to date." He said slowly, smiling, but with an air of menace.

"Of course, Sir." I said.

He looked doubtful. "Mmmm, ok, off you go."

I turned on my heel and resumed my escape from the bridge.

"I think we're in the shit." I announced, as I arrived panting in our cabin.

Steven looked up from his Steam Reciprocating Engines.

"Why?" He said, frowning. "What have you done this time?"

I matched his frown. "Nothing." … Steven still, even now, assumed that, if we were in trouble of some sort, it was because of something I had done. *'He has so easily forgotten the manrope incident. That was entirely his own idea and therefore entirely his fault. Nothing to do with me.'* Unfortunately, that thought didn't help get rid of the feeling I had, that the inference in his question was that any trouble we had been in, had, actually, been mostly my fault. "Nothing." I repeated, loudly. My indignant tone covering any thoughts of inadequacy. "It's just that The Old Man wants to see us about our workbooks and stuff."

Steven's frown deepened. He tutted and raised his eyes heavenwards. (I had seen him do that before… It's not easy, raising your eyes heavenwards and frowning at the same time. I had tried in front of the mirror several times and merely succeeded in looking constipated.)

"I suppose I will have to answer some of those navigation principle questions then." He said.

I held my breath, praying he wasn't going to mention 'The retrograde motion of Uranus'.

"Mind you." He continued, his face brightening. "That thing about the retrograde motion of Uranus was pretty interesting."

"Aagh!" I let out a cry. "Please! No! Anything but that." I said. I am fed up with Uranus!"

There was a chortling noise from behind me and I whirled round to see John, the second mate coming into the cabin.

"Don't go near his anus then if you're fed up with it!" He said laughing.

Steven gawped at him and I blushed and stammered, realising what that sounded like.

"No… No… No…!" I said quickly and far too loudly. "Planets… Planets… He's talking about planets!"

"But of course, he is." Said John, still grinning furiously.

"Tell him." I squeaked looking imploringly at Steven.

"Eh?" He stared at us one at a time and back again, a blank look on his face.

John peered at him, bending forward so his face was about six inches away from Steven's nose.

"No… nothing…" He said straightening up. "Waste of time trying to wind him up." He turned slightly and looked at me, the grin re-appearing. "You, however, are perfect."

"What do you mean?" I stared back at him, an indignant look on my face surrounded by a sullen air. A bit like a bad tempered, immature, grumbling teenager. (Which, really, come to think of it, was an accurate description of my eighteen-year-old self.)

"You are easily wound up. Easily led up the garden path." He was still grinning which made me even more sullen.

"I'm not." I said.

"You are!"

"Not."

"Are." Said John loudly with an air of finality. "Anyway," he said, even louder now and still looking at me. "I just came in to say," he winked at me and turned towards Steven again, "that The Mate wants Steven to show a film in the bar tonight." By this time young Waddington had lost interest in us and had returned to the fascinating, all-consuming world of Steam Reciprocating Engines.

He looked up briefly then turned away again. "No." He said. "Brian is the projectionist now, not me."

"Ah… yes, I know." Said John. "But Albert wants Brian to go up to the bridge and help Dave with something."

"Wha…!" I started to protest but John thumped me in the arm and frowned at me shaking his head furiously.

"Bu…!" He kicked me this time.

Steven continued reading but blew out his cheeks, sighed and said, "Oh alright then, what film is it?"

"Well…" John started to back up towards the door and tugging on my arm, indicating I should do the same. "It is one of the films in the new box that we picked up in Cristobal this time."

"Obviously." Said Steven, still reading. "But what's it called?"

"Ah yes well…erm…" John was grinning again and backing nearer the door.

"…You see…that's the funny thing."

"Yes." Said Steven looking round.

"Well… the ship's agent came with the box and swapped them over."

"Yes." Steven started to look a little tense.

"…And… well the thing is he didn't realise but he bought the same box we dropped off on the way out."

Steven was silent. His shoulders began to stiffen and then his face began to drain of colour. At the same time his hands began to curl and form fists. There was a distinct volcanic feel in the air.

"So…" John backed away a little more. "So… the lads have decided to watch that Mick Jagger film again, you know, 'Ned Kelly'.

Now, as I have said before, Steven never swears. Not ever. Even Jimmy the old Third Engineer who had been with him on his last ship had said that no one had ever… ever heard Steven swear. But then one wouldn't expect the son of a Vicar to run around 'effing and jeffing' all over the place, would one.

There was a short silence. Then the gates of Hell opened, triple headed, raging monsters issued forth and leapt into Steven. He shot to his feet becoming, instantly his full six foot three inches. His hands balled into white knuckled fists and he spread his arms out wide. His face was a picture of pent up fury and uncontrolled rage.

His mouth opened and shut a few times until suddenly he bellowed "FUUUCCKK NO! NO!

FUUUCCKING FUCK FUCKING NO! NO!"

"Run!" Shouted John as he turned tail and fled the cabin. I followed. The chair that Steven had been sitting in narrowly missed me as I hurdled the storm sill. We ran into the alleyway, both turned right after hitting the opposite wall and legged off towards the cross alleyway and the relative safety of the stairs.

Actually, the 'legging down the alleyway' part of the escape was a bit difficult. As we left the cabin we ran straight into JoJo, Barry, two other engineers and Dave. All of whom had been listening, standing outside the door, so there was quite a stampede to that 'safe area' in the cross alleyway.

The cabin door slammed shut.

We stood panting in a huddle by the stairs, and I looked at them all one at a time.

"You were winding him up, weren't you?" I said to no one in particular.

"Of course, I was!" Said John. "We have got some good films this time. We've even got 'The Good. The Bad and The Ugly.'! His voice had a triumphant note to it. As though he had negotiated a multi-million-dollar deal to secure the film exclusively for our viewing.

"Ooohhh!" Exclaimed Barry, his eyes lighting up. "Is that a porn film?" We all turned and stared at him.

He looked at each of us turn. "What?" He said, his head still darting back and forth.

John shook his head slowly. "I don't believe you've just asked that!" He said, incredulously, then he turned and went back down the alleyway towards his cabin.

Barry continued looking at us all in turn. "Well?" he started to frown. "Is it?"

"No!" Dave said, raising his eyes. "Of course not. It's a western."

"Oh." Barry was disappointed. His shoulders sagged and he looked like a little boy that had had his sweets taken away.

"It's a good one." I said, trying to lift his gloom. "It's got Clint Eastwood in it."

"Oh." He said, as he turned and shuffled away towards the engineer's alleyway.

I watched him depart. For some reason I felt sorry for him.

Nobody else showed any signs of sympathy. They all just wandered away towards the rest of their day.

I was left on my own. Not only was I left on my own, but I suddenly realised, I had nowhere specific to go! I was left at the end of an empty alleyway. *'What should I do now?'* I thought. *'I'm left in no man's land!'* Questions started to crowd my brain. *'Should I go back to the cabin? Perhaps I should go to the smokeroom and see about this film? Or was John actually telling the truth about The Mate wanting me to do some job or other on the bridge?'* I was beginning to think that this 'being a Merchant Navy Officer and having to make life defining decisions' thing, might be too much for me. The cabin option was a bit risky, I decided. There was a six foot two, angry Steven, with murderous intent lurking in there. God knows what he might do if I showed my face.

I discarded the 'job on the bridge' idea, The Mate had effectively given us the night off only a few minutes before, so I was pretty sure that was just part of John's wind up. After all he did kick me in the shin when I tried to protest.

So that left the smokeroom. I trotted down the stairs mumbling to myself about the inadequacies of the School of Navigation at Warsash. It was all their fault, I decided, for not having lectures about how to conduct oneself after a wind up turned one's cabin mate into that bloke from 'Psycho'!

I opened the smoke-room door expecting to find it full people getting projectors ready and filling up beer glasses.

Empty. Not a soul.

So, back to the cabin I went and slowly opened the door. No missiles came my way, so I went in. Steven was still sitting reading.

"I'm not showing it." He mumbled without raising his head.

"He was winding you up, they haven't got 'Ned Kelly' at all."

He still didn't look up. "Oh."

"Anyway, I'll show it." I said.

"Oh."

"So…" I said after a short awkward silence. "You're not going to throw anything at me again."

"No." he said, grinning into his book. "As long as you stop talking and let me read."

"Ok." I said, feeling relieved. "Just one thing though."

"What?" He was starting to frown but still didn't look up.

"Our homework, when shall we do that?"

"Our homework?" Now he looked up. "OUR homework?" He was frowning.

"Yes." I said.

Steven stood up.

"WE do not have homework. YOU have homework and I have homework." His arms were spread wide with hands and right angles to the floor, presumably to indicate the vast difference between the homeworks.

"You..." He continued, "...Do your homework." One hand chopped the air. "I..." The other hand chopped the air. "...Do my homework." Both hands chopped the air several times while he said. "We... We... do not do OUR homework. Because WE do not have any 'OUR' homework."

He sat back down with a thump and sort of tossed his head back into his book, keeping his frown permanently etched on his face.

I could see a crisis looming here. One of monumental proportions. There was even a possibility that I would have to do all the remaining work myself! I went all cold and shivery at the thought. Steven would have to be worked on gently, I decided.

"Yes. Yes, you are quite right." I said. "I will have to get cracking on the navigation questions myself." I finished the sentence with a short sigh. "Won't learn anything by letting you do it all eh?"

Steven grunted and continued reading.

"It's just that you're such a natural teacher." I felt a tad false and manipulative saying that, but desperate times need desperate measures, and I could see it had the desired effect. Even though he continued reading with a feigned look of extra concentration there was a definite lightening of his expression with a slightly 'pleased with myself' look around the corners of his mouth.

'That's enough sycophantic fawning for now' I thought. 'Don't want to overdo it.'

There was a knock at the door and the Second Engineer walked in.

"So," he said, rubbing his hands together. "Who's showing this film then?"

"Him." Announced Steven immediately. Again, without even looking up, but flapping a hand in my direction.

"Me." I confirmed.

"Well, come on then." He said marching out. "It's a long film this one. A 'four reeler'!"

Most of the Walport films came on three reels but now and again an epic of some sort would turn up that wouldn't fit on three reels. The Good. The bad and the Ugly was just such a film.

I followed him out.

That was how the first evening of the last leg of our voyage was spent. Engineering watch keepers watched the engine. Bridge watch keepers watched where we were going. Film watchers watched the film and young Waddington read about Steam Reciprocating Engines.

Over the next few days Steven and I were tasked with finishing off the last bits of painting. Various little nooks and crannies that had been missed during the trip needed our expert attention. That was our morning tasks all the way across the Atlantic. Well, until the weather started to get a bit chilly that is. A stiff North Easterly wind that bit at the cheekbones giving you permanently watery eyes and a squint sprang up after about five days and we were given other 'meaningful' tasks indoors.

To my relief, as soon as this colder weather hit, our Chief of all the Officers gave us the afternoons to get some college work done and to my even greater relief, Steven slipped back into teacher mode and helped me with my navigation questions. The only downside was that I had to listen to his long lectures on the navigation principles he found so interesting, and I should have found interesting but didn't.

It was some years later that I became eternally grateful to Steven when I found that facts and figures that he had quoted at me that trip surfaced from my befuddled brain during exams. Only then, after all that time, did I appreciate his depth of knowledge and my lack of maturity.

We were summoned to the captain's cabin one cloudy, windy afternoon a few days before arriving in Avonmouth. The ship was pitching gently but noticeably with the bow punching its way through a grey Atlantic swell as the pair of us trotted up the stairs carrying our completed college work and our big floppy blue Merchant Navy Training Board workbooks.

I had been dreading this day. For one thing, Captain McHale still frightened the socks off me. Secondly, I became a stuttering idiot every time he spoke to me, and lastly, I hadn't completed everything I was supposed to complete. I was feverishly hoping that a; he wouldn't notice the missing learning modules and b; he wouldn't ask me anything.

"Enter!" He bellowed the instant Steven, who I had engineered into the lead coming up the stairs, knocked on the door to his cabin. We both let out small whimpering noises as Steven pushed open the door.

"Ahh, there you are." Said Captain McHale. He was standing by his desk in his shirt sleeves peering over the top of a pair half-moon spectacles and looking fierce. He didn't smile.

"This, I take it, is your college work for the entire trip. Is it?" He took off his glasses and used them to point at the sheaves of paper in our hands.

We both timidly pushed our hands out in front of us like humble peasants offering goods to a tyrannical landowner.

"Yes sir." We said in unison.

"And your workbooks?"

Our hands moved a little further towards him.

"Yes sir."

"Right. Put them on my desk I will review them over the next couple of days, sign what I have to sign and hand them back before you leave the vessel."

"Yes sir."

Relief spread over me and I turned to leave.

"Where d'ya think you're going young man!"

I turned back, relief deserting me even quicker then it came.

"Oh… Ah… Sorry… erm… McSir… Ah Hale… Sir, Captain Sir!" The stuttering idiot had returned. I should say, the bright red, stuttering, idiot had returned.

I added a final "Sir." For no apparent reason before falling silent.

Captain McHale stared at me for a while and then turned and retreated behind his desk. He probably felt safer there. I know I would have if faced with an idiot like me.

"Well." He said finally, after what seemed an eternity while he stared at us one at a time.

"Well, you have both done very well this trip." He paused and moved his head up down in a slow nod. "Yes, very well. You can both be proud of yourselves. You have conducted all your duties well." He frowned slightly. "Most of them, anyway."

We stared at him. More in shocked non-comprehension than anything, really. We had both been expecting a dressing down and to be told "Must do better!" or words to that effect.

"All three officers say good things about you both so your end of voyage reports to the company will reflect that."

This last statement was a bit of a shock. It hadn't occurred to me that there was an 'End of Voyage Report to the company'.

We stood staring at him. He looked at Steven, then at me.

"Well? That's all! Off you go! He said sharply frowning.

Steven was first out the door. He was outside the captain's cabin and down three steps before I had even turned to go. I just managed to catch the door handle before it shut.

"Oh… One other thing young George."

My heart sank as turned back to face him. Captain McHale had sat down by this time and didn't raise his head as he spoke.

"One word of advice." He spoke slowly. "If you make a mistake like breaking something or losing something then tell someone immediately."

"Yes Sir." I managed.

"Just like young Mr. Waddington did when he lost our manropes." He continued.

"Yes Sir."

He was still looking down at something on his desk but waved a hand indicating I could resume leaving so I turned again and quickly grabbed at the door handle trying to pull open the door and leave at the same time.

"Pilot ladders are expensive pieces of equipment." I heard him say as the door closed behind me.

CHAPTER 40

CHANNELS

"Fog! Bloody fog." Our Navigator, or Second Mate as he is occasionally referred to, was not happy. All his calculations and predictions had put us in Avonmouth, tied up by the eleventh of April. Which meant he could be home by the twelfth. This now was looking extremely unlikely. We had crawled our way into the Western Approaches, the area southeast of Ireland and northwest of Cornwall at a slow, chugging six knots, which is about eight miles an hour for those without a nautical twitch. In fact, it wasn't only the fog that had stunted our progress. All the other Weather Gods, in a sort of team effort, had conspired to slow us down as well.

A heavy northerly swell had sprung up out of nowhere when we were midway across the Atlantic and it refused to go away so our ship had heaved, rolled, pitched and wallowed its way North Eastwards, so, once again, everybody had aching knees and tea stains down the front of their white uniform shirts.

Despite this we had maintained a good eighteen knots. Until that night, that is, when I was awoken at about one o'clock by a lack of noise. It had taken me a good half minute to work out where I was and what was happening. The generator hum was still evident, but there was some other noise, something different. My brain, as usual, slowly, began to sort out the confused signals it was getting. *'The engine noise is different.'* It told me. *'We've slowed down.'* I could hear hurried footsteps passing the cabin. They were accompanied by muttered oaths and other bad-tempered noises.

It had occurred to me that perhaps I should go and find out if anything was wrong. Perhaps I could help. Be of some use if there was a crisis of some sort with the engines. However, this was suppressed by the overriding feeling that young George would probably be in the way, as usual. I could imagine myself being told by large fierce looking engineers to "Take the fandanco suppressor off the actilooja valve before it explodes!" And then being moaned at because I didn't know what a valve was. So, I had decided to stay put until told to do otherwise. In fact, I discovered over the course of my cadetship, that this was the thing to do. It kept one out of all sorts of trouble.

However, 'staying put' had proved to be but a few minutes. There had been a knock at the door just before it crashed open. And Derek, one of the Able Seaman who was obviously on watch.

"Wakey, wakey!" He shouted. ... "Old Man wants you on the bridge."

"Me?" I asked, peering down from my top bunk.

"Eh?" Said Derek. My answer had been lost in the cacophony of Steven's range of snoring melodies.

"Me?" I said again. Scrambling out of the bunk.

"Oh…yes… you." He stared at the lump on the lower bunk frowning "Bloody hell! He can't half snore, can't he?"

"Tell me about it." I said landing on the deck with a thump.

We both stared at him for a few seconds.

"Anyway." Derek shook himself out of his reverie. "You're needed."

"What's wrong… have we broken down or something?" I said grabbing a pair of uniform trousers from the chair.

Derek turned and headed for the door. "Nah! Nothing like that." He said. "We've run into some fog."

Steven snored on.

So, there I was, on the bridge, at oh three hundred hours, or three o' bloody clock in the bloody morning.

Actually, I was on the starboard bridge wing, staring out into the night. The ships engine thumped behind me, slowly driving us ever deeper into the fog. Somewhere in front of me the rest of the vessel swished its way through the now gentle swell and rippled water. At least, I hoped and prayed the rest of the vessel was out there in front of me. I couldn't actually see anything passed the first pair of Stulken derricks. The fog was like a thick, grey-black wet blanket enveloping the whole world. The feeling of doom and dread it brought with it was quite intense and spooky. The whole scene was made ten times spookier by the orange glow from the radar in the wheelhouse. It shone upwards giving the person who was looking at the screen that, horror film look, so beloved of small boys trying to frighten their sisters to death by shining a torch up under their chins.

Although I had, by now, been on the bridge many times, in various situations, I still hadn't quite got over the trauma of the first few occasions. The 'tea-stroke-coffee incident for example. Or the heavy weather 'Grab the Captain by the shoulder' episode. So, I felt, even now, a little uneasy.

I stiffened slightly as Captain McHale appeared by the bridge wing door. He was rolling a cigarette one handed again. A procedure that still held me spellbound and somehow gave him that 'John Wayne' aura.

"No use looking at me boy!" He said loudly. His cigarette rolling hand continuing to do its thing while he spoke. "Keep your eyes peeled."

"Yes Sir." I said whizzing my head back forwards and cricking my neck in the process. A sharp pain shot down my left shoulder. An involuntary squeak escaped my lips and Captain McHale frowned at me.

"Eh?" He said.

"Nothing Sir, cricked my neck." I kept looking forward, mainly because any head movement hurt.

"Mmmm," he said, "Just concentrate and keep looking." He turned on his heel and marched back into the wheelhouse.

That's when John had come out. "Fog! Bloody fog!" He stomped up and down for a bit.

"Right, young fella-me-lad," he said when he had stopped muttering. "Go down and wake your mate up, he can come up and do the four to eight with the Mate and you can come up and do the twelve to four with me. With a bit of luck, if this bloody fog goes away and we get a pilot we will alongside before the evening."

"Ok." It was cold up there and I had decided I didn't like fog, so I was on my way into the wheelhouse before the second syllable had left my brain.

"Ah, young man, time for some coffee!" It was the captain.

My heart sank. *Now what do I do,* I thought, *'do I tell him I'm supposed to down and get Steven, or just make the coffee?'* But, as usual, any decision making was taken out of my hands.

"Erm…" I started to say to nobody. He had already turned away and was marching off towards the portside. So, coffee making it had to be. On went the kettle, out came the cups and as we had run out of milk by that stage of the voyage, out came the tinned milk. This was a tin of a disgusting, thick slimy, off white nearly yellow substance that tasted of… of… well… a thick, slimy, off white nearly yellow substance.

"Thought I said go down and get your mate?" John was peering into the chartroom from the wheelhouse with frown on his face.

"Cap'n says make coffee." I said without looking up. "He has more stripes."

It was a good thirty minutes later that I finally got down to the cabin and started the process of 'Steven awakening'. He was snoring as usual. Deep rhythmic snoring that came from his boots.

"Steven!" I bellowed into his ear while shaking his shoulder.

Nothing.

"Steven!" I tried again.

Still nothing. I grabbed his shoulder with two hands and shook.

"Doxford Diesels'!" I shouted and immediately noticed a movement in the tuft of hair protruding from the blanket at the pillow end.

I pressed home my advantage. "Steam Reciprocating Engines!" I roared at the tuft.

Steven sat bolt upright in one movement and stared at the end of the bunk. There was a short silence then his head turned slowly towards me. I, by this time, had sat down on our chair and was watching him slowly take human form.

"Where?" He said, his frowning face a picture of bewildered concentration.

"Where's what?" I said.

"Steam reciprocating engine."

I put on my own bewildered expression. "Eh?"

"Steam reciprocating engines." He said again. "You just said steam reciprocating engines."

I increased by bewildered expression by a factor of at least three. "Why on earth would I say steam reciprocating engines?"

"Dunno," muttered Steven, "but you did."

"Not me mate. I don't know what one is, even!" I raised my hands in the air, palms upward and level with my shoulders. "Wouldn't know one if I fell over it! Anyway, it's your turn on the bridge."

He stared at the end of the bunk again. "What time is it?"

"It is…" I looked at my watch, "Four thirty-two."

His head turned slowly towards me again. This time his facial expression was sort of uncomprehendingly distressed.

"In the morning." I added, helpfully.

"Oh God." He muttered.

I explained all that had gone before while he stared blankly at me yet again. There was one moment when I raised my voice a bit and stood up because it looked as though he was going to go back sleep, but he managed to bring his mind back from the brink and I succeeded in imparting all the information necessary.

Thus, the very last phase of that voyage of the New Zealand Star, the first one with me on it, began.

There had been a strange, sort of, feeling, throughout the ship since we had left Cristobal. A feeling that increased in intensity the nearer we got to our discharge port of Avonmouth. To begin with I couldn't identify what it was. It was just, somehow, different from before Panama. Before the Canal.

The mood seemed lighter but, at the same time there was an air of excitement which brought with it an element of tension. It wasn't until that final afternoon as we approached the port that I discovered what it was.

"Aye, aye, young man, you're doing a lot of pacing." Albert, the Mate had come up to the bridge a little earlier and had been speaking to Captain McHale in earnest tones, presumably about important Captain-stroke-Chief Officer stuff, on the port bridge wing. Now our leader had disappeared into the chartroom and his second in command had wandered across the wheelhouse, stuck his head in the radar for a minute and then wandered out on to the starboard bridge wing.

"Eh?" I responded to his observation.

"Pacing, you're doing a lot of pacing."

The statement took me by surprise. "Oh, erm… am I?" I realised he was right. I had been pacing up and down more than usual. In fact, to this day, I am a renowned pacer. Come to think of it, that's probably the day I began my pacing career.

"Yes," he said, "You are. You look like a man who has a definite case of the channels."

"Pardon!" I said, a little indignantly. It sounded as though he was accusing me of having picked up some nasty social disease.

"The channels." He said again.

I looked at him blankly.

"The channels! The channels!" As usual when the Mate became frustrated with me his arms began to wave about.

I continued to look at him blankly.

"Has nobody told you about 'The Channels'?"

I shook my head, slowly.

He sighed. "Well, you must feel something," he said, "It's the end of the voyage."

It was then I understood. The clouds parted and all became clear. "Ahh, yes," I said, my face brightening, "I see what you mean."

My bosses face mirrored my own and he nodded, smiling. "Ahh good." He said.

I smiled back. "Yes, sort of like... well... the end of term at school." I said, my smile becoming even wider.

His face fell slightly, and I could see him struggling with his thoughts. "Erm... well... no... well... yes, I suppose it is really." He turned away and went back into the wheelhouse. Back into the sanctuary of his work, his career, his professionalism. Away from the alien world, the alien thoughts and realisations of first trip cadets.

I was right though. That's exactly what it was. The end of term. That same feeling of well-being and slight euphoria that invades us all towards the end of something, even if we've enjoyed every minute of it.

"Ahh, young man," it was Captain McHale, "Just nip down and find the Chief Steward for me, would you. Tell him I would like to see him." He returned to his position by the bridge windows and resumed peering through his binoculars.

"Yes Sir." I said and immediately tripped over the rail on the deck that enabled the sliding door to slide. An involuntary "Bollocks!" escaped my clenched teeth as I stumbled into the wheelhouse.

Captain McHale didn't move a muscle. "Mmmm…," He said quietly, maintaining his gaze through the binoculars, "Now is the time to be carefull. End of the voyage you know. Mistakes come easily."

"Yes Sir." I said as went into the chartroom, but it wasn't until I reached the bottom of stairs that I realised I had been given a valuable lesson in professionalism. Well… no… actually, I took no notice whatsoever to what he said. To be truthful it was a lot later in my seagoing experience that that particular piece of advice came back to me. During an uncomfortable conversation with a captain where I was trying to explain some cock-up or other that was directly attributable to my carelessness

The last few hours of my first trip to sea passed by unremarkably. We had passed up the Bristol Channel, having left that particularly persistent fog bank behind to enshroud all the other ships steaming through the Western Approaches and been met by a pilot boat as we approached the place that said Pilot Station on the chart.

I was stationed, as usual, on the bridge with Dave, the Third mate and I was told, as usual, to 'nip down' and escort the pilot up to the wheelhouse I was, as usual, no use whatsoever as the pilot galloped up the stairs with me trailing behind.

Steven went forward with Albert, the Chief Officer and John, the Second Mate had gone aft without the encumbrance of cadet 'assistance'.

Tugs had been 'made fast' fore and aft and in no time at all, we were tying up the dock in Avonmouth with a gentle 'thump' as the ship landed against the quayside, all recorded, inscribed forever in my big blue 'Movement Book'.

'So, that was that.' I thought. My first trip. I did, actually, feel quite pleased with myself. Despite all my mistakes, all my adventures, runs ashore, storms, crocodiles etc., I had survived.

The one thing I was sure about, the one thing that immediately leapt to the front of my mind, was… I wanted more of it!

"Ring 'Finish with Engines'!" Captain McHale came striding through the wheelhouse with the pilot in tow and headed towards the chartroom door.

"Yes Sir." I said and clicked the handle of the telegraph into the correct position.

Down To The Sea. A Cadet's Tale

"Once you have finished up here call in my cabin on the way down and pick up your work-book."

"Yes Sir." I said again and then spent the next twenty minutes clearing up, putting things away and generally fussing around while Dave turned off the radar and all things electric.

Once we were done with all that we left the bridge by the inside door and locked it. There would be no further use for that part of ship for some time.

Meanwhile the rest of the vessel had become instantly alive. Whilst we had been sorting out the bridge, I had seen the gangway being lowered to the quayside and a constant stream of people come dashing up and disappearing into the accommodation. *'Apparently'*, I thought, *'it takes an awfull lot of people to see to the arrival of one ship.'*

I did as I was told and knocked on Captain McHale's door on the way down.

"Come!" he shouted after the first knock. I opened the door and stepped gingerly inside. The memory of my standing in that very same spot being lectured by someone who I had considered to be a 'bobble hatted idiot' all those hundreds of years ago on my first night on board, was still lurking at the back of my mind and was now causing me to feel embarrassed and humbled. Captain McHale had now grown in stature, not physically of course but as my respect for him had grown so had his presence. So now, to me, he could fill a room by being in it and was someone who should be listened to.

"Ahh, there you are young man." He said rummaging amongst the pile of paperwork that adorned his usually clear desk. "Here is your letter from the office about your next voyage, and… somewhere… here… Ahh yes, here is your work -book."

I shuffled forward, took the items and backed away.

"You will be coming back here next trip, but you will have a different Captain." He came from behind the desk and stuck out his hand. "So, I will say goodbye to you and good luck for the future. You have done very well lad, just remember what you've learned and do try to stay out of trouble."

He was grinning as I took his hand. "Yes Sir. Thank you, Sir." I muttered turning bright red as usual and becoming tongue tied yet again.

"Nice to be here." Was all that came out of my mouth. "Sir." I remembered as I tripped over the sill on my way out of his cabin.

I was still red in the cheeks by the time I got down to the cabin. Steven was already there throwing things into a suitcase.

"We can go tomorrow morning." He said. "The Mate just came and told me. Apparently, there is only one cadet coming to do the coast and he won't be here until the day after tomorrow."

I looked round the cabin. Steven had obviously had the usual battle with the suitcase cupboard when he tried to get at his luggage, as all my suitcases (expandable), kitbag, duffle bag etc., were piled in the corner.

It surprised me how much of an anti-climax it was ending a voyage. You would expect there to be farewell drinking sessions with heartfelt goodbyes, promises of continuing friendships and arrangements to meet in the future for further storytelling and beer consumption.

But extraordinarily little of any of that happened. Most people just disappeared quietly in the night or early the following morning, instantly replaced by strangers who functioned as though they had been there for years. It all felt very… well… sad really, I suppose.

I managed to say goodbye to Steven with a brief handshake and "See you again sometime." But Barry escaped during the night and I didn't see or hear of or from him until I sailed with him again some seven years later. JoJo I never saw again but heard some time later that he had only done one more trip and then gone off and joined the army, becoming some sort of Special Forces soldier like his father. I did, however, meet his son, under extremely bizarre circumstances, many, many years later, in an old, abandoned village near Mount Oxa which towers over Elounda on the island of Crete.

Dave was relieved immediately by a newly promoted cadet called Winston on his first ever posting as a Third Mate and was away in a taxi before I had chance say goodbye. John, the Second Mate found that, much to his annoyance, he had to wait for two days before his relief could get to the ship and Albert the Chief Officer wasn't relieved at all. He stayed on the ship for another two weeks until it sailed for Liverpool to start loading for, this time, Australia.

As for the rest of the crew, well, most of them I met again either as shipmates or just in passing. But every time we did meet up and I do mean, every time, there would be laughs, many, many, laughs. All the times shared would be gone over in detail. There would be some exaggeration of course but the stories were funnier and better told for it. All of those times shared were real to us. All the happenings happened to us, they belonged to us and to our time.

Whatever job you did, whatever skills you employed, whatever role you played on a ship, you were, above all, a seaman and it was those shared times, those shared 'happenings' that bound you together.

That's why all seamen go back for more. That's the way it has always been and always will be.

CHAPTER 41

So... Home again

I stood, surrounded by my luggage, looking up the length of the gangway. The same gangway that had stretched before me only three months, one week and two days before. 'Head' had been leaning on the bulwark peering down at me. Dockyard noise had enveloped me then and they did so again now. It was difficult to comprehend. On the one hand it seemed a lifetime away. Something that had happened on another planet. In fact, if I had been standing there in that situation, ten years later, I'd have said; "A long time ago in a galaxy far, far away..." But, as it was only nineteen-seventy-one, Star Wars hadn't been invented yet, so I didn't say that. In fact, I didn't say anything. There was nobody to say anything to. All the goodbyes had been said. All the promises to stay in touch had been promised and already forgotten. All the looking for people to make the promises to had been done. Sometimes successfully, sometimes not. Hands had been shaken. Waves had been waved.

On the other hand, I felt as though I had only been on the looming thing for a few hours. The gangway, the noise, the hustle and bustle, all tried to convince my mind that I was still there, in London. That none of the voyage had happened. It was all an instant dream.

"Oi!" My mind was jolted back to reality. "You George?"

I turned around quickly coming face to face with a large be-whiskered man in a t-shirt at least two sizes too small. A large area of hairy flesh around his midriff was bulging from underneath. Trousers and shirt had obviously given up trying to form any sort of meaningful relationship some time ago.

"Yes". I said.

"Taxi." It was a statement rather than a question. "These yours?" He didn't wait for a reply, just started picking up suitcases (expandable) and heading towards a large green Ford Granada parked by a warehouse door.

Not saying anything I followed him, picking up my fifty-six-pound block of frozen butter. Not for the first time thinking and worrying about the heat that the butter and my chopped-up lamb carcass may encounter between Avonmouth and Lyne Lane, Chertsey, Surry.

"Don't worry young man." Ray, the Chief Steward had said. "It's well packaged. Insulated even. Where are you going?"

Feeling a little less worried I had told him.

"Oh." His smile had faded slightly. "…Erm …yes …well …erm. I am sure it will be fine."

I had felt worried again. Luckily, I thought much later, I was then and had been all the time, entirely focused on the butter and what might happen if it started to melt. It had not, for one minute, occurred to me, the mayhem that might ensue if my lamb carcass, even though it was butchered and did not actually look like a carcass, also started to defrost, and dribble blood over my fellow travellers!

Anyway, it didn't take long for the taxi driver and me to load all the suitcases (expandable), kit bags, rucksacks duffle bags, butter and carcass into the car. The driver did, at one point, look a little worried when he saw how close to the ground the rear of his vehicle, (upon which he relied for his livelihood), was getting.

In no time at all, it seemed, I was hurtling towards the mainline station at Avonmouth.

A strange feeling of reluctance came over me. It felt like I was leaving my home and setting off for somewhere I didn't know. *'How could that be?'* I thought. I was going home. *'You know! Home! That place you wanted to go back to during the first few hours on the looming thing. When you saw Cathy walking round the end of the shed with Ian, the chief of all the engineers!'*

'Ahh Cathy.' There she was again. My Cathy. …Well, not really my Cathy, apparently. Somebody else's Cathy now I suppose.

I shook my head slightly to clear my thoughts and got back to worrying about carcasses and melting butter.

Avonmouth station was all hustle and bustle. People rushing in every direction, flooding off trains, flooding on trains, flooding… well… as I say in every direction. But always going in the opposite direction to me. Which meant that it took me ages to get to the ticket office and exchange my rail warrant for a ticket. Having to arrange the movement of suitcases (expandable), rucksacks, butter etc. didn't help. The luggage managed to draw the odd curse and some mild displays of bad temper from some of my fellow travellers. I said, "sorry" every time one of my pieces of luggage touched, or even went anywhere near the legs of another platform user. I even said sorry when the contact was somebody else's fault! This is typical 'Englishman Travelling' behaviour. Going to work on a train involves your typical Englishman in frowning, gasps of exasperation, superior looks at other travellers, bouts of bad temper and lots of staring at a newspaper. On the other hand, give that same Englishman a suitcase and an unfamiliar destination and he becomes little boy lost saying sorry all the time! Anyway, in the end, I stood waiting on number three platform for the express, non-stop train to London's Paddington station and was in a euphoric state of mind due to the fact that I was actually standing still. Well, euphoric, in a hot, sweaty, and exhausted sort of way.

I needn't have been of course. My father had said in the letter I received in New Zealand that he would pick me up when I returned. That would, of course, have been the sensible thing to do. Ring him and get picked up. But the thing was I wanted to get home by myself and walk in all nonchalant as though I had just been to the shops or something and then bask in the oohs and aahs from family members agog with admiration at my having returned from untold adventures on the world's oceans. Even better, the neighbours would see the taxi pulling up outside the house and be saying, in hushed tones "Ahh, he's back. I wonder where he's been this time?" Hail the returning hero!

It had not, at that stage, occurred to me that; (a) everybody would probably be at work so they wouldn't see me arrive, (b) they wouldn't really care anyway and, (c) it was virtually impossible to do anything nonchalantly when carrying a fifty-six-pound block of butter and a lamb carcass, not to mention suitcases (expandable) etc.!

The London train squeaked and rattled its way into the station. Doors were being opened even before the train had stopped. Harassed looking men in suits were leaping off and galloping down the platform towards the exit. All doing the frowning, superior looking, bad temper thing. Without the newspaper staring of course. But everything else required of them was in place. My bags and baggage drew even deeper, more complex frowns from some of the gallopers as they found their usual daily path blocked. One of them actually hurdled a suitcase in his attempt to beat a fellow worker to the exit.

Finally, they had gone, along with all the other passengers, and I was free to start, yet again, the loading process. Luckily an empty compartment had stopped opposite where I was standing. It was one of those compartments with a corridor on the far side. Just like the one I had occupied with Delbert and company, all those eons ago when I was heading to London to join the 'Looming Thing.'

Again, in fairly short order, I was camped in the compartment, luggage stowed in various places. In the overhead racks, under the seats, on the seats, between my legs. I did a quick check. No. no sign of melting butter.

It was a strange journey. Heading home. I had, of course, done it before. Three times actually. Going home at the end of each term while at the Nautical Collage at Warsash (Southampton). But, somehow, this was different. I felt as though I was someone else now. Unfortunately, I couldn't quite determine who.

A state of mind, which, I now understand, invades all seventeen year olds. Whether they are on a path to profitable suburban normality or are intent on a life of fun and debauchery. I think at that stage I was at a bit of crossroads. Part of me, the part that had been influenced by so many years of normal family life and schooling, wanted a trouble-free normal life of work, duty, pipe and slippers. While another part of me had been awoken by…well… real life… no other way of putting it! So many people, so many places, so many experiences! The New York Bar swam into view at that point. I could feel myself frowning. Actually, frowning at myself. Me admonishing me! Disappointed at myself for being led astray by… by… well by real life, I suppose.

And then Cathy appeared. My lovely Cathy… That's who I was really thinking about at that moment. I could see her lovely face drifting towards me, I closed my eyes. Oblivious to all that was assaulting my senses. The carriage doors opening, and slamming shut, the clackerty clack of the train wheels over the track, the swooshing of the masts, pylons and track side buildings as they raced by. I could see her face drifting closer, golden hair billowing behind her as a breeze sprung from nowhere. She did her lovely head tilting thing as she moved to kiss me. I could feel my lips start to respond, stretching themselves towards her, beginning to form a sort of loose 'O' shape.

She spoke.

"Tickets please!" She said in a gravelly West Country accent. "Tickets please!"

My lips smacked themselves back into place around my teeth. My eyes shot open and found themselves staring into the be-whiskered face of a ticket inspector. He was looking at me with a questioning frown, which I suppose would be a normal look, if a young sweaty man with his eyes closed looked as though he was about to give you a passionate smacker on the lips.

"Ahh… Ooh… Yes." I said for no reason whatsoever while I rummaged around my person for the ticket. Yet again the colour of the brightest red traffic light in the universe.

Ticket found at the third frantic scrabbling in the same pocket, I handed the crumpled paper to the man who took it between thumb and forefinger as though it had just come out of a particularly unpleasant public toilet bowl. He peered at it, clipped it with his clipper thing in a deft, 'Only ticket inspectors of great experience can do it this way,' sort of flourish and dropped it back into my outstretched palm. Where upon it wriggled its way to the edge of my hand and drifted casually to the floor avoiding my flapping, grasping fingers with ease.

The ticket inspector turned on his heal and marched out. "You should look after your ticket." He sniffed as he left the compartment. "Important document that is."

I stared after him suppressing a terrible urge to smack him in the nose and pull his beard.

The urge passed and I folded my dust streaked, crumpled, torn

Down To The Sea. A Cadet's Tale

important document, and put back in a pocket. My thoughts were now far away from the lovely Cathy and her hair and lips. For the next five minutes I was totally occupied with angry thoughts of *'Important documents and pompous ticket men'*.

Anyway, if the bloody thing was so 'Important' why make holes in it with a clipper thing? Surely, he should have a huge ring on his finger with a British Rail seal embossed on it. Crossed signal gantries or something. A small battery powered blow torch to heat some wax carried in a little tin could complete the ticket stamping equipment solemnly handed to graduates of the British Rail Academy of Superior Ticket Collectors in a red carpeted ceremony on Crewe fuckin' railway Station!

My ire had subsided by the time the train rattled through Reading. Unfortunately, it had cause to return due to the 'Non-stop Express' stopping suddenly just past Farnham. A half hour wait did nothing to ease the troubled minds of anybody on board and I could hear the odd raised voice in the other compartments of the carriage. No doubt, I thought with an evil smile, giving ticket man a hard time.

The Express rolled into Paddington station and stopped with a final jolt that caused several people who were eager to do the platform gallop and had stood up before the train had stopped to stagger back and forward in that comic ungainly shuffle dance that must take place during a million or so train stops per day. In fact, I think there is a special class at Train Driver School that potential drivers have to attend to develop their sudden halt skills. Certificates are issued only when students are sufficiently adept at sending three or more passengers to the floor and causing two bags of shopping to topple over and send the contents at least four yards down the carriage. Special commendation is reserved for those who can cause blood to flow from a passenger that 'nose buts' a complete stranger standing in front!

I manhandled all my luggage from the train, frowning slightly, having become aware that I was becoming dangerously obsessed with British Rail Schools of Train Management. I vowed there and then never to let such thoughts cross my mind again.

Finding a trolley, I loaded up and pushed it to the barrier where I was forced to stop and scrabble about for my ticket by another be-whiskered official. My anger started to return as he adopted the same superior, disgusted look when he saw the state of my 'Important Document' as the previous Ticket Person. It must have been ok though, because he decided to keep it and drop it unceremoniously into his 'Important document' bin.

Feeling as though I was already home, I finally arrived at Waterloo station. A place I had been through a thousand times. The taxi driver waited patiently while I discharged my cargo, grabbed my offered five-pound note and drove off assuming the extra pound on top of the fare included in the fiver was for him. "Cheer's mate!" I heard drifting back behind the sound of squealing tyres.

A trolley was at hand, abandoned and shoved to one side by big blousy women with a blue rinse who was heaving her ample self into a cab. I grabbed it as it trundled in my direction and loaded up. All that now remained was to find the Chertsey train and get home.

It was then that my British Rail ire returned with a vengeance. It dawned on me that the ticket collector at the barrier had taken my ticket and thrown it in the bin. All well and good... but... seeing as the bloody ticket was from bloody Bristol to bloody Chertsey not from bloody Bristol to bloody Paddington... I was now without a bloody ticket from bloody Waterloo to bloody Chertsey!

"Oh bother!" thought nice Brian.

"Fuck! Fuck! Fuck!" Said bad Brian out loud, drawing some frowns from passers-by.

My thoughts returned to *'Things to do to British Rail staff that would cause them maximum pain and suffering',* until I finally calmed down and slowed my pace to less than an angry gallop.

I was back to, more or less, normal, by the time I had waited forlornly on the appropriate platform for an hour and then climbed aboard the Chertsey train having had to part with eight shillings and sixpence for another ticket.

More carriage time was endured after the familiar battle with luggage. More waiting for the train to start moving. Seemed like an hour but was probably only fifty-eight minutes. More clackerty clack over endless rails, points, and junctions. Until a final stop, a final luggage/train battle... and there I stood on the platform at Chertsey station. The train clanked its way down the track and as it cleared the platform, I found myself staring across at the opposite platform. Staring at the exact spot I had said goodbye to my father all those decades ago.... Or was it a couple of days ago. I couldn't decide. It seemed like both at the same time. In fact, it was 3 months, one week, two days and eight hours since I had first battled with suitcases (expandable) duffle bags and the like.

All these thoughts fighting for dominance in my shattered brain, I struggled down to the road outside and then saw the driver of the private hire Ford Granada stare in horror when he saw the amount of cargo he was going to have to fit in the interior of his vehicle. His shoulders drooped as he obviously wished he had been second in line.

...And so... some seven hours after standing by the gangway of the 'Looming Thing' I was, at last, staring into the driveway of our house in Lyne Lane. An eleven-year-old me cycled up the drive and tore off up the road. A five-year-old me stood in the driveway wailing on top note, clutching a severely wounded finger. It having been viciously attacked by a rogue stinging nettle. Finally, a sixteen-year-old me stormed up the path and out onto the road presumably after a thoughtless parent had suggested a sensible course of action that would have meant me appearing 'uncool'.

But apart from the procession of 'me' people my mind had conjured up to greet me, I had been right in my prediction that there would be not a single soul to witness my triumphant return.

I sighed a resigned sort of sigh and began, one last time to transfer the luggage, suitcases (expandable) and all to the front door of the house which took a good ten minutes, if not longer. Throughout that time no sound could be heard from inside the house.

My tired brain was just concluding that not even my mother was in when I heard a yelp of delight behind me and there stood mother arms outstretched grinning from ear to ear.

"Ooohhh, your home!" she said.

'At last!' I thought, 'Hail the conquering hero!'

"When are going back?" asked mother.

Now then. Every single Merchant seaman, every single service man, every single person engaged in a profession that involves spending time away from home will recognise that scene.

I had witnessed it three times already when returning from college.

The first. The very first question mothers, fathers, loved ones, friends and even enemies ask is, "When are you going back?"

Not… "How are you?" Not… "Did you have a good trip/voyage/journey/time?" Not even… "Where have you been?" It is always "When are you going back?"

Why this is so, has been perplexing the psychological professions for eons, I'm sure.

Misses Da Gama probably asked the same question of old Vasco when he came home from discovering some continent or other.

"Ooohhh… Lovely to see you dear… When are you going back?"

CHAPTER 42

MY CATHY?

"I am home for about three weeks."

I had answered my mother's age-old query after an odd sort of pause. Again, an inbuilt natural human response to an in built natural human question asked by one human being of another when said human returns to the cave. My delicate feelings recovering from being asked such a question and mother also recovered quickly from feeling she had asked the wrong thing.

Anyway, awkward moment over, we started the luggage and groceries transfer the few feet from doorstep to hallway. I hefted the butter box in then went back for the carcass. Mother's curiosity was immediately aroused when she saw the plastic covered, heavy weight that I was carrying.

"I've brought you some butter." I announced proudly at the same time as she asked.

"What's in the box?"

"Eh?" We both said at once.

I got in first. "Butter." I said.

"Pardon?"

"Butter." I said again.

She frowned slightly, looking a little bewildered.

"…And lamb." I continued, stepping over the box and picking up the odd shaped cardboard covered parcel of meat.

"Oh," she said. Her frown deepened and she now looked totally bewildered. Which is fair enough, I suppose. The very last words a mother would expect to hear from her only son on his triumphant return from voyages to strange lands is "Lamb" and "Butter."

"This is the lamb," I nodded towards the parcel in my hand and then tossed my head in the direction of the box. The box with the word BUTTER emblazoned on the side in big red letters, "…and that's the butter."

"Oh." She managed through her confusion.

"Fifty-six pounds." I continued proudly.

"The lamb!" she exclaimed. Shock appearing amongst the confusion.

"No!" I said slightly exasperated, "the butter!"

"Oh." She turned her gaze to the butter box. "That's an awful lot of money!"

I could feel my triumphant homecoming slipping into confused pantomime mode.

"No! … No… fifty six pounds OF butter… you know… weight… of butter."

"Oh," she said again, now taking on a worried look with a hint of panic. "Is it all frozen?"

'Ah!' I thought. 'Now we're getting somewhere.'

"Yes." I said.

Mother thought for a moment. Her frown now reached her chin. 'O-Oh.' I thought. I had seen that look many times before. 'There's a question coming that I am not going to be able to answer.'

… "Erm… Where are we going to keep it all?"

Long silence.

A long silence while the significance of her question sank in!

A long silence while the horror washed over me.

The fact that we didn't own a freezer had not, for one second, entered my head!

So… Nowhere to keep the fifty-six pounds of butter and an entire lamb carcass.

My triumphant homecoming was now totally in the realm of, "Oh fuck!" It had continued its slide and had reached full pantomime status. All it needed now was for my father to appear in a full Widow Twanky costume and that would complete the scene!

"I'll phone your father," said mother, "he might know where to put it."

Down To The Sea. A Cadet's Tale

A vision of my Father in the panto costume, answering the phone in his office briefly crossed my mind. I quickly put it away. Too horrible!

"Yes." I said. I couldn't think of anything else to say.

Mother headed for the telephone on the window ledge by the front door. I heaved the rest of the luggage into the house and then wandered into the living room and gazed around. It was exactly as it was when I left it twenty thousand years ago. Or was it yesterday? My mother's voice was still echoing around the room.

"Vests! You haven't got enough vests!"

I sighed, suddenly very, very weary. Tired and worn out. Flopping into an armchair and stared straight ahead into the middle distance. I could hear one side of the conversation between my parents as information about the looming frozen grocery crisis was passed.

… "Frozen… Yes! …Yes! … All of it… Fifty-six pounds!... No… silly… in weight… you know… pounds and ounces. …. Yes… A carcass… whole thing… Yes… dead."

I imagined briefly that I could hear muffled oaths and curses coming down the telephone line. But I couldn't have done. My father didn't do oaths and curses of any kind. Muffled or not.

The phone went down, and mother came into the living room.

"It's alright," she said. "The Greenfields over at Ottershaw have just bought a freezer." She looked relieved. "Your father's going to ring Frank now and ask him if he has got any space." She turned around and headed back through the dining room towards the hall. "He should have. They haven't had it long enough to fill it up." I heard the sounds of my suitcase (expandable) being opened and I imagined the look of horror on her face as she was confronted with all the dirty washing and stuff while at the same time part of my brain was wondering if there was some sort of time scale for filling freezers. Some formulae for calculating and plotting a space/time curve or something. I gave up all thought processes as my eyes began to close and the total weariness took over. Another question suddenly popped into my brain as sleep took over. "…Yes… dead." Mother had said! What kind of question had my father asked to warrant her saying "Yes… dead!"? I couldn't be bothered trying to answer that one. My eyes stayed shut.

"I'll empty this suitcase, shall I? … I'll get your washing on." I could tell by the tone in her voice she was holding an item of disgusting looking laundry between thumb and forefinger while she was speaking.

I made a sort of non-committal grunting noise and started to drift away again.

"Oh…by the way" Mother was back in the room. I became instantly awake but managed to keep my eyes closed, "this came for you… It's a magazine. A company one… You know… your company… Blue Star."

I opened one eye, took the offered publication, glanced at it and let it drop onto my lap. It didn't stay there. I picked it up again. Something had caught my attention. My one open eye had detected something and told my brain to take notice. I opened the other eye and lifted the magazine so I could see it without having to go to all the effort of moving my head.

Captain Jonathan McHale glared at me from the photograph on the front cover. *'Good God!'* I thought. *'He's still with me! I'm at home… and he's still with me!'* Glaring! I flicked through several pages to find out what he was doing on the front cover. There was a full colour spread in the centre pages, All about Captain McHale's life at sea. I could see from the headings it included his war record, his many voyages of all ranks from cadet to Master. I flicked a couple more pages and one headline jumped out at me. It had something to do with his latest command, the *New Zealand Star* and how this trip was going to be his penultimate trip before retiring and moving to New Zealand.

I woke up a little more then. *'I have just been on that very trip!'* I thought. An element of completely undeserved pride entering my thinking processes. *'Just this very minute got home!'* I felt… well… sort of famous I suppose. Silly really.

I flicked back a page. There was another picture of himself in full rig with a young girl smiling by his side and a caption about a dinner held in his honour that he had attended with his daughter Katherine in January. The day before sailing for New Zealand.

Weariness started to overtake me again and my eyelids began to droop. I started to enter snooze mode. That time between nodding off and full mouth open, dribbling, snoring slumber.

They say that the human brain is at its most active when sleep begins. That's when it does all its admin. All its sorting and filing. Its analysing and creating.

Mine, apparently, was not exempt from this process.

Something, some file, some piece of information began to connect with another stored file somewhere in the bowels of my cranium.

A spark fizzed to my eyelids and they flew open. At the same time other sparks set off a chain reaction in the rest of my body causing it to convulse into full wide awake, and I do mean wide awake, very wide awake, status.

My brain managed a full start in a millisecond. Straight from neutral to fifth gear.

Captain McHale! ...

New Zealand Star! ...

Last January! ...

Katherine...

I scrabbled on the floor for the magazine. My fingers became the size of baby marrows as I tried desperately to flick quickly through the pages. The page I wanted, the one with the picture of Captain McHale and his daughter at the dinner thing, passed through my baby marrows three times before I managed to stop it.

I stared at the picture. I stared at the girl standing by Captain McHale's side. The beautiful blonde girl. The beautiful blonde girl with her head tilted to one side.

The world came to a standstill. I could still hear my mother tipping stuff out of my suitcase in the hall. I could hear the clock ticking on the mantelpiece. I could hear cars passing on the road beyond our driveway. Everything else around me seemed suddenly detached from reality.

My body left my skin and my heart stopped when the phone in hall suddenly started ringing at a full three thousand decibels. But this did, at least, draw a squeaky whimper from my mouth and my brain began to do the calculations necessary to bring sense to what I was looking at.

Captain McHale in full uniform!

New Zealand Star!

Last January!

The night before sailing!

Daughter!

Katherine!

Cathy by the dock gates.... Cathy... Katherine...

Cathy... My Cathy... Captain McHale's daughter!

I stared at the picture again.

The phone had stopped ringing. I was aware of my mother talking.

"Oh yes… yes… Who? … Yes… Yes… He's here now… just come in…asleep in the chair… Who shall I say! …Oh ok… just a moment I'll get him."

I continued to stare at the picture.

Cathy.

Mother bustled in, a crumpled evil looking black stained boilersuit in one hand.

"There's someone on the phone for you" she said with a knowing half grin across her face. "It's a girl!"

There was a mild shock in her tone when she said, "It's a girl." Her face held that half grin, but she added a knowing nod to go with it. The knowing nod mothers give their sons when they think there is a hint of romance in the air. "Cathy, I think she said."

I transferred my stare from the picture to my mother. Mouth still open. Mother did her nod thing a couple more times before frowning.

"Well… don't keep her waiting. Go and answer it!" She tutted, turned on her heal and went out.

"By the way" she said over her shoulder, "I've emptied the suitcases." (Expandable)

… But I can't find your vests."

The End

…. of the beginning.

Acknowledgements

I must, of course, firstly give heartfelt thanks to all the staff at The Author House for all their valiant attempts at turning my scribblings into a book. Also, I should mention the Author Learning Centre for all those webinars and advice pages. Many thanks, they helped a lot.

Many people have been instrumental in helping me write, not only this first book, but also the follow up tomes. They, of course are not yet finished, but work had to be done on them in order for this book to be completed and tie in with the others.

So, thanks Elys for your editing skills early on in the process.

Many thanks also to the rest of the Welsh family that adopted me and looked after me since that terrible day in April 2013. Kelly, Gemma and Rhys, along with all their families. You have all encouraged and helped me over the past few years. It was their mother, Angie, my partner of eight years until she passed away at such a young age, who set me on the road to completing this book. I shall, of course, be forever grateful to her.

To all the people in Her Majesty's Coastguard who read the original article and pestered me over many years to write more, I say thank you for the pestering! In particular all the staff at my own station, Liverpool, who were particularly vociferous about their desire to learn how my... erm... relationship with Cathy would develop.

Special thanks to my parents, sadly, no longer with us, for their encouragement.

Lastly, I must give thanks from the bottom of heart, for all the encouragement, understanding, time and completely unselfish commitment given to me by my lovely partner, Trude. Thank you so very much love. Also, thank you for just being you. Over these past years you have been a constant source of inspiration to me.

Brian.

The saga will continue…

DOWN TO THE SEA

A tale of Brazil!

"Starboard five," said George, repeating my helm order. I watched as the ship's bow moved slowly towards the setting sun.

"Midships."

"Midships," said George. The starboard movement of the bow slowed.

"Steady."

"Steady... on... on two six five." George, looking even more gnarled and leathery than usual in the rapidly decreasing daylight, repeated each one of my helm orders in a bored, gravelly voice that sounded like a cross between a bad-tempered lion and a ships hooter.

The ship steamed slowly towards the bay.

"Nearly there George" I said staring out of the wheelhouse window.

"Aye," he replied.

"Going up the road tonight?" I enquired.

"Aye," said George.

I heaved myself out of the pilot's chair (sitting in which was punishable by slow death if caught by the old man) and walked past the wheel and compass binnacle towards the starboard wheelhouse door.

I turned and looked at George. "We should be alongside by midnight.

"Aye" ...Man of few words our George.

He had been at sea since Noah was a second mate and been here... Santos ...in Brazil... more times than you could shake a hairy stick at. Everybody here knew George... from the head stevedore to the pockmarked old harridan that ran the sleaziest bar on the strip, and all of them, every single one of them, treated him with a reverence normally reserved by royal servants for visiting heads of state. Even the captain of our fine vessel seemed to be in awe of him. I, on the other hand, as an old salt of a mere six years was not treated with such deference. However, I always thought it wise to stick reasonably close to old George in case some of the regard in which he was held floated in my direction.

The ship continued towards the bay. I squinted into the sun and could see the lights on the shoreline beginning to twinkle, the high-rise buildings of the business quarter looming over the beachfront like great prehistoric beasts. Their shadows lengthening and darkening as the sun began to dip behind the deep, dark, green jungle clad hills beyond.

Having been here myself on quite a few occasions, I could see, in my mind's eye, beyond the buildings to the waterfront on the other side of the long low peninsular that swept northwards between the open sea and the river. I could imagine the bend in the river, the long, low, wide bodied sheds full of stacked timber, bales of wool, cases of corned beef and barrels of menthol. I could see the ancient cranes grinding, squeaking and rattling on the wharves. This was where 'The Strip' was… a street full of… of…

…I was jolted from my reverie suddenly by a voice from the chartroom.

"Is anybody there?" Captain Shinfield loped into the wheelhouse with his usual question. Not for the first time I wondered what he would do if he found that, actually, nobody was there.

"Starboard bridge wing." I shouted back.

I had called him to the bridge, as instructed, once the lights of Cabo Frio had appeared abeam of the vessel some thirty minutes before. He loped out onto the bridge wing, nodding in polite reverence at George as he passed.

George, as usual, ignored him.

"Evening Captain," I said as he appeared in the bridge wing door, resplendent in his normal attire, light blue baggy shorts, grubby, off white vest and flip flops.

"Lovely evening young man." he stated, hands behind his back, leaning forward and peering intently at me over the top of his half-moon glasses.

"Yes sir."

"You have, I take it, been here before?" he said. A sort of statement with a questioning lilt at the end of his sentence.

"Yes sir."

"You will, therefore, be aware of the… ahmm… shall we say… dangers …of the … ahmm… strip area?"

When he said the words *'strip area'*, it was as though it bought a bad taste to his mouth… as though he was talking about some sort of disease-ridden den of iniquity… a dilapidated, muddy, cobbled street crowded with muggers, robbers, gangsters, pimps, prostitutes and various other ne'er do wells.

…Which come to think of it, I suppose, was what it was.

The *'strip area'* to which he referred could be found just outside the dock gates, at the bend in the river. Right outside the gate to Number twelve berth, known to merchant seaman of all nationalities as "Hellfire Corner". One could stroll down the gangway… should one be fortunate enough to be on a vessel berthed at twelve… out of the gate, and straight "Up the strip."

One also had the advantage and peace of mind to know that one's ship, one's place of safety, was close to hand should one fall foul of the aforementioned ne'er do wells.

Hardly an hour would go by during an evening on the strip without seeing some poor unfortunate jolly jack, bereft of funds, eyes bulging, little legs a blur, 'toeing it' for all he was worth in the direction of the dock gates, hotly pursued by several swarthy, snarling, weapon wielding Latinos demanding money. In the background a fierce looking woman covered in tattoos and old scars, arms akimbo, transformed from the dainty, polite, sexy, demur little thing that had persuaded our jolly jack to accompany her to a 'hotel', shouting abuse at the unfortunate and encouragement at the gangsters in equal measure.

"… Erm… Yes sir."

I was 'fully aware'. In fact, I was rather looking forward to being made 'fully aware' again very soon.

My reply must have betrayed my thoughts, he frowned and leaned closer, trying to determine whether I was being facetious.

"Mmmmm," he said, "well, I have a task for you… I want you to make sure our two first trippers are made aware of the dangers of…of…of…of… erm… that… that place. I don't want them going home damaged in mind or body…" he paused. "Do you understand?"

All this was accompanied by a dismissive flapping of a bony left hand in the general direction of the land.

"Yes sir." I mumbled. I could see a good run ashore turning to ratshit before we'd even got alongside.

"But shouldn't the Mate do that… after all, he is in charge of training?"

"Training! Training! It's hardly training young man."

"No sir."

He was right, of course, so there was nothing I could say really.

"Ahh. Mr. MacRose, the very man." Captain Shinfield had turned towards the wheelhouse as John appeared in the doorway.

"Yes," he continued, "I was just saying to young Mr. George here, I want him to make sure our young cadets, both first trippers, you know…" John nodded his head and furrowed his brow as though he was receiving important new information. "…Erm, make sure they understand all about that strip." He flapped his hand in the general direction of the land again. "Very dangerous place, you know."

I was, at this point, standing behind the Captain and could see John's face. A picture of seriousness and concern.

"Yes sir," he nodded his head, "good idea, we wouldn't want them damaged in mind and body would we."

"Certainly not." Said our leader.

"Don't worry Sir, I will make sure your instructions are carried out." John smiled a concerned fatherly smile in my direction.

I smiled a different smile back at him and mouthed a suitable, silent response. The second word being "…Off."

John just widened his smile.

"…Erm sir," I paused until Captain Shinfield looked in my direction. "…it's quite a responsibility to look after youngsters like that when they are ashore." Another pause while I arranged my face into a picture of worried concern.

"I think it best if Mr. MacRose helps me in that task."

John's face dropped and it was his turn to mouth obscenities.

"Yes, I think you're right, young man."

I smiled sweetly at John.

"Anyway, said the captain, turning and marching into the wheelhouse, "let's first get the ship to the anchorage eh."

Evening turned to night and by ten o'clock the ship was safely anchored between an Argentinian Bulk Carrier and a small, scruffy looking French vessel of some sort.

I stayed on watch as usual until midnight and was a bit peeved when the VHF radio burst into life and I was informed by Santos Port Control that a pilot was on the way and we would be berthing in a couple of hours.

"No fucking sleep again." I grumbled to Harry who had just appeared on the bridge to start his midnight to four watch.

"Since when did you need sleep?" he chortled as I opened the door to the alleyway.

"Not the point…" I said. "I need beauty sleep."

"Agreed." He shouted as the door closed.

As I feared there was no sleep for me that night. The pilot arrived on board and we all went to stations. The anchor was raised, and we proceeded towards the entrance to the river. Then, of course, it all went wrong, and we had to go back to the anchorage for a couple of hours. Apparently, a Brazilian vessel had broken down while unberthing and was swinging about in the buoyed channel.

We finally entered the river at about five in the morning and steamed slowly along the channel, past Fortaleza at the entrance, then past the rusting hulk of some vessel that had collided with something and caught fire in the dim and distant past, its twisted, rotting superstructure being a grotesque reminder to all ships crews of what can happen if you make a mistake.

We docked at berth Twelve 'A'. Berth Twelve was just before the bend in the river. Twelve 'A' was just after the bend in the river, so we were close enough to 'The Strip'.

To please everybody.

Everybody, that is, except Captain Shinfield who's deeply held religious beliefs caused him to shudder every time he caught sight of the place.

Berthing took no time at all and as soon as the gangway was lowered dockers streamed aboard and began rigging gear, opening hatches and as usual asking for things.

"…Hey Mr Mate, you give for me one this…"

"…Hey my friend, you give for me one that…" Everybody wanted something to do with hatches, cargo, equipment, other equipment to handle the equipment and so it went on into the afternoon. At two o'clock they all disappeared for two hours to eat. I disappeared for two hours to sleep!

I was awoken by the sound of cranes moving about on the dock, so I staggered back out into the sunlight and joined in the mayhem until six o'clock when Harry arrived to relieve me. Normally I would be the one to work through the night but, Harry, being recently married and apparently, therefore unable to allow alcohol past his lips or even glance at woman, did not feel like going ashore so we had agreed that, in this port anyway, he would work 'nights'.

Once I had told him all I knew about what was going on, which wasn't much, I raced along to my cabin and started undressing *'Just time for a quick snooze'* I thought. There was a knock on the door. It was James, one of the first trip cadets.

"Are you going ashore? Can we come?" His face was full of hope and excitement.

"No, and no." I said. "I need some sleep first. On top of that the 'Old Man' says I have to speak to you about going ashore, but it'll have to wait til I've had a kip. So, be a good chap and fuck off for an hour."

He looked totally crestfallen.

"Mind you," I added, feeling guilty, you can ask the Mate, he can give you a talking to as well."

"OK," he said and disappeared.

I finished undressing, wrapped a towel round my middle and went along the alleyway to the showers and let the hot water rain down on me for ten minutes, washed myself and went back to my cabin. I was just about to land on my bunk when the door flew open, and the Mate walked in.

"Come on hurry up and get ready." He said looking me up and down. I stared at him. He was fully rigged out in his 'Going Ashore' rig. Light blue flared trousers and a red T shirt.

I continued to stare.

"Come on," he repeated. "We're going ashore, we have to take the cadets up 'The Strip'".

"We can't do that!" I gasped. The Old Man said they weren't to go. We are supposed to tell them about it and make sure they understand."

"Ahh yes," said John grinning and pointing his finger in the air. "He didn't say they weren't to go. What he said was…" he stuck his chin forward for dramatic effect, "...And I quote... '...*Make sure they understand all about that place.*' So... after we have taken them there, I guarantee they will 'know all about that place'!"

He sat down on my bunk heavily. "So, stop fuckin' about, get dressed, and let's get going." Grinning he added, "Anyway, that bird you were with last trip will be waiting for you. You know what they're like, they always know what ships are in, and who's on them."

I gave in and continued dressing. *'Mind you'* I thought *'He does have a point about the cadets learning the ways of the world.'*

Education. Education. Education!